WORKING WITH
ECONOMICS

A CANADIAN FRAMEWORK

THIRD EDITION

H. RICHARD HIRD
DURHAM COLLEGE

Copyright © 1992 Maxwell Macmillan Canada Inc.

Maxwell Macmillan Canada
1200 Eglinton Ave. East, Suite 200
Don Mills, Ontario M3C 3N1

Canadian Cataloguing in Publication Data
Hird, H. Richard
  Working with economics

3rd ed.
ISBN 0-02-954024-0

1. Economics   2. Canada—Economic conditions.
3. Canada — Economic policy. I. Title.

HB171.5.H57 1991   330   C91-095268-X

Cover art: John Mantha
Design: D. Fiszel, Jane A. Clark

Printed and bound in Canada by John Deyell Company

  2 3 4 5   96 95 94 93 92

Preface

Organization and Approach

For many students, their only formal exposure to the study of economics is the introductory course. Only a small percentage of students who enrol in an introductory principles course proceed with further study of the subject. The introductory economics course must, therefore, not only familiarize students with economic principles, but should provide them with an appreciation of the major economic issues in our society such as unemployment and inflation, as well as with programs and regulations created to deal with these issues.

This textbook is intended for an introductory college course in economics. It was written with three assumptions in mind about such a course. First, an introductory course need not cover all topics in the field of economics, but rather should emphasize basic principles. Many existing texts are too large and cover topics rarely discussed in an introductory course. Although sometimes interesting, these topics are best left to an intermediate or more advanced course. This textbook does not include such topics, but does provide the student with the basic tools necessary to analyse most economic issues.

The second assumption is that students learn best by doing rather than simply by reading. Understanding economics is not easy and most students must work at it. This textbook emphasizes an applied approach by inserting review questions throughout each chapter. If students can master these questions, they are well prepared to move on to the next topic. More questions are provided at the end of each chapter, and these can be used to introduce classroom discussion about economic principles.

Third, students gain a better understanding of economic principles when they can apply them to everyday events. Each chapter contains special set-off material, typeset in colour. This special material can provide the basis for interesting classroom discussion. The issues dealt with in these sections are meant to highlight the theoretical concepts contained in the chapter without affecting the continuity of the text itself.

Changes to the Third Edition

For the third edition, the tables and the references to legislation have been updated. Recent information is presented on unemployment insurance, immigration, political parties, competition law, banks, excise taxes, and the stock market. Definitions of key terms now appear in the margin as well as in the Glossary. There are additional graphs, especially in the chapter on international trade. A new profile featuring entrepreneur Kaaydah Schatten is included. The tables on the calculation of marginal values have been improved, and the "Questions for Review and Discussion" sections have been expanded.

In addition to the above-mentioned changes, several new topics have been introduced. They include:

- the Goods and Services tax;
- measures of productivity;
- cabotage;
- pay equity;
- zero inflation;
- the Canada-U.S. Free Trade Agreement;
- income elasticity;
- price cross-elasticity of demand;
- defence of marketing boards;
- sunk costs; and
- privatization.

Pedagogical Features

This textbook contains several features aimed at improving the student's understanding of economic principles. These are as follows:

- Chapters begin with the objectives and key terms clearly stated. This clarifies the pedagogical goals within the chapter and relates the chapters to each other;
- A definition for each key term appears in the margin adjacent to the term's first text appearance, as well as being listed in the Glossary. The new margin definitions provide an explanation on first reading of the material; the Glossary offers a summary and quick reference;
- Questions for review are positioned throughout each chapter at the end of the text sections. By attempting to answer these questions, students will be able to check their comprehension of new material immediately;

- Questions are included in the issues (colour) sections that are set off from the rest of the text, reinforcing the purpose of these sections—to provide the opportunity for further exploration of the topic;
- Questions for review and discussion appear at the end of each chapter. Review questions help to summarize the topics covered in the chapter and to reinforce understanding of the content before proceeding.

Acknowledgements

No textbook is written without the assistance of others. My wife Nancy and my children Matthew and Heather did not complain about the time allocated to the rewriting of this textbook. They fully appreciate the concept of opportunity cost. I am also grateful for the assistance provided by the reviewers of the first two editions of this text. Their suggestions are an integral part of the book's success and acceptance in educational institutions. I appreciate the comments from my colleagues at Durham College who have used the book in their classes. Included in this group are Peter George, Craig Thomas, Rod Lee, Colin Lockey, Gary Weaver, Lewis Presner, Henry Klaise, Peter McKeracher, Virginia Colling, and Mike Conte. Instructors at other institutions who provided helpful comments were: John Thompson of Seneca College; Teresa Menzies of Niagara College and Brock University; Don Garrie of Georgian College; Neil Kaplash of the University of Victoria; Anastasia Gotsis of Jarvis Collegiate; Bill Jennings of Frontenac Secondary School; Robb Palmer of Trafalgar Castle School; and Manford Wasson of Miramichi Valley High School.

I would also like to acknowledge the assistance that I was given by the staff at Maxwell Macmillan, especially the editor in charge of this project, Jane Clark. And for their assistance on the last two editions of this book, thanks to Gaynor Fitzpatrick and Patrick Gallagher. Thanks also to my friend David Lawson for his work on the cover.

I hope that you will find this text extremely useful in explaining economic concepts. If you have any comments, I would be delighted to hear from you.

For Nancy, Matthew, and Heather

Contents

Chapter 4:
Government in Canada   105

Chapter 7:
Money and the Canadian
Banking System   201

Chapter 8:
Stabilization Policy   239

Chapter 9:
International Economics   273

Chapter 12:
Perfect Competition:
Theory and Practice   373

Chapter 13:
How Imperfect Competition Functions   399

Chapter 14:
The Pricing of Resources   437

Chapter 1

Introductory Concepts

Chapter Objectives

After successfully completing this chapter, you will be able to:

- relate the concept of scarcity to the science of economics
- understand what is meant by the term "resource"
- differentiate between direct and opportunity costs
- use the concept of opportunity cost in your everyday life, as well as relate it to the allocation of Canada's resources
- construct a production-possibilities curve and identify the assumptions under which the curve was drawn
- define the law of diminishing returns, using an example of conditions under which it would apply
- understand the differences between the two basic approaches to economic decision-making: the free market approach and the command approach
- understand why it is necessary to make certain assumptions when developing economic theories
- identify and present in graphic form positive and inverse relationships between two variables

Key Terms

scarcity
opportunity cost
production-possibilities curve
law of diminishing returns

free market approach
command approach
positive relationship
inverse relationship

What is Economics?

Why is it so difficult to find a job? Why is Canadian money worth less than American money? Should governments in Canada enact more strict pollution-control legislation? Why are there differences between the wages paid to men and those paid to women? Why do many athletes earn more than the prime minister of Canada? Should medical care be free of charge to all residents of this country?

These are some of the questions that concern Canadians. To many of us, they may seem unrelated, yet the answers to all of them fall within the subject matter of economics. An adequate understanding of economic issues is becoming more and more essential to everyday living. This book is an introduction to the science of economics: it helps provide the information and skills that will enable you to answer the questions raised above, and many others as well.

The dictionary defines economics as the science that deals with the production, distribution and use of goods, money, natural resources, and services. But this definition does not provide a real understanding of the subject. One important element of economics is missing from the definition. If it were not for the concept of **scarcity**, there would be no need to study economics. As a starting point for our definition, let us discuss scarcity.

Scarcity

In economics, the term scarcity *refers to anything that is available only in a limited supply.*

The dictionary tells us that scarcity is "an insufficient amount or supply." In economic terms, anything that has a limited supply is referred to as scarce. As a result, almost everything is scarce because very few things are available in unlimited quantities. The only items that cannot be considered scarce are air and sunshine—at certain times of the year. If there is only a limited amount of a commodity, then a decision has to be made as to how that commodity will be used.

On an individual basis, time and money are always scarce commodities. There are only 24 hours in a day. Regardless of how many things we plan to do each day, we are restricted by the number of hours available. For example, time has to be set aside for sleeping, eating, studying, and recreation. A decision has to be made about how best to use the time available. Also, not many of us have an unlimited supply of dollars on hand. Because the amount of money that we possess is limited, we must decide how to allocate it among various purchases. It is only when things are not limited in supply that we do not have to make such decisions.

People who are in business also have to deal with scarcity. Farmers are restricted by the amount of land available and must decide what crops they are going to grow. Store owners have a limited amount of space to use, which means they must make decisions about what products they will or will not stock on their shelves.

Manufacturers must decide what products they will produce with a given quantity of machines and equipment. Again, the fact of scarcity requires that decisions be made.

On a much larger scale, it can be said that Canada has a limited amount of *resources.* The dictionary defines a resource as something that a country or state can use to its advantage. Resources are used to produce goods and services, and can be classified into three groups: *land, labour, and capital.*

When we refer to land as a resource, we mean more than the ten million square kilometres that comprise Canada's land mass. We include such natural resources as minerals, wild animals, vegetation, and water. Canada is the world's largest producer of asbestos, zinc, silver, and nickel. It is the second-largest producer of potash, gypsum, molybdenum, and sulphur, and is a major producer of uranium, titanium, aluminium, cobalt, gold, lead, copper, iron, and platinum. Our country also has abundant oil and natural gas reserves. Wild animals form the basis of our fur and hunting industries. One form of vegetation—trees—covers about 3.1 million square kilometres. This resource provides Canada with its lumber, newsprint and pulp-and-paper industries. As mentioned above, water is also a resource. The minerals and vegetation that are present under water make up part of the resource that we refer to as land. Approximately one million tons of fish are taken annually from Canadian waters. Although Canada's land resource is extensive, it still has its limitations and decisions must be made regarding its use.

The population of Canada forms the basis of our labour resource. Canada's population in 1991 was approximately 26.8 million people. Our population is continuing to grow, but not at the rate that it has in the past. The reason for the slower rate of growth is that the fertility rate in Canada has been declining. In 1959 there were an average of 3.9 births per woman, but by 1989 the fertility rate had fallen to 1.7 births per woman. The fertility rate is the average number of births a woman can be expected to have over her lifetime. In some provinces (Quebec, for example), the decline in the fertility rate has been significantly greater than the national average. In 1989, the fertility rate in Quebec was 1.4 births per woman. Even though women are having fewer children, our population is still growing because of the large number of women who are in their child-bearing years. A steady flow of immigrants is also responsible for increases in the population of Canada.

As well as growing, the Canadian population is also aging. In 1971, people aged 65 and over comprised 8.2 percent of the population. By 1986, this figure had risen to 10.7 percent, and by the year 2001, it is projected to be 14 percent. Elderly individuals are not expected to be part of our labour resource.

The population of Canada by province for 1991 is listed in the following table.

Table 1.1 / Population of Canada by province 1991

	Thousands
Newfoundland	572.7
Prince Edward Island	132.3
Nova Scotia	896.6
New Brunswick	723.0
Quebec	6 779.4
Ontario	9 879.8
Manitoba	1 095.7
Saskatchewan	1 004.8
Alberta	2 467.8
British Columbia	3 167.9
Yukon	26.7
Northwest Territories	53.7
Canada	26 800.3

Source: Estimates taken from *Canadian Markets 1991,* (Toronto: Financial Post Information Service) p.7.

Our labour resource includes more than just the number of people in Canada. It refers to the variety of skills, level of education, and technical training of the Canadian population. Those people who are working and those who are willing to work are all included in the labour force.

Capital resources, which form the third classification, refer to man-made items that are used to produce goods and services. Buildings, factories, equipment, computers, tools, lathes, drill presses, fork-lift trucks, and conveyor belts are examples of capital resources. Also included under the heading of capital resources are steel and paper mills, nuclear and hydro-electric power plants, train stations, and airports. Transportation vehicles such as trucks, railway cars, buses, and airplanes are further examples of capital.

Despite the abundance of these various resources, Canada still has a limited amount of each. These limitations require that Canadians decide how best to use our available resources. What products will we produce? What services will we provide? How will these goods and services be produced? Who will receive these goods and services? These are just some of the decisions that must be made as a result of the limits on productive resources.

Whenever a resource is scarce or available only in limited supply in relation to the demand for it, a decision must be made about how the resource will be used. *Economics is the study of how we make decisions regarding the use of our scarce resources.*

Water: An Inexhaustible Resource?

It may seem unbelievable to suggest that Canada could face a water shortage. Canada has fourteen percent of the world's lakes and nine percent of the world's river flow serving less than one percent of the world's population. Seven percent of our country is covered with water. The Great Lakes contain 22 800 cubic kilometres of water, or about 18 percent of the fresh water on this planet. Lake Superior is the world's largest freshwater lake.

Despite these impressive statistics, Canada may soon be facing a water crisis. Why is this so? Much of the problem in Canada centres on matching the demand for water with the available supply. On average, each Canadian uses 7100 litres of water a day — taking into account household, industrial, and agricultural use. The demand for water by Canadians is quite high. In fact, we are the second-highest water users in the world, following only the Americans. Apart from needing water to drink, Canadians also require a great deal of water for their modern conveniences. For example, one flush of a toilet uses 23 litres of water; a shower uses about 25 litres a minute; a dishwasher uses about 65 litres; an automatic clothes washer uses 230 litres; and a garden hose uses 1500 litres or more per hour.

In addition to our domestic use of water, industry and agriculture require water. Water is needed to separate oil from the tar sands, for potash mines, for hydro-electric developments, for food-processing factories, for coal-burning power plants, and for countless other industrial purposes. Agriculture uses large amounts of water to grow food. Shortages have made it necessary to have extensive irrigation systems installed in farming areas. Western Canada alone has 5400 hectares of land that is now irrigated as a result of drought conditions that have devastated crops in the Prairie provinces. Irrigation in these areas has made possible the planting of such crops as soft wheat, sugar beets, and alfalfa hay. It is estimated that irrigation accounts for up to 60 percent of the water consumption in Canada.

The demand for water clearly exists. But what about the supply? The opening paragraph in this section suggests that the supply of water in Canada is extensive; however, this fact must be examined in more detail. The majority of Canada's water flows north, but most of Canada's population lives in the south, close to the U.S. border. Much of the water is not accessible to our population. There are regional shortages of water. For the following basins, the annual reliable flow of water is insufficient to meet present or projected demands: Okanagan (southern British Columbia); Milk (southern

Alberta); North Saskatchewan; South Saskatchewan; Red-Assini-boine (southern Manitoba); and southern Ontario. There is also a limit to the amount of clean, fresh water available, because water pollution from sewage and acid rain is a continuing and growing problem.

What can be done about obtaining an adequate supply of fresh water? The answer to providing these supplies is primarily finan-cial. Money is definitely required to clean up chemical-waste leaks and to reduce acid-rain sources. Money is needed to repair old water-distribution systems. Money is needed to provide adequate sewage-treatment systems. Money is required to provide dry farm-lands with water—possibly by diverting northern rivers to flow south. Money may also be required to prevent damage to aquatic wildlife. Regardless of which methods are chosen, money has to be made available in order to preserve this resource. Money has to be taken away from other uses in order to ensure that we maintain an ade-quate water resource.

Questions

1 Is water a scarce resource? Explain.
2 The water crisis is worse in the western United States than in Canada. In your opinion, could the fact that Canada has relatively more fresh water than the United States be a source of conflict between the two nations?
3 Can you suggest ways that Canadians could reduce their demand for water?
4 Canadians use more water on average than do residents of warmer climates. Why is this so?
5 What impact might the "greenhouse effect" have on the problem of an inadequate water supply?

Direct Costs / Opportunity Costs

Opportunity costs represent the value of the best possible alternative that is given up in the decision to use a resource.

The process of decision-making involves costs, which can be divided into two groups: direct and opportunity. *Direct costs* can be defined as the out-of-pocket expenses that are required to do something. For instance, deciding to attend college involves certain expenses, such as paying for tuition, books, and supplies. Living away from home makes room and board an expense, too. Transportation is also a major cost of attending college. These are all direct costs. However, possibly the biggest expense of the decision to attend college is not a direct cost. The biggest expense is the salary, or income, that you could have earned had you not decided to further your education. The income thus sacrificed has to be considered as part of the expense of a college education and is referred to as **opportunity cost.**

Every time you spend money you not only incur a direct cost but an opportunity cost as well! Consider another example: assume that you saved $8000 and decided to spend this money on a car. What is the opportunity cost of this decision? If this money were to be deposited in a savings account at a bank, it could earn interest. The opportunity that was sacrificed was the chance to earn interest on the $8000 had it been deposited in a bank account. The opportunity cost is the value of the lost alternative—the interest. If the interest rate paid on a savings account was ten percent per year, you would have sacrificed $800 a year by withdrawing $8000 from the bank. The opportunity cost of this decision is $800 a year, or the opportunity that was sacrificed. The total cost of the car would be the sum of the direct and opportunity costs—$8800. Every decision carries with it an opportunity cost, since in order to do one thing, something else must be sacrificed.

There are opportunity costs involved in making decisions regarding Canada's scarce resources. If we decide to construct a housing development on good agricultural land, we have to give up the farm produce that could have been grown on the land. The opportunity cost of the housing development is the value of the farm produce that was sacrificed. If someone decides to accept a job as an electrician, he or she cannot be an accountant or a computer programmer at the same time. The opportunity cost of being an electrician is the earnings that were forgone by not working at another occupation. There are also opportunity costs associated with machines and other capital resources. If a wood lathe is used to make salad bowls, it cannot be used to make table legs at the same time.

There is an opportunity cost associated with every decision. This cost is present because resources are scarce; when a decision is made regarding resource use, something has to be sacrificed. Thus, opportunity cost is defined as the value of the most expensive alternative that is sacrificed when resources are allocated to a specific use.

In reality, every time a decision is made to put a resource to a certain use, several other options have to be sacrificed. If $8000 is withdrawn from a bank in order to purchase a car, the money cannot be used to take a vacation, buy a swimming pool, put a down payment on a house, or earn interest on an investment. If all of these options must be sacrificed, what is the opportunity cost of purchasing a car? *The opportunity cost is the most expensive alternative that is given up.* In this example, therefore, the opportunity cost is the lost interest that would have been earned had this money been invested.

1.1   Why is scarcity so important to the study of economics?
1.2   What is the opportunity cost of going to a movie on the night before an economics exam?

Production-Possibilities Curves

The production-possibilities curve represents all the possible combinations of levels of production for two products, assuming that all available resources are used efficiently.

The choices that Canadians have to make about the use of scarce resources, and the associated opportunity costs, can be depicted by a **production-possibilities curve.** This curve will be introduced using a simple society as an example. Assume that this society can produce only two products—an agricultural product, corn, and a hunting product, spears. If every individual concentrates on the production of corn, the group could produce 100 bushels of corn from the available land each year. On the other hand, if everyone uses all of the available materials to make spears, the group could manufacture 27 spears in one year. If both corn and spears were produced in the same year, lesser amounts of the two products would be available. The more spears produced, the more corn that would have to be given up. Land and labour previously used to produce corn would be turned over to the production of spears. An increase in the production of corn, on the other hand, would require the use of some land, labour, and materials that were previously used to make spears. Various combinations of corn and spears could be produced. Five of these combinations are given in table 1.2.

Table 1.2 / Alternative combinations of corn and spears that could be produced in one year

Option	Corn (bushels)	Spears
A	0	27
B	20	25
C	50	19
D	85	10
E	100	0

This table indicates five of the options that are available to the society under discussion. As the amount of corn produced increases, the number of spears decreases. There is an inverse relationship between the two products: when one goes up, the other goes down.

The information from table 1.2 is plotted on a graph in figure 1.1. Joining the points plotted on the graph creates a line called the production-possibilities curve. This curve shows all the possible combinations of corn and spears that can be produced by this simple society in one year. In order to draw this curve, it is assumed that all of the resources available to this society (land, people, tools, and equipment) are being used in the most efficient way. If resources are not being used efficiently (for example, if some workers are unemployed), the level of production of corn and spears would be less than the optimum. The level of production resulting from such an inefficient use of resources can be represented by a point to the left of the curve. This point is indicated as **G** in figure 1.1. At **G**, 15 spears and 20 bushels of corn are produced, well below capacity, since according to table 1.2, 25 spears can be produced along with 20 bushels of corn. Any combination of corn and spears to the left of the production-possibilities boundary represents an inefficient use of available resources.

**Figure 1.1
The production-
possibilities
curve**

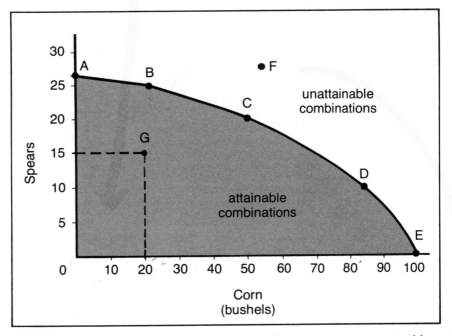

The possible combinations of spears and corn are represented by the curve. The combinations to the left of the curve (e.g. **G** in the shaded area) are attainable, while those to the right of the curve (e.g. **F**) are not.

What about combinations to the right of the production-possibilities curve, as indicated by point **F** in figure 1.1? This combination of corn and spears is currently unattainable since the production-possibilities curve shows the maximum amount of these two products that can be made using available resources.

Will the combination of corn and spears as indicated by point **F** ever be attainable? Yes; this society will not always be limited to the choices on the present production-possibilities curve. Over time, the ability to produce both corn and spears is likely to increase. Any increase in the amount of available resources will permit the increased production of both commodities. For example, as the population increases, more workers would be available to work both in the corn fields and in spear manufacturing. More corn and spears could be produced, causing the options listed in table 1.2 to change. Increases in the amounts of corn and spears that can be produced will cause the production-possibilities curve to shift to the right (see figure 1.2).

**Figure 1.2
Effect of a
population
increase on the
production-
possibilities
curve**

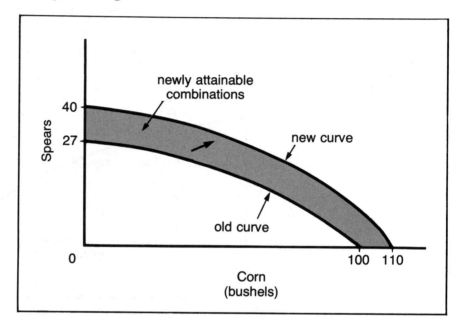

The increase in population permits more of both spears and corn to be produced. The shaded area shows the newly attainable combinations of spears and corn.

Increases in production will also occur if a new method of producing either product is developed. For example, a new way to plant corn may be discovered that increases its yield. This would also cause a change in the options presented in table 1.2 and, therefore, in the production-possibilities curve. The effect of this change is shown in figure 1.3. In the diagram, the maximum amount of corn attainable from available resources is now 120 bushels, whereas previously it was only 100 bushels. The maximum amount of spears that could be produced has not changed and remains at 27. Any change in production methods or technology will cause the production-possibilities curve to shift to a new position.

The concept of opportunity cost can be applied to the production-possibilities curve. In order to produce more spears, a certain amount of corn will have to be sacrificed. Assume that this society is producing the combination of corn and spears indicated by option **D**

**Figure 1.3
Effect of
technological
change on the
production-
possibilities
curve**

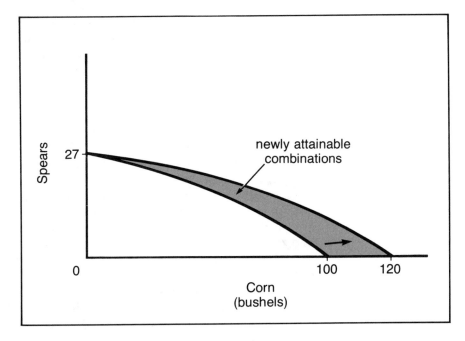

A change in the technology of corn production allows more of both spears and corn to be produced. The newly attainable combinations are represented by the shaded area.

in table 1.2. If the society decided to shift production to is producing the combination of corn and spears indicated by option **D** in table 1.2. If the society decided to shift production to option **C**, an additional nine spears could be produced. In order to make nine additional spears, 35 bushels of corn have to be given up. The 35 bushels of corn could be referred to as the opportunity cost of producing the additional spears.

Is the concept of the production-possibilities curve relevant for a complex country like Canada? The answer is yes. Canadians have to decide between thousands of goods and services, not just two. We have a wide variety of resources and must decide how these resources are to be employed. Canadians also have a series of production possibilities, whereas our numerical example was limited to only two products—corn and spears. Further, the graph that was used to plot the various options is limited to two dimensions—vertical and horizontal. If we were to draw a production-possibilities curve for Canada, we would require more than two axes, since our choices would not be limited to two products. Changes in Canada's production-possibilities can also take place if more resources become available or if new technology is developed to make better use of existing resources.

The choices that Canadians are faced with are almost endless. Farmers must decide which crop to plant for the next year. Businesses must decide which product line to pursue. Homemakers must decide how to best utilize a limited amount of money while trying to provide for their families. For each of these decisions, the concept of a production-possibilities curve could be used in order to map out the various options.

Canada's production-possibilities curve shows the maximum amount of goods and services available to Canadians. It is a reflection of our potential standard of living. In order to improve our standard of living, it is necessary to shift Canada's production-possibilities curve to the right. This can be accomplished by increasing the amount of resources available to produce goods and services. The most likely resources that can be increased are labour and capital. Improvements in the quality of these resources will also allow the production of goods and services to increase. Government expenditures on education are aimed at improving the quality of our labour resource. Improvements in capital equipment and technological change also permit production to expand. In order to encourage technological improvements, governments in Canada have assisted in the financing of industrial research and development. Canada's production-possibilities horizon can also be expanded through foreign trade. A discussion of the impact of foreign trade on the standard of living in Canada appears in Chapter 9.

The shape of the production-possibilities curve is significant when analysing the ability of the simple society to trade off spears for more corn, and vice versa. If it is desirable to give up some spears in order to produce more corn, the society will discover that more and more spears have to be sacrificed for the same amount of corn. For example, if this society was producing at option **A** (27 spears; 0 corn) in table 1.2, the sacrifice of two spears would enable corn production to increase by 20 bushels—option **B**. On the other hand, if the society was producing at option **D** (10 spears; 85 bushels of corn) and decided to increase corn production, the sacrifice in terms of spears would be much greater. At point **D,** 10 spears would have to be given up in order to acquire 15 more bushels of corn. The opportunity cost of acquiring more corn increases as the amount of corn produced increases. Why is this so?

The reason is that different resources in different quantities are used in the production of each product. The production of spears requires mainly labour, while the production of corn requires mainly land. Furthermore, not all of the same resource is of identical quality. Some people are good spearmakers, others are not. Some land is good agricultural land, some is not. Any attempt to increase corn production will necessitate the use of land that is less suited for corn production. More and more spears must be given up in order to acquire more food.

The differences in resource quantity and quality partially account for the shape of the production-possibilities curve. Another factor influencing the shape of the curve is the law of diminishing returns.

1.3 With reference to the simple society, what is the opportunity cost of growing more corn?

1.4 In the society referred to above, someone could develop a new method for making spears. Show the effect of this change on the production-possibilities curve.

1.5 The production-possibilities curve is drawn assuming that all resources are fully employed. If there were unemployed workers in this society, why would the production-possibilities curve not shift?

The Law of Diminishing Returns

The simple society in our example faces several constraints in its attempt to produce more corn and more spears. The resources available to it, mainly labour and land, are limited. As the population increases, it will be necessary to produce more food. With more workers, the ability of this society to supply food should increase, but the gains in food production will be limited by the amount of land available. The amount of land is a fixed resource not subject to change, while population is not a fixed resource and is subject to change. Eventually, a point will be reached beyond which the addition of more workers adds very little to the total output of food.

This analysis also applies to complex societies like Canada. Our country has a limited amount of land available for food production; as our population increases, more food will be required. Our ability to produce food will be constrained by the amount of land available. Even though one resource (the number of workers) may be increasing, another resource (land) remains fixed. Eventually, the increases in food production that can be achieved by the addition of more workers to the land will start to decline. Each successive worker will contribute less food to the total amount produced because he or she has less and less land to work with.

When a fixed resource is combined with increasing amounts of a variable resource, the law of diminishing returns states that increases in total output will eventually become smaller and smaller.

This important economic principle is known as the **law of diminishing returns.** It applies when one resource used in the production of a commodity remains fixed. When other resources (workers) are combined with the fixed resource (land), total production will increase. A point will be reached, however, beyond which the increases in total production associated with the increases in other resources become smaller and smaller.

The law of diminishing returns applies as well to a business firm. Assume that a company has rented a building in order to manufacture chairs. In this case, the building is the fixed resource and cannot be changed. Chair production could increase by employing more workers and more machines. Yet the ability of the company to increase chair production is restricted by the size of the building. Even though more workers are hired, increases to the number of chairs produced by increasing the labour resource in this way will eventually begin to decline.

The law of diminishing returns states that when increasing amounts of a variable resource are added to a fixed resource, the increases in total output will eventually become smaller and smaller. The presence of the law of diminishing returns influences the shape of the production-possibilities curve. In our example, as more and more workers begin to produce corn, a point will be reached at which the additional corn produced by adding one more worker is less than the additional corn provided by the previous worker. This causes the production-possibilities curve to bow in as more corn is produced. The law of diminishing returns is an important concept in the study of economics. Its impact on a company's production costs will be discussed in Chapter 11.

1.6 What condition has to be present for the law of diminishing returns to have any impact on the production of goods and services?

Malthus and Live Aid

The idea of diminishing returns was first introduced by an English clergyman and economist, Thomas Robert Malthus (1766-1834). He lived in England during the time of the Industrial Revolution and witnessed its effects. Machinery was beginning to displace many qualified craftsmen from jobs, and unemployment was a serious problem. Many people had come to the conclusion that England was overpopulated.

Despite the reports of misery created by technological change, many believed that society would eventually progress to a point at which everyone would live in happiness and comparative leisure. In fact, technological change had improved the lot of many people. Malthus believed that these forecasts of happiness and leisure were wrong, and in 1798 he published his *Essay on the Principle of Population*. Malthus based his pessimism on two assumptions: first, that food was necessary to human existence, and second, that sexual passion between males and females was necessary and would remain so, and people would, consequently, continue to reproduce and increase the population.

Malthus argued that the population of the world would increase faster than the ability of the world to produce food. The world's population would increase in a geometric progression (1, 2, 4, 8, 16, 32, 64 ...) whereas food production, at the very best, could increase only at an arithmetic rate (1, 2, 3, 4, 5 ...). The end result is too many people and too little food.

In order to prove his point, Malthus used the example of North America, where the population had doubled over a period of 25 years. This was his estimate of how quickly the population would increase on a world-wide basis if it remained unchecked. However, he did not expect this population expansion actually to take place because there are certain checks that prevent the population from increasing at this rate. These checks include war, disease, and famine. Nonetheless, he believed that population increases would continue to outstrip food production.

Malthus had several proposals to improve the situation. He advocated moral restraint in the form of later marriages and smaller families. He was also opposed to giving any type of relief to the poor. If they were kept alive by charity, they would continue to propagate and make conditions worse. In a sense, charity, according to Malthus, was cruelty in disguise. Malthus would, however, give charity to those who were poor because of some undeserved calamity. These came to be known as the "deserving poor."

The ability of population increases to surpass food production was the basis for the law of diminishing returns. There was no question that a given piece of land would yield more produce with the application of fertilizer and the use of more labour. There comes a point, however, beyond which it does not pay to add any more fertilizer or labour to the land. Additional increments of fertilizer and labour will not bring about corresponding increases in production. In fact, a point may be reached beyond which additional workers may even reduce production.

Some changes in the world have clearly delayed the confirmation of Malthus' predictions. For example, family size has decreased, and in this century, birth control has become more prevalent. In industrialized countries, people are marrying at a later age. Advances in technology have increased the agricultural yield per hectare and have improved the world's ability to produce food.

Are Malthus' theories dead or are they still alive? The projection for the world's population in the year 2000 is approximately 6.1 billion people. World population is continually growing; however, the rate of population growth in most of the world is declining. Dramatic declines in the birth rate are apparent in China and Cuba. Rates are also falling in Thailand, Malaysia, Indonesia, South Korea, Colombia, and Chile, among others. Governments have supported birth control in traditionally Roman Catholic countries such as Mexico and Brazil. However, the birth rate has failed to decline in Africa; on that continent, large families are still desirable.

What is happening to food production? World food output is increasing ahead of population growth. Usable crop land is, however, reaching its limit and the world fish catch is levelling off. The problem is not, in fact, one of food production, but one of distribution. When food prices increase, the poor cannot afford to buy. Also, a large percentage of the world's grain is fed to livestock. In Africa, where the population continues to grow rapidly, food production is declining. The problems related to food production in Africa have been exacerbated by recent droughts and wars. During 1985, the drought in Africa was brought to the attention of the rest of the world through magazines, television specials, records, and notably, the Live Aid concert on 13 July of that year.

Are Malthus' theories dead?

Questions

1   Relate Malthus' ideas on population to the law of diminishing returns.

2   There is some evidence that increased educational levels among females are associated with declining fertility rates in many countries. Why do you think this may be the case? (Hint: consider the concept of opportunity cost.)

3   In Africa there has been a tendency for people to move from rural areas to the cities. By the end of the century it is expected that one-half of Africa's population will live in urban areas. What will this development do to Malthus' predictions?

4   In many African countries, governments have followed policies that keep food prices low. How do you think African farmers would react to low food prices? (Hint: again consider the concept of opportunity cost.)

Economic Systems

The free market approach in economic decision-making is based on private ownership of property and resources.

The production-possibilities curve outlines all of the possible combinations in the production of goods and services that are available. The problem facing each society is which combination to select. How does a group of individuals make decisions about the use of scarce resources? In the terms of our example, which option from table 1.2 should this society select? There are basically two approaches that may be followed in economic decision-making: the **free market approach** and the **command approach.** These approaches to economic decision-making will be discussed under resource ownership and the decision process.

Resource Ownership

The command approach describes a situation in which resources—land, labour, and capital— are jointly or publicly owned.

In a free market system, the nation's productive resources are privately owned by individuals and businesses. Farmers own their land, businesses own their factories and equipment, individuals own their homes, and so on. The free market system is based on private ownership of property. In contrast, the command approach requires public, not private, ownership of all resources. Land, labour, and capital are all jointly owned and not possessed by any one individual or business.

In Canada we have a combination of these two approaches. The majority of our resources are owned privately. However, a substantial portion of our resources is publicly owned. Examples of publicly-owned resources include parks, government office buildings, electricity-generating stations, military equipment, and certain educational institutions. In addition, Crown corporations such as Canada Post Corporation and the Canadian Broadcasting Corporation own a large amount of our nation's resources.

The Decision Process

In a free market economy, the decisions of individuals and businesses determine how our resources are to be used. Consumers are the major determinant of resource use. If they continue to purchase a certain product or service, resources will be allocated to the production of that item. If consumers stop purchasing a certain product, the resources used in its production will go elsewhere.

In a command system, decisions are more centralized and not left up to individuals. Since individuals do not own the resources, it is difficult for them to decide on resource use. Decisions must be made by a group of individuals with official status. Such a group must determine what goods and services will be produced and who will receive them.

Again, in Canada we have a combination of these approaches. *Basically, individuals make decisions regarding privately-owned resources and government makes decisions regarding publicly-owned resources.* Government may also make decisions regarding the use of privately-owned resources. For example, certain provinces have enacted rent-control legislation that limits the amount that a landlord can charge for rental accommodation. Also, minimum-wage laws require that employers provide a certain minimum wage per hour to every worker, and municipal zoning regulations put restrictions on land use.

No country in the world adopts either of these approaches to decision-making exclusively. Countries where the free market approach predominates, such as the United States, are referred to as *capitalist*. Even in capitalist countries, the government plays a significant role in economic decision-making. For example, in the United States, the government operates the post office, the airports, the military, and many other services.

Countries that stress the command approach are referred to as *socialist* or *communist.* In socialist countries, the ownership of the nation's productive resources is in public hands. In communist countries, private ownership of property is not permitted. In major communist nations such as China and the USSR, however, private ownership has not been completely eliminated. Some small farms and businesses are privately owned and the decision on what to produce is made by the individual owner.

All countries combine the free market and command approaches to economic decision-making. Therefore, we can say that all countries have *mixed economies,* even though the nature of the mix between free market and command decisions varies by country.

1.7 How do the free market and command systems vary in the area of resource ownership?

Canada's Political Parties

A political party is an organization whose aim is to form the government of Canada or of a province through the electoral process. Once in control of government, the party can decide what public policy on various matters will be. In deciding upon public policy, the party will be presenting its ideas on how economic decisions should be carried out.

Political parties are divided in their approach about how economic decisions should be made. Some parties are strong proponents of the free market system and allocate only a very small role to government. Others believe that the free market system needs to be modified a great deal by government policies. Still others advocate the elimination of the free market system.

In Canada, two political parties have dominated the scene since Confederation: the Liberals and the Progressive Conservatives. The philosophical approaches of each party do not vary significantly. Both parties see a role for government in our economy, as well as a role for private enterprise. Where the two parties differ is in the areas of leadership and specific issues. Personalities play a large role in political activity and the personality and image of one party's leader may be the reason for its public acceptance. On such issues as energy prices, constitutional reform, and economic policy, the two parties may differ on a pragmatic, but not an ideological basis.

The New Democratic Party (NDP) does differ ideologically from the other two. This party has its roots in the Co-operative Commonwealth Federation (CCF), which had a philosophy counter to the free market approach. The NDP, like the CCF, is a socialist party, but recently has been trying to broaden its appeal to voters by relaxing its socialist stand on some issues.

The Social Credit Party is distinguished from the two major parties by its different views on money management. The Libertarian Party is a proponent of the free market system and advocates very little government intervention in the economy. The Communist Party of Canada is at the other extreme, advocating government decision-making in most areas of our society.

In recent years, several new political parties have entered candidates in both federal and provincial elections. Among these parties are the Reform Party, the Green Party, the Confederation of Regions Party, the Family Coalition Party, and the Christian Heritage Party.

Questions

1 Draw a line, labelling the free market approach at the right-hand side and the command approach at the left-hand side. Situate each of Canada's political parties on the line in accordance with their views on economic decision-making.
2 What political party holds power in your province? What are its views on economic decision-making?

Economics as a Science

Economics is a science. A dictionary definition states that science is the body of knowledge and theory dealing with things in nature and the universe, and with the forces that create, shape, and form them. Science is based on facts that are obtained from careful study of experiments. Economics fits this definition. There is a major difference, however, between the science of economics and other sciences such as chemistry and physics. In chemistry, most of the environmental conditions can be controlled during the experiment. That is, in the process of conducting an experiment, the scientist can control the air temperature, the amount of solution, the filtration process, and so on. Since economic experiments must be conducted in the course of everyday events, this type of precision and control is impossible. Economic experiments are conducted under conditions that cannot be easily controlled. In our economic environment, changes are taking place each day that will influence the results of experimentation.

For example, assume that a company wanted to determine how consumers would react to lower prices for its products. It could set up an experiment whereby it systematically lowered prices and recorded the sales at each price. If sales increased after a price reduction, the company could assume that there is a relationship between the number of sales and prices. This assumption may not be correct, however. At the same time that the company lowered prices, people's incomes may have increased, their tastes may have altered, or the prices of other products may have changed. Any or all of these adjustments could have resulted in higher sales. The company may believe that lower prices increase sales, yet it cannot be sure unless it takes other factors into consideration. Unlike an experiment in chemistry, it is not possible for the company to control all the external factors that could influence the economic experiment.

In order to avoid this problem of a changing environment in the study of economics, we assume that all external factors affecting the outcome of an economic experiment remain constant and do not influence the results. If the company wants to determine how sales are going to be affected by lower prices, it will have to assume for practical purposes that all other factors remain constant. Although this assumption is unrealistic, it aids in the understanding of possible economic consequences of certain actions. Therefore, just as in scientific experiments, it will be necessary throughout this text to assume that factors surrounding economic issues are remaining constant.

An Introduction to Graphs

It may appear strange to be beginning an economics textbook with a discussion of graphs. Yet graphs provide us with a useful aid in explaining economic concepts. If you are not familiar with graphs, it would be advantageous to read this section and attempt the exercises. Even if you are comfortable with the use of graphs, it may be wise to review the concepts presented in this section. The material is sufficient for understanding any graph used throughout the book.

Graphs are simply a visual way of communicating information in a manner that assists in the presentation of economic theories. The statement that a picture is worth a thousand words applies very well to graphs. Graphs represent a relationship between two sets of figures and can only be drawn if the background information is available.

A graph consists of two numbered lines, or axes, which intersect at a 90° angle. The intersection point is called the origin. It has the numerical value of zero and is the starting point for all measurements. It is possible to measure two variables on a graph. For convenience, the axes are labelled x and y. Positive and negative values of x and y are measured as shown in figure 1.4. The following two examples will demonstrate the use of graphs.

Example No. 1: Positive Relationships   Suppose that Mason's Department Store decided to collect information on the number of umbrellas sold in relation to the amount of rainfall in the area so that the store could have a better

Figure 1.4
Axes of a graph

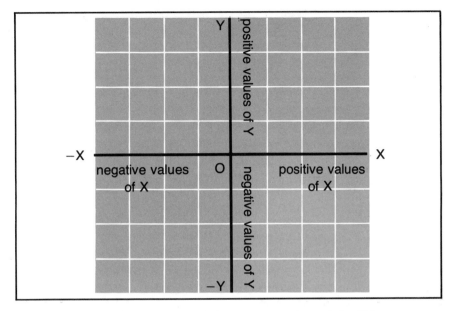

The axes (X and Y) of a graph intersect at the origin (O).

A positive relation-ship is one in which an increase or a decrease in one variable results in a corresponding increase or decrease in the other variable.

understanding of factors that influence umbrella sales. Assume that the store collected the information shown in table 1.3 for the months from April to October.

Upon reviewing the information, the store could determine that in the months when the rainfall was highest, the number of umbrellas sold was also highest. In the month of September, when the amount of rainfall was lowest (0.5 cm), the least number of um-brellas (three) was sold. The relationship between the amount of rain-fall and the number of umbrellas sold is referred to as a **positive relationship.** In other words, as the value of one increases, the value of the other increases. Conversely, as the value of one decreases, the corresponding value of the other decreases.

This information collected by the store can be depicted on a graph. In figure 1.5, the number of umbrellas sold is measured along the vertical axis and the centimetres of rainfall are measured along the horizontal axis.

The information in the table is plotted in figure 1.5 by recording the data for each month separately. For example, in the month of April, there were five centimetres of rainfall and 25 umbrellas were sold. This point, shown as **April** in figure 1.5, was obtained by first measuring along the horizontal axis to the point referring to five centimetres of rainfall. From this point, locate the point on the vertical, or y, axis that corresponds to 25 umbrellas sold. Repeat this proce-dure for each of the remaining months. Once all the points are plotted, they can be connected as shown in the diagram. The line that is drawn on the graph represents the relationship between umbrellas sold and centimetres of rainfall. There is a positive relationship between these variables. Any line or graph that proceeds away from the origin into the positive quadrant represents a *positive relationship* between the variables measured on the axes.

Table 1.3 / Relationship between centimetres of rainfall and umbrellas sold

Month	Centimetres of rainfall	Number of umbrellas sold
April	5.0	25
May	3.0	20
June	2.0	10
July	1.0	5
August	2.5	15
September	0.5	3
October	1.5	7

**Figure 1.5
Graphical
representation
of a positive
relationship**

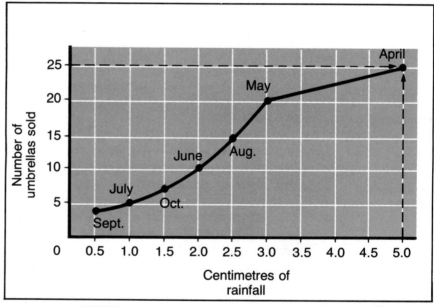

A positive relationship is indicated by an upward-sloping curve away from the origin.

**Example No. 2:
Inverse
Relationships**

Suppose that Mason's Department Store wanted to find out how the price of bicycles affected bicycle sales. Assume that the store varied the price on a certain type of bicycle and recorded the sales at these prices.

In an inverse relationship, an increase in the value of one variable results in a corresponding decrease in the value of the other.

As shown in table 1.4, when the price of bicycles decreased, the number of bicycles sold increased. This is referred to as an **inverse relationship.**

The graphical presentation of an inverse relationship is shown in figure 1.6. The price of the bicycles is measured along the vertical axis and the number of bicycles sold along the horizontal axis. When the information from the table is plotted and the points joined, the line slopes down to the right. Any line on any graph that slopes down to the right indicates that an *inverse relationship* exists between the two variables being measured.

Table 1.4 / Relationship between number of bicycles sold and the price of the bicycles

Price	Number of bicycles sold
$200	10
$190	15
$180	20
$170	25
$160	30

**Figure 1.6
Graphical representation of an inverse relationship**

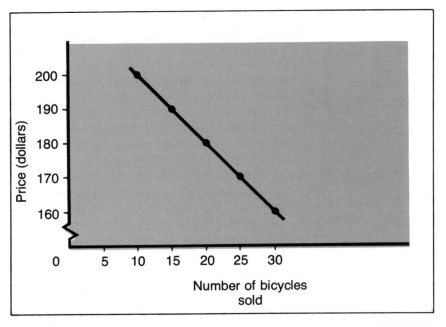

An inverse relationship is indicated by a downward-sloping curve.

You will note that the line drawn in figure 1.6 is a straight line. For many of the graphs throughout this textbook, a straight line will be used as a matter of convenience. In reality, the relationship between any two variables can seldom be represented by a straight line.

A graph is simply a visual presentation of the relationship between two variables. Graphs do not exist without numerical information. They are constructed from this available information. In order to construct the graph, some numerical information had to be collected beforehand.

1.8 Draw a graph to indicate each of the following relationships. In each instance, make up your own numbers and put them in the form of a table before drawing the graph. Be sure to label your axes. Plot:

 i the relationship between the number of litres of gasoline used and the number of kilometres driven;

 ii the relationship between an individual's age and height; and

 iii the relationship between the number of potatoes and the number of carrots that can be grown on the same plot of land.

Summary

The key word in the study of economics is scarcity. Since resources are available only in limited quantities, decisions must be made regarding their use. Economics is concerned with how these decisions are made. An opportunity cost is associated with each decision. It refers to the value of the best alternative that is sacrificed when resources are allocated to a specific use.

The production-possibilities curve allows us to put these decisions into perspective. The curve shows the maximum possible combinations of two items that can be produced using all available resources. The citizens of a country must select which combination is most acceptable or desirable. Any change in a country's resources or a change in technology will change the combinations of items that can be provided. This is shown graphically as a shift in the production-possibilities curve.

Like other peoples, Canadians must make decisions regarding the use of scarce resources. We allocate our resources through a combination of individual and government decisions. Some of our resources are privately owned, and owners must decide how they will be used. For example, each individual is free to decide what type of job he or she would like to pursue. Government also commands control over some of our resources, and uses them to provide such services as hospitals, schools, and defence.

Economics is a science. As in other sciences, economists are interested in conducting experiments and developing theories. The difference between economics (a social science) and the physical sciences is that external factors influencing experiments are more difficult to control in economics. Experiments cannot be done under controlled conditions in a laboratory. The theories developed from these experiments must take these external factors into consideration. For purposes of explanation and demonstration, economic theories are usually stated with the assumption that all other factors remain unchanged.

Questions for Review and Discussion

1 If something could be obtained without giving up anything, is there an opportunity cost? Explain.

2 Is a free sample of cheese handed out in your local supermarket actually free in economic terms? Is it possible for some things to be free from the point of view of the individual, but not from the point of view of society? Explain.

3 Assume that a country had only two products it could produce: bananas and radios. Draw a production-possibilities curve showing the various combinations in the production of these two products that are available to this country. Show what the impact on the production-possibilities curve would be if the population of this country increased.

4 The Pinetree Furniture Company produces two products: pine tables and pine cupboards. The company employs ten carpenters in its factory. Each carpenter can work on only one product at a time. Pinetree management has calculated that the company's daily production of furniture has to be one of the following options:

Option	Tables	Cupboards
A	8	0
B	6	1
C	4	2
D	2	3
E	0	4

Plot a production-possibilities curve for the Pinetree Furniture Company. What is significant about the shape of the curve? Would you expect many production-possibilities curves to look like this? Why or why not?

5 Classify the following countries as either capitalist, socialist, or communist:

  i Great Britain   iv Japan
  ii Cuba   v Poland
  iii Sweden   vi France

6 Almost everything in this world is scarce. Can you list some items that are not scarce (available in unlimited quantities)?

7 Classify the following resources as either labour, land, or capital:

  i grain elevator
  ii waitress
  iii screwdriver
  iv natural gas
  v electrician
  vi railway car
  vii trees

8 The Canadian government spends money on military equipment. What is the opportunity cost of this spending?

9 The Espanola Manufacturing Company only produces metal chairs. Some chairs are sprayed with red paint and the remainder are sprayed with green paint.

  i Draw a production-possibilities curve for the Espanola Manufacturing Company. Would this curve be similar to the curve drawn for corn and spears? Explain.

  ii If the Espanola Manufacturing Company were not producing at capacity and an order arrived for 100 red chairs, what would be the opportunity cost associated with filling this order?

10 Identify the economic resources that are available in your community. Classify these resources as land, labour, or capital.

11 List the resources that are required to make a hamburger and have it served at your favourite restaurant. Classify these resources as land, labour, or capital.

12 At a vegetable-canning plant several varieties of vegetables are processed and put in cans, although only one type of vegetable can be processed at a time. Explain how the concept of opportunity cost would apply to this plant.

13 Some politicians argue that health care should be free for all Canadians. Can health care ever be free? Explain your answer.

14 The law of diminishing returns states that because resources are not of equal quality the production-possibilities curve has a shape concave to the origin. Evaluate this statement.

15 Draw a production-possibilities curve showing the various combinations of television and video-cassette recorders that can be produced by an electronics company. Show the impact on the production-possibilities curve of a technological break-through in the production of television receivers.

16 Explain why economics cannot be considered as a science in the same category as physics and chemistry. What implications does this have for economic experiments and the theories derived from these experiments?

17 The time required to travel from Toronto to Montreal by air-plane is one hour at a cost of $100. The time required to drive

from Toronto to Montreal by car is five hours and costs $30. Which method is cheaper for someone who values his/her time at a) $10 per hour; b) $20 per hour?

18 In 1990, it was decided that the 1996 Summer Olympics would be held in Atlanta, Georgia. The city of Toronto and other levels of government had worked for three years putting together Toronto's application for these games. On September 18, 1990, there were 40 representatives from Canada in Tokyo, Japan to hear the decision of the Olympic Committee as to the 1996 site. What was the opportunity cost associated with Toronto's bid to host the 1996 games? What would have been the opportunity cost of hosting the Olympics had Toronto's bid been successful?

19 List two services provided by each level of government—federal, provincial, and municipal—in Canada. Do any of these services compete with services being offered by privately-owned businesses in your community?

20 For how long should you continue to look for a lost $10 bill?

21 In many nations the military is comprised of volunteers. Often the military has a greater proportion of volunteers from the less-wealthy segments of society than from the more-wealthy segments. Can the concept of opportunity costs be used to explain this situation? Explain.

22 Consider the resources available to Japan. Why do the Japanese emphasize education and training?

Suggested Readings

Block, Walter E. and Michael A. Walker. *Lexicon of Economic Thought*. Vancouver: The Fraser Institute 1989

Christian, William, and Colin Campbell. *Political Parties and Ideologies in Canada*. Toronto: McGraw-Hill Ryerson 1974.

Dumas, Jean. *Current Demographic Analysis: Report on the Demographic Situation in Canada in 1986*. Catalogue 91-209E Annual, Ottawa: Statistics Canada 1987

Foster, Harold D. and W. R. Derrick Sewell. *Water: The Emerging Crisis in Canada*. Ottawa: Canadian Institute for Economic Policy 1981.

Friedman, Milton. *Capitalism and Freedom*. Chicago: Phoenix Books 1962.

Heilbroner, Robert L. *The Making of Economic Society*. 6th ed. Englewood Cliffs: Prentice-Hall Inc. 1980.

LeBlanc, Ronald C. *Values, Value Clarification and Economic Understanding*. Toronto: Canadian Foundation for Economic Education 1986.

Priest, Gordon, "The Demographic Future," *Canadian Social Trends,* Catalogue 11-008E, No. 17, Summer 1990, Statistics Canada, Ottawa, 1990.

Romaniuc, A., *Current Demographic Analysis: Fertility in Canada: From Baby-boom to Baby-bust.* Catalogue 91-524E Occasional, Ottawa: Statistics Canada 1987.

Soule, George. *Ideas of the Great Economists.* New York: Mentor 1952.

Chapter 2

The Operation of a Market

Chapter Objectives

After successfully completing this chapter, you will be able to:

- define the concept of a market
- understand that the law of demand shows an inverse relationship between price and quantity and the law of supply shows a positive relationship between the same variables
- graphically show the impact on price and quantity of changes in demand and supply
- differentiate between a change in quantity demanded (supplied) and a change in demand (supply)
- explain the interaction of demand and supply in the marketplace
- graphically show the determination of price in the marketplace
- relate the concept of a market to real-world markets such as the stock and futures markets
- understand the concept of price elasticity and recognize its determinants
- use the formula for determining price elasticity and the total revenue approach for elasticity in relating to real-world market conditions

Key Terms

market

demand

supply

equilibrium price

stock market

futures market

price system

elasticity

One approach to economic decision-making is the free market system. This chapter discusses the operation of such a system, which includes the concepts of supply and demand.

What is a Market?

A market describes the interaction of buyers and sellers for the purpose of making an exchange of goods or services and establishing a price for them.

The local farmers' market in your area provides a good example of how a **market** works. It is normally located in a historic part of the community and is the focal point for the exchange of farm produce. The central location of the market has advantages for both buyers and sellers: shoppers are exposed to a wide variety of farm products of differing qualities; farmers save time and energy in selling their produce by reaching many potential customers at one location.

Apart from bringing the buyers and sellers of farm products together, the market performs another function. It establishes a price at which the products will be sold. The determining of a price, as will be pointed out in this chapter, is the most important aspect of a market.

An antique auction also provides a good example of how a market operates. Periodically, buyers and sellers of antiques are brought together through the notice of an auction. Unlike other markets, where the price may be set by the seller, at an auction the buyer actively participates in the determination of a price. Antiques are offered for sale and the bids of buyers determine the ultimate price. The more buyers at the auction, and the more money they have to spend, the higher the prices will be. Buyers are not, however, solely responsible for determining the price. Sellers at an auction may influence the price by establishing a minimum below which they will not sell the antique article. This is one example of how the price is set. Regardless of how the price is determined, each market establishes a price and provides for an exchange of goods and services.

Markets exist for any commodity or service that has a price. It is easy to understand the concept of markets, but often difficult to identify the actual market. For example, where is the market for rare coins? Since these coins are bought and sold, a market must exist, but its location is probably scattered all over the globe. In fact, there are many products sold in an international market. As Canadians, we know that not all of our food is grown locally; some food items (e.g., oranges, bananas) come from a variety of foreign countries. For these products, Canadians are buyers in the international marketplace. Canadian manufacturers, such as those producing steel and paper, often seek customers outside of Canada, and therefore are suppliers to international markets.

A market, therefore, is the interaction of buyers and sellers for the purpose of making an exchange, which establishes a price for the goods or services exchanged.

Markets do not need money in order to operate, although money is used as a medium of exchange in most markets. Prior to the introduction of money, exchange was carried on through a system of trading goods and services. This is referred to as *barter,* and is better suited to a more primitive economy than a modern industrialized one. Under a barter system, individuals need to have something to trade. Many people in today's society do not produce anything tangible to trade. For example, after a day's work, an office worker does not have anything tangible to offer in the marketplace. During the day, the worker may process hundreds of paper forms, but cannot take the forms home to trade for other products. Money solves this problem by providing something of value in return for the worker's services. This money can then be exchanged by the worker for goods and services.

Trades are difficult to make in the barter system. In order to complete a trade, a buyer of a certain product has to locate a seller interested in what he or she has to offer. Money again solves the problem. Since money is acceptable to both buyers and sellers, the exchange of goods and services is facilitated. The barter system, although inefficient, is not dead. It is still used in many parts of the world and appears to be making a comeback in industrialized countries. Rapidly rising prices and a desire to lessen the burden of personal income tax have resulted in the increased use of barter. Professional people and store owners appear to be best suited for participating in this type of exchange, since they have a service or a product that may be attractive to others. For example, an electrician may do some electrical work on his or her dentist's house in exchange for a certain amount of dental care. Since no records are kept, nor money transferred, the services will not be counted as income for either the electrician or the dentist.

The market for any good or service is divided into two sections: the demand side, representing those who are willing to purchase the product; and the supply side, representing those who are willing to sell the product.

In order to analyse the operation of a market in more detail, it is necessary to review the actions of buyers and sellers separately. The buyers' side of the market is referred to as the demand side. In other words, buyers have a certain **demand**, or desire, for various goods and services. This demand is represented by the quantity of goods and services that they are willing and able to purchase. The sellers' side of the market is referred to as the supply side. It represents the quantity of goods and services that sellers are willing and able to **supply**, or offer, to the market.

The Concept of Demand

You may have heard the phrase, "the consumer is king." This reference to royalty implies that consumers have the power to decide what products are supplied to the market simply by making their preferences known to manufacturers. Consumer preferences are transferred to the market in terms of the goods and services that they buy. If they continue to buy a certain product, it will continue to be produced. On the other hand, if they do not purchase a product in sufficient quantity, it will disappear from the market.

In actual fact, the consumer is not king. The decision about which products will be offered for sale is made jointly by the consumer and the supplier. Nonetheless, *consumer demand* and changes in this demand are an important aspect of any market. In circumstances where consumer demand has changed, the nature of the market changes as well. The automobile market provides a good example. The high cost of gasoline has changed driving habits, increasing the demand for small fuel-efficient cars, while the demand for "gas-guzzlers" has fallen off. These changes in demand have forced automobile manufacturers to increase the production of smaller cars.

Factors Affecting Demand

Many factors can cause consumer demand for a product to change. These can be summarized as follows:

Price: the fact that stores hold "clearance sales" attests to the importance of price to the consumer. Under normal circumstances, a person will buy a larger quantity of a product if the price is low. A lower price allows the consumer to buy more. Also, a lower price enables the consumer to substitute the lower-priced product for a more expensive alternative.

Change in the price of substitute products: since a number of products are fairly close substitutes for each other, changes in the price of one product will likely influence the demand for another. For example, in the past, sharp increases in the price of coffee have convinced some consumers to drink more tea and less coffee. Television sets provide another example. As the price of colour television sets dropped, they became more attractive substitutes for the conventional black and white set.

Change in the price of complementary products: the demand for a product is also influenced by any changes in the price of a complementary product. A complementary product is one that is used in conjunction with the product in question. As the price of gasoline increased, the demand for big cars declined. When mortgage interest rates increase, the number of houses that consumers buy declines.

Incomes: changes in the general level of income have an effect on product demand. Under most circumstances, the more money consumers have to spend, the greater the demand for the product. This is shown in the increased demand for luxury items such as backyard swimming pools and foreign vacations. The demand for luxury products has increased as the level of consumer income in Canada has increased. In periods when the real incomes of Canadians are declining, the demand for luxury items declines as well. This relationship, however, does not hold for all products. If a product is seen as cheap or inferior, consumers may purchase less of it as their incomes increase and be forced to buy more of it when their incomes decrease. For example, as a person's income increases, he or she may eat less hamburger and more steak; when income declines, hamburger outsells steak.

Tastes and preferences: individual tastes, preferences, and needs also influence demand. A major influence on individual tastes is advertising. Manufacturers have resorted to advertising in various media in order to maintain or increase the demand for their products. If consumers are constantly exposed to a certain brand through advertising, their purchase choices are likely to be affected. Advertising is not always aimed at persuading the consumer to buy the product. A certain amount of advertising simply provides information, which is especially true of government service ads.

Some industries do a more effective job of influencing consumer tastes than others. The fashion industry has been successful at constantly changing styles in apparel and footwear. These changes convince consumers that their present wardrobe is not satisfactory, creating a demand for new lines of clothes.

Consumer preferences may also be altered by receiving more information about a product. In the area of nutrition, medical research continually provides more data on the harmful effects of various food additives. For example, red dye and nitrites have been linked to cancer. The importance of consumer information has made such an impact that the federal government has established the Department of Consumer and Corporate Affairs in order to provide more information on product safety and quality. This department has also enacted legislation to eliminate misleading advertising.

Expectations of future prices: if consumers believe that the price of a product will increase in the near future, they are likely to buy more of the product in the present. In the early 1980s, the expectation of rapidly rising house and mortgage costs increased the demand for houses. With housing being the important consumer item that it is, buyers were anxious to purchase houses at the lowest possible price. The expectation of future prices also drastically influenced the gold and silver markets during the latter part of 1979 and early 1980. Rapidly rising prices led to the belief that prices would continue to rise. On the other hand, if people expect prices to be lower in the near future, they will postpone purchases until a later date.

Number and characteristics of buyers: as the population increases, the demand for most products increases as well. There is a greater need for food, clothing, housing, and so on. For certain products, it is not only the number of potential buyers but also the characteristics of those buyers that are important. For example, the age of the population affects product purchases. The greater the number of young people, the greater milk sales will be. The age of our population also influences the sales of running shoes, CDs and cassettes, home video equipment, houses, toys, and other such items.

The factors discussed above do not remain constant. They are continually changing and continually altering the demand for products. These changes complicate the analysis of demand. The effect of a change in any one of these factors on product demand is difficult to determine when several other factors are changing at the same time. In order to simplify the analysis of demand we assume that all factors influencing demand, other than price, remain constant. It is as if the analysis of demand refers to one specific moment in time, before any changes can take place. After reviewing the reaction of consumers to price changes, we can relax this assumption and see how demand responds to other changes.

Consumer Response to Price Changes

How do consumers respond to changes in the price of a product? Under most circumstances, they will buy more of a product if the price is low and less of it if the price is high. When the price of a product increases, less of the product can be purchased with the current level of income. Also, when the price of a product increases, consumers may substitute another, cheaper, product for it. The inverse relationship between the price of a product and the quantity of the product demanded can be presented by means of a *demand schedule.*

In order to better analyse the changes on the demand side of the market, let us derive a demand schedule for submarine sandwiches. This schedule is shown in table 2.1. It shows the number of sandwiches that would be demanded in your town at various prices during one week. The table shows an *inverse relationship* between the price and the quantity demanded. If the price of sandwiches was $2.90, consumers would be willing to buy 500 in a week; if the price was $3.30, consumers would only want to purchase 300.

The information in this table is presented in graphical form in figure 2.1. In the graph, price is presented on the vertical axis and the number of sandwiches demanded per week is shown on the horizontal axis. After plotting the relationships from table 2.1, and connecting the points, we can see that the graph shows a line representing an inverse relationship between the price and the quantity demanded. In figure 2.1, this curve is labelled **D¹** and is known as a *demand curve*. Remember, the demand curve does not provide any more information about the consumer demand for sandwiches than the demand schedule does, since it is derived from the schedule. The demand curve will, however, facilitate our future discussions of demand.

Table 2.1 / Demand schedule for sandwiches

Price of sandwich	Quantity demanded in one week
$2.90	500
$3.00	450
$3.10	400
$3.20	350
$3.30	300

**Figure 2.1
The demand
curve**

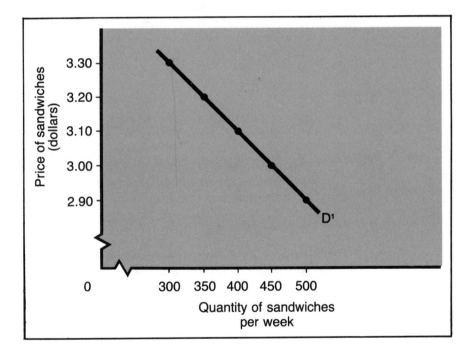

The inverse relationship between the price and the quantity demanded is represented by a downward-sloping curve.

The inverse relationship between price and quantity demanded is referred to as *the law of downward-sloping demand*. This means that consumers are willing and able to buy more of the product the lower the price, and less of the product the higher the price. When the price of sandwiches changes, the quantity of sandwiches demanded changes as well, but the demand curve itself does not.

Changes in Demand

Consumer demand for a product is not likely to stay constant over time. The factors that influence consumer demand are constantly changing. For example, individual tastes do not remain the same. The demand for submarine sandwiches may decline, while the demand for another fast food increases. Changes in consumer incomes will also affect the demand for sandwiches. During the summer, when students are working and earning money, the demand for submarine sandwiches will likely be higher than in other months. Changes in the price of other fast foods will also affect the demand. If the price of hamburgers increases, the number of sandwiches demanded at submarine shops may increase as people substitute sandwiches for hamburgers. The demand schedule derived for sandwiches in table 2.1 would no longer be applicable if any of these changes were to take place. We were able to draw this table only under the assumption that everything else stayed the same. Assume that the price of hamburgers has changed and that a new demand schedule for submarine sandwiches has to be drawn up. This schedule is presented in table 2.2. After an increase in the price of hamburgers, consumers also would be willing to buy 600 sandwiches at a price of $2.90. At all other prices, consumers would be willing to buy more sandwiches. How will a change in the demand schedule affect the demand curve?

Figure 2.2 translates the new demand schedule into a new demand curve (D^2). An increase in the price of hamburgers has resulted in a shift of the demand curve to the right. This is called an *increase in demand.* In other words, consumers are willing to buy more sandwiches at the same price than they were prior to the change in the price of hamburgers. Other changes in the submarine sandwich market may cause the demand curve to shift to the left.

Table 2.2 / Demand schedule for sandwiches (after an increase in the price of hamburgers)

Price of sandwich	Quantity demanded last week	Quantity demanded this week
$2.90	500	600
$3.00	450	550
$3.10	400	500
$3.20	350	450
$3.30	300	400

If consumer tastes change and they are less anxious to purchase sandwiches, the demand curve for sandwiches would move to the left. In this situation, regardless of the price, consumers would buy fewer sandwiches. A shift to the left in the demand curve is called a *decrease in demand*. In fact, any time there is a change in one of the factors held constant when drawing the curve, the demand curve for a product shifts. This shift is referred to as a *change in demand* and must be distinguished from a change in the quantity demanded. The latter occurs in response to a change in the price of the product. In order to determine consumer reaction to a change in the price of submarine sandwiches, we do not draw a new curve, but refer to a new point on the existing curve corresponding to the new price. That is, a change in demand occurs when one of the constant factors changes and results in a shift of the demand curve. In contrast, a change in the quantity demanded occurs in response to a change in the price of the product and is shown by moving along the demand curve.

**Figure 2.2
A shift in the
demand curve**

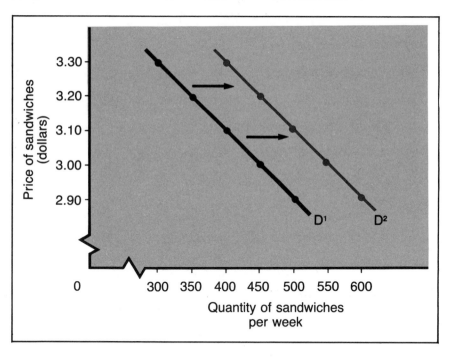

An increase in the price of a substitute product has shifted the demand curve to the right. More sandwiches will be demanded, regardless of the price, than previously.

2.1 For each of the following changes show the effect on the respective demand curve. Draw a separate graph for each answer, being sure to label your axes:
  i the effect of an increase in the price of tea on the demand for coffee;

ii the effect of a decrease in consumer incomes on the demand for new cars;

iii the effect of an advertising campaign by the Ontario Egg Marketing Board on the demand for eggs; and

iv the effect of a shoe price increase on the demand for shoes.

The Demand for Houses in Toronto

A classic example of the increase in demand for a product is the case of houses in Metropolitan Toronto and vicinity in the 1970s and 1980s. A number of factors combined to increase the demand for houses and, ultimately, to raise prices significantly. Some of the factors that resulted in the large price increase were:

The "baby boom": the baby boom era is the name given to a period of time after World War II (1945-1960) in which there was a large increase in the number of births. By the early 1970s, children born during this period were marrying and looking for their own homes.

Immigration and migration: Toronto is the destination of many immigrants to Canada, and migrants from other provinces. The increase in the population of the city increases the demand for accommodation.

Increase in incomes: the increase in the number of families with two wage-earners enabled more couples to purchase a home.

NHA mortgages: not many people purchase a home without taking out a loan. These loans are called mortgages. During the 1970s, mortgage restrictions were relaxed, making it easier for many people to obtain a mortgage. Since mortgages are a complementary product, changes in mortgage availability influenced the demand for housing.

Corporate transfers: Toronto is the head office location for many Canadian and international companies. People who acquire promotions are often asked to move to the head office.

Increased desire to live near city centre: increased commuting time and increased transportation costs revitalized the demand for homes near the centre of the city.

Questions

1 Draw a demand curve for Toronto houses. Show the effect on the curve of the changes discussed above.

2   What additional factors could alter the demand for houses in
    Toronto? In your home town?
3   What effect would an improved public transportation system
    have on the demand for houses in Toronto? Would your answer
    depend on whether you were referring to houses in downtown
    Toronto versus those in the suburbs?
4   There have been suggestions that home owners be allowed to
    deduct part of their mortgage interest payments from their income
    tax. If such a policy were adopted, what effect would it have on the
    demand curve for houses?

The Concept of Supply

Changes are also taking place constantly on the supply side of the
market. The number and variety of products available to consumers
is constantly increasing. For example, the kinds of pocket calculators
offered in the marketplace have increased rapidly in recent years.
There has also been an increase in the number of fast-food outlets
available to consumers. On the other hand, some items have disap-
peared from the marketplace, or are in the process of disappearing:
the energy crisis has reduced the number of big cars on the highway, and the introduction of the ball-point pen has almost eliminated the use of fountain pens.

**Factors Affecting
Supply**

There are several factors affecting the supply side of the market:

Price: the higher the price that a supplier can receive for a product,
the more of the product the supplier will offer to the market. When
the price is high, the time and effort involved in supplying the product
become more worthwhile. The opportunity cost of not providing
the product is also greater when the price is higher. That is, when
the price is high, the amount of money given up by not supplying
the product is greater. At low prices, the time and cost involved in
supplying a good or service may be too great in relation to the reward
(the price). For example, when the price of pork increases, farmers
are encouraged to increase their stock of pigs. It becomes worthwhile to spend more time and money raising pigs. In addition, farmers not previously engaged in pork production may decide to enter
the business. Therefore, with the higher prices, there will be more
pork offered to consumers in the marketplace. On the other hand,
when pork prices fall, some farmers may decide to get out of pig
farming and concentrate their efforts in other areas. The end result
is that less pork is sent to the marketplace.

Production costs: supplying a product to the market involves many
expenses, including raw materials, transportation, rent, wages, salaries,

energy, machines and equipment, interest payments on loans, and taxes. A change in any of these costs influences the supply of a product. If the wages paid to employees increase, the cost of supplying the product will increase. The supplier may only be willing to supply the product after granting a wage increase if a higher price for the product is received.

Technological change: businesses employ both workers and machines to produce their products. Changes in the type of machinery or equipment available could influence the supply of the product to the market. Improvements in equipment are referred to as technological changes. The impact that these changes can have on supply can again be shown with reference to farming. The development of pesticides like DDT reduced the damage to crops by insects and increased the yield that farmers could expect from a given acreage.

The development of computer technology has changed the production techniques of many businesses. The recent introduction of word processors has revolutionized office procedures. The new equipment has increased the demand for certain office skills, while reducing the demand for others. There is more need for people with a knowledge of computers and their capabilities, and less need for outdated skills in such areas as manual inventory control. Computer technology has also introduced robots on the production lines of certain manufacturing companies.

Psychology of owner: although it is assumed that all suppliers are in business to make a great deal of money, there may be other reasons. Some individuals may be in business in order to be their own boss, or to reduce their taxable income. Any change in the psychological aspects of business will ultimately affect supply.

Weather conditions: for agricultural products in particular, weather conditions have an important influence on supply. Extremely wet or dry conditions may reduce the volume of farm output and ultimately affect market conditions.

Prices of other products: the supply of some products on the market can also be influenced by the prices of other products requiring the same resources to produce. Agriculture provides a good example. In some situations, several different crops can be grown on the same type of farmland. If the price of one crop rises in relation to the others, its production is likely to increase at the expense of the others.

The approach to the analysis of the supply side of the market is the same as for demand. It is difficult to analyse the supply side of the market when everything is changing. Therefore, it is assumed that all factors influencing supply, other than price, remain constant. The reaction of suppliers to changes in the price of the product will be analysed first.

Supplier Response to Price Changes

The quantity supplied of a product to the market increases when the price of the product is higher. The additional costs of supplying more of the product to the market begin to increase beyond a certain level of output. Since costs increase, a higher price must be obtained in order for the supply to be increased. In the case of submarine sandwiches, the supplier's costs will increase if more sandwiches are to be provided beyond a certain number. These costs could include storage and refrigeration capacity, seating space, and the supplier's time.

The *positive relationship* between the price of sandwiches and the quantity supplied can be represented in a supply schedule (table 2.3). The schedule assumes that all other factors influencing supply (eg. rental costs, workers' wages, the price of buns, etc.) remain constant. At a price of $2.90, submarine store owners are only willing to supply 300 sandwiches per week; if the price increased to $3.30, 500 sandwiches would be provided.

Table 2.3 / Supply schedule of sandwiches

Price per sandwich	Quantity supplied in one week
$2.90	300
$3.00	350
$3.10	400
$3.20	450
$3.30	500

The supply schedule can be depicted in graphic terms, as in figure 2.3. The price of sandwiches is represented on the vertical axis, and the quantity of sandwiches on the horizontal axis. By plotting the points and joining them, a line is formed, indicating the positive relationship between the two variables. This upward-sloping line, designated by S^1, is called the *supply curve*. With all the other factors that influence supply remaining constant, an increase in the price of sandwiches will lead to an increase in the quantity supplied. A decrease in the price will lead to a decrease in the quantity supplied.

**Figure 2.3
The supply
curve**

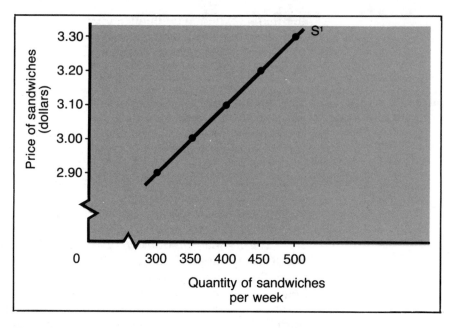

The positive relationship between the price and the quantity
supplied represented by an upward-sloping curve.

**Changes in
Supply**

The supply of a product to the market will change over time because
of changes in the factors that influence that supply. For example,
an increase in the rent that a store has to pay will affect supply. It
will result in a change to the supply schedule because submarine
shop owners will want a higher price for sandwiches. The supply
schedule in table 2.3 is now obsolete, and a new schedule is required.
Assuming that rent increases apply to all suppliers, a new schedule
is presented in table 2.4 and translated into a graph in figure 2.4.
Under the new conditions, suppliers would supply 300 sandwiches
at a new price of $3.00 per sandwich. Similar price increases would
be necessary for other quantities.

**Table 2.4 / Supply schedule of sandwiches
(after the increase in rent)**

Price per sandwich	Quantity supplied in one week
$3.00	300
$3.10	350
$3.20	400
$3.30	450
$3.40	500

**Figure 2.4
A shift in the
supply curve**

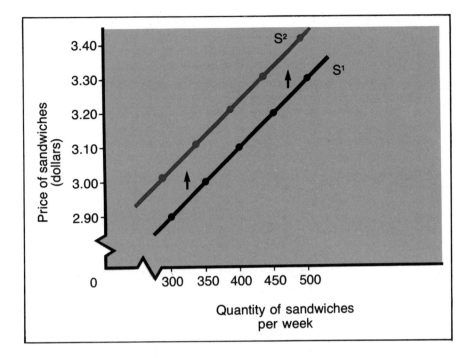

An increase in production costs results in a shift of the supply curve to
the left. The sandwiches will only be supplied to the market at a higher
price.

The new supply curve is represented by **S²**. A change in rent
has shifted the supply curve to the left. Proprietors are only willing
to supply the same amount of sandwiches at a higher price. Another way to say this is that for the same price, suppliers will put
fewer sandwiches on the market after the increase in rent. This is
referred to as a *decrease in supply*. In contrast, any change that will
lower costs results in a move of the supply curve to the right. This is an
increase in supply. Any change in a constant factor, such as production
costs, will cause the supply curve to shift. This circumstance is referred to as a *change in supply* and must be distinguished from a
change in the quantity supplied. The latter occurs in response to a
change in the price of the product. In order to determine supplier
reaction to a change in the price of submarine sandwiches, we do
not draw a new curve, but refer to a new point on the existing
curve corresponding to the new price. That is, a change in supply
occurs when one of the constant factors changes; this results in a
shift of the supply curve. In contrast, a change in quantity supplied
occurs when the price of the product changes and is shown by a
movement along the existing supply curve.

2.2   Using your knowledge of supply curves, show the impact of the following changes on the respective supply curves;
   i   an increase in construction workers' wages on the supply curve for new houses;
   ii   the development of a new pesticide on the supply curve for wheat;
   iii   the effect of a drought on the supply curve for corn;
   iv   the effect of a price increase on the supply of shoes.

The Supply of Oil

One of the most pressing problems facing Canada in recent years has been the use and supply of energy. The energy crisis began in 1973 after the Arab-Israeli conflict. At that time, the Oil Producing and Exporting Countries (OPEC) reduced the supply of oil and drastically increased the price. (The OPEC nations are Algeria, Ecuador, Gabon, Indonesia, Iran, Iraq, Kuwait, Libya, Nigeria, Qatar, Saudi Arabia, the United Arab Emirates, and Venezuela.) This move produced greater concern in Western industrialized countries over the possibilities of oil shortages in the future.

At the time of the OPEC price increase, the Canadian government had been following a policy of low oil prices, which were substantially below world oil prices. The result of these low prices was a reduction in the amount of money being spent on oil exploration. Because the return on their investment was low, oil companies were investing in other countries where the return was greater.

The federal and provincial governments both realized that Canada's oil-pricing policy would have to change. If the supply of oil in Canada was to increase, prices would have to start increasing toward the world level. The higher oil prices stimulated exploration in the Arctic and off the shores of the Atlantic provinces. Development continued in the oil sands of Alberta.

The higher prices for oil were necessary in order to increase the supply and assist Canada in becoming more self-sufficient in energy. Higher oil prices, however, had a different impact on the demand side of the market. Consumers were forced to adapt to higher prices for energy and did so by decreasing their demand for oil. By the early 1980s, the world found itself facing an oil surplus. Some OPEC nations began to see their oil revenues decline and thus increased the production of oil in order to increase revenue. With more oil on the market, the price fell. In order to keep up the price, Saudi Arabia, the largest oil-producing member of OPEC, decided to decrease production. This strategy failed because other nations continued to increase their production.

Faced with declining revenues, in 1985 Saudi Arabia increased oil production with the intention of driving the price of oil down and driving these countries who could only produce oil at a high cost out of the market. In Saudi Arabia it costs less than $2 to get a barrel of oil out of the ground. Production costs are much higher in other parts of the world. In Canada, costs ranged from $3 to $20 a barrel in 1986.

Iraq's takeover of Kuwait in the summer of 1990 resulted in sharp increases in oil prices. As the threat of war escalated, the price of a barrel of oil increased. Oil prices declined during the war, once a Coalition victory seemed certain.

What do low oil prices mean for Canada? Cheaper gasoline and home-heating costs are welcomed by consumers. Producers are not as happy. If low oil prices do not make oil exploration and production feasible, companies will close down and jobs will be lost. The impact of low oil prices is not felt equally across Canada. Alberta, Saskatchewan, the Atlantic provinces, and the Arctic will suffer the most. The livelihood of many communities depends on continued oil exploration and production. It is also less likely that Canada will become self-sufficient in energy with low oil prices continuing on the market.

Further information on the topic of oil supplies can be obtained from the Petroleum Resources Communication Foundation in Calgary.

Questions

1　Draw a supply curve for oil in Canada. From the point of view of the Canadian economy, why is it necessary for oil prices to increase?
2　What will be the effect of higher oil prices on the demand side of the market?
3　As the price of oil increases, what will be the impact on other sources of energy such as electricity and solar power?
4　In your opinion should the Government of Canada become involved in the exploration for and the production of oil?
5　Why would exploration costs increase as the search for oil continues?

The Interaction of Demand and Supply

The primary function of a market is to bring buyers and sellers together in order to establish a price and to make an exchange. Now that they have been discussed separately, it is time to join the demand and supply sides of the market. This is done in table 2.5 and figure 2.5, using the demand and supply curves previously developed for submarine sandwiches. The demand and supply curves on the same graph represent the market for that particular product or service. We can use these curves to show how the buyers and sellers in a market get together in order to establish the price and quantity exchanged.

Table 2.5 / Comparison of demand and supply schedules for sandwiches

Price	Quantity demanded	Quantity supplied	Price change
$2.90	500	300	↑
$3.00	450	350	↑
$3.10	400	400	no change
$3.20	350	450	↓
$3.30	300	500	↓

Suppose that the suppliers of sandwiches decided to sell sandwiches for $3.30. At this price, they are willing to supply 500 sandwiches per week. How would consumers react to this price for subs? According to table 2.5, consumers would be willing to buy only 300 sandwiches a week at that price. As a result, suppliers would find that they could not sell all of their sandwiches. One possible solution would be to lower the price. Suppose that the price was dropped to $3.20. Consumers would be willing to buy an additional 50 sandwiches a week. Suppliers, on the other hand, would reduce the number of sandwiches that they were prepared to

Figure 2.5 Equilibrium

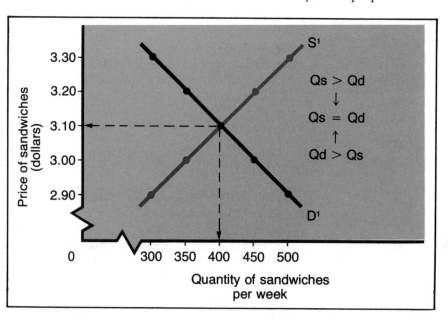

The intersection of the demand and the supply curves for a product. At equilibrium there is no tendency for the price or quantity of sandwiches to change.

make. The lower price would still leave proprietors with a surplus of 100 sandwiches. In fact, until the price drops to $3.10, there will be a surplus of sandwiches. At $3.10, the quantity of sandwiches demanded is just equal to the quantity of sandwiches supplied. Therefore, there is no reason for the price to change.

What would happen if suppliers started selling sandwiches for $2.90? At this price, they would be willing to supply 300 sandwiches, but the consumer demand would total 500 sandwiches per week. Consumers would be willing to purchase more sandwiches than are available at that price. There is a shortage of sandwiches. Suppliers would be willing to supply more sandwiches, but only at a higher price. The price of subs will continue to rise until it reaches $3.10. At this price, the quantity of submarine sandwiches demanded is equal to the quantity supplied. Since there is no tendency for the $3.10 price to change, it is referred to as an **equilibrium price.** This equilibrium price is determined by the intersection of the demand and supply curves for a product. If the price of the product is not at the equilibrium level, it will constantly be moving toward equilibrium. The only stable price in a market is the equilibrium price.

The equilibrium price is the price at which the quantity demanded of a product is equal to the quantity supplied.

Prices change as they move toward equilibrium. They also change when changes take place in the factors that affect the demand and supply sides of the market. For example, what effect does an increase in the price of hamburgers have on the price of submarine sandwiches? It increases the demand for sandwiches, a substitute product. This is shown in figure 2.6. An increase in the price of hamburgers shifts the demand curve for sandwiches to D^2. The new demand curve now intersects the supply curve at the new equilibrium price of $3.20. The increased demand for sandwiches forces up the price under the existing supply conditions.

It should also be noted that at this new price, more sandwiches are purchased (450 compared to 400 before demand increased). Is this a contradiction of the law of downward-sloping demand? How can the price of sandwiches increase, and the quantity purchased increase as well? This is only an apparent contradiction. It was stated earlier that—all things remaining the same—any increase in price would decrease the quantity demanded. However, not all things have remained the same. The price of hamburgers has increased, and as a result, consumers must reassess their demand for submarine sandwiches. The new conditions have convinced them to purchase more sandwiches than before. Under the new conditions represented by D^2 in figure 2.6, consumers will still purchase fewer sandwiches if the price goes above $3.20 and more sandwiches if it falls below $3.20. That is, the law of downward-sloping demand applies to the new curve D^2, just as it did with the previous curve D^1.

**Figure 2.6
A new
equilibrium
position (shift in
the demand
curve)**

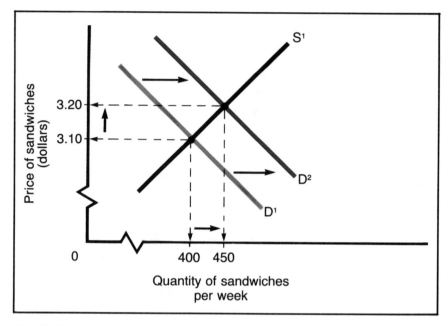

A shift in the demand curve to the right results in a higher equilibrium price and quantity.

**Figure 2.7
A new
equilibrium
position (shift in
the supply
curve)**

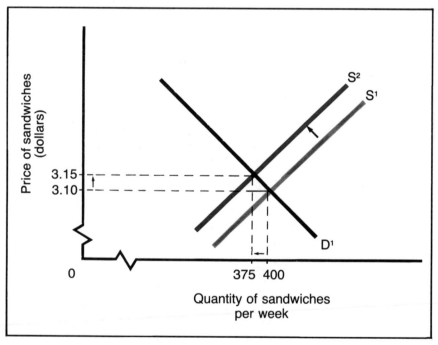

A shift in the supply curve to the left results in a higher equilibrium
price and a lower equilibrium quantity.

How will changes in supply affect the price? Suppose that the price of butter used in the sandwiches increases. Suppliers are going to ask a higher price for the same number of sandwiches. This is represented in figure 2.7 as a shift in the supply curve to S^2. The new supply curve intersects demand at a higher equilibrium price ($3.15). In this case, fewer sandwiches (350) are purchased by consumers then before the shift in supply. A decrease in supply (shift of the supply curve to the left) results in a higher price and a lower quantity exchanged under constant demand conditions.

2.3 Using your knowledge of both demand and supply curves, show the impact of the following:
  i   an increase in consumer incomes on the price of restaurant meals;
  ii an increase in the cost of steel on the price of new cars;
  iii a decrease in the price of tea on the price of coffee;
  iv the development of new pesticides on the price of corn; and,
  v   the expectation of future price increases on the present price of houses.

Gold and Silver

An interesting example of the interaction of markets and the role that expectations can play on market prices was provided by the gold and silver markets in the fall of 1979. Concern over the declining value of paper money prompted investors to exchange their paper currency for gold. Enough money was exchanged for gold to drive the price of gold above the $300 (U.S.) per-ounce mark for the first time. The expectation that gold prices would rise even higher pushed the price of gold above the $600 (U.S.) per-ounce mark before the end of the year. The gold market was also highly influenced by the uncertain political climate at the time. In Iran, American citizens were held hostage in the American embassy; the USSR had sent troops into Afghanistan. This uncertainty convinced investors to look for a safe place to store their wealth.

What happened to the silver market during this time? Higher and higher prices for gold turned some investors away from that market. As a result, they redirected their demand to a cheaper metal, namely silver. The price of silver then increased drastically to more than $50 (U.S.) per ounce early in January 1980 from a price of around $7 (U.S.) per ounce a year earlier. The increase in the price of silver was augmented by the large purchases made by the Hunt brothers. This American family wanted to control silver prices by owning a large quantity of the metal.

By March 1980, the fortunes of gold and silver investors had turned. The price of gold had dropped from a price of more than $800 per ounce in January to less than $500 per ounce in March.

The drop in silver prices was even more dramatic. The price fell to $10 per ounce by the end of March. Since 1980, the prices for gold and silver have not remained stable. Price fluctuations have occurred, although not as dramatically as during the 1979-80 period. By the early 1990s, the price of gold was about $450 per ounce and silver was selling for approximately $8 per ounce.

Questions

1   Using demand and supply curves, show the impact on the gold and silver markets during this time period. Which side of the market was affected?
2   What would be the effect on gold prices if South Africa, the world's major gold producer, decided to increase the volume of gold it put on world markets? Use demand and supply curves in your answer.
3   What would account for the big drop in gold and silver prices?
4   What effect do you think these prices had on gold and silver mines?
5   Can you name any other markets that are as closely interrelated as the gold and silver markets?

Dutch Auction

It has been stated in this chapter that a market is where buyers and sellers get together in order to exchange a product or service and to establish a price. One type of market that many of us are familiar with is an auction. We have probably seen antique auctions, car auctions, farm auctions, art auctions, or possibly, auctions of property. In each of these auctions, potential buyers constantly bid up the price that the item will be sold for. Eventually the selling price is reached.

Not all auctions, however, are conducted in this manner. In situations where the auction must be conducted quickly, it may be beneficial to operate the auction in reverse. That is, to start at a high price and to have the price steadily drop. This is known as a "Dutch auction," one example of which is the flower auction conducted by the Ontario Flower Growers' Cooperative Limited. Flower growers bring their flowers to the auction in order to sell them to retail florists. The auction begins early in the morning and must be conducted quickly so that retailers can transport the flowers back to their shops.

Retailers bid on flowers offered for sale by the growers. The starting price is set on a large clock, and as the second hand of the clock moves, the price begins to fall. The amount that the price drops each second depends on the type of flower or plant being auctioned and the original starting price. For some items the price may drop by $1 a second, while for others the price may drop by only 10 cents a second. When a retail florist, or wholesaler, feels that the price has dropped far enough, a button can be pressed in order to stop the clock. At this point a sale is made. A flower grower can also stop the clock if he or she feels that the price is falling too low.

Questions

1 Prior to the introduction of the Dutch auction and the clock, how do you think flower growers got in touch with retail florists? Would your answer explain why both buyers and sellers are willing to pay in order to participate in this auction?

2 Would the auction help growers who produce better quality products receive a higher price than other growers receive for the same type of flower? Why or why not?

3 How would you draw a supply curve for the flowers offered at this auction on a given day?

The Stock Market

The exchange of shares, or ownership, in public corporations takes place in a stock market.

The **stock market** represents the organized trading of shares, or ownership, in public corporations. As with other markets, the stock market's primary purpose is to bring the buyers and sellers of these shares together.

In Canada, individuals interested in share trading are brought together by means of five stock exchanges, located in Toronto, Montreal, Vancouver, Calgary, and Winnipeg. The exchanges are central locations where the stocks that are listed are bought and sold. Each exchange is owned by the members, usually *stockbrokers*.

Individuals who are interested in acquiring or disposing of shares cannot deal with the exchange directly. They must deal through a stockbroker who transmits their order to the exchange. At the exchange, all requests to buy and sell shares in a certain company are co-ordinated. The actual share trading is done on the floor of the exchange by employees of the exchange members called floor traders. On a certain day, if someone is willing to sell shares for the same price someone is offering to buy shares, an exchange takes place.

How does an individual find out the price of a share for a particular company? The exchanges publish daily price information for all companies listed on the exchange. This information can be found in many newspapers across the country. A sample of this information from the Toronto Stock Exchange (TSE) follows:

52-week High	Low	Stock	Div	High /bid	Low /ask	Close /last	Change	Vol
330	165	Bema Gold o		193	190	193	+ 7	28700
18½	14½	Benetton ads	ka .385	$15	21	18		nt
70	30	Bethlehem Res		31	31	31	− 2	1000
26	490	Biochem IAF		$23⅝	22½	22⅝	− 1⅛	4200
11⅞	130	Biomira Inc o		$11¼	10⅝	11⅛	+ ½	21300
125	37	Bionaire Inc		125	125	125	+ 5	900
35	10	Black Cliff Mines o		22	22	22	+ 2½	5000
75	26	Black Hawk Mng o		40	44	40		nt
22	6	Black Swan Gold		7	7	9		z400
185	100	Blue Range Res A		185	190	175		nt
27	14¼	Bombardier Inc A	.32	$25¾	25⅜	25¾	+ ⅛	500
27	12⅞	Bombardier Inc B f	.345	$25¾	25½	25¾	+ ¼	41060
24	21⅝	Bombardier Inc p A	1.875	$24	24¾	24		nt
70	30	Bonanza Oil & Gas		50	60	55		nt
26½	23	Bonar Inc	.20	$23½	32	23½		nt
170	50	Bovar Inc		140	135	135		9149
15	12¾	Bow Valley Inds		$14½	14½	14⅝	− ¼	50703
16	13½	Bow Valley $0.56 p A	.56	$15½	16	16		nt
30½	27	Bow Valley $1.875 p C	1.875	$28¾	30½	28¼		nt
30½	26⅝	Bow Valley $2.025 p B	2.025	$29½	30½	29½		nt
23	17½	Bow Valley $2.05 p D	2.05	$23	22¾	23	+ ¾	11200
25	21⅛	Bow Valley $2 p U		see below.				

52-week High	Low	Stock	Div	High /bid	Low /ask	Close /last	Change	Vol
13¾	11	Cdn Satell Comm o	.20	$11⅞	12⅛	11⅞		nt
20	4	Cdn Spooner Res		14	14	14		z334
27½	21½	Cdn Tire	.40	$24½	24½	24½		z50
26	19⅞	Cdn Tire A f	.40	$23¼	22¾	23¾		23431
440	155	Cdn Turbo		185	178	185	+ 7	2156
48	42	Cdn Util 4.25% p A	4.25	$48⅞		45		nt
58	52	Cdn Util 5.00% p B	5.00	$58¼	64	56½		nt
71	60	Cdn Util 6.00% p C	6.00	$70	74	70½ ·		nt
24½	21¼	Cdn Util C 2nd p G	1.825	$23¾		23½		nt
21⅜	18⅝	Cdn Util Cl A f	1.38	$20⅞	20½	20¾	− ¼	13000
21¾	18⅝	Cdn Util Cl B X	1.38	$21	21½	21½		nt
26½	24¾	Cdn Util I 2nd p N	2.185	$26¼	26	26		9700
26¾	23¾	Cdn Util K 2nd p O	1.95	$26¾	26	26	− ½	1400
26½	23½	Cdn Util L 2nd p P	1.925	$25½	27½	26½		nt
25¾	23¾	Cdn Util M 2nd p Q	1.77	$25¼	26¼	25		nt
25	23	Cdn Util N 2nd p R	1.775	$25¼	26	25		nt
26¼	25	Cdn Util P p S	2.00	$25¼	26	25¾		nt
5⅞	370	Cdn Western Bank		420	410	410		1700
9½	8	Cdn West NG 4% p A	.80	$9¼	9½	9¼		nt
12½	10¾	Cdn West 5-1/2% p B	1.10	$12¼	12¾	12½		nt
425	205	Canam Manac Grp A f	.10		300	245		nt
63	26	Canamax Res		32	35	33		nt

Source: *The Globe and Mail* and the Toronto Stock Exchange.

For each company listed, the information provided is as follows:

52-week High Low	Stock	Div	High /bid	Low /ask	Close /last	Change	Vol.
The highest and lowest values that the shares of this company have traded during the last 52 weeks.	Company name	If dividends have been paid, it is indicated in this column.	On a given day, shares may trade for several different prices. The TSE information indicates the highest and lowest values that the stock trades for during that day. It also shows what the final trading value was on that day, and the change from yesterday's closing price. For shares not traded (nt), the bid and asked prices are quoted as well as the last price the shares traded for. The final column shows the volume of shares traded during the day.				

The stock exchanges also publish information on the total number of shares traded each day and the overall trend in share prices. For the Toronto Stock Exchange, the trend in stock prices is revealed with the daily publication of the TSE Composite. This is an index of stock prices for that day and is simply the price of a selected set of 300 stocks listed on the exchange. When the TSE 300 Composite is increasing, the share prices for most stocks are increasing. When the TSE 300 Composite is decreasing, there is a trend toward lower prices on the stock exchange.

2.4 Why do we call the operation described above "the stock market"?

2.5 Using your knowledge of demand and supply curves, what factors would cause the price of a company's shares to increase? To decrease?

2.6 Why is it necessary to centralize the buying and selling of shares at a stock exchange?

Glossary of Investment Terms

Bear market: A market in which share prices are falling.

Blue chip stocks: Stocks with good investment qualities. They are usually common shares of well-established companies with good earnings records and long-time dividend payments.

Bull market: A market in which share prices are rising.

Capital gain or loss: Profit or loss resulting from the sale of a security. The capital gain or loss is the difference between the buying and selling price of the security.

Common shares: Securities issued by a company that represent part ownership in the company. Common shares sometimes carry a voting privilege and entitle the holder to a share in the company's profits, usually issued in the form of dividends.

Dividend: A portion of a company's profit paid to the common and preferred shareholders. The amount is decided upon by the company's board of directors and may be paid in cash or stock.

Equities: Those shares issued by a company that represent ownership in the company. Common and preferred shares are usually called equity stock.

Liquidity: The measure of how quickly an investor can turn his securities into cash. A security is liquid if it can be bought and sold quickly with small price changes between transactions.

Margin account: A special type of brokerage account that allows the client to pay a portion of the price of the securities and borrow the balance from the broker. The word "margin" refers to the difference between the market value of the stock and the loan that the broker makes against it.

Options: Contracts that give the holder the right to buy ("call" options) or sell ("put" options) a fixed amount of a certain stock at a specific price, within a specified time.

Over-the-counter: The O-T-C or "unlisted" market is the market maintained by securities dealers for issues not listed on a stock exchange. Trades are made over the telephone.

Portfolio: The securities owned by an individual or institutional investor. An investor's portfolio may contain common and preferred shares, bonds, options and other types of securities.

Preferred shares: shares issued by a company to raise additional capital, after the issuance of common shares. Preferred shares carry dividends at predetermined rates, which must be paid before any dividends are paid to common shareholders.

Prospectus: A legal document describing securities being offered for sale to the public. It must be prepared in accordance with provincial securities-commission regulations.

Security: A legal certificate providing evidence that the buyer has loaned money to the issuer (in the case of a bond), or has purchased part-ownership of the issuing body (in the case of stock).

Right: A temporary privilege granted to existing common shareholders to purchase additional shares of a company from the company itself at a stated price.

Short sale: The sale of shares that the seller does not own. The shares are first borrowed from an investment dealer and then sold. The seller is speculating that the stock price will fall in the hope of later purchasing the same number of shares at a lower price, thereby making a profit.

Underwrite: The purchase by an investment dealer or group of dealers of a new issue of securities from the issuing company at a fixed price. The dealer or dealers then arrange the sale of the shares to the public.

Warrant: A certificate giving the holder the right to purchase securities at a stipulated price within a specified period of time. Warrants are usually attached to a new issue of securities to assist in the initial sale. They are often detachable and may be traded separately. Like "rights," warrants expire after a specified time, although the term is usually longer for warrants.

The Futures Market

Some of the most volatile markets in terms of price and quantity are the commodity, or **futures markets**. *Commodities are primarily agricultural products and metals.* They are traded at commodity exchanges located in Canada and the United States. Winnipeg is the centre of commodity trading in Canada. At the Winnipeg Commodity Exchange, trading is undertaken in feed wheat, feed oats, feed barley, rye, flaxseed, rapeseed, and gold. The main commodity trading exchanges in the United States are in New York and Chicago. Futures contracts are negotiated at these exchanges. This type of contract is a firm commitment to deliver, or accept delivery of a given quantity and quality of a commodity at a specified time in the future at a price established today. The primary reason for making this arrangement is to avoid the uncertainty of future price changes. The buyer knows the price to be paid regardless of what happens to the price in the meantime. The seller is assured of selling the commodity and is also guaranteed a price.

Why are futures contracts so popular in the commodities markets? The reason is that sharp price swings can occur from day to day in these markets. On the supply side, adverse environmental conditions such as drought, frost, or volcanic eruptions make it difficult to forecast future supply. Crop damage may also occur through insect infestation or plant disease. Man-made barriers such as war or strikes may also restrict supply. Changes may also occur on the demand side of the market, although these are normally not as drastic as those on the supply side.

A wider variety of products is traded on the American exchanges than on Canadian ones. The following products, for example, have futures trading at the New York Commodities Exchange Center: copper, gold, silver, cotton, frozen orange-juice concentrate, coffee, sugar, Maine potatoes, platinum, petroleum products, and international currencies.

In order to understand the workings of the futures markets, let us focus on one of the most important food items—corn. It is used as human food, but more importantly, it is a major source of animal feed. Without an adequate supply of corn, the hog, cattle, and poultry industries would be affected. Meat-packing plants would slow down production and lay off workers. The shifts that occur in demand and supply in the corn market cause price fluctuations that create a risk for corn growers and the users of corn products. Among those affected are farmers, producers, export merchants, feed manufacturers, and grain-elevator operators. Fluctuations in supply can result from weather conditions, the number of hectares planted each year, advances in agricultural technology and plant genetics, and government farm policy. Changes in demand can come from animal-feed requirements, changes in the demand for meat, and price changes for competitive feeds.

Information on price changes for futures contracts is available in the business section of many newspapers. The price changes for wheat futures as traded on the Chicago Board of Trade (CBT) are listed below. The basic trading unit is 5000 bushels and the prices listed are per bushel. The delivery months for wheat are May, July, September, December, and March. The delivery month may be as much as 18 months in the future. Information in the listings is for Tuesday 29 October 1991. For futures contracts to be completed in May 1992, the price varied from a high of $3.4050 per bushel to a low of $3.3500 per bushel. It closed the day (Settle) at $3.3650 per bushel, which was down $0.0650 from the previous day's closing price. The column "Opint" indicates how many contracts for May still have to be completed. Seasonal high and low prices are provided in the extreme left-hand columns.

Chicago Board of Trade

SeaHi	SeaLo	Mth.	Open	High	Low	Settle	Chg.	Opint
WHEAT 5,000 bu minimum- dollars per bushel								
3.69¼	2.72½	Dec	3.61	3.63	3.57	3.57½	—.07¼	29,268
3.70¾	2.79	Mar	3.59	3.61	3.54	3.55¼	—.07	21,448
3.52½	2.80½	May	3.40	3.40½	3.35	3.36½	—.06½	5,275
3.37½	2.79	Jul	3.21	3.23	3.18	3.19¼	—.05½	8,089
3.41	2.92	Sep	3.25½	3.27	3.23¼	3.24	—.05¼	581
3.51	3.38	Dec	3.36	3.38	3.34	3.35½	—.06	411
Est Sales				Prv Sales		Prv Open Int		Chg.
18,000				19,140		65,072		+372

Source: *The Globe and Mail*

Apart from those parties mentioned above who are interested in the future price of wheat, speculators may also participate in this market. Speculators purchase futures contracts with the expectation that the price of wheat will increase. Should the market price of wheat increase above the price stated in the futures contract, the speculator would be able to sell the contract for a profit. There is no guarantee, however, that the price of wheat will increase, and this makes speculation a risky adventure.

2.7 What differentiates the futures market from other markets?

2.8 Why would most individuals who have some money to invest be more likely to purchase common shares rather than a futures contract?

The Operation of a Free Market System

The markets described in this chapter accomplish two things in our economy. They co-ordinate the exchange of goods and services by bringing buyers and sellers together and they establish market

The price system is the technique by which scarce resources are allocated to the production of those products and services that provide the greatest return to the resource owner. In this way, the system of prices, rents, wages, and interest organizes economic activity.

prices. It is the system of prices that emerges from the various markets that makes the free market approach to economic decision-making effective.

You will recall from Chapter 1 that Canadians have to decide how to use the scarce resources that they have available. What products and services are these resources going to produce? Who will receive these products and services when they are available? The **price system** is the technique by which all of these questions are answered.

Resources will be allocated to the production of those products and services that provide the greatest return to the owner of the resource. Individuals seek out jobs that pay the highest salary. Others use their land in the most profitable manner. They rent their buildings under circumstances that provide the highest return. The complete system of prices, rents, wages, and interest organizes economic activity. Price changes also assist in the necessary adjustments that have to be made in any economy. If there is a shortage of a product, the price will rise until the shortage is effectively eliminated. Surpluses are eliminated through price reductions.

How will the various commodities be produced? Resources will be combined in such a manner that the good or service can be produced at the lowest possible price. When competition is present, suppliers are forced to offer their goods or services at a competitive price. Consumers purchase more at lower prices so suppliers are interested in keeping prices as low as possible.

Who will receive the goods and services that are produced? The items produced will be distributed to those who are willing and able to pay for them. Individuals will use their limited incomes to purchase those products that have a high priority for them. Therefore, the products that are produced and purchased will be items that consumers want. These wants are made known by purchases.

The price system has two distinct advantages in allocating resources. First, it is *efficient*. It allows thousands of individuals to co-operate in making economic decisions. These people do not necessarily know each other or have the same attitudes and beliefs. Each individual is making decisions based on prices and price changes. Secondly, the price system permits a great deal of individual freedom in the decision-making process. Actions of individuals on what job to take and what product to buy are all voluntary. Prices do not tell people what to do, yet they do influence their decisions and induce them to act in a certain way.

Second, the price system *transmits information* to buyers and sellers. The price differences between products assist consumers in allocating their limited income to various purchases. When prices decrease, consumers are able to purchase more of the product with the same amount of income. Price changes also provide information to suppliers. Higher prices identify products that may be profitable to produce. Competition from other suppliers forces businesses to be price-conscious. They are encouraged to adopt the least costly and most efficient means of production.

If the price system is prevented from operating, information is not being transferred to buyers and sellers. As a result, these participants in the market are not able to make knowledgeable decisions about product choices. Under such circumstances, shortages and surpluses tend to persist. For example, when prices are not allowed to increase (possibly due to government regulations) in response to a shortage, suppliers are not encouraged to put more of the product on the market. In countries where the price system does not organize economic activity, shortages and surpluses tend to be consistent problems.

Our knowledge of the free market system provides insight into the *concept of value.* What is the value of a diamond ring? a new car? a compact disc? a glass of water? The only indicator of value that we have is the price established for these products in the marketplace. If a diamond ring costs $700, then its value is said to be $700. The same applies to all other products.

Using this definition of value, it follows that a diamond ring has more value than a glass of water. Yet, we can survive without diamond rings, but we cannot survive without water. Surely water has more value than a diamond ring. Why is the price of water not higher than that of diamonds? The answer lies in the concept of relative scarcity. Although there is a tremendous demand for water, there is also a great supply. The demand for diamonds is less than the demand for water, but the supply of diamonds is relatively more scarce than the supply of water. The interaction of demand and supply therefore results in a higher price for diamonds than for water.

Elasticity

Price Elasticity of Demand

The law of downward-sloping demand states that, all other factors remaining constant, the quantity demanded of a product increases as the price falls. For most goods and services, this relationship holds. However, price changes for different products affect consumers in different ways. For example, a five-cent increase in the price of milk is not likely to have a significant impact on the quantity of milk that consumers buy. For many families, especially those with small children, milk is a necessity. They will continue to buy milk even at higher prices. In contrast, a five-cent increase in the price of a chocolate bar may greatly reduce the number of chocolate bars that consumers are willing to buy. Since chocolate bars are not a necessity, some consumers may be reluctant to pay the higher price. The demand curves for both milk and chocolate bars are downward-sloping, but their shapes are different. The exact shape of the demand curve and consumer response to price changes are of great concern to those on the supply side of the market—the manufacturers and retailers. The different responses of quantity demanded to price changes are shown in figure 2.8.

The demand curve for milk is D^1, while D^2 represents the demand curve for chocolate bars. A reduction in the price from P_0 to P_1 causes a greater increase in the quantity demanded in the case of D^2 as opposed to D^1. The price reduction increased the quantity demanded from Q_0 to Q_2 in the case of D^2, but only from Q_0 to Q_1 in the case of D^1. Although both demand curves show an inverse relationship between price and quantity demanded, the nature of the relationship is different.

**Figure 2.8
Price elasticities
of demand**

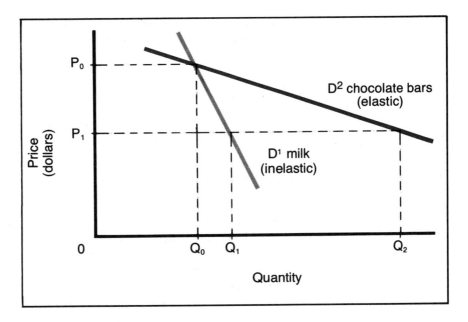

A drop in price from P_0 to P_1 brings about a greater change in the quantity demanded for D_2 than D_1. The demand for products with elastic demand curves responds more to price changes than it does for products with inelastic demand curves.

The elasticity of demand measures the extent to which the quantity of a product demanded responds to a change in price.

In order to measure to what extent the quantity demanded of a product responds to a change in price, economists have developed the concept of elasticity. **Elasticity** measures the reaction of consumers to price changes, or, more specifically, elasticity measures the responsiveness of quantity demanded to a change in price. An *elastic demand* is one in which a price change brings about a more-than-proportional change in the quantity that consumers demand. A small increase in the price of chocolate bars is likely to have a large impact on the number of bars sold. In cases where the quantity of a product demanded does not vary a great deal with the price, it is considered an *inelastic demand.* Milk has an inelastic demand curve, since price changes appear to have little effect on the quantity of milk sold. The determination of whether a product has an elastic or inelastic demand is made through the use of a formula:

$$\text{price elasticity of demand coefficient } (E_d) = \frac{\text{percentage change in quantity demanded } (Q_d)}{\text{percentage change in price } (P)}$$

$$E_d = \frac{\% \Delta Q_d}{\% \Delta P} \text{ (where } \Delta = \text{change in)}$$

For example, if a 10 per cent cut in the price brought about a 20 percent increase in the quantity demanded, the elasticity coefficient would be:

$$E_d = \frac{\% \Delta Q_d}{\% \Delta P} = \frac{20}{10} = 2.0$$

If, on the other hand, the same price cut encouraged only a one percent increase in quantity demanded, the elasticity coefficient would be:

$$E_d = \frac{\% \Delta Q_d}{\% \Delta P} = \frac{1}{10} = 0.10$$

If the elasticity coefficient (E_d) is greater than one, the demand is said to be elastic. If the coefficient is less than one, the demand is inelastic. Finally, if the elasticity coefficient equals one, the demand is said to be unitary elastic.

Some characteristics of a product that help to determine whether it has an elastic or inelastic demand are:

Luxury or necessity: generally items that are necessities have an inelastic demand. Consumers have to buy them regardless of the price. Conversely, luxuries have an elastic demand. Food and clothing are necessities, while event tickets and video-cassette recorders are luxuries.

The number of close substitutes: the more close substitutes a product has, the more elastic its demand. If the price increases, the consumer has several alternatives to turn to. There are many restaurants in the larger Canadian cities. The demand facing any one restaurant is likely to be elastic, as the consumer has many alternatives. Conversely, if a product has few substitutes, its demand is usually inelastic. Milk is a product with very few substitutes. There are also few substitutes for the services of a dentist. The demand for dental care is inelastic. The demand for the services of a certain dentist is likely, however, to be elastic.

Percentage of budget spent on product: if a product takes up only a small fraction of a consumer's budget, price changes are not likely to have a great impact on quantity demanded. As a result, the demand for the product will be inelastic. An example of such a product is pepper. Products that comprise a large percentage of one's budget have an elastic demand. Changes in the prices of these products will force a reaction on the part of consumers. For many people, rent comprises a large portion of the budget. An increase in rent may result in a search for alternative accommodation.

It should be noted that a product need not possess all of the above characteristics in order to be classified as having either an elastic or inelastic demand. For example, it has been determined that cigarettes have no substitutes according to cigarette smokers, and this is the main reason for their inelastic demand. Yet it can be argued that cigarettes are not a necessity and, in some cases, compose more than a small percentage of one's income. One of the above characteristics may be sufficient to determine the elasticity of demand for a product or service.

2.9 Assuming that income and all other conditions remain the same, state whether the demand for the following items is elastic or inelastic. Give your reasons.

i   gasoline
ii salt – *In*
iii cigarettes – *In*

iv restaurant meals – *E*
v   milk – *In E*
vi newspapers –

The Numerical Calculation of Elasticity

Price elasticity of demand has been defined as the responsiveness of quantity demanded to a change in price. The formula presented in the chapter was

$$\text{price elasticity of demand coefficient } (E_d) = \frac{\% \text{ change in quantity demanded } (Q_d)}{\% \text{ change in price } (P)}$$

It should be pointed out that under normal circumstances, the value of the elasticity coefficient will always be negative. This is because of the inverse relationship between price and quantity demanded. Since discussions about elasticity refer to positive values, it is necessary to insert a negative sign in front of the calculation, as follows:

$$E_d = -\frac{\% \triangle Q_d}{\% \triangle P}$$

Inserting the negative sign converts the value of the coefficient to a positive number.

One further change has to be made to this formula before it can be used to calculate elasticity coefficients. In order to understand this change, refer to figure 2.9. When the price increases from \$5 to \$8, the coefficient of price elasticity of demand, according to our formula, is equal to 0.83. When the price decreases from \$8 to \$5, the value of the elasticity coefficient becomes 2.67. Thus there are two different values of elasticity for the same section of the demand curve. In order to avoid this problem, it is necessary to calculate all elasticities using an average price and an average quantity demanded. Using averages and calculating the price elasticity of demand for a price increase from \$5 to \$8, the formula becomes:

$$E_d = - \left[\frac{\dfrac{\Delta Q}{Q_1 + Q_2}}{\dfrac{2}{\dfrac{\Delta P}{P_1 + P_2}}} \right] \qquad E_d = - \left[\frac{\dfrac{-5}{5 + 10}}{\dfrac{2}{\dfrac{3}{5 + 8}}} \right] \qquad E_d = - \left[\frac{\dfrac{-10}{15}}{\dfrac{6}{13}} \right]$$

$$E_d = - \left[\frac{-10}{15} \times \frac{13}{6} \right] \qquad E_d = - \left[\frac{-130}{90} \right] \qquad E_d = \frac{130}{90} \qquad E_d = 1.44$$

**Figure 2.9
Numerical
calculation of
price elasticity
of demand**

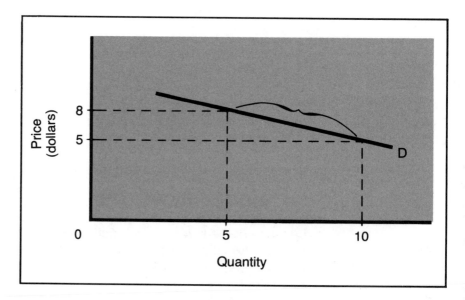

The numerical value of elasticity for one section of the demand curve should be the same regardless of whether it is calculated for a price increase or a price decrease.

Question

1 Calculate the price elasticity of demand coefficient for a product if the increase in price from $0.50 to $0.70 causes quantity demanded to fall from 400 to 300 units. Does this represent an elastic or an inelastic demand?

Total Revenue Approach to Price Elasticity of Demand

The concept of price elasticity of demand can also be discussed in terms of any change in the total amount of money people spend on a product when the price changes. The amount of money people spend on a product is referred to as total revenue (TR) and is calculated by multiplying the price times the quantity demanded.

$$TR = P \times Q_d$$

If the demand for a product is elastic, any decrease in price will increase total revenue; conversely, any increase in price will decrease total revenue.

elastic: when P↑, TR↓
           when P↓, TR↑

If the demand for a product is inelastic, any decrease in price will cause total revenue to fall, and any increase in price will cause total revenue to increase.

inelastic: when P↓, TR↓
              when P↑, TR↑

Finally, when the elasticity of demand is unitary, any change in price leaves total revenue unchanged.

unitary elastic: when P↑ or P↓,
                    TR remains the same

The total revenue approach to elasticity has important consequences for business. For example, it is known that a lower price will increase the quantity demanded of a product, but will it increase the revenue that the store receives from selling the product? This depends on the elasticity of demand. If the demand for a product is inelastic, the store owner would be reluctant to lower the price, even if more of the product could be sold. Why? For an inelastic demand, any drop in price will be accompanied by a decrease in total revenue. If a product has an inelastic demand, consumers do not respond significantly to price changes. It is unlikely, then, that store owners would have sales on goods with an inelastic demand (such as cigarettes).

Conversely, where a product with an elastic demand is involved, sales may be more commonplace. Any decrease in price should generate additional revenue. Automobile manufacturers regularly have sales on cars with the hope of stimulating sales.

2.10 Why does total revenue (TR) decline when there is a price increase for a product with an elastic demand?

2.11 If your local bus company was losing money and decided to increase fares, what is the company's view of the elasticity of demand for its products?

Differing Price Elasticities for the Same Product

It is technically incorrect to state that the demand for a product is inelastic or elastic. This is only true within a certain price range. Within another price range, the coefficient of elasticity is likely to change.

In order to prove this point, refer to figure 2.10. The demand curve in this case is a straight line so that a five-cent change in the price of the product will bring about a ten-unit change in the quantity demanded. The *elasticity coefficient* in the range $0.55-$0.60 is less than one, or inelastic. The elasticity coefficient in the price range $1.95-$2.00 is greater than one, or elastic. The elasticity of demand becomes greater as the price rises.

A good example of how price ranges can affect elasticity is gasoline. In recent years the price of gasoline has been steadily increasing. At lower prices for gasoline, the demand appeared to be relatively inelastic. Even when price increases did occur, people still drove big cars and drove at high speeds. Now that gasoline prices have increased substantially, changes are taking place in the amount of gasoline consumed. People are driving smaller cars. They are making greater use of public transportation, and they are moving closer to their place of work.

The elasticity of demand for a product also increases over time. Substitutes are developed and become more readily available. This results in a more elastic demand for the product. Often price increases encourage the development of substitute or competing products. This takes time, but as more substitute products come onto the market, the price elasticity of demand increases. For example, higher energy costs have stimulated an interest in the development of new energy sources. As these new sources appear on the market, the price elasticity of demand for home-heating oil increases. The elasticity of demand also increases over time because it often takes consumers a while to adjust to the higher prices.

2.12 Why does the price elasticity of the demand coefficient increase over time?

**Figure 2.10
Price elasticity
for various
sections of the
demand curve**

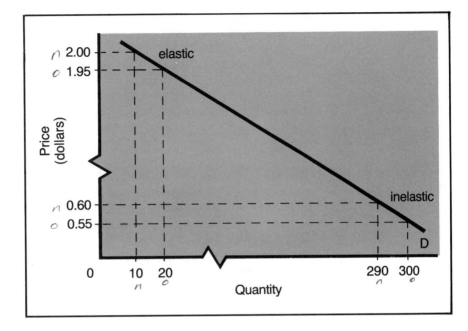

The elasticity of demand varies within different price ranges for the
same product. At higher prices, the elasticity of demand becomes
more elastic.

**Some Calculated
Price Elasticities
of Demand**

The following list of price elasticity coefficients of demand was
obtained from the Economic Council of Canada.

New passenger cars	1.20	Toilet articles and cosmetics	0.18
Recreation, sport, and camping equipment	0.40	Drugs and sundries	0.36
Men's and boys' clothing	1.08	Gasoline	0.68
Women's, girls', and infants' wear	0.23	Travel services	1.40
Footwear and repair	0.70	Recreational services	0.59
Books, newspapers, and magazines	0.56	Laundry and dry cleaning	0.12
Semi-durable household furnishings	0.73	Domestic services	0.27
Jewellery, watches, and repairs	0.38	Education and cultural services	0.37
Food and non-alcoholic beverages	0.38	Expenditure on restaurants and hotels	0.45
Alcoholic beverages	0.84	Purchased transportation	0.65
Tobacco	0.38	Financial, legal, and other services	0.26
Non-durable household supplies	0.35	Gross rent paid	0.18

Source: Unpublished preliminary estimates of price elasticity from the
Candide Model 3.0, Economic Council of Canada, Ottawa, Mar. 1985.

Questions

1 Explain why each product has either an elastic or an inelastic demand.
2 What factors do you think would account for the difference in price elasticity of demand between men's and women's clothing?
3 The above price elasticities of demand were calculated over a relatively short period of time. What do you think would happen to the elasticity values for many of these items if they were to be calculated over a longer period of time?

Special Cases of Price Elasticity of Demand

The general principle of demand states that as the price of the product falls the quantity demanded of that product increases. When the price rises, the quantity demanded decreases. The degree to which quantity demanded reacts to change in price is a measure of the price elasticity of demand. There may be two special cases of a demand curve where the price and quantity demanded are not inversely related.

In figure 2.11a, the demand curve is horizontal. At the set price P_1, the quantity demanded is unlimited. The price elasticity of demand coefficient (E_d) in this case is ∞ (undefined).

**Figure 2.11a
Perfectly elastic
demand curve**

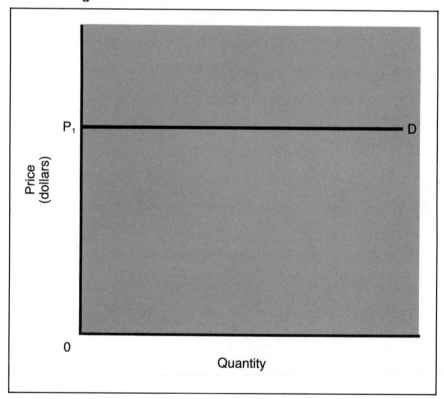

A horizontal demand curve implies that at price P_1 an unlimited quantity of this product would be demanded.

**Figure 2.11b
Perfectly inelastic
demand curve**

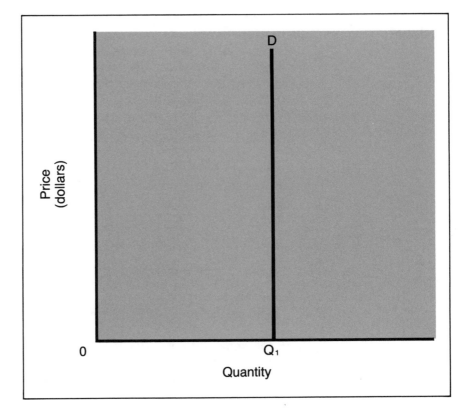

A vertical demand curve implies that an unlimited price would be
paid for a set quantity (Q$_1$) of this product.

Although situations similar to this one are limited in the real world,
there are applications of such a demand curve, known as a *perfectly
elastic demand curve*. In Chapter 12, the discussion of perfectly competitive pricing employs such a demand curve. Another real-world example of a perfectly elastic demand curve occurred during the 1950s
and 1960s in the United States in relation to gold. It was illegal for U.S.
citizens to possess gold and they were required to sell their gold to the
government at $35 an ounce. The government agreed to purchase an un-
limited amount of gold at this price.

In figure 2.11b, a vertical demand curve is shown. A certain
quantity (Q$_1$) of this product is demanded and any price will be paid
to acquire that amount. The price elasticity of demand coefficient is
zero and is referred to as *perfectly inelastic*. Such a curve may reflect
the demand for a necessary drug or medicine. A person may require a
certain amount of this medicine and would be willing to pay any price
in order to acquire it.

Price Elasticity of Supply

Since suppliers also differ in their capacity to respond to price changes, the concept of price elasticity can also be applied to the supply curve. The terminology used in discussing supply price elasticity is similar to that of demand. If a supplier is able to adjust supply readily when the price changes, the supply is referred to as elastic. If the quantity supplied does not respond to price changes, supply is said to be inelastic.

The numerical determination of supply elasticity is as follows:

$$\text{price elasticity coefficient of supply } (E_s) = \frac{\text{percentage change in quantity supplied } (Q_s)}{\text{percentage change in price } (P)}$$

$$E_s = \frac{\% \, \Delta \, Q_s}{\% \, \Delta \, P}$$

If the coefficient is greater than one, supply is elastic; if less than one, it is inelastic; and finally, if the coefficient is equal to one, the supply is unitary elastic.

What are the major factors determining the price elasticity of supply?

Time: the primary determinant of supply elasticity is time. For a single moment in time, supply is fixed and cannot be adjusted to price fluctuations. The longer the time allowed to adjust to price changes, the more it is likely that existing firms will be able to increase production. They will be able to attract the necessary resources in order to increase output. Also, the longer the time allowed for adjustment, the more new firms will be able to enter the industry in response to a price increase.

Consider a farmer bringing his fresh produce to market. The supply of produce is fixed for that day. This can be represented by curve S^1 in figure 2.12. The curve S^1 is perfectly inelastic, and the price elasticity coefficient of supply is zero. Over a period of time the farmer will be able to adjust the supply that he brings to market depending on the price that he can get for his produce. If the price of a certain product increases, the farmer will likely grow more of that product in the future. The supply curve over a longer period of time is represented by curve S^2 in figure 2.12. The supply curve S^2 shows a greater ability to respond to price changes than does S^1, and is therefore more elastic.

Ability to store product: some products such as food items are perishable and cannot be stored for long periods of time. Since the items cannot be kept off the market until the price rises, their elasticity of supply is inelastic. Regardless of the price, they must be sold. This also applies to products that are expensive to store. For example, if a product requires extensive refrigeration, it is not likely to be stored indefinitely. The elasticity of supply for products that can be stored will be more elastic.

**Figure 2.12
Price elasticity
of supply**

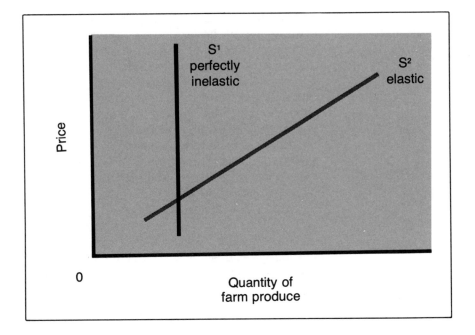

The price elasticity of supply for a product can change over time.

Ability to substitute during production: the ability of suppliers to react to price changes also depends on whether or not production can be easily shifted to an alternative product. Automobile manufacturers may be able to switch production levels between two similar types of cars. However, they may not find it so easy to switch from producing large cars to producing small cars. If the switch from one product to another is relatively easy, the supply elasticity is likely to be elastic. If the switch is not easily made, or cannot be made quickly, then the elasticity of supply will be inelastic.

2.13 Why is the primary determinant of price elasticity of supply the time period being considered?

**Other Types
of Elasticity**

We have calculated elasticity values based on changes in the price of a product and the resulting impact on the quantity demanded or supplied. Economists also rely on other elasticity measures when analysing markets.

Income elasticity measures the responsiveness of the change in quantity demanded to changing income levels. How is the quantity demanded of a product affected when incomes increase or decrease? If more of a product is purchased when incomes increase, the product is a normal good and has a positive value for income elasticity. If a product has a negative value for income elasticity, increases in income result in less of the product being purchased. Products with negative income elasticities are called inferior goods. They are not inferior in the sense of quality, rather in that consumers switch to other products when their incomes increase. As a student with a limited income, your diet may lack variety. You may choose to consume more of certain foods because they are less expensive. When your income increases, you may switch from buying these foods to buying others that cost a little more. Finally, products with income elasticities close to zero are necessities. Their consumption is not affected by income levels.

Economists are also interested in the impact that changes in the price of one product have on the quantity demanded of another product. This is referred to as *cross-elasticity of demand*. By calculating cross-elasticities, economists can better identify substitute and complementary products. If the value of cross-elasticity is positive, the two products are substitutes. That is, increases in the price of product A lead to increases in the quantity demanded of product B. If increases in the price of product A lead to reductions in the quantity demanded of product B, the two products are complementary. For complementary products, the value of cross-elasticity is negative. Values of cross-elasticity close to zero indicate a lack of association between the products.

Summary

Markets serve two functions in our economy. They are the focal point for exchanges of goods and services, and they establish prices. The system of prices determined in the various markets is a key component of a free market system.

The market for any good or service is divided into two sections. The demand side of the market represents those who are willing to purchase the product. The supply side represents those who are willing to sell the product. Through the interaction of both sides, exchanges take place and prices are established.

The prices and quantities exchanged in each market are constantly moving toward a stable position called equilibrium. If the quantity that people are willing to buy at a certain price does not match the quantity supplied at that price, then adjustments begin to take place. The price either rises or falls, signalling changes on both sides of the market. Equilibrium is attained when the quantity demanded of a product at a certain price is equal to the quantity supplied at that price. This equilibrium position may, however, only be temporary. A change in any one of several factors will cause the market to seek out a new equilibrium.

An important concept in the study of markets is that of price elasticity. This measures the response of buyers and sellers to price changes. If consumers do not react very much to price changes in terms of the amount of a product purchased, the demand for the product is said to be inelastic. In contrast, if consumers react significantly to price changes, then the demand is said to be elastic. The same terminology applies to the supply side of the market.

There is a market for any commodity or service that has a price. In some instances the price is referred to by another name such as rent, interest, or wages.

Two markets were discussed in some detail in this chapter. The stock market represents the organized trading of shares, or ownership, in public corporations. The futures market represents the buying and selling of commodities contracts that specify the future delivery of given quantities at a price established today. The free market system of economic decision-making is comprised of thousands of operating markets. The markets described in this chapter operate free from government intervention. In reality, very few markets operate without some form of government intervention, and the rationale behind this intervention is presented in the following chapter.

Questions for Review and Discussion

1. How would an increase in the price of beef affect the demand for beef? How would it affect the supply?
2. "Higher prices for houses will cause the demand for houses to decline. This will eventually result in lower prices for houses." Comment on the validity of this statement.
3. It has been stated that the consumer is king. What does this statement mean when referring to the operation of a market?
4. In 1990, 2000 units of a commodity were purchased at a price of $3.00 per unit. In 1991, 3000 units were purchased at a price of $4.00. Does this contradict the law of downward-sloping demand? Explain.
5. Why are some commodities more likely to be involved in futures trading than others? What are the characteristics of these commodities?
6. Why would individuals be interested in purchasing ownership in a company through the stock exchange?
7. If the demand for many farm products is inelastic, why would a bad crop be to the advantage of farmers? Use demand and supply curves in your answer.
8. Draw a demand curve for wanting and having children. What factors would cause the demand curve to shift?
9. In the discussion of price elasticity of demand, it was shown that changes in total revenue could shed some more light on the question of demand elasticity. Why will a review of total revenue, similar to that used for demand, not work with the

concept of elasticity of supply?

10 What would happen to the price of a product if there were a simultaneous increase in both the demand and the supply? Explain, using a graph in your answer.

11 Why do sellers lower the price when there is a surplus? Why do buyers bid up the price when there is a shortage?

12 The stock and futures markets both use brokers in order to conduct buying or selling. Are there any other similarities between the two markets?

13 Draw the supply curve for a limited-edition print or plate. What is the elasticity of supply for such an item?

14 Using demand and supply curves in your answer, show the impact of the following:
    i   an increase in wood prices on the market for new houses
    ii a decrease in the incomes of consumers on the market for new clothes
    iii an increase in players' salaries on the market for hockey tickets
    iv an increase in the price of butter on the market for margarine

15 In the 1970s a severe frost hit Brazil and damaged much of the coffee crop of that country. Since Brazil is one of the world's leading coffee producers, what impact might this frost have had on world coffee prices? Use demand and supply curves in your answer.

16 Which of the following would lead to an increase in the current demand for beef?
    i   higher pork prices   iii higher prices for cattle feed
    ii higher consumer incomes   iv   an increase in beef prices

17 "We cannot allow gasoline prices to rise too high because gasoline is an essential product, especially for poor people." Comment on this statement using your knowledge of demand and supply.

18 Using your knowledge of demand and supply, explain why parking garages in the downtown core of Canadian cities have several levels, whereas in the suburbs parking lots tend to be only one level.

19 The disappearance of anchovies off the coast of Peru in 1972 caused a scramble for protein-rich substitutes, notably soybeans. Because soybeans are used in cattle feed, higher soybean prices eventually were translated into higher cattle prices. Use demand and supply diagrams to illustrate what happened in the anchovy, soybean, and cattle markets. Indicate which curves shifted in each instance and show the effects on the equilibrium price and quantity in each market.

20 Although higher prices are not welcomed by consumers they are good for producers. Some communities depend on high prices for the natural resources located in their vicinity. Name

some communities that depend on

i high oil prices	iv high nickel prices
ii high lumber prices	v high fish prices
iii high iron-ore prices	

21 For each of the following goods and services, state whether the demand would be elastic or inelastic:

i postal service	iv textbooks
ii soft drinks	v houses
iii theatre tickets	vi home computers

22 Why do motels and hotels lower their rates in the off-season and raise their rates in the peak season?

23 Fire destroyed one-half of the trees on a certain tract of land in New Brunswick. The remaining lumber was worth more than the value of the trees before the fire. What does this say about the elasticity of demand for lumber?

24 Donor organs for transplants are in short supply. What would happen to the supply of organs if donors were paid in advance for their body parts?

25 In order to reduce the cost of medicare to the public, it has been suggested that individuals pay one dollar for each visit to the doctor. Discuss the impact of this user fee on the demand for medical services. Refer to the price elasticity of demand in your answer.

26 The cost of mailing a letter is constantly increasing. Postage is now subject to the G.S.T. In your opinion, is the demand for stamps elastic or inelastic? Explain.

27 Provide examples of products with the following characteristics:
   i   positive cross-elasticities (two products)
   ii negative income elasticity.

28 In March 1990, McDonald's Restaurants announced a reduction of up to 30 percent in the price of hamburgers and other items. A McDonald's spokesperson stated that although the lower prices will pinch profits, the increase in customers will ultimately compensate for the decline in earnings. What is McDonald's view of the price elasticity of demand for its food? Do you think that this view is correct? Explain.

Suggested Readings

Campbell, Robert. *People and Markets*. Menlo Park: Benjamin/ Cummings 1978.

Cheveldayoff, Wayne. *The Business Page*. Toronto: Deneau and Greenberg 1977.

Downes, John and Jordan Elliot Goodman. *Dictionary of Finance and Investment Terms.* Woodbury: Barron's Educational Series 1985.

Elzinga, Kenneth (ed.). *Economics: A Reader,* 3rd ed. New York: Harper and Row 1978.

Friedman, Milton, and Rose Friedman. *Free to Choose.* New York: Harcourt Brace Jovanovich 1980.

Heyne, Paul. *Microeconomics.* Chicago: SRA 1988

Heyne, Paul. *The Economic Way of Thinking.* Sixth Edition New York: Macmillan 1991

Chapter 3

The Role of Government in a Market Economy

Chapter Objectives

After successfully completing this chapter, you will be able to:

- appreciate the advantages and shortcomings of the free market system
- describe in your own words the concept behind Adam Smith's invisible hand
- understand the rationale behind government intervention in the free market system
- graph the impact of price floors, price ceilings, and excise taxes on various markets

Key Terms

invisible hand	privatization
natural monopoly	price ceiling
third-party effects	price floor
unmet public goods	excise tax

Government and the Free Market

In Chapter 2, we discussed how a free market system works and that price changes are the vehicle by which the market system operates. Not only do price changes provide information and incentives to the marketplace, they also determine the distribution of the products in our industrial society. Now let us look at how and why government becomes involved in the operations of the market.

The Writings of Adam Smith

The advantages of the free market system were first highlighted by Adam Smith, a Scottish philosopher, in 1776. In his book, *An Inquiry into the Nature and Causes of the Wealth of Nations,* (usually referred to as *The Wealth of Nations*), Smith stressed the advantages to society of *individual self-interest* and decision-making. He believed that the free market system would channel selfish, egoistic motives toward the betterment of society. In his words, each producer

> intends only his own security; and by directing that industry in such a manner as its produce may be of the greatest value, he intends only his own gain, and he is in this, as in many other cases, led by an invisible hand to promote an end which was no part of his intention. Nor is it always the worse for the society that it was not a part of it. By pursuing his own interest he frequently promotes that of society more effectually than when he really intends to promote it. I have never known much good done by those who affected to trade for the public good. It is an affectation, indeed, not very common among merchants, and very few words need be employed in dissuading them from it [p. 423].

Philosopher Adam Smith introduced the term invisible hand *to describe the effect that a free market economic system has of directing the self-interests of individuals toward a common goal.*

Smith believed that society would be better off if everyone pursued his or her own self-interests and was not concerned about the effects of their actions on society. He felt that self-interest promotes the public good more than actions that are intended only for the betterment of society. He thought that it was as if an **"invisible hand"** directed the affairs of individuals toward a common goal.

How can Adam Smith's philosophy, written more than 200 years ago, be related to the 1990s? What are the consequences of an individual seeking to acquire wealth in today's society? In order to answer these questions, it is best to review the means by which you could become wealthy. You could win a lottery, marry into a wealthy family, inherit a fortune, or start your own business. Of these, starting your own business is the most common approach and has the greatest impact on the economy.

If you were to start a business, which one would you choose? This is a difficult question to answer. There are thousands of small businesses operating in Canada today. To be successful, you will have to provide a product or a service that consumers want. If people buy your product in sufficient quantities you will be able to earn a living. Both parties are happy—consumers receive a product they want, and you succeed in making money. In this way, you are not only improving your own welfare but also that of your customers. When deciding to start a business, you do so with a great deal of uncertainty and you take a risk in assuming that people will want whatever you have to offer. You may guess wrong and not make a success of your endeavour; thousands of small businesses fail each year for this reason. The fact that you have started a business does not guarantee success, because not enough consumers may want your product. If you cannot increase consumer welfare, your individual welfare does not increase.

If you succeed, your success is likely to attract the attention of others: it will attract competition! If you can make money, why can't they? In order to continue to sell your product or service, it will be necessary to make it more attractive than the product or service that the competition provides. This can be done by either lowering prices or by improving the quality of your good or service. Regardless of which option you choose, the consumer will benefit, because competition ultimately benefits the consumer.

This sequence of events has so far been undertaken without any government involvement. You are not told what business to enter, how to make your product, or what price to charge. Yet, through the pursuit of your own selfish interests, a product or service is provided and distributed to consumers. Just as you are successful in your business, others will be successful in their business pursuits if they satisfy consumer wants. The pursuit of individual self-interest through the free market system results in the needs of the consumer being fulfilled. In economic terms, we say that the free market will tend to allocate resources (land, labour, materials) to their most efficient use. Adam Smith believed that any interference with the free market system could only have negative consequences for society.

> No regulation of commerce can increase the quantity of industry in any society beyond what its capital can maintain. It can only divert a part of it into a direction into which it might not otherwise have gone; and it is by no means certain that this artificial direction is likely to be more advantageous to the society than that into which it would have gone of its own accord [p.421].

Smith assumed that consumers know what they want and will spend their money accordingly.

The free market system guarantees a great deal of individual freedom, allowing people to be guided by their own self-interest and to do things that maximize their own satisfaction. Many believe that having freedom in economic matters is essential to having freedom in political matters. A major proponent of this philosophy is economist Milton Friedman, whose views on the market system of capitalism are presented at the end of this chapter.

3.1   What did Adam Smith mean by the term "invisible hand"?

3.2   Is there any significance in the fact that the United States became an independent country in 1776, the same year that *The Wealth of Nations* was published? On what principles was the United States established?

Possible Shortcomings of the Free Market System

Even though the free market system is efficient at satisfying consumer needs, it does have some shortcomings as an economic system. These deficiencies have led to some government involvement in the economy.

Market Imperfections

The free market system described in Chapter 2 was a perfect system. In reality, however, there are certain imperfections that impede the operation of a market. We will review two of these imperfections.

Information

The theoretical explanation of the free market system assumes that buyers and sellers have adequate information with which to make decisions. In reality, however, *satisfactory information* is not always available. Consumers may not know where they can find products that they are looking for and they may not know the price differences between different suppliers. Buyers also may not be aware of any differences in product quality. If suppliers have difficulty obtaining information, they may not know the best way to reach potential customers. They may not know where to find competent employees or what wage to pay them. For both consumers and producers, information is often inadequate.

Advertising helps to fill this information gap. Through advertising, suppliers are able to provide information to potential buyers, and consumers can find out more about the product, including the price. Advertising is influenced by economic conditions so that it more closely meets the needs of consumers. For example, with the current concern over energy conservation, automobile manufacturers are forced to promote the fuel-saving features of their cars in addition to their different design features. Consumers are also concerned about automobile safety and, as a result, manufacturers are beginning to promote such features as air bags and anti-lock brakes.

Unfortunately, advertising does not completely close the information gap. More often than not, advertising is meant to persuade rather than to inform. Government has intervened in the workings of the market system in order to improve the information available to both the consumer and the supplier. It has also made misleading advertising illegal. Government regulations insist on certain labelling, especially in the area of food packaging. Food products are required to have a list of their ingredients on the package, in the order of their importance. Consumers often lack information in other areas, as well. For example, they may not know whether or not standards of cleanliness are maintained in the kitchens of restaurants. For this reason, the government has introduced *health standards* for eating establishments. New home buyers cannot be sure how their home was constructed; government building codes are designed for consumer protection in this area. Perhaps you could think of other areas in which government has intervened in order to improve information in the marketplace. In Canada, many of these regulations and others are administered by the Department of Consumer and Corporate Affairs. This federal government department works in conjunction with other federal departments and with provincial consumer affairs' departments to increase consumer information and protection.

Information is also inadequate in the labour market. Job seekers may not know where available jobs can be found; employers may not know where to find employees with the necessary skills. Within the free market system individuals have taken some steps to improve this situation. Private placement agencies have been established in order to assist in the matching of workers and jobs. However, many of these agencies operate in specialized job markets only; e.g., accounting, secretarial, engineering, and data processing fields. For most occupations and skills, no specialized job-finding assistance is provided. In order to fill the information gap, the federal government operates a network of Canada Employment Centres (CECs) across the country. These centres provide job information and *employment counselling* services. Information on job opportunities across the country is made available at each centre. Employers can also use the services of the CEC in their search for qualified workers.

Competition

A second type of imperfection in the marketplace is competition. If the market system is working as it should, new firms will set up in industries that are profitable. The resulting competition will improve the quality of the product or service and help to keep prices down. The entry of new companies in the ball-point pen market helped lower the price from its original $12.95 in the 1940s to what it is today. New firms have also had a restraining effect on prices in the pocket calculator and running-shoe markets. What would happen if new firms were prevented from entering the industry? There would be less competition. There would be higher prices and less of the product available. Quality might also deteriorate.

Competition in the marketplace can be restricted in several ways. Firms may get together in order to fix prices. Some companies may sell their products at a loss for a short period of time with the sole purpose of eliminating competitors. Manufacturers may refuse to sell to retailers who do not charge a set price for the product. All of these practices, and others that intentionally limit competition, are illegal in Canada under the Competition Act. This act will be discussed in more detail in Chapter 13.

Despite the advantages of competition, it may be more efficient in some industries to have a single supplier of the product or service. For example, imagine the difficulties of having competing telephone companies in the same town. You may be required to keep several telephones in your house in order to be able to phone whomever you wish. There would be a great deal of duplication in setting up telephone lines, switchboards, and so on. Similarly, how many companies would be required to effectively provide sewer and water services to a municipality? It would be inefficient to have more than one. In situations like these, referred to as **natural monopolies**, the government either provides the service or regulates the company that does provide the service. The regulation of natural monopolies is another role that government plays in the market system. A more detailed discussion of natural monopolies appears in Chapter 13.

Natural monopolies are those industries in which it is more efficient to have only one company or supplier of a product or service.

3.3   Provide an example of a government service whose purpose is to provide more information to the consumer.

3.4   What do we mean by a natural monopoly?

Third-Party Effects

Market transactions benefit two parties—the buyer receives a desired good and the seller receives money. In many transactions, however, these are not the only parties to be affected. *A third party may be affected in either a negative or a positive manner.*

Let us first discuss possible negative **third-party effects**. Consider the case of a paper mill. In the process of making paper, the mill may pollute the air and the water in the surrounding area. The mill will continue to pollute as long as it is cheaper simply to dump the waste than to dispose of it in any other way. Because the paper mill faces competition from other manufacturers, it has to be concerned about costs, and will not be inclined to install pollution-control equipment. Higher costs mean higher prices. The paper mill would prefer not to raise the price of

A transaction between a buyer and seller also may have an impact on others, creating either positive or negative third-party effects.

paper because such a move would turn away customers.

There are additional costs to making paper not contained in the price of the paper. These are third-party, or external, costs that people in the surrounding area will suffer, such as ill health due to the pollution. Fish in the river will no longer be fit to eat. Acid rain may destroy some of the surrounding lakes and cropland.

In a free market system, there would be no need for the paper mill to take steps to solve its pollution problem. The company is free to make paper the way it wants to. Governments believe that they have a responsibility to intervene, since not all the costs associated with making paper are being considered. In the case of the paper mill, the government could force the mill to install pollution-control devices, or it could tax the mill in order to pay for pollution clean-up. Either way the negative effects of paper-making on the third party would be reduced. The effect of government intervention on the price of paper is shown in figure 3.1.

Figure 3.1 Government reaction to negative third-party effects

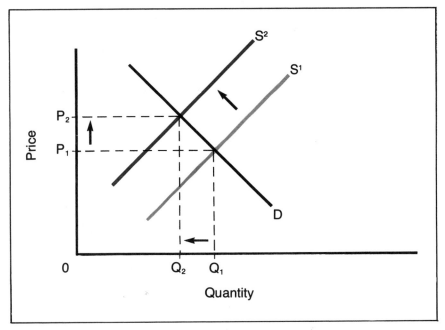

In order to account for third-party costs, the government undertakes action to decrease the supply of the product. This increases the equilibrium price and decreases the equilibrium quantity.

Government action, either in the form of a tax or the requirement to install new equipment, would cause the supply curve for paper to shift to the left (S^2) because of increased costs. This results in a higher equilibrium price in the market (P_2). The higher price would then reflect the total cost of providing this product. Pollution has negative third-party effects because its costs spill over to a third party.

Transactions between buyers and sellers may also have positive third-party effects. Assume that polio vaccinations were being offered in the free market for a price. Those people who were concerned about their health and could afford it would probably get the necessary vaccinations. They would purchase the vaccination from a doctor or health clinic. In this transaction, both parties benefit. The doctor is paid for services and the consumer receives immunization against the disease. Because polio is a contagious disease, this transaction also benefits others. Those who come into contact with the immunized person now run a smaller risk of getting the disease. Many people benefit from this type of transaction and it would be beneficial to society if more vaccinations could be provided. In this situation, a government may step in to ensure that more of this service is provided. This intervention may be accomplished by using tax dollars to subsidize the doctor or the health clinic. The impact of such subsidization is shown in figure 3.2. The supply curve has shifted from S^1 to S^2. The price of polio vaccinations has decreased from P_1 to P_3. Another option would be to pay for the vaccination on behalf of those who could not afford it. The effect of this on the polio vaccination market is also shown in figure 3.2. If the original price was P_1 in the market and the government assisted consumers in the

**Figure 3.2
Government
reaction to
positive third-
party effects**

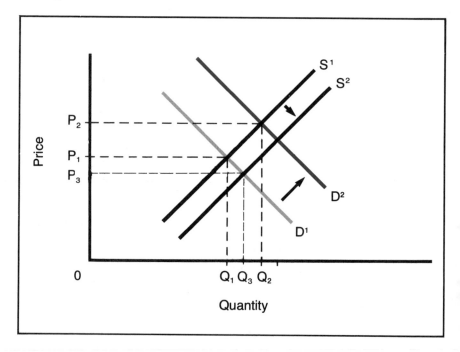

In order to account for third-party benefits, the government undertakes to increase the demand for or increase the supply of this product.

purchase of this product, then the demand for vaccinations would increase. This would cause the demand curve to shift to D^2 and increase the equilibrium price to P_2. The new price would better represent the value of the service to society. Polio vaccinations are referred to as a positive third-party effect since their benefits spill over to a third party.

3.5 Define third-party effects.

3.6 Why does government feel it is necessary to intervene in the market when the third-party effects are present?

Unmet Public Goods

The market system may not be able to provide a number of goods and services—such as national defence, police protection, municipal water supply and sewage treatment—that are important to society. This is because the benefits from these services are spread over such a large segment of the population that it is difficult to charge a fee for their use based on the benefits received. It may not even be possible to determine who receives the benefits. It is also difficult to divide these services up into units that can be sold in the marketplace. In the case of national defence, it would be impossible to charge each individual who benefits from the service. It is more efficient to have a government provide the service and pay for it from general tax revenue. If national defence were left up to the free market, only certain individuals would decide to purchase the service. Those who chose not to purchase the service would still benefit, since it would be difficult for the military to protect only those who had purchased the national defence service; if everyone benefits, then everyone should pay for it.

Unmet public goods describes those goods and services not provided by the free market system due to the difficulty of charging a fee to the beneficiaries of the good or service.

It is not necessary that government should own and operate all such services defined under the heading of **unmet public goods**. In many situations, it may be more efficient to contract out the service to private companies. Regardless of whether the service is government-run or contracted out, the government cannot rely on the free market to provide the service, because it may not be profitable to do so. Government has played a role in the free market by directing some of our resources toward the provision of these kinds of services.

3.7 Roads and sidewalks have been categorized as unmet public goods. Why?

3.8 Does a lighthouse qualify as an unmet public good? Explain.

Privatization

Privatization is the transfer of control of a company from government to private ownership.

Encouraged by the success of **privatization** efforts in countries such as Britain and France, the federal government sold a number of Crown corporations to private interests in the latter half of the 1980s. Among the companies that were sold, in whole or in part, are de Havilland Aircraft, Canadian Arsenals, Canadair, Teleglobe Canada, Nanisivik Mines, CN Route, and Air Canada.

What is the rationale behind the selling of Crown corporations? Some argue that the rationale lay in the ideology of the Conservative party, which states that government should not compete in the private sector. That is, why should the government own a company that makes airplanes? Can this type of manufacturing not be done in the private sector? Others have argued that the motive for privatization is profit. The money received for Crown corporations can be used to help pay off the government debt. A third possible rationale, and the one adhered to by the federal government, is that private ownership will make Crown corporations more efficient and competitive. If Crown corporations are freed from government policy decisions, they would be more efficient.

Privatization of a Crown corporation is not easy. Apart from the legal and accounting difficulties, the concerns of those who have a strong interest in retaining the Crown corporation have to be addressed before the privatization can be called a success. The interests of four groups have to be taken care of while the privatization is being carried out. These groups are the bureaucrats who are responsible for the Crown corporation, the work force, the people who benefit from the program or company, and the legislators who must be ready to face the complaints when the Crown corporation is being sold. Privatization is not so much an economic issue as it is a political issue. If the concerns of these groups can be addressed, the privatization effort will run more smoothly. For example, in order to address the concerns of the work force, workers could be offered shares in the new private corporation. By offering shares to the workers, the shares would initially be more widely dispersed and not be held by a few individuals or groups.

Privatization efforts are worldwide. Apart from Canada, Britain, and France, privatization efforts are under way in Germany, Japan, Italy, the Netherlands, Austria, Denmark, Turkey, Chile, Bangladesh, the United States, Kenya, Sweden, Portugal, Pakistan, South Korea, Mozambique, and India, among others.

Questions

1   Can you suggest some Crown corporations that you would not want the government to sell to private interests? What is your rationale? Is it economic or political?

2   Do you believe that giving shares to workers would reduce their concerns about privatization?

3 It has been suggested that Canada privatize some of its international airports. How would a private company operate an international airport?

Distribution of Income

One of the main advantages of the free market system is competition. In a free market system, there is not only competition between businesses, but between individuals. In the pursuit of earning an income, individuals compete with each other for jobs. Because not all jobs pay the same wage, there will be differences in individual incomes. Some workers earn more money because they are more highly skilled, have more initiative, or live in the right part of the country. Some workers earn less, or are unable to find a job. In fact, the reasons for differences in incomes are numerous, and are discussed in more detail in Chapter 14.

In a free market system, some people may not be able to compete. For example, many elderly people may not be able to compete with younger people for certain jobs, especially those requiring heavy manual labour or new technological skills. Some disabled persons may not be able to participate in the labour force at all. If a person is not able to compete in a free market system, he or she will not be able to earn an income. Because our society has a conscience about these matters, government has intervened in the free market in order to achieve a more equitable distribution of income. A number of *social welfare programs* have been put into effect. These include assistance for the elderly and the disabled, unemployment insurance, and financial assistance to single parents. In order to help finance these programs, the government has introduced a *progressive income tax*. This type of tax requires that an individual pay taxes in relation to personal income. Someone with a higher income will pay a higher percentage of their income in taxes. The rationale behind our income tax system is presented in Chapter 4.

The extent of income differentials in Canada is presented in table 3.1. In 1989, five percent of unattached individual Canadians earned less than $5000 per year. At the other end of the income scale, 10.7 percent of unattached Canadians earned $40 000 per year or more. Significant sex differentials appear when reviewing the figures in table 3.1. The average income in 1989 for an unattached man was $24 098 and for an unattached woman it was $18 675. A greater percentage of men than women are in the higher-income brackets. The data, however, should not be seen as evidence that females are discriminated against in terms of income. There may be other reasons for the higher percentage of women in the lower income categories. A higher percentage of women work part-time. On average, women have not been in the labour force as long as men because of family responsibilities.

Table 3.1 / Percentage distribution of unattached individuals by income groups and sex, Canada 1989

Income group ($)	Percent		Total
	Male	Female	
Under $5 000	5.0	5.0	5.0
$ 5 000–9 999	16.0	21.8	19.2
$10 000–14 999	15.5	27.1	21.9
$15 000–19 999	11.1	11.7	11.5
$20 000–24 999	11.6	9.4	10.3
$25 000–29 999	9.8	8.0	8.8
$30 000–39 999	16.1	9.7	12.6
$40 000 and above	14.9	7.3	10.7
Total	100.0	100.0	100.0
Average income	$24 098	$18 675	$21 138
Median income	$20 822	$13 997	$16 598

Source: *Income Distribution by Size in Canada 1989,* catalogue no. 13-207, annual (Ottawa: Statistics Canada, November 1990), pp. 92, 95.

Table 3.2 / Percentage distribution of families by income groups, Canada 1989

Income group ($)	Percent
Under $10 000	2.4
$10 000–14 999	4.5
$15 000–19 999	7.4
$20 000–24 999	6.4
$25 000–29 999	7.0
$30 000–34 999	7.3
$35 000–39 999	8.1
$40 000–49 999	15.2
$50 000–59 999	12.6
$60 000–69 999	9.5
$70 000 and above	19.6
Total	100.0
Average income	$50 083
Median income	$44 460

Source: *Income Distribution by Size in Canada 1989,* catalogue no. 13-207, annual (Ottawa: Statistics Canada, November 1990), pp. 56.

Income differentials also exist when comparing family incomes. The data in table 3.2 refer to the percentage distribution of families by income group for 1989. In that year, 2.4 percent of all families in Canada had incomes less than $10 000. Another 4.5 percent of families had incomes between $10 000 and $14 999. At the other end of the income scale, 19.6 percent of families had incomes of $70 000 per year and above. Another 9.5 percent of families had incomes between $60 000 and $69 999. These wide differences in income prompt government to intervene in the free market system in order to redistribute income. Despite government initiatives in this area, tables 3.1 and 3.2 point out that income differentials continue to exist.

The existence of income differentials in Canada would not be a serious problem if every Canadian earned enough money to meet his or her basic needs. This, however, is not the case and many Canadians are forced to live in a state of poverty. What exactly do we mean by poverty? Several organizations in Canada have derived a definition of poverty in terms of a *minimum income necessary* for an individual or family. When one's annual income falls below this income standard it can be said that the person is living in poverty. One set of income standards prepared by the Canadian Council on Social Development appears in table 3.3. The council's income standard is based on 50 percent of the national average family income and varies according to family size. The council established a poverty line of $12 800 for a single person in 1990. According to table 3.1, almost 50 percent of all unattached individuals had an income of less than $15 000 in 1989. From the information provided in table 3.2, it is more difficult to establish what proportion of families fall below the poverty line, because family size is not given in the table. Yet we can see that approximately 16 percent of families had an annual income of less than $20 000, which is close to the poverty line for a family of two persons. The income standard in table 3.3 is a national figure and should provide an adequate income in all areas of the country. The actual income necessary to escape poverty will vary by province and by regions within a province. The poverty line will also be affected by health considerations in the family unit.

Incomes also vary across the various regions of Canada. Table 3.4 shows the average and median family incomes for the provinces in 1989: Ontario had the highest average family income and Prince Edward Island the lowest. In general, family incomes were lower in the Atlantic provinces and higher in Ontario and the western provinces of Alberta and British Columbia. The presence of regional income differences has prompted the federal government to transfer tax dollars to the lower-income provinces and to undertake economic development projects in these provinces.

3.9 What factors do you believe would account for income differences between individuals?

Table 3.3 / The Canadian Council on Social Development and Statistics Canada: poverty lines by family size and area, in dollars, 1990

Family size (no. of persons)	CCSD	Statistics Canada			
		A	B	C	D
1	12 800	14 200	12 500	12 200	11 100
2	21 300	19 300	17 000	16 600	15 100
3	25 600	24 500	21 500	21 100	19 200
4	29 800	28 200	24 800	24 200	22 100
5	34 100	30 900	27 100	26 500	24 100
6	38 300	33 500	29 400	28 700	26 200
7	42 600	36 000	31 600	30 900	28 200

Source: *Perception.* Winter 1990, Vol. 14, No. 1 (Ottawa: Canadian Council on Social Development) p. 48. The estimates were calculated from 1988 data using inflation rates of 5.4 percent from 1988 to 1989 and 5.0 percent from 1989 to 1990.

A: Quebec, Montreal, Ottawa, Toronto, Hamilton, Winnipeg, Calgary, Edmonton, Vancouver.
B: St. John's, Halifax, Saint John, Chicoutimi-Jonquiere, Sherbrooke, Trois Rivieres, Sudbury, Oshawa, St. Catharines-Niagara, Kitchener, London, Windsor, Thunder Bay, Regina, Saskatoon, Victoria.
C: Communities with populations from 30 000 to 99 999.
D: Communities with populations less than 30 000.

Table 3.4 / Average and median family incomes by province, 1989

Province	Average family income ($)	Median family income ($)
Newfoundland	39 648	35 652
Prince Edward Island	38 726	34 548
Nova Scotia	43 123	37 649
New Brunswick	40 670	36 344
Quebec	44 860	40 187
Ontario	57 330	50 464
Manitoba	46 551	41 257
Saskatchewan	42 978	38 068
Alberta	49 734	44 867
British Columbia	49 442	46 028
Canada	50 083	44 460

Source: *Income Distribution by Size in Canada 1989,* catalogue no. 13-207, annual (Ottawa: Statistics Canada, November 1990), pp. 56-7.

Economic Stabilization

The market system is not free of economic fluctuations. There have been periods of economic expansion and periods of economic decline. Possibly the most famous economic decline was the depression of the 1930s, the Great Depression. At the beginning of the depression period, governments did not see their role as one of influencing business conditions. However, as economic conditions deteriorated, governments were influenced by the writings of John Maynard Keynes and became more involved in the state of the economy. Keynes proposed that government involvement in the economy could help bring an end to depressed economic conditions. If government were to increase the level of its spending, business activity would pick up. On the other hand, increased taxes or reductions in government spending would slow down economic activity.

After World War II, the Government of Canada adopted Keynes' philosophy. It issued a statement accepting responsibility for maintaining high levels of employment, reasonably stable prices, and sufficient economic growth. Chapters 6 and 8 of this book discuss the role of government in stabilizing economic activity.

Impact of Government Intervention

We have discussed the operations and results of the free market system. It is important to determine the effect of government involvement on these results. Using the demand and supply analysis developed in Chapter 2, it is possible to analyse the impact of government intervention in the marketplace.

Price Ceilings

A price ceiling is a government-imposed maximum price.

In certain situations, government may not approve of the price established in the product market. Government officials may feel that the equilibrium price is too high. It may be that many people believe that they cannot afford to buy the product. In these situations, the government may legislate a price lower than the one established in the marketplace. This legal maximum price for a product is referred to as a **price ceiling**. It would be illegal to sell the product at a price in excess of the maximum price. Price ceilings have been introduced in Canada on apartment rents and oil prices. The impact of such a decision is shown in figure 3.3. P_0 is the market price. Government may decide to set the maximum price that can be charged for the product at P_c. At this price the quantity demanded increases to Q_d and the quantity supplied drops to Q_s. This results in a shortage of the product ($Q_d - Q_s$).

Figure 3.3
Price ceiling

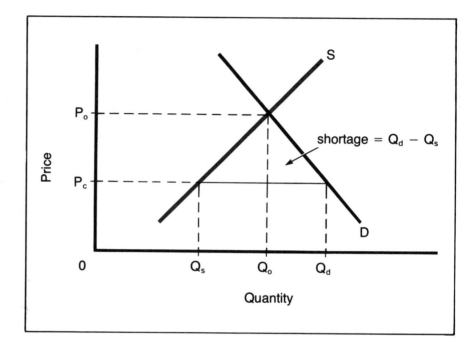

The imposition of a price ceiling (P_c) results in a shortage of the product (Q_d-Q_s).

When shortages exist in the free market system, the price increases and the shortage is eliminated. With government price ceilings in effect, it is illegal to raise the price above P_c. The shortage remains and government must find another way to eliminate it. Somehow either the demand curve or the supply curve will have to shift in order to establish a new equilibrium price at P_c. One possible way is for the government to offer a *subsidy* to the producers of the product. This would shift the supply curve to the right, with more of the product being offered on the market.

When controls are established, the allocation function of the free market system is destroyed. An equilibrium situation in terms of price and quantity cannot be attained without further government involvement.

3.10 Using demand and supply curves, show the impact of the government imposing a price ceiling on bread.

Rent Controls

One of the foremost examples of price ceilings is that of rent controls. Attempts to regulate accommodation have been applied in several countries in order to assist low-income families to afford reasonable housing.

In Canada, the problem is not one of a shortage of decent housing. We are probably one of the best-housed nations in the world and rank very high on a scale that compares living space per person.[1] The problem centres around the inability of some individuals to afford available accommodation. Governments in various countries, including Canada, have placed a ceiling on rents as a solution to this problem. In this country, only Alberta, British Columbia, and New Brunswick do not have a program for rent control. Rather than provide money to low-income individuals and families, governments have introduced rent controls in order to supplement the incomes of these people. If rent controls keep apartment rents below the free market rents, individuals who rent apartments are better off financially. In addition to helping low income persons, rent controls also assist apartment-dwellers who can afford more highly-priced accommodation. This is due to the fact that rent controls are placed on the apartment unit and not on the occupant's income.

How do rent controls work? The exact form that rent controls can take varies from province to province. The usual practice is to limit annual rent increases to a percentage of existing rents. Increases above the allowable limit may be granted if the landlord can demonstrate higher operating costs. Any increases above the annual limit must be approved by a rent-review commission.

Do rent controls assist people in obtaining affordable accommodation? In order to answer this question, the impact of rent controls on the rental accommodation market needs to be studied. If rent increases are prevented or regulated by a government, then the incomes of apartment owners are also regulated. Owners may respond by refusing to maintain the building in order to increase their income. Carpets may not be cleaned, walls may not be painted, and repairs may not be undertaken. It is likely that the quality of residential accommodation will deteriorate. Apartment-building owners may decide to convert the building to another use not subject to rent controls. Hotels, condominiums, and offices have been the end product of many apartment-building conversions. In some cases, the existing building has been demolished in order to convert the land to another use.

Not only are existing buildings affected, but the regulation of rent increases also affects the construction of new apartment units. Contractors may not want to put up apartment buildings if the government is regulating the rent. They may direct their efforts into other types of construction, such as office buildings, retail stores, and houses. They may also decide to build condominiums, luxury apartments, or co-operatives, which are not likely to be subject to rent restrictions.

[1] *Rent Control: A Popular Paradox* (Vancouver: Fraser Institute 1976), p. 10.

As the population increases, the quantity of apartment units required will become greater than the available supply. Rent controls will have resulted in a shortage of apartment units. When this happens, governments feel obligated to assist in the construction of new rental units. Government may undertake the construction of new buildings or offer subsidies to private contractors for rental-unit construction. One such program, Convert-To-Rent, exists in the province of Ontario. Under this program, interest-free loans can be obtained for converting non-residential property (for example, a vacant warehouse, school, or retail space) into rental accommodation. Governments, after imposing rent controls, are forced to participate in the construction of new residential units. It has been stated that 95 percent of all units built in Ontario since the introduction of rent controls in 1975 have received some form of government assistance.

Do rent controls have any other impact? The shortage of apartments created by rent controls leads to other consequences. Prospective home buyers who now rent apartments may be reluctant to buy a house, preferring to live in a rent-controlled unit. At the present time, no protection exists for the home owner from higher property taxes or mortgage-financing costs. The shortage may also encourage landlords to ask prospective tenants for more money than they are legally allowed. In more popular locations, landlords have asked for "key money" when offering an apartment for rent. "Key money" is the name for a practice whereby landlords ask for money in addition to the rent, in order to get a price closer to the true market value of their apartment.

If the shortage is severe enough, some people will be willing to pay more in order to guarantee accommodation. A shortage of units will also make it easier for landlords to discriminate against prospective renters. It is easier to refuse accommodation to students, families with young children, or members of certain ethnic groups under these conditions. A group of landlords is already compiling a database on the personal and financial backgrounds of thousands of tenants in order to screen prospective tenants more closely than in the past.

Why do governments continue with rent-control programs in light of these undesirable consequences? It is easier to introduce rent controls than to remove them. If rent controls were to be suddenly removed, the built-up demand for rental units would result in a drastic increase in rents. There would be a great deal of tenant opposition to the removal of rent controls. Since there are more tenants than landlords, governments interested in re-election are likely to pay more attention to the tenants' point of view. In some instances, provinces originally introduced rent controls as a temporary measure, but now find them difficult to remove.

Questions

1 Draw demand and supply curves showing the imposition of rent controls on the market for apartments.

2 How can governments solve the shortage problem created by rent controls? Show this using demand and supply curves.

3 "Rent controls represent a special tax on apartment owners." Explain what is meant by this statement.

4 Would a better solution to the housing problem be to give low-income families a subsidy with which to purchase acceptable accommodation, rather than to control rents? What are the problems with this approach? Draw a demand and supply diagram to show the impact of such a subsidy.

5 A group of landlords opposed to rent controls is appealing to home-owners in their attempt to have rent control legislation overturned. Why would home-owners be concerned about rent controls?

Price Floors

A price floor is a government-imposed minimum price.

In contrast to a situation where a price ceiling is imposed, the government may feel that the market equilibrium price for a product is too low. This is quite often the case with agricultural products. If the equilibrium price is too low, a **price floor,** or minimum price, could be legislated, making it illegal to sell the product at a price below the legal minimum price. The effect of a price floor on the market is shown in figure 3.4. The market equilibrium price is shown as P_0 and the price floor as P_f. At P_f the quantity demanded is Q_d and the quantity supplied is Q_s. There is a *surplus* of the commodity on the market, i.e. Q_s is greater than Q_d. If this price floor were established in the egg market, there would be a surplus of eggs.

In a free market situation, a surplus would be disposed of by lowering the price. With a price floor, however, a lower price is out of the question. Another way must be found to rid the market of the surplus. That is, something has to happen in this market to shift either the demand or supply curve so that a new equilibrium price is found at P_f. One method may be to restrict the amount of the product that can be produced. For example, in terms of egg production, farmers could be limited in the number of hens they are allowed to have. This would shift the supply curve to the left. Another solution would be to try to shift the demand curve to the right. One way in which the demand curve may be shifted is through advertising. Regardless of which alternative is chosen, the government becomes further involved in regulating market conditions. The imposition of a price floor results in a disequilibrium situation (i.e. a surplus) and the government has to intervene further in order to restore the balance.

Figure 3.4
Price floor

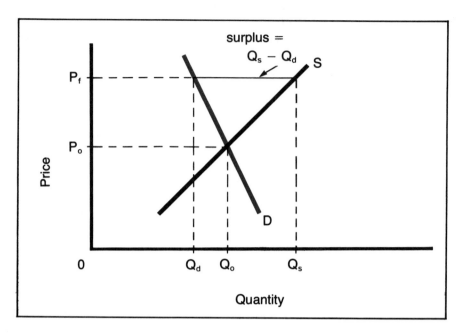

The imposition of a price floor (P_f) results in surplus of the product (Q_s - Q_d).

3.11   Using demand and supply curves, show the impact of government imposing a price floor on the market for wheat.

Minimum Wage and Poverty

The introduction of a minimum wage is an example of a price floor in the market for workers. At the present time, all ten provinces as well as the federal government in Canada have minimum-wage legislation. There are several reasons for introducing a minimum wage into the labour market. One objective is to help reduce the level of poverty among the working poor. For some workers, an increase in the minimum wage will increase their hourly wage rate and their income.

Does the minimum wage reduce the level of poverty? There is strong evidence to suggest that it does not. First, low hourly wages are only one cause of poverty. Other factors contributing to poverty include unemployment, low hours of work, a large number of family members, and the health of family members. The minimum hourly wage rate cannot be raised high enough to solve all these problems.

A second criticism of using the minimum wage to fight poverty is that increases in the legal minimum wage result in unemployment for some workers. Since the minimum wage is a price floor, it will create a surplus of labour in the market. Employers will want to hire fewer workers if they are forced to pay higher wages and yet, at higher wages, more workers will be willing to offer their services. Any program that increases the level of unemployment cannot be considered an anti-poverty device.

Third, in most provinces, there are certain groups of employees (such as some farm workers and domestic servants) who are exempt from minimum-wage coverage. For these workers, increases in the minimum wage are irrelevant and do not aid their financial situation.

Fourth, in order to be an effective anti-poverty device, the minimum wage should permanently redistribute income among wage earners; that is, minimum wage increases should narrow the wage differentials between low- and high-wage workers. Studies have shown that an increase to the minimum wage is only effective in reducing wage differentials for a short period of time. Within a year, previous wage differentials among workers are usually restored.

Finally, it is important to have an understanding of the characteristics of workers who earn the minimum wage. A survey of low-wage workers has shown that women and young people are most heavily represented in this wage group. Many of these individuals would be better off working at the minimum wage than not working at all. That is, if they were not working, they may not qualify for public assistance, and the benefits received by those who qualify would not be as much as their earnings at the minimum wage. Increases in the minimum wage are not beneficial to these individuals if employment opportunities are reduced.

Questions

1 Using demand and supply curves, show the impact of a minimum wage on the labour market.
2 Can you suggest anything that might improve conditions for the "working poor"?
3 Why are women and young people most likely to be earning the minimum wage?
4 Why would wage differentials among workers re-establish themselves within a year after a minimum-wage increase?

Excise Taxes

An excise tax is one levied by government on the suppliers of certain products.

Excise taxes are extra costs imposed by government on the sale of particular commodities. These taxes may be used as a revenue source for government, or as a means of curbing the use of a particular commodity. For example, the excise tax on liquor and tobacco is a *source of revenue* for government, while the tax on air conditioners in automobiles is meant to reduce the sales of air conditioners, for environmental reasons. The manufacturer is required to pay the tax and to submit it to the appropriate government agency.

The effect of an excise tax on a market can be shown in figure 3.5. Assume that the government decides to impose an excise tax of one dollar on each baseball hat that is produced. The equilibrium retail price for baseball hats prior to the imposition of the tax was five dollars per hat.

The impact of the excise tax will be to shift the supply curve upward by the amount of the tax. The supply curve shifts because the cost of producing the hats has gone up. In this case, the supply curve shifts vertically by one dollar. Suppliers will now want to receive one dollar more per hat than they had been receiving prior to the tax. What will happen to the price? More than likely, the price will increase, but by how much? Initially, suppliers may respond to the tax by raising the price of baseball hats to six dollars each. At six dollars, however, only Q_1 hats are wanted by consumers even though suppliers are still supplying Q_0 to the market. This surplus will force the price down to $5.60, the new market equilibrium price.

At this new price, Q_e baseball hats will be exchanged in the market. At this price, the quantity of hats demanded equals the quantity of hats supplied. The effect of the tax has been to raise the price of baseball hats. The price, however, has not risen by the full amount of the tax, but only by 60 cents. Since the supplier must still forward one dollar to the government from each hat sold, the consumer is paying 60 cents of the tax.

Part of the burden of paying for the tax has been shifted to the consumer. The ultimate burden of the excise tax is referred to as the *incidence* of the tax. In our example, the incidence of the tax is that the consumer pays 60 percent and the supplier 40 percent. Tax incidence varies by product. The price elasticities of demand and supply are major determinants of the incidence of a tax. For example, if the price elasticity of demand is inelastic, it is probable that the consumer will bear the greatest burden when an excise tax is imposed. If the demand for a product is inelastic, consumers will not decrease the quantity demanded a great deal when the price increases. If consumers continue to purchase the product in spite of the price increase, it will be easier for the supplier to shift the major burden of the tax to the consumers. If the demand for a product is elastic, suppliers will assume the greatest burden of an excise tax. Consumers will respond to price increases by reducing significantly the quantity demanded, and therefore suppliers will be reluctant to raise the price when an excise tax is imposed on their product.

On what products would the government impose an excise tax? The answer depends on the objective behind the tax. If the objective is to raise revenue, then a product with an inelastic demand (e.g. tobacco, liquor) will be chosen. Even after the imposition of the tax,

**Figure 3.5
The effect of an
excise tax**

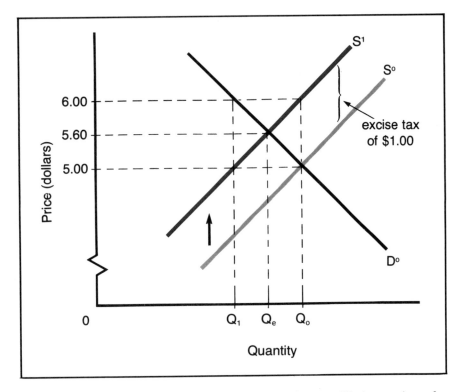

The imposition of an excise tax increases the equilibrium price of
the product ($5.60) and reduces the equilibrium quantity (Q_e).

consumers will continue to buy the product. If the objective was to
discourage consumption, then a product with an elastic demand
would be chosen. An example of a product with an elastic demand is
the automobile air conditioners. By imposing an excise tax on this
product, the government hopes to decrease the number purchased
and, ultimately, to save energy.

3.12   Using demand and supply curves, show the effect of government imposing a 50-cent excise tax on each ticket to a rock concert.

**Excise Taxes in
Canada**

Excise taxes at the federal government level in Canada are included in two pieces of legislation: The Excise Act and the Excise
Tax Act. Excise duties are imposed under the Excise Act and excise
taxes are imposed under the Excise Tax Act. Excise duties apply
to domestic alcohol and tobacco products only, whereas excise
taxes apply to various domestic and imported products. A further
difference is that excise duties are more closely related to the production process and are paid at various stages of production. In

contrast, excise taxes are paid at the end of the month following sales of the product.

Federal excise tax rates for 1991 are listed below:

gasoline (motor and aviation)
- for personal use .... 7.5 cents/litre
- for commercial use .... 4 cents/litre
diesel and aviation fuel .... 4 cents/litre
cigarettes .... 10.888 cents/5 cig.
manufactured tobacco $15.214/kg
cigars .... 40 percent
wine
- alcohol 1.2% or less .... 2.05 cents/litre
- alcohol 1.2% to 7% .... 24.59 cents/litre
- alcohol over 7% .... 51.22 cents/litre
automobiles .... $60/45 kg
automobile air conditioners $100/unit
jewellery .... 10 percent
watches, clocks .... 10 percent

Federal excise duties as at January 1,1991 are as follows:

distilled spirits .... $11.066/L alc.
mixed beverages (up to 7% alcohol) ... 24.59 cents/litre
beer
- up to 1.2% alcohol .... $ 2.591/hL
- 1.2% to 2.5% alcohol $13.9909/hL
- over 2.5% alcohol $27.985/hL
cigarettes
- up to 1361 g/1000 .... $27.475/1000
- over 1361 g/1 000 .... $29.374/1000
cigars $9.189/1000
manufactured tobacco $15.333/kg
raw leaf tobacco .... 97.70 cents/kg

Source: *The National Finances 1990* (Toronto: Canadian Tax Foundation 1991), pp. 7:49, 7:51.

There is a certain amount of controversy surrounding the imposition of excise taxes. If some luxury items are singled out for taxation purposes, why are not all luxury items taxed? For example, jewellery is taxed, but fur coats are not. Also, tobacco products are subject to both excise duties and excise taxes. Is it necessary to have double taxation on these products?

Questions

1 In your opinion, why are watches subject to excise tax?
2 Why does the government concentrate on tobacco products for both excise duties and excise taxes? Do they want people to refrain from smoking? Relate your answer to the concept of elasticity.
3 In the case of jewellery, who is likely to bear the greater burden of the excise tax, the consumer or the producer? Why?

Views of Government Involvement

Although there is a trend toward increasing government involvement in the economy, Canada still basically adheres to a market economy (a capitalistic system). Individuals own the means of production and make their own decisions on how available resources will be used. Not everyone sees the free market system approach as the best possible one. This section summarizes the theories of three writers on the market system. Karl Marx and John Kenneth Galbraith can be considered critics of the free market approach to economic decision-making, while Milton Friedman is considered a proponent of it.

Karl Marx

Possibly the most well-known critic of the free market system was Karl Marx (1818-1883). He was a journalist of German descent who lived in France and England as well as in Germany. His philosophy was outlined in *The Communist Manifesto* (1848) and *Das Kapital* (1867).

Marx believed that society was divided into two groups, and that the conflict between these groups would eventually lead to the destruction of the capitalist system. The first group, the *bourgeoisie,* was comprised of those individuals who owned property, yet did not work. The second group, the *proletariat,* included those who worked, yet did not own property. During the time of Marx, political power rested with the bourgeoisie who owned the means of production. Marx believed, however, that the size of the proletariat would continue to grow and that a social revolution would take place.

Marx predicted that as the age of industrialization progressed, smaller businesses would no longer be able to compete in the system and economic power would become concentrated in fewer hands. The small-business owners (who were part of the bourgeoisie) would end up joining the proletariat. As industrialization developed and the production process became more mechanized, the wages paid to workers of the proletariat would be reduced. The introduction of new machinery would also eliminate the jobs of some workers. Marx believed that conflict between the two groups would increase until workers united to form trade unions. The uniting of the workers would eventually lead to social revolution and the demise of the capitalist system.

John Kenneth Galbraith

A modern-day critic of capitalism is John Kenneth Galbraith (1908-). More than just a critic of the capitalist system, Galbraith is a critic of the market theories of demand and supply. It is his contention that economic theories developed in the 1800s are not suitable for analysing current economic problems.

Galbraith's ideas are incorporated in a number of popular books, two of the most well known being *The Affluent Society* (1958) and *The New Industrial State* (1967). He is also known as the author of the television series "The Age of Uncertainty." Galbraith criticized the classical economic belief that competition would improve conditions for society and prevent the concentration of economic power in only a few hands. Galbraith held that the reverse was true and that economic power was becoming more concentrated— as evidenced by the decline in the number of firms in certain industries. The cause of this increased concentration was the economics of large-scale production. In order to compete, companies had to become technically more efficient. Once the company had grown and held a dominant position, it could exercise more control over the marketplace. The consumer was no longer "the king." He was being replaced by big business.

According to Galbraith, competition would remain but would be channelled into other areas. These included the non-price areas of business: advertising, salesmanship, service, and new-product development. The promotion of brand names and salesmanship by large firms is regarded by Galbraith as a waste of resources. Galbraith views increasing government intervention in the economy as the necessary element in controlling the trends to further concentration of business.

Milton Friedman

A contemporary proponent of the free market approach is Milton Friedman (1912-). The views of Friedman are very similar to those of Adam Smith and are spelled out in two of his more popular books, *Capitalism and Freedom* (1962) and *Free to Choose* (1980). In contrast to other writers, Friedman believes that many of our economic problems could be solved through less government involvement in the economy. Government regulation and control (e.g. the use of price ceilings and floors) has not allowed the market system to function effectively. The advantages of the market system are therefore not realized in our society.

Friedman is primarily concerned about the erosion of individual freedoms as government becomes more involved in economic decision-making. If government is to be effective in regulating the economy, it must have control over more and more resources. As resources fall under government control, fewer of them are under individual control. Individuals gradually lose the freedom of decision-making concerning the resources that they own. For example, government zoning regulations outline what type of development may occur in various areas. If you are a landowner, your ability to use your land as you want to is restricted by the zoning law.

In his books, Friedman proposes changes to many existing social institutions, including social security, medical care, and education. In the area of education, he believes that the current dissatisfaction with the educational system would disappear with more private involvement in the school system. He points out that the desire for more government intervention in education did not originate with unhappy parents but with teachers and government officials. The increasing enrolment in private schools, even where public schools are provided, is, according to Friedman, an indication of the parents' dissatisfaction with the present situation.

The argument for more tax dollars going into education hinges on the positive third-party effects of education. If a greater proportion of the population were highly educated, it is argued, greater increases in economic growth would take place. Friedman disagrees and believes that most of the benefits from further education accrue to the individual and not to society.

Summary

The free market approach to economic decision-making has several advantages. First, there is a great deal of individual freedom in the decision-making process. Second, the free market approach is efficient at allocating resources to various uses. This efficiency is achieved through the price system. Changes in prices act as signals to buyers and sellers and direct their behaviour. Third, the competition among sellers inherent in a free market system provides for lower prices and better quality products.

Government becomes involved in the operations of the market due to certain shortcomings in a free market system. First, markets are not always perfect in their operation. Buyers and sellers often do not have adequate information with which to make decisions. As well, competition may be circumvented by companies getting together to set prices and divide up the market. In other situations, competition in an industry may not be the ideal competitive situation; it may make more sense to have only one seller.

Second, transactions between two parties may affect a third party. Negative third-party effects are costs imposed on a third party while positive third-party effects are benefits provided to a third party.

Third, the free market system may not provide certain services that society considers important (unmet public goods). These services are not provided by the free market because it is difficult for companies to charge people individually or directly for the benefits that they receive from a service. An example is police protection.

Fourth, incomes may not be distributed equitably in a free market system. Those individuals who cannot compete in the marketplace will earn little or no income. Our social conscience dictates that this situation is not acceptable. Finally, the free market system is not immune to fluctuations in the level of economic activity.

As a result of these market imperfections, government intervenes in our free market system. Examples of this intervention include the imposition of price ceilings, price floors, and excise taxes.

Questions for Review and Discussion

1 For each of the following activities that has a significant amount of government involvement, identify the economic rationale for government participation.
   i   Canada Post
   ii police departments
   iii Canadian Broadcasting Corporation
   iv Petro-Canada
   v   unemployment insurance
2 One reason for the strong participation of government in education is the presence of third-party effects. Identify these third-party effects.
3 One reason that we have rent controls is that there are more tenants than landlords. Does this statement make sense?
4 Price floors tend to result in surpluses. With a given supply curve would you get a larger surplus by putting a price floor on a product with an elastic or an inelastic demand? Use a graph in your answer.
5 Are some goods and services better able to be provided by government than by private companies? Explain your answer.
6 If competition is good for the consumer, why is it illegal in Canada to set up your own post office? Is there any competition for Canada Post?
7 Discuss the consequences of government imposing stringent pollution controls on paper mills. In your answer, you should consider the competition that paper mills face.
8 Why do local governments run the fire department? Does it have anything to do with third-party effects? Could fire protection be offered adequately by the free market?
9 What is the connection between positive third-party effects and unmet public goods?
10 Income differentials are one reason for government intervention

in the free market system. Would it be good for Canada if everyone earned the same level of income?

11 Draw two graphs with similar supply curves. On one graph draw a relatively inelastic demand curve, and on the other a relatively elastic demand curve. Assume a similar excise tax is imposed on each product. Under what circumstances is the price increase greater? Why?

12 In some respects, a subsidy can be considered the opposite of an excise tax. Using demand and supply curves, show the effect on the Canadian book market of the government offering the publishers a subsidy of 25 cents per book.

13 Much of the criticism of capitalism is that, if left unchecked, it will tend to concentrate economic power in too few hands. Do you agree? Why is this considered to be a negative aspect of capitalism?

14 In the Soviet Union privately-owned farms account for only three percent of the cropland and yet produce 27 percent of the country's food. Why do you believe this happens?

15 Should the responsibility for the poor be turned over to concerned citizens, charitable organizations, and churches and not be the responsibility of the government? Discuss this possibility.

16 Is there justification for natural monopolies in areas such as electricity and telephones? Would opening up the market to competition improve the variety and quality of service?

17 In socialist nations such as the Soviet Union, Poland, and Romania, food prices have been kept low by the government. What impact does this have on the food supply? What action must the government then take?

18 One of the responsibilities of the price system is to allocate resources to various uses. Why might the price system not be an efficient allocator of resources when third-party effects are present?

19 Public goods are defined as those goods or services for which it is not possible to exclude anyone from using the good or service whether they pay for it or not. Which of the following are public goods?
    i   North American air defence system
    ii   public school
    iii Banff National Park
    iv   fire department
    v   tickets to BC Lions football games

20 If people cannot be excluded from using a service, is the incentive to provide the service reduced? Explain.

21 In Ontario, the practice of extra-billing by doctors above the specified fees has been banned. What impact will this ban have on the supply of medical services in Ontario?

22 Many years ago Milton Friedman proposed a voucher system for education. Parents would be given an education voucher by the government that could be used to purchase education for their children. Parents would have the freedom to use the voucher at whichever school they desired. Such a system is being experimented with in some U.S. cities. What would be the impact of such a system on the education system as we now know it?

23 In most provinces, there is a price ceiling on college tuition. With a price ceiling in effect, how are places at a college rationed to those who want them?

Suggested Readings

Block, Walter E. ed. *Economics and the Environment: A Reconciliation*. Vancouver: The Fraser Institute 1990

Block, Walter, and Edgar Olsen (eds.). *Rent Control: Myths and Realities*. Vancouver: Fraser Institute 1981.

Friedman, Milton. *Capitalism and Freedom*. Chicago: Phoenix Books 1962.

Friedman, Milton, and Rose Friedman. *Free to Choose*. New York: Harcourt Brace Jovanovich 1980.

Galbraith, John Kenneth. *The Affluent Society*. New York: Mentor 1958.

Marx, Karl. *Capital: A Critique of Political Economy. Vol. I: The Process of Capitalist Production. Vol. II: The Process of Circulation of Capital*. New York: International Publishers 1967.

Not Enough: The Meaning and Measurement of Poverty in Canada. Report of the CCSD National Task Force on the Definition and Measurement of Poverty in Canada. Ottawa: Canadian Council on Social Development 1984.

Osberg, Lars. *Economic Inequality in Canada*. Toronto: Butterworths 1981.

Ross, David P. *The Canadian Fact Book on Poverty - 1983*. Canadian Council on Social Development Series. Toronto: James Lorimer and Company 1983.

— *The Working Poor: Wage Earners and the Failure of Income Security Policies*. Canadian Institute for Economic Policy Series. Toronto: James Lorimer and Company 1981.

Rydenfelt, Sven. *A Pattern for Failure: Socialist Economies in Crisis*. New York: Harcourt Brace Jovanovich 1984.

Smith, Adam. *The Wealth of Nations*. New York: Modern Library 1937.

Chapter 4

Government in Canada

Chapter Objectives

After successfully completing this chapter, you will be able to:

- appreciate the different responsibilities of the federal and provincial governments
- explain the reasons for the growth in government spending
- relate which taxes are collected by each level of government
- differentiate between the ability-to-pay and benefits-received approaches to tax equity
- differentiate between progressive, regressive, and proportional tax systems
- calculate marginal tax rates using your own figures

Key Terms

federalist system
law of increasing state activity
direct tax
indirect tax
indexing
benefits-received approach
ability-to-pay approach

progressive tax
proportional tax
regressive tax
marginal tax rate
gross public debt
equalization payment
stabilization payment

Constitutional Framework

A federalist system of government is one in which two levels of government have jurisdiction over each citizen.

Canada has a **federalist system** of government, which means that two levels of government—central and provincial—have jurisdiction over each citizen. On matters affecting the entire country, the federal (central) government has authority, while provincial governments have responsibility for their own smaller geographic areas. The powers and responsibilities of each level of government are outlined in the Constitution Act, which was originally the British North America (BNA) Act. The BNA Act, originally enacted in Great Britain, has only recently been patriated and renamed the Constitution Act, 1867. On 17 April 1982, the Constitution Act, 1982 was proclaimed and amended at a special ceremony in Ottawa. It contains the Charter of Rights and Freedoms.

At the time of Confederation (1867), it was the intention to create a powerful central, or federal, government in Canada. This level of government was awarded the major responsibilities of the time, as well as authority over major revenue sources. Matters of war, foreign relations, foreign trade, customs duties, and the postal service are under the jurisdiction of the federal government. It is also responsible for such matters as the regulation of trade and commerce; navigation and shipping; penitentiaries; weights and measures; currency and coinage; and banking. Any residual powers, not specifically granted to the provinces, were also given to the federal government. Section 91 of the Constitution Act, 1867, allows this level of government "to make Laws for the Peace, Order, and good Government of Canada, in relation to all Matters not coming within the Classes of Subjects by this Act assigned exclusively to the Legislatures of the Provinces." In order to match these responsibilities with financial authority, unlimited taxing power was given to the federal government.

To the provincial governments were allocated matters of more direct local importance. Provincial responsibilities are outlined in sections 92 and 93 of the Constitution Act, 1867. Provinces are responsible for hospitals; for the licensing of businesses; for the management and sale of public lands; and for local works. In section 93 of the legislation, provinces also were awarded responsibility for education. As these matters were seen as having less importance at the time of Confederation, provinces were given less command over revenue sources than was the federal government. Provincial governments were restricted to the collection of direct taxes; that is, taxes on the people who should pay them. In 1867, many of the provincial responsibilities were relatively unimportant, but in the 1980s they are of major importance. Hospitals and education, for example, now comprise a large portion of total government spending.

We described Canada's system of government as federalist. In fact, it is probably best described as quasi-federalist. The jurisdictions of the federal and provincial governments are not totally separate. The federal government has the power to interfere, or check, the authority of the provinces. For example, under section 95 of the Constitution Act, 1867, the provinces are awarded responsibility for agriculture and for immigration. The same section of the act also gives the federal government the power to legislate in these areas, and states that provincial legislation cannot conflict with that of the federal government concerning these matters. In providing the federal government with the authority to make laws regarding the peace, order, and good government of the country, section 91 of the Constitution Act, 1867 made it possible for the federal government to intervene in traditionally provincial matters, such as natural resources.

It was difficult for the architects of the constitution to foresee the situation in Canada 100 years later. The division of powers outlined in the legislation has resulted in some confusion and overlapping. There are areas of responsibility in which both the federal and provincial governments have authority. This overlapping has also occurred in the field of taxation, which is discussed later in this chapter. Difficulties arise because matters awarded to provincial government jurisdiction in 1867 have increased in importance, while some matters awarded to federal government control have decreased in relative importance. The changes in these areas have not been matched with changes in the ability of the provinces to collect revenue. The federal government still has unlimited taxing power, while the provinces are restricted to collecting only direct taxes.

The Meech Lake Accord, signed by all ten provincial premiers and the federal government, was an attempt to change some of the constitutional arrangements between the federal and provincial governments. The Accord, however, was not passed by all provincial legislatures and it expired on June 23, 1990. On September 25, 1991 the federal government introduced new proposals; at the time of publication these proposals were still being debated.

Government Spending By Function

Federal

The importance of various government responsibilities can be assessed by reviewing data on government spending. Information on federal government spending is presented in table 4.1. The largest component of federal government spending is the cost of paying off the *public debt*. This refers to all costs relating to unmatured debt, as well as annual amortization of bond discounts, premiums and commissions, servicing of the public debt, and costs of issuing new loans. Unmatured debt consists of marketable bonds, Canada

Savings Bonds, Canada Pension Plan investment fund, treasury bills, and notes and loans payable in foreign currency. In 1989, unmatured debt amounted to more than $277 billion, and interest payments were in excess of $26 billion. The second largest component is *social services spending,* which accounts for 24.0 percent of total expenditure. The main social program is *old age security payments,* which in 1990/91 amounted to 17.5 billion, or about ten percent of all federal government spending. Upon reaching the age of 65, individuals are eligible for assistance under this program and receive $343.13 per month (as of January 1990). To be eligible for assistance, an individual must have resided in Canada for at least ten years. Certain low-income individuals are also eligible for a guaranteed income supplement to their old age security benefits. This extra payment was set at a maximum of $407.77 per month for a single person. On March 31, 1990, 45.2 percent of all pensioners received a supplement to the old age security payment.

The *Canada Pension Plan (CPP)* is also available to persons at age 65 who have been employed and contributed to the plan. In addition to the regular CPP benefits, supplementary benefits are also available for orphans and spouses. In the fiscal year 1990/91, over $10 billion was spent on CPP benefit payments.

Table 4.1 / Gross general expenditure for the fiscal year ending 31 March 1991, federal government[a]

Function	Millions of dollars	Percent of total
debt charges	41 150	29.4
social services	33 620	24.0
defence	12 093	8.7
health	8 067	5.8
general-purpose transfers to other governments	9 702	6.9
general government	4 592	3.3
transportation and communications	3 706	2.7
natural resources, agriculture, and environment	4 395	3.1
education	4 015	2.9
foreign affairs and international assistance	3 406	2.4
protection	3 719	2.7
other	11 381	8.1
Total gross general expenditure	139 846	100.0

[a]Canadian Tax Foundation estimate.

Source: *The National Finances 1990* (Toronto: Canadian Tax Foundation 1991), pp. 6:15-6:16.

The second major program in the social services area is *unemployment insurance*. Almost $13 billion was spent on unemployment insurance in the fiscal year 1990/91. The unemployment insurance program is financed by both employer and employee contributions. Individuals who have been terminated or who have been temporarily laid off from their job are eligible for unemployment insurance benefits. Women who are on maternity leave from their job and individuals who are away from work due to illness are also eligible for benefits. Eligibility depends on the number of weeks that one has paid unemployment insurance premiums. The amount of the weekly benefit depends on the average weekly wage that a person was earning while paying the premiums. In 1991 the maximum weekly benefit was $408.

Two government departments are responsible for social service programs. The Department of National Health and Welfare is responsible for old age security and several other programs. Included among these programs are family allowances, the Canada Assistance Plan, and vocational rehabilitation for disabled persons. Under the Family Allowance program, payments are made to families on behalf of each child under 16 years of age. Effective 1 January 1991, the monthly Family Allowance payment was $33.93 per month per child. The Canada Assistance Plan is a comprehensive program that co-ordinates public assistance programs in the provinces. This includes assistance for blind and disabled persons, assistance to needy mothers and dependent children, assistance for needy persons in homes for special care, and assistance for needy unemployed persons. The vocational rehabilitation program is a cost-sharing program with the provinces.

The Department of Employment and Immigration is also responsible for social service programs. In addition to unemployment insurance, the department provides training allowances for adults taking training under the National Training Act. These allowances depend on the location of the training and the number of dependents that a trainee has.

Defence spending in Canada amounted to more than $12 billion in 1990/91. In addition to our own defence forces, Canada participates with other countries in the North Atlantic Treaty Organization (NATO), co-operates with the United States in the defence of North America, and provides peacekeeping forces in various parts of the world. A detailed description of all federal government spending can be found in *The National Finances,* an annual publication of the Canadian Tax Foundation.

Provincial

Expenditures of the provincial governments are listed in table 4.2. Spending on health programs accounts for about one-quarter of provincial government expenditure. The health services provided by the provinces fall into three categories: public health services; medical care; and hospital insurance. Public health services encompass a wide range of activities, including programs for mental health, occupational health, disease control, maternal and child care, cancer treatment, and diagnostic laboratory services, among others. All provinces have hospital care insurance schemes partly financed by the federal government. The insurance covers services in hospitals, including accommodation and meals. Provinces also have medical care insurance plans that are also partly funded by the federal government. In order to receive federal government assistance for health care, provinces must comply with certain guidelines.

Five provinces and the territories finance their share of the costs of the provincial health insurance plans from general taxation; two provinces (Alberta and British Columbia) levy premiums, augmented by general taxation; and Manitoba, Ontario, and Quebec levy a payroll tax on employers, augmented by general taxation.

Table 4.2 / Estimated provincial expenditure by function for the fiscal year 1989-90[a]

Function	Millions of dollars	Percent of total
health	35 991.8	25.9
education	26 024.4	18.7
social services	24 335.4	17.6
debt charges *Cost of borrowing*	17 052.3	12.3
transportation and communications	7 060.2	5.1
protection	4 665.8	3.4
other own source expenditure	23 522.2	17.0
Total gross expenditure	138 652.1	100.0

[a]Includes Yukon and Northwest Territories.

Source: *Provincial and Municipal Finances 1989* (Toronto: Canadian Tax Foundation 1990), p. 3.13.

The second most important provincial program is education. All provinces look after elementary and secondary education, although policies and programs may vary by province. Assistance is also provided by provinces to local (municipal) governments for capital expenditures related to education.

Social welfare programs account for almost 18 percent of provincial government spending. These programs are operated in co-operation with the federal, and in some cases, the municipal governments. The Canada Assistance Plan co-ordinates welfare spending in each province.

Provincial governments also borrow money; debt charges accounted for more than $17 billion in 1989/90. Transportation and communication expenditures also accounted for more than $7 billion of total spending. Most of this money is spent on roads and highways. A more detailed description of provincial government spending can be found in *Provincial and Municipal Finances*, an annual publication of the Canadian Tax Foundation.

Municipal

A word should also be said about municipal, or local, government spending. The authority of local governments to spend money comes from the provincial legislature. In other words, local government can only undertake spending in areas approved by provincial governments. The main area of local government spending is *education*, which accounts for approximately 40 percent of total spending. Other important services include maintenance of roads, protection of persons and property, and environmental programs. Local governments also borrow money, and debt payments in 1988 amounted to approximately seven percent of total expenditures.

4.1 What is a federalist system of government?

4.2 Which level of government in Canada has the primary responsibility for i) education, ii) hospitals, iii) national defence, and iv) banking?

4.3 In what areas do federal and provincial government spending overlap?

The Growth of Government Spending

In Canada, government expenditures have been rising in relation to the overall level of economic activity. Government spending on goods and services accounts for nearly one-quarter of Canada's total spending. In addition, money is redistributed by government throughout the country in the form of *transfer payments*. These are monies paid out by government to individuals where no service was performed for the money. These payments include such items as unemployment compensation, pensions, and Family Allowance payments. Prior to 1930, government spending, including transfer payments, had risen to almost 17 percent of total spending in the economy. By 1976, this had increased to more than 41 percent. In other words, more than two-fifths of our national output is actively controlled by government. The figures do not take into consideration the maze of rules set up by government for regulating business activity.

Theories about why government is playing a greater role in our economy have been around for a long time. One of the earliest theories was proposed by a German economist, Adolph Wagner, in

Adolph Wagner's law of increasing state activity states that in industrialized economies, government spending can be expected to grow at a faster rate than the total output of goods and services.

1883. Wagner's **law of increasing state activity** postulated that government expenditures could be expected to grow at a faster rate than the total output of goods and services in industrialized economies. One reason was that the complexities of economic development would require the establishment of a centralized authority. Increased frictions between individuals as a result of greater urbanization would necessitate more money being spent on law and order. Wagner believed that government would also become involved in trying to correct market imperfections and in financing large capital projects. Finally, he believed that cultural and welfare expenditures were luxury items, and as the level of national income grew, more money would be allocated to these luxury services.

In general, Wagner's theory seems to hold for Canada. Our transition from a rural to an urban country has made government more prominent. People in the cities require more services than do people in rural areas. Governments normally provide the following services in urban areas: water and sewers, garbage pick-up, sidewalks, street lights, and transportation services.

Increases in the amount of goods and services produced in Canada have also been accompanied by increases in social welfare payments. Canadians appear to have a strong social conscience and have become more concerned about those who are less fortunate. Social welfare expenditures now represent the biggest category of federal government spending, as well as approximately 18 percent of all provincial government expenditure. These expenditures cover such programs as pensions, disability and unemployment compensation, Family Allowance payments, and general welfare assistance.

Wagner was also correct about the increasing complexities of economic development. The rapid pace of technological change is constantly altering the types of products available, as well as the production process itself. These changes require a skilled and trained labour force that is able to undertake research and development, and to maintain and service new equipment. Government has become increasingly involved in the education process, particularly at the post-secondary level, in order to provide this labour force. Advances in technology can also create an increased demand for services that government traditionally supplies. For example, increased air travel has created a demand for improved airport capacity.

Wagner's theory helps to explain much of the increase in government spending. Yet there are still other factors to consider. One of the most significant is the political process itself. In order to get elected, candidates are likely to promise certain services that will be provided once they are in office. Promises cost money. The more promises that are made, the more money that is required to carry them out. Once in office, politicians are concerned with re-election, and government programs already in existence tend to continue. Since these programs benefit a certain segment of the population, the elimination or reduction of programs may lose potential voter support. The rising cost of government is sustained because of a reluctance to reduce or eliminate programs that are no longer necessary. An example is worth noting: the Family Allowance program distributes a monthly cheque to every family, the amount depending on the number of children in the family. This cheque is sent to the mother in the family, and is added to the family's income when calculating income tax. If the family is in a high income tax category, much of the family allowance will be returned to the government in the form of taxes. It is obvious that higher income families are not in need of this government assistance in order to raise a family. Why do they receive government assistance? One reason may be that it is easier to have a universal program in which everyone receives assistance rather than a selective one. If only certain families were to receive assistance, a means test for assistance would have to be established. A second reason for maintaining the program in its current state is that changing it would alienate many voters. It would especially alienate those women voters who are accustomed to receiving a monthly cheque.

Another reason for increased government spending is *military conflict*. During a war, government spending has to increase, yet it may not come down to previous levels once the war is over. Changes in spending as a result of war form part of a theory on government spending put forth by Alan Peacock and Jack Wiseman. They believe that the level of government spending depends on what taxpayers believe to be an acceptable level of taxation. In the event of war, when funds are needed, the concept of an acceptable level of taxation increases. Peacock and Wiseman believe that after a war, the acceptable level of taxation remains above its prewar level and government continues to collect more money in taxes. The Peacock-Wiseman hypothesis, however, cannot really be proven in the case of Canada. In 1939, prior to World War II, government spending represented 21.4 percent of total spending in Canada. This increased to 50.5 percent of total spending in 1944, during the war. Yet by 1950, it represented only 22.1 percent of total spending in Canada. Wars cause changes in government involvement in the economy, but whether or not these changes are permanent is not clear.

Much of the increase in government spending may result from the increase in tax revenue that government is receiving. With a progressive income tax structure (discussed later in this chapter), the percentage of income that an individual pays in taxes increases as the level of income increases. As Canada's production of goods and services rises, so do incomes; thus government receives more money from income tax revenue. With more money available to spend, government spends it. A trend of rising prices also helps tax revenues to increase, since income increases are often linked to price increases.

Finally, the nature of government services itself can lead to increased costs and increased government spending. Productivity increases have been harder to achieve in providing government services than in the provision of goods and services in the private sector. Productivity can be defined as the amount of work accomplished per person. If productivity increases match wage increases, then costs and prices do not have to increase. In the public sector, there is little incentive to increase productivity. The services provided by government are not in competition with those provided in the private sector, and the lack of competition means that government can be less cost-conscious in providing its services. In fact, several reports of the auditor general have criticized the federal government for a lack of concern over steps to reduce government expenses.

4.4   Explain Wagner's theory of increases in government spending. Does it apply to government spending in Canada?

4.5   How does the political nature of our government affect its level of spending?

Sources of Government Revenue

Constitutional Authority

A direct tax is one imposed on the individual who should pay the tax, whereas an indirect tax is one levied against one individual in the expectation that it will be paid by another individual.

The taxation powers of the various levels of government are contained in the Constitution Act, 1867. The act gave unlimited taxing powers to the federal government while restricting the provincial governments to collecting only direct taxes. The administrative arrangements of the tax determine whether it is a direct or an indirect tax. A **direct tax** is a tax imposed on a person who it is intended should pay the tax. For example, an income tax is a direct tax since the individual receiving the income is expected to pay the tax. An **indirect tax,** on the other hand, is one that is levied against one person in the expectation that it will be paid by another person. An excise tax is an example of an indirect tax. It is levied on the supplier of a product, yet it is expected that the supplier will try to pay for the tax by charging a higher price to the consumer for the product. In 1867, direct taxes were not very common and so were given to the provinces as a source of revenue. The majority of government revenue at that time came from two indirect taxes: excise taxes and customs duties. These taxes became the responsibility of the federal government.

Today there is a myriad of direct and indirect taxes at both the federal and provincial levels of government. The conditions of the

Constitution Act, 1867 have been altered through federal/provincial tax-sharing arrangements. Municipal government tax responsibilities, not mentioned in the constitution, have also clouded the tax picture. Municipalities receive their taxing authority from their respective provincial governments.

Table 4.3 / Federal budgetary revenue for 1989-90

Source	Millions of dollars	Percent of total
tax revenue		
personal income	51 895	45.6
corporate income	13 021	11.5
sales	17 672	15.5
customs import duties	4 587	4.0
unemployment insurance		
contributions	10 738	9.4
non-resident tax	1 361	1.2
gasoline excise tax	2 154	1.9
other excise taxes		
and duties	3 685	3.2
energy taxes	57	0.1
miscellaneous	226	0.2
total taxes	105 396	92.7
return on investments	5 850	5.1
other non-tax revenue	2 461	2.1
Total budgetary revenue	113 707	100.0

Source: *The National Finances 1990* (Toronto: Canadian Tax Foundation 1991), p. 7:1

Federal

Sources of federal government revenue are listed in table 4.3. The *personal income tax* accounts for more than 45 percent of all revenue. This tax applies to all individuals living in Canada. Tax is payable on all sources of income, whether earned in Canada or not. Individuals may receive income in various ways. Some earn income through employment; others earn income from investments; and others earn income from government assistance such as unemployment insurance and Family Allowance payments. All sources of income are taxable, even though they may be taxed at slightly different rates.

    Corporation income tax provided the government with more than $13 billion of revenue in 1989/90. Corporation tax rates vary depending on the type of business and the ownership. For the calendar year 1990, the basic federal tax on corporate income in a province was 28 percent. There is also a three percent surtax on all corporate income tax payable. A lower rate of tax (12 percent) is levied on small-business income earned by Canadian-controlled private corporations. For the particulars of these programs, reference has to be made to the Income Tax Act.

Other federal government taxes include *excise taxes* and *customs duties*. Excise taxes are levied on certain items classified as luxuries. The tax may be on an *ad valorem* (e.g. ten percent) basis, or on a specific (e. g. three cents per item) basis. A list of federal excise taxes was presented in Chapter 3. Customs duties, or tariffs, are applied in conjunction with the General Agreement on Tariffs and Trade (GATT), discussed in more detail in Chapter 9.

The federal government also receives 7.3 percent of its revenue from non-tax sources. These include the profits earned by Crown agencies, interest on loans, and bank interest. Also included is revenue from licences, fees, and proceeds from the operation of the Royal Canadian Mint.

The federal Goods and Services Tax (GST) came into effect on January 1, 1991. This tax replaced the Manufacturers' Sales Tax (MST) and federal taxes on telecommunications. This section discusses why the MST was replaced and how the GST works.

The MST was introduced in 1924. By 1990, Canada was the only industrialized country to still have a special tax on manufactured products. There were several problems associated with the MST. The MST had a narrow tax base since only manufactured items were taxed. Services, which account for the majority of production in Canada, were not covered. In addition, there were many exemptions to the tax among manufactured items. With a narrow tax base, the MST rate needed to be set at a high enough level to generate sufficient revenue for the federal government. Prior to its demise, the MST tax rate was 13.5 percent. The Goods and Services Tax has a broader tax base and a lower rate of seven percent.

Canadian manufacturers trying to sell products in foreign countries were subject to the MST. This increased the price of Canadian exports and made market penetration for Canadian companies in foreign countries more difficult. Imports into Canada that did not pay a similar tax in the home country were able to sell for less than Canadian-made products subject to the MST. When importers paid the MST, the tax was often applied to a price that excluded distribution and marketing costs in Canada. Canadian producers tended to pay the MST on a price that included distribution and marketing costs. As a result, Canadian firms tended to pay higher MST taxes than did comparable importers. Thus, the MST hurt Canadian exports and put Canadian manufacturers at a competitive disadvantage within Canada as well.

The MST was a hidden tax. It was included in the price of the product but most Canadians were unaware that they were paying it. In fact, many retailers were unaware of the extent of the MST contained in purchases from wholesalers. When retail firms marked up the price of an item, the original price being marked up included the MST. In effect, the MST was being marked up as well. Consumers were paying higher prices for products than would have been the case without the MST.

The MST also had administrative difficulties. There were over 22 000 interpretations issued by Revenue Canada to keep track of the exemptions to the tax. The auditor-general estimated that MST loopholes were costing the federal treasury about $300 million annually. It was clear that something had to be done about the MST. The government's response was to replace it with the GST.

The GST is a value-added tax—one which imposes a tax at each stage of the production and distribution chain. The tax is imposed only on the value added to the product at each stage in the process. The tax is applied to services as well as manufactured products. The GST is paid by consumers at the time of the purchase of the final good or service. Producers who buy inputs for the production process are able to obtain a refund on the GST paid. For example, if I purchase paper in order to publish a book, I am entitled to a refund of the GST that is included in the purchase price. If you purchase paper to use in school, you will pay the GST as you are the final consumer of this product.

The following example relating to the cost of producing a wooden chair illustrates the impact of the GST.

	Purchase			Sale			
	price paid ($)	GST(1)	total	price charged ($)	GST(2)	total	amount paid to govt. (2)-(1)
forester	0	0	0	10	0.70	10.70	0.70
mill	10	0.70	10.70	40	2.80	42.80	2.10
manufacturer	40	2.80	42.80	60	4.20	64.20	1.40
wholesaler	60	4.20	64.20	80	5.60	85.60	1.40
retailer	80	5.60	85.60	100	7.00	107.00	1.40
consumer	100	7.00	107.00	-	-	-	-
total tax							$7.00

As shown in the above example, the tax is applied to the value added at each stage of the production process. Businesses are essentially tax exempt, since they obtain a refund for any GST paid on purchases that they make, provided that the items purchased then receive further processing. Non-business purchases, that is, the final consumer, are not eligible for tax refunds, and thus pay the entire tax.

Certain goods and services are exempt from the GST. Basic groceries, prescription drugs, residential rents, daycare services, and most health and dental services are not subject to the GST. Some observers argue that there should be no exemptions from the GST. This policy of no exemptions would permit the rate to be lowered. Also if all goods and services were taxed, there would less confusion concerning what is exempt and less time spent on arguing for exemptions. Products destined for export are essentially tax-free as well, allowing Canadian companies to be more cost-competitive in foreign markets.

In order to reduce the impact of the GST on the purchasing power of some Canadians, a GST Credit is available for families earning up to $30 000 per year. The amount of the credit depends on family size and income.

The federal government cites the following advantages to the GST. Unlike the MST, the GST is not a hidden tax. Both consumers and businesses know how much tax they are paying. The GST improves the competitiveness of Canadian exports since exports are essentially free of tax. The GST allows Canadian companies to compete with imports more effectively in the Canadian market. The prices of many manufactured products in Canada now should be lower since the 13.5% MST was replaced by the 7% GST. By taxing services as well as manufactured items, the tax is fairer and more broadly based. The GST Credit helps reduce the impact on low-income families.

There are criticisms of the GST as well. The GST will add to inflation since more items are currently taxed than was the situation with the MST. Union members have begun to ask for GST protection in contract negotiations with employers. These wage increases will be inflationary as well unless offset by productivity improvements. The GST is time-consuming for small business. All companies must make adjustments to accommodate the GST. Changes need to be made in financial statements, costing procedures, pricing, accounting systems, and the budgeting process. Critics argue that once the GST is in place at 7%, it will be easy to raise the rate in the future. Provincial governments can also increase tax revenue by applying provincial sales taxes on top on the consumer price that includes the GST.

Provincial

Provincial sources of revenue are provided in table 4.4. Provinces receive about half of their revenue from taxes, while the other half is divided between non-tax sources and transfers from the federal government. Transfers from other governments (mainly the federal government) accounted for about 19 percent of provincial government revenue in 1989/90.

Table 4.4 / Estimated provincial revenue by source for the fiscal year 1989-90[a]

Source	Millions of dollars	Percent of total
Taxes on		
personal income	33 076.5	24.4
corporate income	6 798.9	5.0
retail sales	18 014.41	13.3
motive fuels	4 546.2	3.4
natural resources	5 443.0	4.0
Other own source revenue	41 714.2	30.8
Transfers from other governments		
general purpose	9 488.9	7.0
specific purpose	16 467.2	12.1
Total gross general revenue	135 549.3	100.0

[a]Includes Yukon and Northwest Territories.

Source: *Provincial and Municipal Finances 1989* (Toronto: Canadian Tax Foundation 1990), p. 3:13.

Table 4.5 / Provincial personal income tax rates, 1990

Province	As a percent of basic federal tax
Newfoundland	62.0
Prince Edward Island	57.0
Nova Scotia	59.5
New Brunswick	60.0
Ontario	53.0
Manitoba	52.0
Saskatchewan	50.0
Alberta	46.5
British Columbia	51.5
Yukon Territory	45.0
Northwest Territories	44.0

Source: *The National Finances 1990* (Toronto: Canadian Tax Foundation 1991), p. 7:12.

Personal income tax provided the main source of revenue for the provinces. All provinces, except Quebec, have agreed to let the federal government collect provincial personal income tax. The nine remaining provinces apply a percentage tax rate to the basic federal tax. These percentages, which vary by province, are listed in table 4.5. Rates range from 62 percent of the basic federal tax in Newfoundland to a low of 44 percent in the Northwest Territories and 45 percent in the Yukon. The lowest provincial rate is 46.5 percent in Alberta.

Provinces also levy a corporation income tax. All provinces except Alberta, Ontario, and Quebec allow the federal government to collect corporation income tax. Corporations are subject to provincial income tax if they have a permanent establishment in the province. Corporate tax rates also vary from one province to another.

A major source of provincial government revenue is the retail sales tax. All provinces except Alberta have such a tax, although Alberta has a sales tax on hotel and motel accommodation. Each province sets its own retail sales tax rate. Provinces also vary in the exemptions allowed from retail sales tax. The retail sales tax itself may vary depending on the item being taxed. For example, in several provinces, alcoholic beverages are subject to higher taxes than other goods.

The major source of provincial non-tax revenue is revenue from natural resources. Money is obtained from the provincial renting of land and from royalties on the minerals produced. Other sources of non-tax revenue include return on investments, liquor board profits, and money from licences and permits.

Municipal

Municipal governments also levy taxes and receive transfers of money from the other levels of government. The major source of tax revenue for municipal, or local, governments is the *property tax,* which accounted for approximately 37 percent of local government revenue in 1988. Transfers from other levels of government represented 47 percent of local government revenue.

4.6 Define what is meant by direct taxation.
4.7 In what areas do federal and provincial government taxes overlap?

Government Profits from Inflation

Inflation is defined as an increase in the overall level of prices. Because some government taxes are assessed on a percentage basis, the revenue collected from taxation increases as prices increase. For example, the provincial retail sales tax, applicable in all provinces except Alberta, is a percentage of the retail selling price. When prices are increasing, the money that consumers pay in retail sales tax is also increasing. Certain excise taxes are also levied on a percentage basis. Government revenue, therefore, increases along with inflation.

The most celebrated example of government profiting from

inflation concerns the personal income tax. In Canada the personal income tax is a progressive tax. As one's income increases, a higher percentage of income is paid in income tax. In a period of rising prices, individual incomes are likely to increase as well. Many workers, particularly those who are members of trade unions, want to ensure that their wage increases keep up with price increases. As wages and incomes increase, individuals move into higher tax brackets and pay a greater percentage of their income in taxes. Much of the gain from a wage increase is thus taken away. In fact, if wage increases only keep pace with inflation, the individual could be worse off than before, since a greater percentage of the individual's income is now paid in taxes.

The process of indexing taxes or payments involves making adjustments according to changes in the rate of inflation.

In 1973, the federal government, under public pressure to do something about inflation, introduced **indexing** of the personal income tax. Indexing took the form of adjustments to the personal exemptions and the tax brackets. In order to adjust for price increases, personal exemptions were increased annually in line with inflation. For example, the basic personal amount used to calculate tax credits, which was $6066 in 1989, was increased to $6169 in 1990 as a result of indexing.

The indexing of personal income tax has been a benefit to the individual but a cost to government. Tax revenues are lower than they would have been without indexing. Provincial governments also receive less revenue, since their personal income tax is based on a percentage of the basic federal tax (except in Quebec). The loss of revenue from indexing is a major concern to government. The federal government has toyed with the idea of removing indexing entirely from personal income taxes, but strong public reaction has delayed this move. Apart from the personal gain that indexing provides, the public favours its maintenance in order to control the possibility of government profiting from inflation. If indexing was removed from the tax system, government tax revenues would increase right along with rising prices. However, the federal government has partially removed indexing from personal income taxes. Beginning with the 1986 tax year, the indexing factor was reduced to the rate of inflation less three percent.

Questions

1　Why does government tax revenue increase in times of inflation under a progressive income tax structure?

2　Do you think that indexing helps control government spending?

Theory of Taxation

There is a saying that there are only two things in life that are certain: death and taxes. It appears as if taxes have been around forever. The Bible tells stories of taxes and tax collection. In Britain, public reaction to taxes led to the signing of the Magna Carta more than 700 years ago. The English tax on tea helped fuel a revolt in the colonies that lead to the creation of the United States of America. Taxes are also part of Canadian history, and responsibility for taxes was written into the Constitution Act, 1867.

Taxes are imposed in order to provide revenue for government, and also to influence economic conditions. It is hoped that taxes will not be imposed indiscriminately, but will adhere to certain principles. Two of the major principles of taxation are maintenance of social justice and consistency with economic objectives.

Social Justice

Taxes should be equitable or fair. The Royal Commission on Taxation in Canada during the 1960s concluded that the primary objective of any tax should be *equity*. Although this is not in dispute, the problem remains in defining what equity or fairness means. One approach to defining equity is to insist that all individuals who are in similar circumstances pay the same amount of tax. For example, all those who earn $20 000 per year should pay the same amount of income tax. All those who smoke one package of cigarettes per day should pay the same tax on cigarettes. Treating like people in a similar manner is referred to as horizontal equity. There is basically no argument over this approach.

The problem in terms of equity arises where individuals in different circumstances are concerned. In order to be fair, how do you treat individuals who have different amounts of wealth, income, and children? How should people in unlike circumstances be taxed in order to be fair? This is the problem of vertical equity.

There are two approaches to vertical equity: benefits received and ability to pay. The **benefits-received approach** proposes that people be taxed on the basis of the benefits that they receive from government programs. Those who benefit most from government spending should pay more taxes. Although this proposal appears equitable, two problems are associated with it. First, it is very difficult to determine who receives the benefits from various government programs. For example, who receives the benefit from a government-provided modern highway system? The benefits are spread out among many people. Those who use the highway obviously benefit. If food and other products travel by truck, then store owners and consumers also benefit from faster service. Those who live in residential areas of the city may benefit from less traffic and less pollution in their neighbourhood. Pedestrians may benefit because there is less traffic on residential streets. If people are to be

The benefits-received approach to taxation proposes that individuals be taxed on the basis of the benefits they receive from government programs.

taxed on the benefits they receive, it must first be determined who receives the benefit. In addition, the amount of the benefits has to be decided.

The second difficulty with the benefits-received approach relates to the composition of government spending. The biggest expenditure from the point of view of the federal government is social welfare. These expenditures go to those individuals who are not as fortunate as others, and who may not be able to provide for themselves. It is unreasonable to expect these individuals to pay for the benefits that they receive.

These problems with the benefits-received approach do not mean that this approach is useless. For some taxes, the benefits-received principle may be the most practical and equitable principle. A tax on airplane tickets forces those who use the airports to pay for their maintenance. Gasoline excise taxes help pay for the roads and are paid by those who use the roads. The more one drives, the more gasoline is used, and the more tax is paid.

The ability-to-pay approach, whereby individuals are taxed based on their ability to pay taxes, is an alternative approach to taxation theory.

The alternate approach to vertical equity is to tax individuals on their **ability to pay** taxes. Those with a greater ability to pay should pay more in taxes. How is ability to pay determined? This is where problems with this approach arise. Some economists argue that a person's wealth is the best measure of ability to pay. Personal wealth includes real estate, stocks, bonds, paintings, bank accounts, etc. Others believe that the best measure of ability to pay is income. This represents the flow of money coming to an individual in a given year. Finally, ability to pay could be measured on the basis of expenditure. The more money that one spends, the more one should be able to pay taxes. Individual spending can be related to standard of living, and a higher standard of living represents a greater ability to pay taxes.

In Canada, all three approaches to ability to pay are used for taxation purposes. Federal and provincial governments tax corporation and individual income. Municipalities tax property, which is an indicator of wealth. Provinces impose retail sales taxes on consumer purchases. The major source of tax revenue, however, comes from income. Approximately 45 percent of federal government revenue and 24 percent of provincial government revenue come from personal income taxes. Corporation income taxes contribute another 11 percent and 5 percent respectively.

A progressive approach to taxation is one in which the percentage of income an individual pays in taxes increases as the individual's level of income increases.

Even though income taxes provide the greatest source of revenue for government, there is still discussion about how income should be taxed. It is agreed that those with higher incomes should pay more tax, but how much more? There can be several relationships between one's income and the percentage of income paid in taxes. If the percentage of income paid in taxes rises along with income, it is referred to as a **progressive tax.** If the percentage paid

A proportional tax is one in which the percentage of income paid in taxes remains constant regardless of an individual's level of income, whereas a regressive tax describes one in which the percentage of income paid in taxes decreases as the level of income increases.

in taxes remains the same regardless of the level of income, it is a **proportional tax.** Finally, if the percentage paid in taxes declines as income increases, it is called a **regressive tax.** Regardless of which approach to taxation is used, individuals with more income will pay more in income taxes.

In Canada, the progressive form of taxation is used on income. It is the belief that this type of tax is best suited for extracting an equal sacrifice from each individual. Even though someone with a higher income pays more in taxes than someone with a low income, the sacrifice that each has to make in paying taxes is thought to be the same. The proportional and regressive approaches do not accomplish this. In the proportional approach, individuals in low-income groups will make a greater sacrifice in paying their taxes because the money they pay in taxes means more to them than the amount paid by higher-income groups. With the regressive approach, the low-income individual pays a higher percentage of income in taxes and thus is making more of a sacrifice than someone in a higher-income tax group.

A regressive tax does not mean that low-income people pay more taxes; they just pay a higher percentage of their income in taxes. For example, assume that someone earning $50 000 per year pays ten percent of his or her income in taxes, and someone earning $10 000 per year pays 20 percent of his or her income in taxes. The amount of money paid in taxes is $5000 and $2000 respectively. The higher-income person pays more tax, but the lower-income person pays a higher proportion of tax on that lower income. Thus even under a regressive approach, the taxation principle of ability to pay could still hold.

When taxes are referred to as progressive, regressive, or proportional, they are not always based on income, but the actual amount of the tax is related to income. For example, the municipal property tax is often called a regressive tax, even though it is not based on income. Individuals who live in the same type of house on the same amount of property pay the same amount of property tax. The individuals who live in these houses may not earn the same income, and if this is the case, then the low-income person will be paying a greater proportion of his or her income in taxes. The regressive nature of the property tax should not be over-emphasized or criticized. This tax is not based on income but based on *wealth*. The fact that two individuals have similar real estate wealth indicates that they should pay the same amount of tax in order to preserve horizontal equity.

Consistency with Economic Objectives

The imposition of taxes has economic consequences. As discussed in following chapters, taxes can be used by government to control price increases and unemployment. Tax increases tend to reduce spending and are used to lower price increases. By doing this, tax increases may lead to more unemployment. Taxation changes therefore have to be in tune with economic objectives.

Government tax policy also has to be consistent with a desire for economic development. If it is desirable to see the petroleum industry expand in Canada, it may be consistent to give it a tax break not given to other sectors. If it is desirable to promote the Canadian publishing industry, the sales tax on books could be reduced or eliminated. Government has certain objectives for the economy, and taxation policy should be consistent with these objectives.

Government tax policy can also be used to influence the allocation of resources. If government does not want consumers to purchase air conditioners for automobiles, then it can put an excise tax on this product. If government would like consumers to drink Canadian wine as opposed to imported wine, the excise tax policy could reflect this objective. The tax on imported wine could be increased, while the tax on domestic wine could be eliminated or reduced.

4.8   What is the difference between vertical equity and horizontal equity?
4.9   For what type of taxes is the benefits-received approach most appropriate?
4.10 What is the difference between a progressive and a regressive tax?

Marginal Tax Rates

A marginal tax rate defines that percentage of any additional income that is paid in taxes.

One of the most important aspects of a progressive income tax system is that of **marginal tax rates.** The word "marginal" is used regularly in the study of economics and means extra or additional. The marginal tax rate is the extra income tax paid in relation to an increase in income. An example will best serve our purpose here. The following table outlines a hypothetical progressive income tax structure.

Taxable income	Tax rate (percent)	Taxes paid	Marginal tax rate (percent)
$10 000	10	$1 000	-
$15 000	15	$2 250	25
$20 000	20	$4 000	35

In the above example, an individual earning $10 000 per year would pay $1000 in tax for that year. If that individual's income increased to $15 000 per year, $2250 would be paid in taxes. The individual's income, which increased by $5000, resulted in an increase in taxes paid of $1250. Twenty-five percent of the increase in income was paid in taxes. This is the marginal tax rate. For an increase in income from $15 000 to $20 000, an additional $1750 is paid in taxes. This represents a marginal tax rate of 35 percent.

How is it possible to have a marginal tax rate of 35 percent when someone is only in a 20-percent tax bracket? The answer is that when your income increases from $15 000 to $20 000, the 20-percent tax rate does not apply only to the increase in income, it also applies to the $15 000 that you were already earning. You end up paying extra taxes on the money that you earned prior to your increase in income.

Combined (federal and provincial) marginal tax rates for personal income tax for selected taxable incomes, 1990

Province	Combined marginal tax rates % for minimum net incomes of			
	$12 050	$30 001	$52 073	$94 638
Newfoundland	28.39	43.42	43.42	49.30
Prince Edward Island	27.54	42.12	42.12	49.50
Nova Scotia	27.97	42.77	42.77	50.30
New Brunswick	28.05	42.90	42.90	48.72
Quebec	32.91	46.01	47.01	50.54
Ontario	26.86	41.08	41.08	48.23
Manitoba	30.69	44.82	44.82	50.40
Saskatchewan	33.35	42.30	44.10	49.80
Alberta	30.46	39.89	40.86	46.38
British Columbia	26.61	40.69	40.69	46.26
Yukon Territory	25.50	25.50	39.00	44.37
Northwest Territories	25.33	25.33	38.74	44.08

Source: *The National Finances 1990* (Toronto: Canadian Tax Foundation 1991), p. 7:20.

Marginal tax rates for personal income tax are given by province in the table above. For a net income of $12 050 per year, marginal tax rates range from 25.33 percent in the Northwest Territories to 33.35 percent in Saskatchewan. For a net income of $94 638, marginal tax rates range from 44.08 percent in the Northwest Territories to 50.54 percent in Quebec.

Questions

1   Calculate the marginal tax rates from the following example.

Taxable Income	Tax rate (percent)
$20 000	25
$30 000	30
$40 000	35

2 Under a progressive income tax structure, what effect may marginal tax rates have on an individual's willingness to take on a second job or to work overtime?

3 What is the marginal tax rate under a proportional income tax structure?

4 As an aid to understanding marginal tax rates, obtain a copy of the general tax guide from Revenue Canada. Refer to the tax tables at the back of the guide and calculate a couple of marginal tax rates.

Government Borrowing

The major alternative to taxation as a source of government revenue is borrowing. Taxation is compulsory, whereas borrowing is voluntary. Governments borrow from individuals, banks, and other financial institutions. All levels of government in Canada borrow money, yet only the federal government can borrow from the *Bank of Canada*. Borrowing from the Bank of Canada has special significance. It is commonly referred to as printing money. Money borrowed from the Bank of Canada is not in circulation. When the government spends this money, it is put into circulation. When the government borrows from other groups, e.g. individuals, the money is removed from circulation before being put back in by government. Thus borrowing from the Bank of Canada is similar to printing money.

Government borrowing is done by selling various types of securities to the public. These securities can be of various maturities, ranging from a couple of months in the case of treasury bills to the longer term government bonds. The most familiar government security is the Canada Savings Bond—the major source of borrowed funds. These bonds are sold to individuals and non-profit institutions and represent about 20 percent of the borrowing by the federal government.

Gross public debt is defined as unmatured bonds, treasury bills, and other liabilities of government.

Gross public debt refers to unmatured bonds, treasury bills, and notes, as well as other liabilities, including annuity insurance, pension accounts, and other special accounts. *Net debt* is gross public debt after deductions of recorded assets; it equals the overall deficit of the federal government since Confederation. The final column in the table presents net public debt as a percentage of GNP. The term GNP, discussed more fully in Chapter 5, represents the value of all goods and services produced by residents of Canada in a given year. In table 4.6 the federal net public debt for selected years is presented.

As shown in the table, the net debt as a percentage of GNP declined until 1975-76. By 1988-89, the net debt as a percentage of

GNP refers to the value of goods and services produced by Canadians in a given year. GNP is discussed further in Chapter 5.

GNP had increased to 53.9 percent. Interest must be paid on this debt; in 1988 the federal government paid in excess of $26 billion interest on its unmatured debt. This amounted to an average rate of interest of 10.50 percent per annum.

The major source of provincial government borrowing has been from the Canada Pension Plan Investment Fund. The second source of borrowing is from non-residents of Canada. Since provinces cannot borrow from the Bank of Canada, much of their borrowing has to be done from individuals outside the country.

Why does government borrow money rather than collect it through taxes? The answer to this question lies mainly in the nature of the political process. Voters can see how much government is costing them when paying taxes. They have no idea, however, of what borrowing is undertaken and how much the borrowing costs, although this information is available. Most citizens are not as concerned about high levels of government borrowing as they are about high levels of taxation, which has a more direct impact on individuals. Through borrowing, government can carry on programs that would only be possible with excessively high levels of taxation.

Table 4.6 / Federal net public debt as at March 31 for selected years

	Net debt (millions of dollars)	Net debt per capita ($)	Net debt percent of GNP (%)
1956-57	11 446	689	35.7
1957-58	11 642	682	34.7
1958-59	12 519	716	36.0
1959-60	13 119	734	35.6
1960-61	13 648	748	35.6
1961-62	14 596	785	35.7
1962-63	15 429	815	34.7
1963-64	16 598	860	34.8
1964-65	16 913	861	32.4
1965-66	16 610	830	28.9
1966-67	16 797	824	26.1
1967-68	17 508	846	25.4
1968-69	17 908	853	23.7
1969-70	17 576	825	21.2
1970-71	18 356	851	20.6
1971-72	19 898	913	20.5
1972-73	21 573	979	19.9
1973-74	23 572	1 054	18.5
1974-75	25 581	1 127	16.8
1975-76	31 318	1 362	18.3

1976-77	37 615	1 616	19.0
1977-78	48 041	2 043	22.0
1978-79	60 658	2 554	25.1
1979-80	72 159	3 001	26.1
1980-81	85 681	3 520	27.6
1981-82	100 553	4 082	28.2
1982-83	128 369	5 158	34.3
1983-84	160 768	6 394	39.6
1984-85	199 092	7 845	44.8
1985-86	233 496	9 118	48.8
1986-87	264 101	10 235	52.3
1987-88	292 184	11 260	53.1
1988-89	320 918	12 224	53.9

Source: *The National Finances 1990* (Toronto: Canadian Tax Foundation 1991), p. 15:4.

The government may also borrow money for large *capital expenditures* such as electric power stations and airports. These projects are too costly to be paid for out of current tax revenue. Since the power station and the airport will be in operation for a number of years, they can be financed over a number of years through borrowing.

Federal/ Provincial Financial Arrangements

Canada's system of government divides responsibilities between the federal and provincial levels of government. The authors of the BNA Act could not foresee some of the problems that these divided jurisdictions would create. Shortly after the act came into effect, the provinces complained that their revenue sources were inadequate. The federal government then agreed to make annual payments to the provinces based on their population.

There have always been differences in provincial abilities to collect tax revenue. Some provinces have a good tax base, while others are not so fortunate. Ontario, British Columbia, and Alberta have high per-capita incomes and a good industrial base. Prince Edward Island and Newfoundland, however, have lower per-capita incomes and less-diversified economies. It is more difficult for the latter provinces to provide the same level of public service as the others.

The federal government, also in need of revenue, introduced taxes in these areas. A major characteristic of the Canadian taxation scene is the overlapping of taxes. Both levels of government have personal and corporation income taxes, as well as various excise taxes. This leads to duplication in administration as well as to the possibility of high tax rates.

The present system may also lead to a conflict in taxation policies. One level of government may pursue a policy of increasing taxes, while the other level of government may introduce completely opposite measures. For example, in order to stimulate the economy, the federal government may reduce personal income taxes, while the provinces are increasing taxes in order to finance new programs.

These difficulties have led to the signing of several federal/provincial taxation arrangements. The first was introduced during World War II, and provided for the provinces to rent their personal and corporation tax powers to the federal government. In return, the provinces received annual rental payments. The tax rental agreements, which lasted from 1941 to 1957, were replaced by tax-sharing arrangements. The major change introduced into the new agreement was that the provinces would receive a percentage of the revenue collected by the federal government instead of a lump-sum payment.

A variety of financial arrangements has existed between the two levels of government. The present system is referred to as Established Program Financing. This arrangement centres on hospital insurance, medicare, and post-secondary education. Under Established Program Financing, the federal government gives the province a percentage of personal and corporation income tax revenue plus a cash payment.

Equalization payments are those made by the federal government to those provinces that are unable to collect sufficient revenue through taxes.

The federal government also makes equalization and stabilization payments to some provinces. **Equalization payments** are a recognition that provinces differ in their ability to collect revenue. The federal government transfers money to the poorer provinces on the basis of 33 revenue sources. In recent years the only provinces to miss out on equalization payments have been Ontario, British Columbia, Alberta, and Saskatchewan.

The federal government may make stabilization payments to ensure that provincial taxation revenues do not decline over those of the previous year.

Stabilization payments are meant to ensure that provincial taxation revenues do not decline substantially from one year to the next. The stabilization payment from the federal government to a province ensures that the current year's revenue at previous year's tax rates amount to 95 percent of the previous year's revenue. Stabilization payments are not made every year.

Questions

1 At the time of Confederation, why were the major responsibilities and sources of revenue given to the federal government?
2 Why do all provinces not have the same ability to receive revenue from taxes?
3 If the distribution of responsibilities and taxing authority in the Constitution Act is not adequate for our present circumstances, why not change the legislation?

Summary

Because Canadians are governed by a federalist system of government, more than one level of government exerts influence over the day-to-day lives of individuals. The powers of the federal and provincial government are outlined in Canada's constitution. The federal government was awarded the major responsibilities given to government at the time of Confederation, 1867. Along with these responsibilities, the federal government was given unlimited taxing power. The provinces were awarded lesser responsibilities and were only given the authority to collect direct taxes.

In terms of expenditure, the federal government spends about 30 percent of its budget on interest and service charges on the national debt. The second largest expenditure item is social services. The major component of provincial government spending is health care, followed by education. The major component of municipal government spending is education.

Both the federal and provincial governments obtain revenue from a variety of taxes. The personal income tax, levied by both governments, is the major source of tax revenue. Each level of government also imposes corporation income taxes and excise taxes. The federal government introduced the Goods and Services Tax on 1 January 1991.

A main objective of any tax is that it be equitable or fair. This objective of tax equity is not in dispute; however, the definition of an equitable tax is still in question. It is agreed that all individuals in similar circumstances should pay the same amount of money in taxes. It is not agreed, however, how individuals in different circumstances should be treated. One approach is to tax individuals on the basis of the benefits that they receive from government programs. For some programs, such as highways and airports, the benefits-received approach to tax equity is acceptable. It is not acceptable for other programs, particularly those in the social services area.

The ability-to-pay principle is the alternative approach to vertical equity. It proposes taxing people on their ability to pay taxes. The measure of ability to pay could be either income, wealth, or expenditure. The level of taxation could be either on a progressive, regressive, or proportional basis. Canada's income tax is on a progressive basis: those with a higher income pay a higher percentage of their income in taxes.

Questions for Review and Discussion

1 Which do you believe is the most equitable income tax structure for Canada: progressive, proportional, or regressive? Explain.

2 Define marginal tax rates. Make up your own numerical example to show how marginal tax rates affect taxes paid under a pro–gressive tax system when an individual's income increases.

3 One of the major social service expenditures of the federal government is family allowances (also known as the baby bonus). Should the federal government subsidize families with children?

4 Do you think that the federal government should be responsi–ble for hospitals so that the same level of medical care is pro–vided in each province? Discuss.

5 Explain the differences between the Wagner and Peacock-Wiseman hypotheses regarding government spending.

6 In your opinion what are the disadvantages of a proportional income-tax system?

7 Canada has opted for a progressive income-tax system as the most equitable approach to income taxation. Can you think of any negative aspects of a progressive income-tax system?

8 The second biggest area of federal government spending is social services. Should the federal government turn over some social services to the private sector in order to reduce the size of the federal deficit?

9 Government involvement in the Canadian economy has increased substantially in the last 20 years. Do any of the reasons discussed in this chapter apply to this growth in government spending?

10 The main objective behind Canada's personal income tax is that it be equitable or fair. What problems would arise if many individuals believed the current personal income-tax system to be unfair?

11 In your opinion, should personal income-tax rates be applied to individual or to family income? In other words, should all family members have their income lumped together for taxation purposes? Discuss.

12 Having corporations pay income tax does not make sense. Cor–poration profits should only be taxed when paid out to individuals as dividends. Discuss these statements.

13 In 1867 the responsibilities of government deemed to be most important were given to the federal government. Are those re–sponsibilities the most important today in terms of government spending?

14 Could higher marginal tax rates in one province cause its citi–zens to move to another province? To another country?

15 The town of Whitby, Ontario wants minor sports organizations to pay increased fees for the use of town baseball diamonds and soccer fields. Is this an example of the benefits-received approach to taxation? Are the recipients of the benefits easily identified in this situation?

Suggested Readings

Allan, Charles M. *The Theory of Taxation*. Middlesex: Penguin Books 1971.

Auld, D.A.L., and F.C. Miller. *Principles of Public Finance: A Canadian Text*. 2nd impression. Toronto: Methuen 1977.

Bird, Richard M., and N. Enid Slack. *Urban Public Finance in Canada*. Toronto: Butterworths 1983.

McCready, Douglas J. *The Canadian Public Sector*. Toronto: Butterworths 1984.

The National Finances 1988-89. Toronto: Canadian Tax Foundation 1990.

Pipes, Sally, and Michael Walker, with David Gill. *Tax Facts. The Canadian Consumer Tax Index and You*. 3rd ed. Vancouver: Fraser Institute 1982.

Provincial and Municipal Finances 1989. Toronto: Canadian Tax Foundation 1990.

Rabbior, Gary. "An Overview Of The Goods And Services Tax." Economic Bulletin #3. Toronto: The Canadian Foundation for Economic Education March 1990

Ruggeri, G.C. *The Canadian Economy: Problems and Policies*. 3rd ed. Toronto: Gage 1987.

Strick, J. C. *Canadian Public Finance*. 3rd ed. Toronto: Holt, Rinehart and Winston 1985.

Chapter 5

Economic Indicators

Chapter Objectives

After successfully completing this chapter, you will be able to:

- define the participation rate and the unemployment rate as they appear in the Labour Force Survey
- understand exactly what the unemployment rate measures
- explain the five types of unemployment
- describe the composition of the Consumer Price Index
- explain the causes of inflation
- relate the problems of inflation to the Canadian economy
- calculate items in the National Accounts
- explain why the level of GDP cannot be associated with social welfare

Key Terms

macroeconomics
Labour Force Survey
Consumer Price Index
National Accounts
gross domestic product (GDP)
unemployment rate
participation rate
underemployment
hidden unemployed
demand-deficient
   unemployment
frictional unemployment
structural unemployment

seasonal unemployment
insurance-induced unemployment
demand-pull inflation
cost-push inflation
structural inflation
hyperinflation
circular flow of money
investment
net domestic income
personal income
personal disposable income
real GDP

Definition of Macroeconomics

Macroeconomics is the area of economics concerned with the overall view of an economy, rather than with individual markets.

Macroeconomics is the area of economic analysis concerned with the overall view of an economy rather than with individual markets. In Canada, macroeconomics analyses the effects of all markets acting together. The issues that will be important in this section include those affecting all Canadians: unemployment, inflation, and the level of business activity.

This chapter reviews some of the sources of information that are available to assist our understanding of Canadian macroeconomic issues. These are the Labour Force Survey, the Consumer Price Index, and the National Accounts. All three sources are tabulated by Statistics Canada.

Unemployment

The Labour Force Survey measures the number of unemployed persons in Canada on a monthly basis. An unemployed person is someone who is out of work and looking for a job. The measure of unemployment provides one indication of the state of economic conditions in the country. If people are not working, then Canada is not using its resources efficiently. It means that Canada is producing a quantity of goods and services that falls inside its production-possibilities curve. The Labour Force Survey thus provides an indication of our under-utilized resources.

Unemployment is also a concern on an individual basis. When a worker is unemployed, his or her income is reduced, making it more difficult to support his- or herself or a family. People also like to feel that they are contributing to our society. Unemployment removes this sense of satisfaction.

If high levels of unemployment persist, social unrest can result. Evidence of this was seen in the summer of 1981 in Britain when rioting erupted in several major cities. The consensus was that the frustrations over the lack of jobs led to extreme and unusual behaviour on the part of some young people.

Inflation

The Consumer Price Index (CPI) measures the change in retail prices in Canada each month. Inflation means an increase in the general level of retail prices. Therefore, the Consumer Price Index is regarded as a measure of inflation. The problems of inflation are many and affect different individuals in different ways. Price increases hurt those persons who are on fixed incomes, e.g. pensioners, who have no other means of obtaining income. Rising prices favour people who have borrowed money and do not favour those who have lent money. The money that is paid back at a future date after a period of rising prices will buy fewer goods and services than the amount that was initially borrowed could have bought. The borrower is, therefore, in an advantageous situation. Canada's position in world markets is also hurt by increasing prices. If products made in Canada become too expensive, foreign buyers will look elsewhere. Canada is a country that relies heavily on foreign trade, and remaining competitive in foreign markets is a major concern.

Another disadvantage of inflation is that the rate of price increases may get higher and higher, and become more difficult to control. Rapidly rising prices destroy the purchasing power of incomes. This forces workers to demand higher wages in order to keep up with the cost of living. If companies are forced to pay higher wages, they will likely raise the price of their product. This could set off another round of *wage and price increases.* If price increases continue for any period of time, an *inflationary psychology* may develop in the population. People begin to react as if they expect prices to continue to rise. They spend now before the prices go even higher. The increased demand puts further upward pressure on prices. As prices increase, the purchasing power of money decreases, and if price increases are not constrained, the value of the currency is destroyed.

Level of Business Activity

Gross domestic product (GDP) represents the value of all goods and services produced in a country in a given year.

The National Accounts measure the overall level of business activity in Canada. The most common statistic in the National Accounts is **gross domestic product (GDP).** This is a measure of the market value of final goods and services produced in Canada in a given period of time. GDP figures are produced on both a quarterly and an annual basis. "Final" goods and services are those purchased by their final user as "finished," in contrast to those goods that are used as "inputs" in the production of other goods.

Why is it necessary to measure the level of business activity? The information tabulated in the National Accounts gives an indication of the *standard of living* in Canada. If the amount of goods and services produced is constantly increasing, then Canadian incomes are rising. Increases in incomes are associated with improvements in living standards.

Increases in the statistical measure of gross domestic product and the other tabulations of the National Accounts are, however, not synonymous with improved living standards. It is necessary to relate increases in GDP to increases in our population. Our standard of living will only be improving as long as GDP is increasing at a faster rate than the population. Also, GDP increases have to be compared to price increases. The real value of any increase in GDP may be eroded by rapidly rising prices.

The information available in the National Accounts has more uses than simply defining our standard of living. Businesses use the information for *forecasting market conditions* and for making decisions. If the forecast is that the level of business activity will decline, many businesses can expect a slump in sales and need to manage their affairs accordingly. Governments use GDP and other National Accounts figures to judge the success of their various programs. Many government programs are aimed at stimulating business activity and the success of the program is measured in terms of the changes in such tabulations as gross domestic product.

The words *recession* and *depression* are defined with reference to changes in GDP. A recession is described as a drop in economic activity whereby GDP, adjusted for price increases, declines for two successive quarters. A depression is a more exaggerated slowdown in economic activity.

In this chapter, we will discuss the Labour Force Survey, the Consumer Price Index, and the National Accounts separately. In our economy, however, the three are closely related. For example, if the level of GDP is falling, unemployment is likely to be increasing. When business sales are low, companies will not need as many employees. The level of business activity may also affect prices. When activity is low, prices may fall as a result of special clearance sales and discounts. When business activity is great, prices may rise due to the increased demand for goods and services.

The Labour Force Survey

The Labour Force Survey is a monthly measure of the number of unemployed in Canada. This measure provides an indication of the country's economic condition.

The Labour Force Survey is compiled monthly and is based on a survey of approximately 53 000 households across Canada. The survey excludes residents of the Yukon and Northwest Territories, persons living on Indian Reserves, inmates of institutions, and full-time members of the armed forces. It was first introduced in Canada in 1945 in order to obtain more accurate information about unemployed persons. In January 1976, a revised survey was introduced in order to collect more data. The Labour Force Survey is a compilation of these data concerning the composition and characteristics of the various labour-force groups.

Selected households remain on the survey for six months, with one-sixth of the households being replaced each month. The interviewer gathers information on each member of the household 15 years of age and over, in order to determine labour force behaviour during a reference week. Each individual in the survey population is put into one of three categories based on work-related activities during the reference week. These categories are:

Employed: any person who did any work for pay or profit during the reference week. Also included are unpaid family workers in a family farm or business. This category includes individuals who were on vacation, on strike, or on sick leave during the reference week.

Unemployed: any person who, during the reference week, was without work, looking for work, and available for work. An unemployed person has an immediate interest in finding work, and would be available if suitable work was found. Also unemployed are those who are not actively seeking work but who are on temporary lay-off and those who will have a new job to start in the next four weeks.

Not in labour force: any person who, during the reference week of the survey, was without work, yet not looking for work.

A number of definitions are derived from this categorization of the population. The labour force is defined as the number of persons who are either employed or unemployed. In other words, the labour force is comprised of individuals who are working or looking for work. Those individuals not in the labour force are neither working nor looking for work, and include students, retired persons, and homemakers (according to the Labour Force Survey, work does not include work done around the house).

The percentage of the population that is employed or actively seeking employment makes up the participation rate.

The **participation rate** is defined as the percentage of those people surveyed who are in the labour force. It is a measure of the proportion of the working-age population that is employed or seeking work. The calculation of the participation rate is shown in the formula below, and data on Canada's participation rates are shown in tables 5.1 and 5.2.

$$\text{participation rate} = \frac{\text{labour force}}{\text{population}\,(15\,\text{years}\,+)}$$

Table 5.1 / Participation rates (percent) and unemployment rates (percent) by age and sex, Canada, 1990

	Total			15-24 Years			25 Years +		
	Both sexes	Men	Women	Both sexes	Men	Women	Both sexes	Men	Women
Participation Rate	67.0	75.9	58.4	68.9	71.1	66.6	66.5	77.1	56.7
Unemployment Rate	8.1	8.1	8.1	12.8	12.8	11.4	7.0	6.8	7.3

Source: *Canadian Economic Observer,* February 1991, publication no. 11-010, monthly, vol. 4, no. 2 (Ottawa: Statistics Canada, February 1991), p. 5.41

Table 5.2 / Participation rates (percent) and unemployment rates (percent) by province, Canada, 1990

	Cda	Nfld	PEI	NS	NB	Que.	Ont.	Man.	Sask.	Alta.	BC
Participation rate	67.0	56.0	66.0	62.1	59.8	64.3	69.4	67.6	66.8	72.1	66.0
Unemployment rate	8.1	17.1	14.9	10.5	12.1	10.1	6.3	7.2	7.0	7.0	8.3

Source: *Labour Force Annual Averages 1990,* publication no. 71-220 (Ottawa: Statistics Canada, 1991), pp. A-14-25

As shown in the tables, the participation rate for Canada was 67.0 percent in 1990. There are some definite differences in the rate when analysed by sex, age, and province. Men have traditionally had a higher participation rate than women. Men 25 years of age and over have the highest participation rate (77.1 percent) and women in the same age category, the lowest (56.7 percent). Provincial participation rates range from a high of 72.1 percent in Alberta to a low of 56 percent in Newfoundland. The long-term trend in participation rates has been stable for middle-aged men, declining for younger and older persons, and increasing for women.

These trends are influenced by several variables, which include family size and income, level of education, and general economic conditions. For example, the presence of improved educational opportunities has resulted in a lowering of the participation rate for younger individuals. People are staying in school longer. The declining participation rate of older workers can, in part, be attributed to the higher levels of income and the more lucrative social benefits available. Elderly individuals can more easily afford to retire from the labour force at an earlier age. The state of the economy can also influence participation rates. If unemployment is high, other family members may enter the labour force to look for a job, while some individuals may become discouraged about job prospects and leave the labour force.

The most noticeable trend in participation rates has been in the area of rates for women. In 1953, the participation rate for women was approximately 25 percent, and by 1990, was approaching 60 percent. What factors accounted for this increase? Reasons for the higher labour force participation of women include the following: a higher level of education among women; a higher opportunity cost of not working; the fact that family sizes are getting smaller; and the advances in household technology that have reduced the time necessary to complete household chores. There has also been an increase in the number of white-collar and part-time jobs that are more attractive to women. Economic and financial conditions have also made it necessary for some women to seek employment. Rising prices and unemployment among other family members have forced women to work outside of the home in order to supplement the family income. Women's attitudes about their roles have been changing, as is evident in women's increased involvement in the work force.

Greater government activity in the labour market has improved the attractiveness of employment for women. This government involvement includes the passage of equal-pay and affirmative-action legislation, maternity-leave provisions, and changes to the Unemployment Insurance Act. The latter changes have made it easier for people to receive unemployment-insurance benefits when they are out of a job. This easier access to unemployment-insurance benefits has made labour-force participation more attractive for some women. There is also increased pressure on government to provide more subsidized day care. Changes in legislation may have made it easier for women to enter the labour force, yet these changes would not likely have occurred without the increased labour-force participation of women that was already taking place. Greater participation of women in the labour force has also brought changes in the negotiating of collective agreements between union and management. Changes have been negotiated in pension plans and maternity-leave provisions and in other conditions of employment.

The percentage of the labour force that is not employed yet is seeking employment comprises the unemployment rate.

The **unemployment rate** is defined as the percentage of the labour force that is not working, yet is looking for work. The calculation of the unemployment rate is given below and data on the rate are presented in tables 5.1 and 5.2.

$$\text{unemployment rate} = \frac{\text{unemployed}}{\text{labour force}}$$

As shown in the tables, the unemployment rate also varies by age, sex, and province. The overall unemployment rate for Canada in 1990 was 8.1 percent. There is a significant difference in the unemployment rate when ages are compared. The unemployment rate for those in the 15-24 year age group was 12.8 percent, while for the older age group it was only seven percent. On a provincial basis, Ontario had the lowest unemployment rate in 1990 and Newfoundland had the highest.

Canada's unemployment rate of 8.1 percent in 1990 has not been a typical rate of unemployment for the Canadian economy. Table 5.3 shows the unemployment rates for Canada from 1966 to 1990. The trend over this twenty-four-year period has been for unemployment rates to increase. In 1966, the unemployment rate was only 3.4 percent of the labour force. By 1983, the unemployment rate had reached 11.8 percent. The reasons for this trend are varied and include changes in the composition of our labour force, changes in the unemployment-insurance program, changes in oil prices, changes in technology, and changes in the pattern of world trade. A more detailed discussion of the changes in unemployment rates appears in Chapter 8.

Table 5.3 / Unemployment rates (percent), Canada, 1966-90

Year	Unemployment rate (percent)	Year	Unemployment rate (percent)
1966	3.4	1979	7.4
1967	3.8	1980	7.5
1968	4.5	1981	7.5
1969	4.4	1982	11.0
1970	5.7	1983	11.8
1971	6.2	1984	11.2
1972	6.2	1985	10.5
1973	5.5	1986	9.5
1974	5.3	1987	8.8
1975	6.9	1988	7.8
1976	7.1	1989	7.5
1977	8.1	1990	8.1
1978	8.3		

Source: *Canadian Economic Observer, Historical Statistical Supplement 1989/90,* July 1990, publication no. 11-210, vol. 3, (Ottawa: Statistics Canada, July 1990), p. 34, and Canadian Economic Observer, February 1991, publication no. 11-010 monthly, vol. 4, no.2 (Ottawa: Statisitics Canada, February 1991), p. 5.28.

Although the Labour Force Survey provides monthly data on Canada's unemployment rate, there are still some questions that have to be answered before Canada's unemployment situation can be accurately assessed. The survey provides information on the number of unemployed, but not on the number of *job vacancies.* That is, the solution to the unemployment problem depends on the number of job vacancies available. If there are no jobs available, then jobs will have to be created. If jobs are available, then a way will have to be found to match the unemployed workers to the available opportunities.

Underemployment is the term used to describe a situation in which individuals are employed but not at jobs that fully utilize their skills.

The definition of unemployment used by the Labour Force Survey does not take into consideration **underemployment,** the situation in which individuals are employed, but not at a job that fully utilizes their skills. For example, a qualified plumber may accept a job delivering pizza if no other jobs are available. In terms of the Labour Force Survey, this person is employed, since she or he is working. However, this worker is not as productive as she or he could be. Individuals are also underemployed if they are working fewer hours a week than they want to work. The survey also does not identify those who have more than one job, or are "moon-lighting."

The survey categorizes an individual as unemployed if that person was looking for a job during the reference week. Although the survey questionnaire asks what the person has done to find a job, there is no indication of how hard the person looked for work. Some unemployed workers may have put a great deal of effort into finding a job, while others may have simply gone through the motions. Undoubtedly, unemployment means real financial hardship for some people. The higher the unemployment rate, the greater the degree of financial problems. The survey, however, does not measure the financial hardship suffered by unemployed persons. Some unemployed persons may have a separate source of income or have a spouse that is employed. In order to get a picture of economic hardship in Canada, Labour Force Survey data need to be combined with other data on incomes.

One criticism of the Labour Force Survey is its inability to identify the "hidden unemployed" or "discouraged workers." These persons are interested in employment, but are not actively seeking a job since they believe that a suitable job is not available. Rather than being tabulated as unemployed, they are deemed by the Survey to be not in the labour force. In order to estimate the degree of **hidden unemployment,** Statistics Canada carries out a special survey in March of each year in conjunction with the monthly Labour Force Survey. Since March is normally a period of high unemployment, the maximum number of discouraged workers is likely to show up at this time. Statistics Canada also publishes each month, as part of the labour force data, estimates of the number of people who have looked for work in the last six months, not just the last four weeks.

When the unemployment-rate statistics are released every month, two sets of figures are given. The actual unemployment rate and the *seasonally adjusted unemployment rate* are provided. The actual rate is the unemployment rate derived from survey statistics. The seasonally adjusted rate adjusts the actual rate to account for seasonal fluctuations. It takes into consideration the fact that unemployment is normally higher in the winter months than in the summer. The seasonally adjusted rate is used for month-to-month comparisons of the unemployment situation, and for revealing the underlying trend in the unemployment statistics.

The "hidden unemployed" are those members of the population who are not actively seeking a job because they do not believe there are suitable jobs available.

Types of Unemployment

Demand-deficient

Demand-deficient unemployment results from a lack of overall spending in the economy.

Employers want to hire workers in order to produce the products that they are selling. If employers are having difficulty selling their products, then they will not need to hire as many workers. A decrease in the level of spending by consumers will result in reduced sales for businesses. If consumers are not spending money on goods and services, employers will not need to hire workers. This results in unemployment. Lack of aggregate demand for products in the economy results in **demand-deficient unemployment.**

Frictional

Short-term unemployment on the part of individuals who have voluntarily left one job and are in the process of looking for another is termed frictional unemployment.

Under all types of economic conditions, there will always be individuals who are in between jobs or are just entering the labour force. These persons are classified as being frictionally unemployed. In most cases, the unemployment is of short duration and the individual is expected to find a job relatively quickly. **Frictional unemployment** is peculiar in that it tends to be higher when economic conditions are good. When the aggregate demand for goods and services is high and jobs are plentiful, individuals are more willing to leave one job and look for a better one. When the aggregate demand is low and jobs are scarce, workers are less willing to leave one job voluntarily in order to begin searching for another.

Seasonal

Seasonal unemployment results from the seasonal nature of some industries, such as agriculture, construction, tourism, and recreation.

Some jobs are very seasonal in nature. Employment in many areas of construction, recreation, tourism, and agriculture is only available in the warmer months of the year. For many workers in these industries, alternative employment opportunities may not be available during the winter. Ski instructors, on the other hand, may be employed during the winter months but unemployed for the rest of the year. In both cases, such workers experience **seasonal unemployment.**

Structural

Structural unemployment results from a mismatching of the demand for, and the supply of workers on an occupational or geographic basis.

Structural unemployment results from a mismatching of workers and jobs, rather than from a shortage of jobs. This mismatching has two dimensions: occupational and geographic. In some instances, jobs are available, yet the unemployed individuals do not have the necessary skills to fill the available jobs. The *occupational dimension* of structural unemployment results from a change in the consumer demand for goods and services as well as from changes in technology. As consumers' spending patterns change, some jobs are eliminated. Changes in methods of production or technology have also reduced the demand for certain types of workers. For example, the growth of computer technology has drastically altered the types of office jobs available.

The *geographic dimension* of structural unemployment means that unemployed workers may have the skills to fill the job vacancies, but the jobs may be in another area of the country. There may be unemployed welders in Halifax and a shortage of welders in Edmonton. The solution to the geographic element of structural unemployment is to improve the matching process by increasing worker mobility from place to place.

Insurance-induced

Insurance-induced unemployment is caused by the level of unemployment insurance benefits, which make the effort of looking for work unattractive.

Changes to the Unemployment Insurance Act in 1971 affected Canada's unemployment rate. These changes, which made unemployment insurance easier to collect while at the same time increasing the available benefits, have tended to increase the unemployment rate by generating **insurance-induced unemployment.** For certain groups of individuals, weekly unemployment-insurance benefits may be more attractive than regular employment. Although technically a person has to be actively seeking work in order to be classified as unemployed and to qualify for insurance benefits, these circumstances may not be revealed by the Labour Force Survey. In other words, someone may be classified as unemployed on the survey, although he or she is not actively seeking work.

5.1 Are students classified as being unemployed according to the Labour Force Survey? Why or why not?

5.2 What is the difference between the participation rate and the unemployment rate?

5.3 How does structural unemployment differ from demand-deficient unemployment?

Unemployment Insurance and the Unemployment Rate

The unemployment-insurance program in Canada provides monetary benefits to persons who cease to be employed. Those eligible to collect unemployment-insurance benefits are persons who have been terminated or laid off from their job, who are not able to work because of illness, or who qualify for maternity benefits. In order to qualify for benefits, a person must have been employed and have made contributions to the unemployment-insurance fund. The contributions are automatically deducted from earnings at the person's place of employment. The benefits that one receives when unemployed depend on the amount of contributions that were made. The program is not based on need but solely on contributions. Wealthy and low-income individuals are both eligible for unemployment-insurance benefits under the same conditions.

Although the program is referred to as insurance, it differs from a typical insurance scheme. First, the program is not voluntary, but compulsory. Only certain categories of workers, e.g. the self-employed, are not required to make contributions to the unemployment-insurance fund. If the program were voluntary, many people would refuse to participate. If these people became unemployed, they might seek financial assistance from government in the form of welfare. The inevitability of many people receiving some type of public assistance once unemployed made the compulsory aspect of the program more practical. Second, the contributions to the fund have not been sufficient to meet the benefits that must be paid out. The federal government has subsidized the program out of general tax revenue in order to make up the deficit.

There is some evidence that the unemployment-insurance program has had an impact on the unemployment rate. The program may increase job turnover. Individuals may be encouraged to leave their jobs in order to receive benefits. The opportunity cost of leaving one job in order to search for another is reduced. Others may voluntarily remain unemployed for longer periods of time if financial assistance is still available. They may conduct a job search with less intensity and only be willing to accept high-paying jobs. They may not be willing to incur the cost and trouble of re-training in order to acquire new skills. The existence of unemploy-ment-insurance benefits may also encourage some individuals to enter the labour force because they are attracted by the possibility of receiving benefits if they lose their job.

Since the availability of unemployment-insurance benefits makes leisure cheaper, some individuals who want more leisure may quit their job to get it. This decision to get more leisure in-volves certain costs. First, there is the cost of finding a new job when the benefits run out. Some time must be spent in a job search and this will cut into the leisure time. The length of the job search will depend not only on the individual's skill and experi-ence, but on the labour-market conditions at the time. The sec-ond cost of accepting benefits is the waiting period that must be served before benefits commence. Voluntary job leavers have to wait longer than others before they can begin receiving jobless benefits.

In order to continue receiving benefits, an unemployed per-son must be actively seeking work. The individual has to prove to officials of the Canada Employment and Immigration Commission that a job search did take place. The need to document job-search activities cuts into leisure time and is a third cost involved in deciding to accept unemployment-insurance benefits.

A 1986 provincial royal commission in Newfoundland re-ported that unemployment-insurance was harmful to the work ethic. The commission noted that unemployment-insurance benefits account for approximately eight percent of personal in-come in Newfoundland, compared with two percent in the rest of

Canada. The unemployment-insurance program is regarded as an income supplement and not as temporary income assistance between jobs. The commission suggested that unemployment insurance be retained in the province strictly as an insurance scheme, and that a guaranteed annual income program be established for which everyone is eligible.

The Commission of Inquiry on Unemployment Insurance (Forget Commission) also submitted its report in 1986. The report contained 53 recommendations for changes in the unemployment insurance legislation and other human-resource development programs. The report recommended the introduction of an earnings supplementation program while phasing out the regionally extended benefits and fishing benefits. The problems with the current unemployment-insurance legislation are addressed in the report. The report's first recommendation, however, is that Canada should give a high priority to economic growth rather than focus on restructuring the unemployment-insurance program. A growing economy would create more employment opportunities for Canadians.

In the fall of 1990, changes were made to Canada's unemployment insurance legislation. Government contributions to unemployment insurance ended. Employers and employees now contribute all the money. The government redirected unemployment insurance money away from low-unemployment areas to job-training programs. It is also harder to qualify for unemployment insurance in low-unemployment areas. The benefits for new parents and older workers have increased.

Sources: Chris Green, "The Impact of Unemployment insurance on the Unemployment Rate," paper presented at the Canadian Economics Association meetings, Queen's University, Kingston, Ontario, 3 June 1973; Herbert G. Grubel, Dennis Maki, and Shelley Sax, "Real and Insurance-induced Unemployment in Canada,"*Canadian Journal of Economics* viii, no. 2 (May 1975).

Questions

1 What groups of workers would be most likely to take advantage of the availability of unemployment insurance in order to have more leisure time?
2 Do you think that wealthy individuals should be able to collect unemployment insurance benefits? Discuss.
3 What effect would unemployment insurance have on the mobility of workers across the country?

Consumer Price Index

The Consumer Price Index (CPI) lists the ratio of current prices of consumer products to the prices of those products in a base year. The percentage change in this index from year to year is referred to as the rate of inflation.

Inflation can be defined as a general increase in the level of prices. In Canada, the rate of inflation is measured by the **Consumer Price Index (CPI).** The CPI is a monthly survey of retail prices undertaken by Statistics Canada. The survey covers urban centres with populations of more than 30 000, including Whitehorse and Yellowknife. Three hundred and twenty-five consumer items are surveyed in the categories of food, clothing, transportation, health and personal care, housing, recreation and reading, and tobacco and alcohol. Some specific items included in the survey are restaurant meals, eyeglasses, cross-country skis, floor wax, movie tickets, interest payments on a mortgage, and gasoline. As some items are more important than others in a person's budget, those items are assigned more importance in calculating the index.

Monthly retail-price increases are published in the form of an index. In order to calculate the index, prices in 1986 are given a value of 100.0 and prices in subsequent years are related to 1986 prices. The formula for calculating the index is as follows:

$$\frac{\text{price level in 199?}}{\text{price level in 1986}} \times 100.0 = \text{CPI in year 199?}$$

For example, assume that in 1986 the price of a movie ticket was $5.00 and by 1990 it had risen to $10.00. Calculation of an index for this item would be:

$$\frac{\$10.00}{\$5.00} \times 100.0 = 200.0$$

In other words, this shows that the price of movie tickets increased by 100 percent from 1986 to 1990.

The CPI keeps track of changes in retail prices of goods and services typically purchased by consumers. Since these goods and services change over time, the CPI must regularly update the "basket" of goods and services surveyed. With an increasing number of two-wage-earner families, more money is now being spent in restaurants. With more leisure time available, more money is being spent on recreational activities and equipment. New products such as low-fat foods and video "camcorders" are being introduced in the marketplace. These changes are identified through a survey of family expenditures. Once the results of the survey are known, items surveyed by the CPI are adjusted. The most recent change occurred with the publication of the June 1990 CPI, which used the basket of goods and services identified by the 1986 family-expenditure survey.

Table 5.4 / Consumer Price Index (January 1991) and relative weights for various groups, Canada (1986 = 100.0)

Group	CPI (January 1991)	Relative weights (percent)
housing	124.0	36.32
food	120.9	18.05
transportation	122.6	18.29
clothing	124.4	8.69
recreation, reading and education	128.0	8.84
tobacco and alcohol	143.9	5.60
health and personal care	127.6	4.20
All items	125.0	100.00

Source: *Consumer Price Index, January 1991,* publication no.62-001, monthly, vol. 70, no. 1 (Ottawa: Statistics Canada, February 1991), pp. 16-19.

The group of consumer items and their weighting in the Consumer Price Index are presented in table 5.4. The weighting refers to the importance of that item in the basket of goods and services, and determines the degree of influence exerted by the price change of that basic grouping on the aggregate index. As shown in the table, prices had increased 25 percent from 1986 to January 1991. All items, however, have not increased by the same amount. Tobacco and alcohol prices increased by 43.9 percent over this period, while food prices increased only 20.9 percent.

In table 5.5, the CPI data is provided for 18 Canadian cities for January 1991. It should be pointed out that these data do not allow for comparisons of the cost of living between cities. The figures simply refer to how much prices have increased in each city from 1986. For example, in Toronto the CPI was 127.4, and for St. John's it was 119.6. This can be interpreted by stating that prices have increased 27.4 percent in Toronto and 19.6 percent in St. John's since 1986. It is impossible to compare the cost of living between these cities because there is no information presented on the actual prices in each city in 1986.

The rate of inflation is calculated on the basis of increases in the CPI from year to year. Rates of inflation for Canada for selected years are presented in table 5.6. The table shows that the rate of inflation was in double figures in the mid-1970s and early 1980s. The rates of inflation in 1984 and 1985 returned to the level of the 1960s and early 1970s.

Table 5.5 / Consumer Price Index for selected Canadian cities, January 1991 (1986 = 100.0)

St. John's, Nfld.	119.6
Charlottetown/Summerside	124.7
Halifax	124.8
Saint John	123.5
Quebec City	123.7
Montreal	125.3
Ottawa	124.6
Toronto	127.4
Thunder Bay	123.2
Winnipeg	124.3
Regina	124.0
Saskatoon	124.5
Edmonton	123.9
Calgary	123.9
Vancouver	123.0
Victoria	123.0
Whitehorse	120.3
Yellowknife	121.7

Source: *The Consumer Price Index,* January 1991, publication no. 62-001, monthly, vol. 70, no. 1 (Ottawa: Statistics Canada, February 1991), pp. 28-36.

Table 5.6 / Annual average increases in the CPI, Canada, 1965-90

Year	Annual increase in CPI (percent)	Year	Annual increase in CPI (percent)
1965	2.4	1978	9.0
1966	3.7	1979	9.1
1967	3.6	1980	10.2
1968	4.0	1981	12.4
1969	4.6	1982	10.9
1970	3.3	1983	5.7
1971	2.9	1984	4.4
1972	4.7	1985	3.9
1973	7.8	1986	4.2
1974	10.8	1987	4.4
1975	10.8	1988	4.0
1976	7.5	1989	5.0
1977	8.0	1990	4.8

Source: *The Consumer Price Index,* January 1980, catalogue number 62-001, monthly, vol. 55, no. 1 (Ottawa: Statistics Canada, February 1980), p. 9; ibid., January 1991, p.20.

It should be pointed out that the CPI is a retail price index and not a cost-of-living index. It is impossible to calculate a cost-of-living index since each individual has a different pattern of spending. A different cost-of-living index would be needed for each person. Certain individuals may not purchase all the items included in the index, nor purchase the items in the ratio of assigned weights given in table 5.4. The items that a retired individual would spend money on differ from those of a family of four or of a student attending college. The CPI simply relates the changes in retail prices of a certain basket of consumer goods. In actual practice, however, the CPI is often referred to as a cost-of-living index since no cost-of-living index is available.

5.4 How would you interpret a CPI for Canada of 300.0?

5.5 What could you say about a CPI for Vancouver of 123.0 in January 1991 compared to a CPI for the same month for Regina of 124.3?

5.6 Why is it not correct to call the CPI a cost-of-living index?

Causes of Inflation

In order to understand why prices increase, it is necessary to understand how a market operates. This topic was discussed in Chapter 2. In order for a price to increase, either demand has to increase or supply has to decrease. Each of these causes will be considered separately.

Demand-pull

Demand-pull inflation describes the increase in the general level of prices that occurs when the aggregate demand for goods and services exceeds the supply.

Increases in the demand for a product result in price increases, assuming that nothing else has changed (see Chapter 2). The increased demand could result from a number of factors, including increased incomes and changing expectations about future prices. If consumers expect prices to increase in the future, they will purchase the necessary goods and services right now. The increased demand pushes up today's prices. If individuals are increasing their demands for all goods and services, then the overall level of prices will increase, causing **demand-pull inflation.**

Cost-push

Cost-push inflation describes increases in the general price levels resulting from firms passing on their cost increases to consumers in the form of higher prices.

Anything that causes supply to decrease will result in higher prices, or **cost-push inflation.** With reference to Chapter 2, this includes anything that will shift the supply curve to the left. Factors causing the supply curve to shift in this manner include wage increases, tax increases, raw-material and energy-price increases, and increased borrowing charges. For example, energy costs have been increasing rapidly since the mid-1970s and have put significant upward pressure on the cost of manufactured products.

In reality, it is difficult to separate demand-pull and cost-push influences on prices. They are often interrelated. For example, if the demand for products increases, higher prices will result. Price increases will lead to demands for higher wages, which will push up costs and eventually increase prices. The higher wages received by workers may lead to increased demands for goods and services and this will increase prices. The sequence could continue to repeat itself.

One indicator used by economists to distinguish between demand-pull and cost-push inflation is corporate profits in the manufacturing and commodity-producing industries. These industries are the most sensitive to changes in the business cycle. In times of demand-pull inflation, profit margins tend to widen; during times of cost-push inflation, they tend to narrow. Cost-push inflation is usually preceded by demand-pull inflation. Some economists argue that cost-push inflation does not really identify a cause of inflation. Rather, cost-push pressures are a matter of timing. After demand pressures have increased product prices, the prices for resources used to make the products increase.

Structural

Structural inflation can occur when certain industries or groups of workers who are shielded from competition raise the prices of their products or services even though prices are not increasing in other areas of the economy.

A third type of inflation, **structural inflation,** is caused by certain institutional arrangements in our economy. Certain industries and groups of workers are immune from many of the changes that take place in the economy and can raise the prices for their products or services in spite of poor economic conditions. In each of these areas, competition for the product or for the services of labour does not exist.

An example of such an institutional factor is agricultural marketing boards. As will be discussed in Chapter 12, marketing boards have the ability to regulate the supply and the price of certain agricultural products. Another example is present in the labour market. Certain groups of workers are also not subject to the same type of competitive pressures as others. Many workers in Canada produce products that are subject to import competition. Some workers, such as doctors, lawyers, dentists, and a few others, do not face this type of competition. Many civil servants—for example, teachers or air traffic controllers—are employed in areas not subject to any competition.

Inflation refers to an overall increase in the general level of prices. If certain industries and groups of workers can shield themselves from competition, they can achieve price and wage increases even when others cannot. Price increases in these industries can lead to inflation even if prices are not increasing in the rest of the economy.

Hyperinflation

Hyperinflation is the term used to describe a very rapid increase in the level of prices that leads to a lack of public confidence in the currency.

If rising prices remain unchecked, there is the possibility that **hyperinflation** could result. This is a term that refers to a situation of rapidly escalating prices. In fact, prices in a situation of hyperinflation are increasing so quickly that the value of the country's currency is eroded and the currency becomes useless. Imagine a situation in Canada in which prices increase to a level of 100 times what they are today. The real value of one Canadian dollar in terms of the amount of goods it could purchase would be equivalent to one cent prior to the price increases.

Although these figures seem impossible, there have been several cases of hyperinflation. The most celebrated case is that of Germany in the years after World War I. Inflation in that country started to escalate in 1919 when prices tripled. By November 1923, prices were 1 422 900 000 000 times what they were before World War I (in 1914). Clearly, the German currency had become useless. On 20 November 1923, Germany introduced a new currency. The exchange rate was a trillion units of the old currency to one unit of the new currency.

In recent years, Israel, Argentina, and Bolivia have experienced hyperinflation. In Israel, prices increased 191 percent in 1983, 445 percent in 1984, and approximately 404 percent in 1985. In Argentina, price increases were even higher over those years. In 1983 prices increased by 433 percent, in 1984 by 688 percent, and in 1985 by 771 percent. In 1985, the 10 000-peso note in Argentina had the purchasing power of one cent in Canadian money.

The worst case of inflation in recent years has been that of Bolivia. After experiencing 328 percent inflation in 1983, and 2700 percent inflation in 1984, Bolivia had an inflation rate of 11 894 percent in 1985. Prices were climbing hourly. Since Bolivia had its money printed outside the country, it cost more than 1000 pesos to print a 1000-peso note. In order to purchase a television set with 1000-peso notes, the consumer needed almost 31 kg of money.

How does hyperinflation occur? The main ingredient in all cases is the printing of too much money by the country's central bank. If the amount of goods and services available to be purchased does not increase in the same proportion as the increases in the money supply, then prices will increase. More and more money is made available to buy the same amount of goods. The faster the money supply is increased, the faster prices rise. As consumers see prices rising quickly, they react accordingly. They buy goods and services now, before the prices increase even further. This increased demand, as a result of the expectation of higher prices, also pushes up prices.

Questions

1   In times of hyperinflation, would an individual want to hold his or her wealth in cash?

2   What would happen to the purchasing power of pension income or savings during a period of rapidly rising prices?

3   Could hyperinflation lead to social unrest in the country? Why?

4   Will the present Canadian dollar be worthless someday? If that happens, what will Canadians use for money?

5   In times of hyperinflation, who is forced to sacrifice more—the borrower of money or the lender of money? Why?

The National Accounts

The National Accounts are data compiled by Statistics Canada that measure the overall level of business activity in Canada.

Since Canada's economy has to grow in order to meet the demands of an increasing population, a measure of economic growth is seen as a valuable piece of information. Economic growth takes place whenever a country continues to produce more goods and services. This increase in production is seen as necessary in order to increase standards of living and to provide employment for an expanding population. In Canada, the **National Accounts** is a series of data prepared by Statistics Canada in order to measure economic growth. It is probably best to visualize the National Accounts in terms of a **circular flow of money** diagram like the one presented in figure 5.1.

The directional flow of money in the economy from the business sector to households and back is called the circular flow of money.

This diagram represents the flow of money in the Canadian economy. In our diagram we will assume that the Canadian economy is composed of only two sectors: businesses and households. The direction of the money flow is indicated by the arrows. In order to produce goods and services, businesses have to purchase resources. The money paid out for these resources in the form of wages, rent, interest, etc. is indicated in the lower loop of the diagram. This money finds its way to households. In turn, households spend money on goods and services produced by the business sector. This is shown in the upper loop of the diagram (the product markets).

Households spend money on a variety of items including clothes, food, housing, entertainment, and the like. The prices of these products are determined in the product markets. In these markets, households represent the demand side of the market and businesses represent the supply side.

Businesses must purchase certain resources in order to provide these goods and services. They need workers, raw materials, machinery, and buildings as well as other resources. The lower loop of the diagram represents the resource markets. Businesses represent the demand for resources, while households supply these resources.

The circular flow diagram can be used to measure the level of economic activity in two ways. One measure, referred to as the *expenditure approach,* involves determining the amount of

**Figure 5.1
The circular flow
of money**

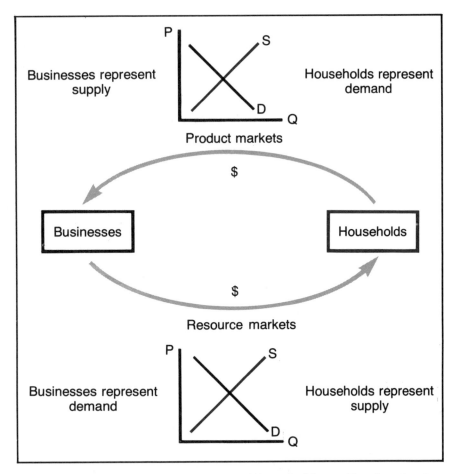

Money circulates from businesses to households and back to businesses. In the product markets, households demand products while businesses supply them. In the resource markets, businesses demand resources that are supplied by households, e.g. labour.

money that households spend on goods and services. This would entail adding up all the money that circulates in the upper loop of figure 5.1. By adding up the dollar value of all consumer purchases, we would have an indication of the level of economic activity.

A second approach to measuring economic activity would be to determine the amount of money businesses pay out for the services they require. This is shown in the lower loop of the diagram and is called the *income approach*. The value arrived at in both approaches is gross domestic product (GDP).

The measuring rod used in each approach is money. That is, GDP is measured in dollars. In order to calculate GDP, we need to add up all of the items that consumers purchase. Yet how could we add T-shirts and tea bags? The only way to do this is to reduce everything to dollars and cents. Therefore, in order for an item to be included in the National Accounts, it must have a price.

Expenditure Approach to Gross Domestic Product

Investment describes business spending on machines and equipment, new residential construction, and any change in inventories.

One way of measuring the level of economic activity in Canada would be to add up the total amount of spending during a calendar year. This expenditure approach, (determining the total amount spent), and the resulting dollar value give the gross domestic product (GDP). In order to determine the total level of spending in the Canadian economy, it is necessary to include other groups that spend money, besides households. These are businesses, government, and buyers from foreign countries (who buy our exports). Businesses make purchases from other businesses for such things as machinery, equipment, and new buildings. This type of spending is referred to as **investment.** Government purchases certain goods and services as well, ranging from the purchase of new fighter aircraft to the hiring of someone to cut the lawn on Parliament Hill. Government also undertakes investment spending. The construction of a nuclear power plant, an airport, and a government office complex are examples of investment spending by government.

Exports are also an important component of gross domestic product. Foreigners buy many products made in Canada. For example, most Canadian-made automobiles are produced for the United States market. Canadians also sell products such as wheat and paper products to residents of other countries. Gross domestic product is the total dollar value of these various types of spending and is calculated as follows:

$$GDP = C + Ig + G + X - M \text{ (see figure 5.2)} \text{ where}$$

C = consumption spending by households on goods and services

Ig = gross investment by business and government, which includes the purchase of machines and equipment, new housing constructed, and any change in inventories

G = government purchases of goods and services

X = exports (foreign purchases of Canadian goods and services)

M = imports (Canadian purchases of foreign goods and services).

Why is it necessary to subtract the amount of money that Canadians spend on imports when calculating GDP? Money spent on imports is not returned to Canadian businesses. In turn, this money is not available to be paid out to Canadian households. The money spent on imported products such as Japanese cars, French wine, and Florida oranges can be said to leave the circular flow of money in Canada.

Gross investment is the term used to represent spending on man-made resources in our economy. This type of spending is undertaken by both business and government. In the National Accounts it is divided into two groups: gross fixed capital formation, and value of physical changes in inventories. *Gross fixed capital formation* is composed mainly of residential and non-residential construction as well as purchases of machinery and equipment. *Inventory changes* are added to the investment calculation because it is necessary to record goods that were produced in a given year, yet not sold in that year. If gross national product is to be an accurate measure of the level of economic activity, then products that remain on the shelves at the end of the year have to be included in GDP since they represent production in that calendar year.

During the process of producing goods and services, some physical deterioration of machinery and equipment takes place. This physical deterioration, or *depreciation,* of equipment, is shown as *capital consumption allowance* in the National Accounts. If the dollar value attached to the capital consumption allowance is subtracted from gross investment, the resulting figure is net investment.

net investment = gross investment − capital consumption
                                            allowance

Not all spending by businesses is included in gross domestic product. Spending on intermediate goods is not included. The definition of intermediate goods can best be explained using an example. In order to build a car, automobile manufacturers must purchase a variety of materials, such as steel and plastic, from suppliers. The cost of these materials is included in the price of the car. If spending by business on steel and plastic were included in gross domestic product, as well as spending by the consumer when buying the car, double counting would take place. The price of the car includes the value of the steel, plastic, and other materials that have been purchased in order to make the car. Only spending on final goods and services is included in the calculation of GDP.

It is also necessary to clarify the government component of GDP. Government spending can be divided into two groups. The first group represents government spending on goods and services. All levels of government are involved in these purchases of machinery, paper, typewriters, landscape services, and so on. The second group is composed of *transfer payments.* These are government expenditures for which a service was not provided. Money is taken from one segment of the population in taxes and transferred to another segment of the population. Examples of government transfer payments are old-age pensions, family allowances, and general welfare assistance. Only those expenditures made on goods and services are included in the calculation of GDP.

Gross domestic product is not the only indicator of economic activity calculated via the expenditure approach. Statistics Canada also calculates *gross national expenditure (GNE)*. The components of GNE are similar to GDP, with one difference. Gross domestic product (expenditure-based) can be defined as the value of all final goods and services produced *in Canada* in a given year, whereas gross national expenditure is the value of all final goods and services produced *by residents of Canada* in a given year.

Gross domestic product, then, is concerned with the economic activity undertaken in Canada, regardless of whether it is done by residents of Canada or not. Gross national expenditure is concerned with the economic activity of residents of Canada, even if they worked outside the country.

Income Approach to Gross Domestic Product

An alternative approach to measuring the level of business activity in Canada would be to determine the amount of money that circulates through the lower loop of the circular flow of money diagram (figure 5.1). This includes business expenses for such items as rent, wages, and interest. Profits are also included in this flow, as they eventually end up in households and are spent on consumer goods and services. Profits can be considered as payment for that resource which represents the productivity of the owner. The lower loop approach to economic activity is referred to as gross domestic product (GDP) and is calculated as follows:

        GDP = wages and salaries
            + interest
            + rent
            + corporation profits before taxes
            + income from unincorporated enterprises
            + indirect taxes
            + capital consumption allowance

Included in our calculation of GDP is a dollar value for capital consumption allowance. In the process of producing goods and services, a certain amount of machinery and equipment was used up. This represents a cost to business, since this machinery will eventually have to be replaced.

Corporation profits can be divided into 1) corporation dividends, 2) corporation income taxes, and 3) undistributed corporation profits. The corporation profit figure, which includes corporation income taxes, is used in calculating GDP. Derivations of this figure are used in calculating other items in the National Accounts.

Not all the expenses of businesses are included in the calculation of GDP. Purchases from other businesses are excluded and only the value added at each stage of production is considered. For example, if a shoemaker buys the leather for a pair of shoes for $40 and sells the shoes for $60, only the $20 that was added to the value by the shoemaker is included in GDP. The other $40 would have been included in GDP on behalf of the company that sold the leather to the shoemaker.

As shown in tables 5.7 and 5.8, the dollar value of GDP is the same whether it is arrived at through the income approach or the expenditure approach. This result occurs because of the nature of the circular flow diagram on which these calculations are based. All of the money spent on goods and services ends up in the business sector of our economy. The business sector has to do something with this money, so it is paid out to individuals in the form of wages, rent, and interest. If profits, which are also returned to households, are added to the other expenses of business, then the dollar value of GDP is the same regardless of the approach used.

GDP (expenditure based) = GDP (income based)

Statistics Canada also used the income approach to calculate *gross national product (GNP)*. The components of GNP are similar to those of GDP with one difference. As with GNE, GNP represents the value of all final goods and services produced by residents of Canada in a given year. Gross domestic product (income based)

Table 5.7 / Gross domestic product, expenditure based, Canada 1990

	$(millions)
personal expenditure on consumer goods and services	402 055
government current expenditure on goods and services	132 456
government investment	16 898
business investment	
- fixed capital formation	124 251
- value of physical change in inventories	-2 687
exports of goods and services	168 435
imports of goods and services	-165 464
statistical discrepancy	1 956
Gross domestic product at market prices	677 900

Source: *Canadian Economic Observer, March 1991*, publication no. 11-010, monthly, vol. 4, no. 3 (Ottawa: Statistics Canada, March 1991), p. 6.3.

Table 5.8 / Gross domestic product, income based, Canada 1990

	$(millions)
wages, salaries and supplementary labour income	383 244
corporation profits before taxes	47 875
interest and miscellaneous investment income	57 941
accrued net income of farm operators from farm production	2 692
net income of non-farm unincorporated business including rent	37 221
inventory valuation adjustment	-2 484
net domestic income at factor cost	526 489
indirect taxes less subsidies	76 451
capital consumption allowance	76 916
statistical discrepancy	-1 956
Gross domestic product at market prices	677 900

Source: *Canadian Economic Observer, March 1991,* publication no.11-010, monthly, vol. 4, no. 3 (Ottawa: Statistics Canada, March 1991), p. 6.3.

represents the value of all final goods and services produced *in Canada* in a given year. If a Canadian citizen living in Windsor, Ontario, works every day in Detroit, Michigan, USA, then that person's income would be included in GNP but not in GDP. Conversely, if someone living in Detroit works in Windsor each day, that person's earnings are included in Canadian GDP but not in Canadian GNP. Since the dollar value of gross domestic product is the same regardless of the approach used, (income or expenditure), the dollar values of GNE and GNP are also the same.

In 1986, Statistics Canada switched from reporting GNP as the main indicator of economic activity in Canada to reporting GDP. Statistics Canada will continue to compute GNP figures; however, emphasis will be put on GDP as an economic indicator.

Gross domestic product is normally greater than gross national product, primarily because a large percentage of Canadian business is foreign-owned. The profits earned by foreign owners of Canadian businesses would be included in GDP since they were earned in Canada but they would not be included in GNP. The annual changes in these two measures do not vary greatly (see table 5.9). Since this is the case, both measures can be used to indicate changes in the level of economic activity.

The value of GDP provides a broad indication of the level of economic activity in Canada. For some uses, the aggregate figures

Table 5.9 / Annual percent changes in gross domestic product, Canada, 1961-90

Year	GDP Percent change	Year	GDP Percent change
1961	3.6	1976	15.4
1962	8.6	1977	10.1
1963	7.4	1978	10.9
1964	9.5	1979	14.3
1965	10.2	1980	12.2
1966	11.9	1981	14.9
1967	7.3	1982	5.2
1968	9.2	1983	8.4
1969	10.1	1984	9.6
1970	7.3	1985	7.5
1971	9.2	1986	5.8
1972	11.7	1987	9.0
1973	17.3	1988	9.4
1974	19.4	1989	8.0
1975	12.8	1990	4.0

Source: *Canadian Economic Observer,* Historical Statistical Supplement 1989/90, July 1990, publication no. 11–210, vol. 3 (Ottawa: Statistics Canada, July 1990), p. 3, and Canadian Economic Observer, March 1991, publication no. 11–010, monthly, vol.4, no. 3, (Ottawa: Statistics Canada, March 1991), p. 6.2.

may not be appropriate. Therefore, Statistics Canada manipulates the information collected in the National Accounts and, in addition to GDP, provides the following information (see figure 5.2):

Net domestic income (NDI): In order to calculate **net domestic income,** the dollar values of the capital consumption allowance and indirect business taxes are subtracted from the value of gross domestic product.

Net domestic income (NDI) is the value of final goods and services produced in a country in a given year, minus an allowance for capital consumption and indirect business taxes.

$$NDI = GDP - \text{capital consumption allowance}$$
$$- \text{ indirect business taxes}$$

Personal income (PI): **Personal income** equals NDI minus corporation income taxes and undistributed corporation profits, while adding government transfer payments. Transfer payments are moneys paid out to individuals for which no product or service was provided, e.g. old-age pensions.

Personal income (PI) is the total of consumption spending and savings in the economy.

$$PI = NDI - \text{corporation income taxes}$$
$$- \text{ undistributed corporation profits}$$
$$+ \text{ government transfer payments}$$

Personal disposable income (PDI) is the level of personal income that remains after income taxes have been paid.

Personal disposable income (PDI): **Personal disposable income** equals PI minus personal income taxes. PDI can also be considered as the total of household consumption plus household savings.

PDI = PI – personal income tax

5.7 Why are government transfer payments not included in the calculation of gross domestic product?

5.8 Why are changes in inventories included in the calculation of GDP?

**Figure 5.2
The National
Accounts**

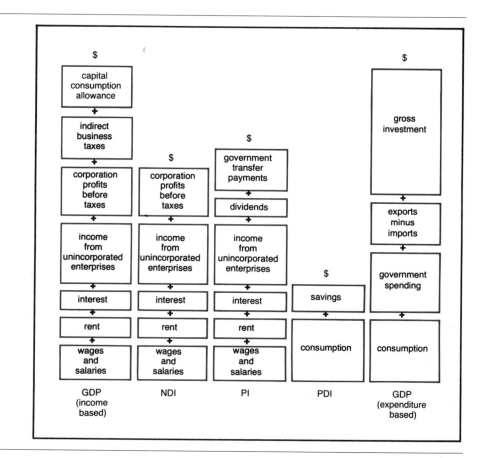

Numerical Calculation of the National Accounts

In order to better understand the National Accounts, the following exercise is provided. Using the following information and figure 5.2, calculate GDP, NDI, PI, and PDI.

Item	$ (million)
consumption	75
corporation dividends	15
capital consumption allowance	15

exports	15
government expenditure on goods and services	25
government transfer payments	5
housing constructed	20
imports	10
income from unincorporated enterprises	25
interest	10
machinery and equipment manufactured	20
net change in inventories	+10
rent	15
savings	25
taxes: corporation income	10
personal income	15
indirect business	5
undistributed corporation profits	15
wages and salaries	45

The easiest calculations to make from these data are personal disposable income (PDI) and personal income (PI).

$$PDI = C + S$$
$$= 75 + 25$$
$$= 100$$

$$PI = PDI + \text{personal income tax}$$
$$= 100 + 15$$
$$= 115$$

It is possible to calculate gross domestic product if we calculate gross investment first.

$$
\begin{aligned}
\text{gross investment} =\ & \text{new housing constructed} \\
+\ & \text{net change in inventories} \\
+\ & \text{machinery and equipment} \\
& \text{manufactured} \\
=\ & 20 + 10 + 20 \\
=\ & 50
\end{aligned}
$$

$$GDP = C + Ig + G + (X - M)$$
$$= 75 + 50 + 25 + (15 - 10)$$
$$= 155$$

$$
\begin{aligned}
NDI = GDP\ & - \text{indirect business taxes} \\
& - \text{capital consumption allowance} \\
= 155\ & - 5 - 15 \\
= 135 &
\end{aligned}
$$

Relationship of GDP to Social and Economic Welfare

Gross domestic product is a measure of the dollar value of final goods and services produced in Canada in a given year. The change in GDP from year to year is an indicator of the amount of economic growth in our country. If our economy is growing and producing more, it is assumed that our standard of living is improving as well. However, increases in GDP do not always represent improvements in our welfare. Some of the reasons why changes in GDP cannot be automatically associated with changes in the standard of living are:

Effect of price increases: since GDP is arrived at by using market prices, the value of GDP will increase each year simply because of inflation. In order to determine whether more goods and services have actually been produced, it is necessary to adjust the dollar value of GDP in order to account for price increases. The resulting figure is referred to as **real GDP** and is expressed in constant, or 1986, dollars.

Real GDP refers to the level of gross domestic product adjusted for increases in the average price level.

The impact of price increases on GDP is shown in table 5.10. In the table, GDP figures in current and constant (1986) dollars are given for the years 1966 to 1989. In all years, the dollar-value growth in GDP was greater than the real growth in GDP. For example, in 1982, GDP increased by 5.2 percent over the 1981 level of GDP in current dollar terms. Yet real GDP, or GDP in constant (1986) dollars, actually fell by 3.2 percent from the previous year. Even in years when the economy is growing, inflation can distort the GDP figures. In 1975, the current dollar value of GDP increased by 12.8 percent over 1974, whereas the constant (1986) dollar value increased by only 2.6 percent.

Effect of population size: each year it is likely that GDP will increase. It is also likely that the population of Canada will increase. In order to determine if Canadians are better off from year to year, GDP has to be calculated on a per capita basis. This is done by dividing the dollar value of real GDP by the population. If this figure increases from year to year, it means that there are more goods and services per person than there were the year before.

Need for a market price: if a good or a service does not have a market price, it is not included in GDP. If you purchase tomatoes at a vegetable market, the value of the tomatoes is included in GDP. If you grow tomatoes in your own garden for your own use, they are not included in GDP. The reason is that the tomatoes from your garden do not have a market price, whereas the other tomatoes do.

Table 5.10 / Gross domestic product in current and constant (1986) dollars, and percentage annual increase, Canada, 1966-90

Year	Current dollars (millions)	Annual percentage increase	Constant (1986) dollars (millions)	Annual percentage increase
1966	64 388	11.9	231 519	6.8
1967	69 064	7.3	238 306	2.9
1968	75 418	9.2	251 064	5.4
1969	83 026	10.1	264 508	5.4
1970	89 116	7.3	271 372	2.6
1971	97 290	9.2	286 998	5.8
1972	108 629	11.7	303 447	5.7
1973	127 372	17.3	326 848	7.7
1974	152 111	19.4	341 235	4.4
1975	171 540	12.8	350 113	2.6
1976	197 924	15.4	371 688	6.2
1977	217 879	10.1	385 122	3.6
1978	241 604	10.9	402 737	4.6
1979	276 096	14.3	418 328	3.9
1980	309 891	12.2	424 537	1.5
1981	355 994	14.9	440 127	3.7
1982	374 442	5.2	425 970	-3.2
1983	405 717	8.4	439 448	3.2
1984	444 735	9.6	467 167	6.3
1985	477 988	7.5	489 437	4.8
1986	505 666	5.8	505 666	3.3
1987	551 336	9.0	526 123	4.0
1988	603 356	9.4	549 237	4.4
1989	651 616	8.0	565 657	3.0
1990	677 900	4.0	570 743	0.9

Source: *Canadian Economic Observer,* Historical Statistical Supplement 1989/90, July 1990, publication no. 11-210 vol. 3, (Ottawa: Statistics Canada, July 1990), p. 3, p.7, and Canadian Economic Observer, March 1991, publication no.11-010, monthly, vol.4, no. 3, (Ottawa: Statistics Canada, March 1991), p. 6.4.

If GDP is to accurately measure production, all tomatoes grown in Canada should be included. Yet, it is only possible to include in the calculation of GDP those goods and services that have a market price.

If Canadians start to do things for themselves—paint their own houses, fix their own cars, grow their own food, and sew their own clothes—the value of GDP will decrease. If Canadians begin to trade goods and services instead of purchasing them, GDP will again decrease.

Types of goods produced: gross domestic product measures the dollar value of goods and services, not the type of goods and services. Some goods and services may be questionable in terms of the benefits that they provide. Nonetheless, all products that have a price are included. The dollar value of all items—guns, chocolate bars, houses, clothes, etc.—are all lumped together in order to arrive at a total figure.

Illegal items: illegal goods and services are not included in the calculation of GDP. Although they are not included in GDP, these items increase the welfare of those who purchase them.

Pollution: it is possible that GDP may increase from year to year. However, it is also possible that increased production is accompanied by more pollution and negative third-party effects. The very real problem of acid rain is a direct result of the increased production that shows up as higher levels of GDP.

Leisure: the calculation of GDP does not consider how hard Canadians have to work to achieve a certain level of output of goods and services. If the number of paid holidays and vacations in Canada increased, it is likely that GDP figures would be lower, since fewer goods and services would be produced. Would this indicate that Canadians are not as well off? No; increased leisure time is a benefit that does not show up in GDP.

Improved product quality: GDP simply measures the value of goods and services produced. No attempt is made to account for changes in the quality of products. Improvements in quality lead to a better standard of living.

Distribution of income: as GDP increases, it is assumed that the population is better off. The GDP figure, however, does not state how this increased production and income is distributed among the population. It is possible that the increases go to only a small segment of the total population. The vast majority of Canadians may not be any better off.

5.9 Why is it necessary to calculate real GDP? Per capita GDP?

5.10 If you fix your own car, is the service included in GDP? Why or why not?

Summary

Three issues that are important to all Canadians are unemployment, inflation, and the level of business activity. An unemployed person is someone who is out of work and looking for a job. The unemployment rate in Canada is measured monthly through the Labour Force Survey. The number of unemployed persons as a percentage of the labour force is called the unemployment rate.

The participation rate is also calculated by the Labour Force Survey. This measures the percentage of the Canadian population who are in the labour force. The most noticeable trend in participation rates has been the recent increase in the women's rate. This increase is a result of several factors, including smaller family sizes, higher levels of education, advancements in household technology, and women's changing attitudes about their involvement in the labour force.

Inflation is defined as a general increase in the level of prices. In Canada, the rate of inflation is measured by the Consumer Price Index, and is calculated on the basis of annual increases in this index. The prices of several hundred consumer items are recorded in the index on a monthly basis. The items are weighted depending on their importance in the consumer budget. It should be remembered that the index is simply a measure of changes in retail prices, not a measure of cost-of-living changes.

The level of business activity in Canada is measured by the National Accounts. The most common statistic in the National Accounts is gross domestic product (GDP), which measures the final value of goods and services produced in Canada in a given year, and is also used as an indicator of the total income earned by Canadians.

Even though GDP is a measure of the level of business activity, it is not necessarily useful as a measure of social welfare. The calculation of GDP does not take into consideration the type or quality of goods produced, how hard Canadians have to work to produce those goods, the negative third-party costs of production (such as pollution), how the increased income is distributed, or illegal goods and services.

Questions for Review and Discussion

1 From the following sets of data, calculate GDP, NDI, PI, and PDI. Treat **A** and **B** as separate problems. Fill in the blanks where necessary.

Item	A $	B $
change in business inventories	+ 8	− 4
consumption	−	33
corporation profits after tax	9	−

Item	A $	B $
corporation profits before tax	–	10
capital consumption allowance	7	–
dividends	5	2
exports	–	10
government expenditure on goods and services	36	15
government transfer payments	3	4
gross investment	–	22
housing constructed	20	10
income from unincorporated enterprises	27	–
interest	15	8
imports	–	12
machines and equipment manufactured	14	16
net investment	–	18
rent	9	7
savings	29	17
taxes, corporation income	10	3
indirect	4	3
personal income	35	–
undistributed corporation profits	–	–
wages and salaries	55	25

2 Do you think that the unemployment rate is a good indicator of the economic hardship that Canadians are facing?

3 Is there any connection between the participation rate and the unemployment rate for various sex and age groups? What about rates for individual provinces?

4 Draw a graph from the information presented in table 5.6. What appears to be happening to Canada's inflation rate?

5 Would the legalization of marijuana increase the value of GDP? Explain.

6 Why does the federal government calculate GDP? Why would private individuals and companies be interested in this information?

7 Why does GDP not measure all the goods and services produce in Canada in a given year?

8 Why do we include only final goods, and not intermediate goods, in the calculation of GDP?

9 "The impact of inflation is not felt equally by all Canadians." Explain this statement.

10 In addition to publishing participation and unemployment rates, Statistics Canada publishes an employment/population ratio. What would trends in such a ratio tell us?

11 Why is it that the seasonally-adjusted level of unemployment is sometimes rising when the actual number of unemployed is falling?

12 Why are the services performed by volunteers not included in the calculation of GDP? Should the work of volunteers be recognized in the National Accounts?

13 It has been argued that the government should provide a pension for homemakers. Why might it be difficult to introduce this proposal? Should the value of housework and the raising of children be included in GDP?

14 Why does a kilogram of beef add more to GDP than a kilogram of potatoes?

15 Why might changes in GDP, when measured in current prices, be a misleading statistic?

16 Some air pollution is the by-product of producing paper. The value of the paper is included in GDP but the air pollution is not. If steps are taken to clean up the pollution, will GDP increase?

17 Which of the following activities would lead to higher prices in Canada?
  i more women entering the labour force
  ii more workers joining labour unions
  iii OPEC setting a higher price for a barrel of oil
  iv the federal government purchasing new aircraft

18 Identify each of the following as either a final good or an intermediate good:
  i a bar of cold-rolled steel
  ii a bag of fertilizer
  iii a pair of shoes
  iv a bag of flour
  v a baseball glove

19 Determine whether or not each of the following is included in GDP:
  i the purchase of building materials by a contractor for the construction of a house
  ii the purchase of building materials by you for the construction of your own house
  iii the sale of vegetables at a local fruit and vegetable stand
  iv growing vegetables in your garden
  v the distribution of food hampers at Christmas by the Salvation Army
  vi a ride on the roller coaster at a local carnival

Suggested Readings

Denton, F.T., A.L. Robb, and B.G. Spencer. *Unemployment and Labour Force Behaviour of Young People: Evidence from Canada and Ontario.* Ontario Economic Council Research Studies. Toronto: University of Toronto Press, 1980.

Gonick, C. *Out of Work.* Toronto: James Lorimer and Co. 1978.

Gunderson, Morley. *Labour Market Economics: Theory, Evidence and Policy in Canada.* Toronto: McGraw-Hill Ryerson 1980.

Robinson, H. Lukin. *Rising Prices.* Toronto: James Lorimer 1978

Trevithick, J.A. *Inflation: A Guide to the Crisis in Economics.* Middlesex: Penguin Books 1978.

Chapter 6

Determination of National Income

Chapter Objectives

After successfully completing this chapter, you will be able to:

- explain equilibrium GDP using the circular flow approach
- use the multiplier formulas to calculate changes in equilibrium GDP
- explain the fiscal policy changes necessary to reach equilibrium GDP
- define the inflationary and recessionary gaps
- explain the paradox of thrift

Key Terms

equilibrium gross domestic product
aggregate demand
aggregate supply
average propensity to consume/save
marginal propensity to consume/save
Keynesian economics
paradox of thrift
expenditure multiplier

tax multiplier
balanced-budget multiplier
foreign-trade multiplier
full-employment GDP
recessionary gap
inflationary gap
Say's Law

Gross Domestic Product

In Chapter 5, the calculation of Canada's National Accounts was reviewed. The most commonly used component of these accounts is gross domestic product (GDP), which refers to the value of goods and services produced in Canada in a given year.

The concept of GDP was first introduced with the aid of a circular flow diagram. Money circulates from the business sector to the household sector in the form of wages, salaries, rent, interest, and profits. This money then returns to the business sector when households purchase goods and services. We measured GDP by the flow of money in the circular flow diagram. If the level of GDP is to change, the flow of money, or the amount of spending in our economy, must change. This chapter discusses the reasons for changes in the level of GDP.

Household Savings and Investment

One way for the amount of spending to change would be for households to increase the amount of money that they save. Households save money by not spending it on goods and services. Savings can be put in a bank or other financial institution, or simply kept at home in a cookie jar. If household savings increase, then the amount of money sent to the business sector in the circular flow (upper loop in figure 5.1) would be reduced. Businesses would react by cutting back on production and forwarding less money to households in the form of wages, interest, and rent. This would reduce the flow of money in the lower loop of the circular flow diagram. Since the flow of money is reduced, the level of GDP is also reduced.

The amount of money in the circular flow would increase if businesses decided to increase their level of investment (spending on machinery and equipment). This increase in spending would increase payments to other businesses, which would, in turn, increase their payments to households. As households receive more income, their spending is likely to increase. As the total level of spending increases, so does the level of GDP.

The procedure of saving money results in a reduction of money in the circular flow, while business investment results in an increase of money in the circular flow. If the overall level of savings is greater than the level of investment, GDP will decrease. If investment exceeds savings, GDP will increase. Finally, if the level of savings and investment are equal, then the level of GDP will not change. This is referred to as **equilibrium GDP** (see figure 6.1). When the amount of money leaving the circular flow is equal to the amount entering the circular flow, the result is an equilibrium, or stable, level of business activity. The term *equilibrium,* first introduced in Chapter 2, refers to a balanced or unchanging position.

GDP is said to be at an equilibrium, or stable, level when aggregate demand equals aggregate supply.

The level of GDP will always be moving toward the equilibrium level. That is, it will always move towards a situation where the amount of money leaving the circular flow is equal to the amount of money coming in. For example, increased savings by households will reduce the flow of income going to the business sector. In turn, businesses will cut back production and lay off workers. The loss of employment reduces the flow of money back to households. With less money available, households will cut back on their spending. With less spending on goods and services, business spending (investment) will also decrease. With less investment, GDP will fall. As GDP drops, households will not be able to save as much, since their incomes will be lower. This process will continue until a new equilibrium level of GDP is reached. This new level, lower than the original level, will be attained when the level of savings and investment again are equal.

Figure 6.1
Equilibrium GDP

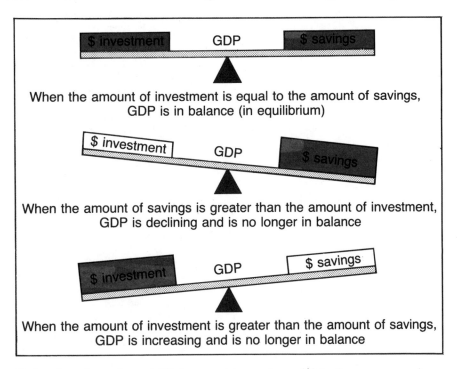

When the amount of investment is equal to the amount of savings, GDP is in balance (in equilibrium)

When the amount of savings is greater than the amount of investment, GDP is declining and is no longer in balance

When the amount of investment is greater than the amount of savings, GDP is increasing and is no longer in balance

Only when investment ($) is equal to savings ($) is the economy in equilibrium.

A point of confusion for students of economics is the source of *investment funds* for business. Where do businesses get the money to spend on machines and equipment? Investment funds can come from one of four sources. First, businesses could use some of their income from sales to purchase new machines from other businesses. Second, they could borrow the money from a bank or other financial institution. Since banks are recipients of household savings, it is quite likely that household savings will be lent out to businesses for investment purposes (see figure 6.2). Savings are taken out of the circular flow and put into financial institutions. When businesses borrow money from these institutions, the money finds its way back into the circular flow. Businesses also borrow money directly from the public by issuing bonds. Third, businesses issue shares in their corporations in order to raise money for investment. Fourth, some investment may come into Canada from outside the country. Decisions by Japanese and Korean automobile manufacturers to locate in Canada are examples of this type of investment.

**Figure 6.2
The circular flow
of money**

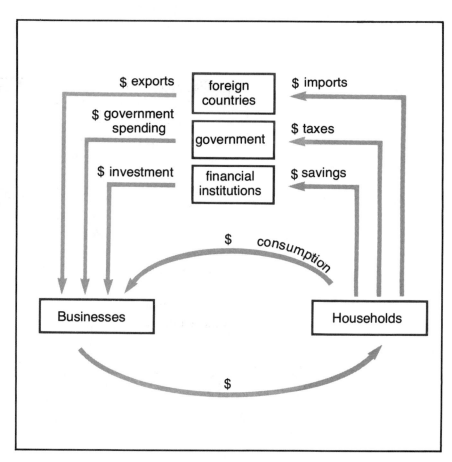

Savings, taxes, and imports represent leakages from the circular flow of money, while investment, government spending, and exports represent injections.

**The Government
and Foreign-Trade
Sectors**

As pointed out in Chapter 5, households and businesses are not the only two participants in the Canadian economy. The government and foreign-trade sectors have also to be considered. Government spending is similar to business investment in its influence on the level of economic activity. Government spends money on equipment and services, and this money (which is paid out to Canadian businesses) will eventually find its way into Canadian households. In order to finance their spending, the various levels of government impose taxes. *Taxation removes money from the circular flow, and government spending puts it back in.*

Sales of goods and services to foreign countries, called *exports,* have the same effect on the level of GDP as do investment and government spending. Foreign purchases represent income for Canadian businesses. Canadian purchases of foreign products, on the other hand, represent a drain on the circular flow of money. These purchases, referred to as *imports,* result in money being paid to foreign businesses rather than to our own. *Exports cause GDP to increase while imports cause GDP to decrease.*

When the total amount of money injected into the circular flow (investment, government spending, and exports) exceeds the leakages from the circular flow (savings, taxation, and imports), the level of GDP will increase. There will be more money circulating in our economy. When the opposite occurs, the level of GDP will decrease. Under circumstances in which the amount of money injected equals the leakages, the level of GDP is in equilibrium.

Condition for equilibrium GDP:

injections ($)	=	leakages ($)
investment (I)+ government spending (G) + exports (E)	=	savings (S) + taxes (T)+ imports (M)

Changes in the level of GDP are also associated with changes in the level of unemployment and inflation. When the level of GDP is increasing, spending is up, jobs are being created, and the unemployment rate is likely to be low. However, when spending is high, the increased demand for goods and services puts pressure on prices, so inflation is likely to result.

We have discovered that whenever the level of spending in the economy changes, the level of GDP changes. What causes spending to change? This question can best be answered by analysing each of the spending components of the economy separately.

6.1 Why do we say that the economy, in terms of GDP, is in equilibrium when savings equals investment?

6.2 Why does the level of GDP always move toward an equilibrium level?

Components of Aggregate Demand

Aggregate demand is the total demand for goods and services in the economy, including consumption, investment, government spending, and exports.

The total level of spending in the Canadian economy is composed of consumption, investment, government spending, and the difference between exports and imports. The total level of spending is referred to as the **aggregate demand** for goods and services produced in Canada.

Consumption

The level of household spending on goods and services is referred to as *consumption*. Some of the factors influencing the level of consumption expenditures are:

Disposable income: possibly the most important determinant of the level of household spending is the level of disposable income. This is the income that remains in the household after taxes have been paid. There is clearly a positive relationship between disposable income and consumption. As disposable income increases, consumption will increase as well.

Interest rates: in order to spend, it may be necessary for some people to borrow money. The decision on whether or not to borrow money often depends on the cost of borrowing. If borrowing costs (interest rates) are high, then spending will probably be reduced. When interest rates are high, households are also encouraged to save money because the return (the interest rate) they get for leaving money in a bank or other financial institution is also high. When interest rates are low, the cost of borrowing is less and the opportunity cost of not saving is also less. Therefore, at low interest rates, consumer spending usually increases.

Wealth: in addition to income, the level of accumulated wealth also influences consumption expenditures. Whereas income can be seen as a flow of money, wealth is seen as a stock or accumulation of money or assets. Wealth can be accumulated and held in many forms: real estate, savings accounts, gold, paintings, and other forms of valuable goods. The greater the accumulation of wealth, the greater the ability to spend, and the higher the level of consumption.

Expectations: a major determinant of household spending is expectation about future prices and future levels of income. If consumers expect prices to increase in the future, they may purchase products now in order to get the product at a lower price. Expectations of future income will also affect spending. If there is a possibility of losing your job, or experiencing a layoff in the near future, you are likely to cut back on your spending and increase your savings. These expectations will cause the total level of consumption to drop.

Psychological: a whole range of psychological factors influences spending. Some families may want to purchase "status" items in order "to keep up with the Joneses." Others may be content with purchasing essential items. Variations in individual tastes and preferences, and in individual motives toward spending, affect consumption. Advertising attempts to persuade households to alter or maintain their consumption habits.

New products: as new products come onto the market, spending patterns may change. The introduction of new products (such as Laserdisc players and VCRs) may change household preferences and alter expenditure plans. The introduction of these products may convince consumers that a change in their lifestyle is required; the money needed to pay for these products may be taken out of savings rather than transferred from other purchases.

Distribution of income: the overall level of consumption in the economy may also be influenced by the distribution of income among households. Whereas high-income families are able to save, poorer families are not able to afford that luxury. Any shift in the distribution of income away from high-income households to low-income households may increase the total level of consumption. Certain government transfer programs redistribute income in favour of lower-income groups (see Chapter 4), and thus influence the overall level of consumption spending.

Prices: prices and price changes are likely to influence the level of consumer spending. It is difficult to assess the effect that price changes will have on spending, since other factors are also involved in the decision to spend money. In some cases, households may cut back in response to price increases. In other cases, they may increase present spending, if it is expected that prices will rise even higher.

Demographic factors: several demographic factors are bound to influence consumption. These include age, sex, race, family size, level of education, occupation, and location of residence.

Of the factors listed above, it is believed that *disposable income* is the most important. We will, therefore, concentrate on the positive relationship between *consumption* and *income*.

The Consumption Schedule

Table 6.1 presents various levels of disposable income, consumption, and savings for similar-sized families. These figures are arbitrary and are only meant to serve as an example. The table shows positive relationships between the levels of consumption and of disposable income. As the level of income increases, the level of consumption increases as well. Savings are also positively related to disposable income. In this particular example, a hypothetical family of four would break even with an income of $40 000 per year. At this level of disposable income, the family is consuming $40 000 worth of goods and services and saving nothing. At levels of disposable income below $40 000, families are in fact "dissaving" (that is, their spending, or consumption, is greater than their disposable income). The money needed to pay for this spending must come out of accumulated savings or else must be borrowed. In these situations, the level of consumption exceeds the level of disposable income. Positive savings levels appear at incomes above $40 000 per year. For example, at a disposable income of $50 000, this family manages to save $5000 per year.

Table 6.1 / Levels of disposable income, consumption, and savings for hypothetical families of four

Disposable income $/year	Consumption $	Savings $	APC	APS	MPC	MPS
20 000	26 000	-6000	1.3	- 0.3	-	-
30 000	34 000	-4000	1.13	- 0.13	0.8	0.2
40 000	40 000	0	1.0	0	0.6	0.4
50 000	45 000	5000	0.9	0.1	0.5	0.5
60 000	48 000	12 000	0.8	0.2	0.3	0.7

APC = average propensity to consume
APS = average propensity to save
MPC = marginal propensity to consume
MPS = marginal propensity to save

The average propensity to consume (APC) represents the ratio of consumption to income (or gross domestic product).

The average propensity to save (APS) represents the ratio of savings to income (or gross domestic product).

From the table, it is possible to calculate two additional statistics that relate consumption to income. The **average propensity to consume (APC)** is the ratio of total consumption to total income. For example, the average propensity to consume (APC) for a family earning $50 000 per year is 0.9. This family is spending $45 000 per year or 90 percent of its income. The **average propensity to save (APS)** is the ratio of savings to disposable income. Since there are only two things that can be done with one's income—to consume it and/or to save it—the average propensity to save (APS) for a family earning $25 000 per year is 0.1, or ten percent.

$$\text{average propensity to consume (APC)} = \frac{\text{consumption}}{\text{disposable income}}$$

$$\text{average propensity to save (APS)} = \frac{\text{savings}}{\text{disposable income}}$$

$$\text{APC} + \text{APS} = 1.0$$

The marginal propensity to consume (MPC) represents the proportion of any increase in income that is used for consumption.

More important than the concept of average propensities is the concept of *marginal propensities,* which refers to the change in consumption resulting from a change in disposable income. According to table 6.1, a family of four with an income of $50 000 per year has a **marginal propensity to consume (MPC)** of 0.5. The calculation can be made by looking at what would happen to consumption if a family's income increased from $40 000 to $50 000 per year. Consumption would increase from $40 000 to $45 000, representing an increase in consumption of $5000 per year. Fifty percent of the increase in disposable income went for consumption spending. The **marginal propensity to save (MPS)** relates changes in the level of savings to the changes in the level of income.

The marginal propensity to save (MPS) represents the proportion of any increase in income that is used for savings.

$$\text{marginal propensity to consume (MPC)} = \frac{\text{change in consumption}}{\text{change in income}}$$

$$\text{marginal propensity to save (MPS)} = \frac{\text{change in savings}}{\text{change in income}}$$

By definition,
$$\text{MPC} + \text{MPS} = 1.0$$

As indicated in table 6.1, it is expected that the MPC would decline as the level of income increases. Those families in the higher income brackets can afford the luxury of saving more of any increase in income. Those in the lower income categories may need to consume almost all of any increase in income and can afford to save very little. Empirical studies have shown that although the MPC is slightly lower for higher-income Canadians, the difference in MPCs between income groups is not very great. Several studies have estimated the MPC for Canadians. The value of the MPC for Canada for the years 1961–1985 was estimated by Statistics Canada to be 0.77.

6.3 Discuss five factors that influence the level of consumer spending.

6.4 If your disposable income went up by $6000 per year and you increased your spending by $4000, what would be your marginal propensity to consume? To save?

Savings: Canada versus the United States

Canadians have always been known as big savers. The percentage of disposable income Canadians save exceeds that saved in many other industrialized countries. In 1991, Canadians saved over ten percent of their after-tax income. The comparable figure in the United States was a little over four percent. Why is the level of savings so high in Canada?

Some analysts have concluded that the higher rate of unemployment in Canada encouraged more precautionary savings on the part of Canadians. The high rate of inflation at the time convinced consumers to postpone spending. The high interest rates paid on savings accounts also encouraged people to save money. Although this seems like a logical response to the situation, Americans did not react in the same manner to their high rates of inflation and high interest rates. Why are Canadians and Americans different in terms of saving money?

Part of the answer lies in the differing income-tax regulations in each country. During the 1970s, Canada introduced several incentives for savings in the Income Tax Act. These included the Registered Retirement Savings Plan (RRSP) and the Registered Home Ownership Savings Plan (RHOSP). Both plans enabled individuals to reduce the amount of tax payable if savings were deposited to one of these registered plans. Another change to Canada's Income Tax Act allowed Canadians to earn a certain amount of interest on their savings before the interest became taxable.

By contrast, the American income-tax system was, until recently, geared more toward spending. For example, Americans were allowed to deduct the interest charges on mortgages, bank cards, other general-purpose credit cards, and charge accounts from their taxable income. Now, only the interest payments on mortgages are tax deductible. Residents of the U.S. can now reduce their taxable income by putting money into Individual Retirement Accounts. These accounts, which are similar to Canadian RRSPs, encourage savings.

Another reason for the higher level of savings in Canada may be the approach to paying for social services like medical care. In Canada, a higher percentage of medical costs are paid for out of tax dollars than in the United States. Medical care is basically a private expense in the United States. Since Canadians have already paid for these services through taxes, they can afford the luxury of saving more of their after-tax income.

In recent years, the higher level of savings in Canada has been attributed to the fact that real interest rates have been higher in Canada, than in the U.S. Real interest rates are determined by subtracting the rate of inflation from the nominal, or actual, rate of interest.

Questions

1 What group of Canadians would benefit most from RRSP plans? Why?
2 Why would Americans have been more willing to borrow money in the past for consumer purchases than Canadians?
3 What would be the effect on the economy if the government took steps to encourage more Canadian savings?

Investment   Investment is defined as business purchases of machines and equipment, new housing construction, and any change in business inventories. It is the most volatile component of GDP and is also the most difficult to predict. There are two major reasons for this. First, many investment decisions are based on business expectations about the future. Quite often these expectations are subjective in nature and open to change. Second, there are several variables that influence the level of investment spending. Changes in any of these variables alter investment spending. These variables are:

The interest rate: in order to purchase new equipment many businesses are forced to borrow money. High borrowing costs, or interest rates, are likely to discourage borrowing and, therefore, to reduce the level of investment spending. Some equipment purchases may be regarded as only marginally profitable and if interest rates are too high, these projects will be abandoned. On the other hand, lower interest rates may encourage spending on projects that were not feasible at the higher interest rates.

Innovation and changes in technology: as new products are developed, companies may want to purchase them in order to improve the efficiency of their operation. For example, the introduction of the laptop, the personal computer, and word-processing equipment has revolutionized office procedures. In order to be able to compete, companies are forced continually to update their equipment and methods of operation.

Government policy and taxes: many government policies affect business spending. For example, rent controls may reduce the number of new apartment buildings being constructed. An excise tax on a product, which increases the price, will influence consumer demand and, ultimately, business investment. Changes in the Income Tax Act may change the conditions under which businesses can depreciate capital purchases. The switch from the Foreign Investment Review Agency (FIRA) to Investment Canada has changed the image of Canada from a foreign investor's point of view. These decisions and others will have an impact on investment. The philosophy of the political party in power can also influence investment. Investors will be more willing to spend money if the government in power leans toward the free market approach rather than one advocating government control in order to solve economic problems.

Expectations: expectations about the future business environment influence spending. Changes in the level of sales, profits, and GDP affect business expectations about the future. For example, if GDP was forecasted to increase significantly, companies would expect their sales to increase. If sales are expected to increase, investment will increase. Conversely, expectations about depressed economic conditions will reduce the level of investment.

Replacements: in the process of producing goods and services, some equipment will wear out and have to be replaced. The spending required to replace this equipment is investment. Some economists believe that spending on replacement equipment is the major reason for the fluctuations in investment and ultimately in GDP.

Cost of capital goods: as with the purchase of any product, the price is also important. Price increases would tend to discourage the purchase of new equipment.

Gross domestic product: when GDP increases, it is an indication that the total level of income in the economy is increasing. If total income is increasing, spending is increasing, and companies will need to buy more equipment in order to be able to keep up with the increased demand. Investment spending will be required unless business already has unused productive capacity.

Government and Foreign Trade

The third component of aggregate demand is government spending. In order to carry out its mandate, government spends money on goods and services in a manner similar to any other business. The variables that influence the level of government spending were discussed in Chapter 4. The final component of aggregate demand is the difference between exports and imports. The factors that influence Canada's foreign trade will be discussed in detail in Chapter 9.

Aggregate Demand Curve

In Chapter 2, we learned that a demand curve for a specific product or service is drawn with the price of the product or service on the vertical axis and the quantity on the horizontal axis. We can draw a demand curve for all products in much the same manner. The aggregate demand curve (**AD**) is shown in figure 6.3. On the vertical axis the price level for all products is measured. On the horizontal axis is real gross domestic product (**RGDP**).

Why use real gross domestic product instead of quantity on the horizontal axis? Actually, RGDP is a measure of quantity. As stated in Chapter 5, GDP is a measure of the flow of money from the business sector in our economy to the household sector. It is a measure of the total amount of income earned in our economy in a given year. It is also a measure of the total amount of goods and services produced. Since we cannot add up bushels of apples, tons of steel, houses sold, lawns cut, and so on, we convert all these products and services to money. Adding them up in money terms provides us with GDP. Because GDP is a measure of production, it can be used as a measure of quantity in deriving the aggregate demand curve.

**Figure 6.3
Aggregate
demand and
aggregate
supply**

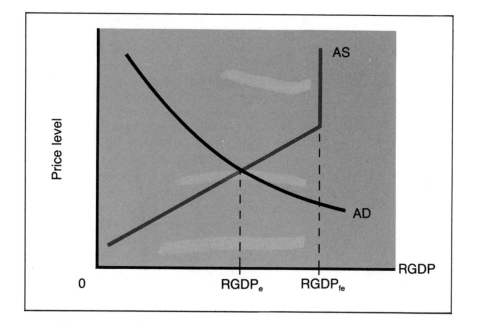

The aggregate demand curve (AD) shows an inverse relationship
between the price level and RGDP, whereas the aggregate supply
curve shows a positive relationship.

Because price increases alone can result in an increase in GDP, an
adjustment for price increases is necessary so that GDP will adequately
reflect the amount of goods and services produced. Adjusting GDP for
price increases gives us real gross domestic product (RGDP).

The aggregate demand curve (AD) is similar to the individual
demand curves introduced earlier. As the price level increases, the
quantity of goods and services demanded, represented by RGDP, decreases. As the price level falls, RGDP increases. Individual demand
curves shift when one of the factors influencing demand, other than
the price, changes. Similarly, the aggregate demand curve will shift
when one of the components of aggregate demand changes. For example, if businesses decide to increase the level of investment spending, then the AD curve will shift to the right. If consumers decide to
increase the amount of their savings, the AD curve will shift to the left.

Aggregate Supply

*Aggregate supply is the
total production of goods
and services available in
the economy over a cer-
tain period of time.*

In order to discuss the concept of equilibrium gross domestic product, it
is necessary to introduce the concept of **aggregate supply.** Aggregate
supply represents the summation of all the individual supply curves in the
economy. The aggregate supply curve (**AS**) is shown in figure 6.3. It

bears a resemblance to the market supply curves introduced in Chapter 2. The price level is measured on the vertical axis. The horizontal axis measures quantity in terms of real gross domestic product (**RGDP**). In a fashion similar to individual market supply curves, the aggregate supply curve (**AS**) shows a positive relationship between price and quantity supply. As the price level increases, the quantity of goods and services produced increases as well. The AS curve, however, does not continue to increase indefinitely. There is a physical limit to the amount of goods and services that Canadians can produce. This maximum is shown in figure 6.3 as **RGDP$_{fe}$**, which represents the production of goods and services that would be possible if all available resources were fully employed. **RGDP$_{fe}$** refers to the full employment level of real gross domestic product.

Apart from price change, what determines the level of aggregate supply in our economy? It is primarily determined by the quantity and quality of resources available. An introduction to Canada's resources was presented in the first chapter of this text. *The more resources (land, labour, and capital) available to Canadians, the greater the amount of goods and services produced.*

The quantity and quality of land will determine Canada's ability to supply goods and services (the definition of this resource is in Chapter 1). Land means more than square kilometres; it includes such natural resources as minerals, wild animals, vegetation, and water.

Human resources are also necessary for production. Increases in the population will normally lead to increases in the labour force. Changes in labour-force participation rates, such as those discussed in Chapter 5, may also increase the size of the labour force.

The productivity of our resources also influences production levels. If members of Canada's labour force receive better instruction, better training, and better education, they will be more productive. If management techniques are updated and improved, increases in productivity will occur. Improvements in technology will also result in increased production.

If businesses invest in new factories, machinery, and equipment, our capital resources will increase. If businesses fail to invest, then our capital resources may be reduced as existing machinery and equipment wears out. Business investment not only represents a major component of aggregate demand, but has a significant impact on aggregate supply as well.

Government regulation may also influence aggregate supply. Many Canadian industries are strictly controlled by government in terms of the number of companies allowed to operate in the industry. Examples of such industries are telephone, cable television, and natural gas. In agriculture, the number of producers of eggs, chickens, tobacco, milk, and turkeys is also restricted by marketing boards. Alternatively, government may also act in order to increase aggregate supply. Tax changes may make it more attractive for businesses to increase production. Government promotions like those being undertaken by Investment Canada may encourage more foreign companies to locate in Canada.

Equilibrium Gross Domestic Product

Equilibrium in an individual market is achieved at the price level at which the quantity demanded and the quantity supplied are equal. A similar situation occurs with aggregate demand and aggregate supply. The level of RGDP at which they are equal is referred to as equilibrium RGDP (figure 6.3). At this level of economic activity there is no need for RGDP to change. The amount of goods and services demanded will be equal to the amount of goods and services supplied. Once achieved, the equilibrium level of RGDP will only change when either AD or AS changes.

If RGDP is not at equilibrium, how does it get there? Assume that the level of aggregate demand was greater than the level of aggregate supply. This is shown as **RGDP$_1$** in figure 6.4. In this situation, inventories would be depleted and suppliers would need to increase production in order to meet the demand. As new employees are hired and new machinery put into use, production levels will increase. Real gross domestic product will increase. If the level of aggregate supply were greater than the level of aggregate demand (as shown by **RGDP$_2$** in figure 6.4) inventories would begin to accumulate. Companies would cut back on production and lay off employees. The level of gross domestic product would decline. Only at a level of RGDP where AS and AD are equal **(RGDP$_e$)** would the economy be in equilibrium. That is, only at this level of economic activity would the total level of spending and the total level of production remain the same.

How does the equilibrium level of RGDP change? Anything that would cause aggregate demand or aggregate supply to change would change the equilibrium level of RGDP. For example, if consumers decide to increase their spending on goods and services, the AD curve will shift to the right (**AD^2** in figure 6.5). At the present level of equilibrium, **RGDP$_1$**, the aggregate demand now exceeds aggregate supply. This circumstance will cause production to increase and the RGDP to rise until it reaches **RGDP$_2$.** Conversely, a drop in aggregate demand caused by a decline in investment would shift the AD curve to the left. This would cause the level of equilibrium RGDP to decline.

**Figure 6.4
Equilibrium real
gross domestic
product**

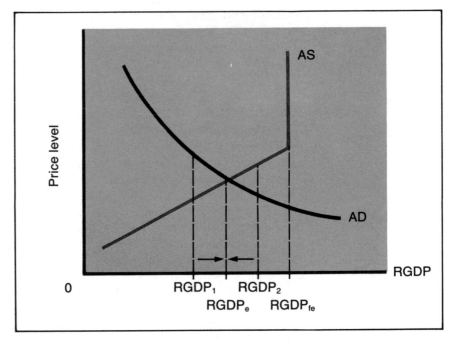

Equilibrium real gross domestic product occurs where the aggregate demand and aggregate supply curves intersect.

**Figure 6.5
Changes in the
equilibrium level
of real gross
domestic
product**

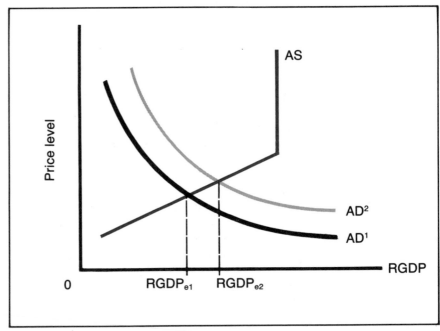

An increase in aggregate demand will increase the level of equilibrium RGDP.

Paradox of Thrift

The paradox of thrift states that an increase in the level of savings in the economy can lead to lower levels of income, and ultimately, to lower levels of savings.

An interesting aspect of the consequences of saving is the **paradox of thrift.** According to the dictionary, a paradox is "a statement that appears to be contradictory, but in fact may be true." The contradiction in relation to savings is that by attempting to save more, we may end up saving less. The result would be a lower level of equilibrium RGDP. As RGDP moved toward this new equilibrium level, the total income earned in Canada would begin to decline. Some people would only be able to work part-time, some would experience lay-offs, and others would simply lose their jobs. As the level of income in Canada fell, the ability of Canadians to save money would fall as well.

In terms of the circular flow of money diagram (figure 6.2), when households decide to increase their savings, less money will circulate to the business sector. In turn, businesses pay out less money to households in the form of wages, rent, interest, and profits. With a reduced level of income, households will not be able to save as much. As a result, the total level of savings would be reduced.

The paradox of thrift only applies if a significant number of people decide to increase their savings. If only a few people decide to save more, then there will be a negligible impact on gross domestic product, and on the total level of savings. It should be noted that not everyone will suffer a reduced level of savings. Some individuals may not suffer a drop in income when the level of gross domestic product declines. Civil servants are an example of people whose incomes do not depend on the level of business activity or, more specifically, on the sales and profits of their company.

6.5 Why is RGDP a better indicator of the amount of goods and services produced than GDP?

6.6 What factors might cause the aggregate demand curve to shift to the right?

6.7 If AS is greater than AD at the current level of RGDP, will the level of RGDP move toward equilibrium? Explain.

6.8 In your own words explain the paradox of thrift.

The Multiplier

What impact do changes in aggregate demand have on GDP? Any increase in aggregate demand will cause GDP to increase because GDP is a measure of the total level of spending in the economy. By how much will the level of GDP increase? Surprisingly, the level of GDP increases by more than the initial increase in aggregate demand.

The Expenditure Multiplier

Assume that you decide to spend $1000 on some new stereo equipment. What is the impact on GDP? Your initial spending will cause GDP to increase by $1000. Your spending also represents income to the owner of the stereo shop. The owner may spend some of that money on other purchases. The amount that the owner spends depends on his or her marginal propensity to consume (MPC). Another person will be the recipient of this spending and will, in turn, spend part of what he or she receives. Every time that spending takes place, GDP increases. In fact, your decision to spend $1000 on a stereo has started a chain reaction that results in an increase in the level of GDP of more than $1000. How much more? The ultimate impact on GDP can be shown as follows:

$$\Delta \text{ GDP} = \$1000$$
$$+ (\text{MPC}) \text{ x } \$1000$$
$$+ (\text{MPC}) \, (\text{MPC}) \text{ x } \$1000$$
$$+ (\text{MPC}) \, (\text{MPC}) \, (\text{MPC}) \text{ x } \$1000$$
$$+ \ldots \ldots \ldots$$

This formula assumes that everyone has exactly the same MPC, and spends the same percentage of any increase in income. It is possible to add up these expenditures using a short mathematical formula. This formula is known as *the sum of a geometric progression.* Assume that the MPC is equal to 0.8.

$$\Delta \text{ GDP} = \Delta \text{ AD} \times \frac{1}{1 - \text{MPC}} \text{ (where } \Delta \text{ means "change in")}$$

$$\Delta \text{ GDP} = \$1000 \times \frac{1}{1 - 0.8}$$

$$\Delta \text{ GDP} = \$1000 \times \frac{1}{0.2}$$

$$\Delta \text{ GDP} = \$1000 \times 5$$

$$\Delta \text{ GDP} = \$5000$$

The expenditure multiplier is the amount by which a change in aggregate demand is multiplied in order to determine the change in GDP.

Your initial decision to spend $1000 could have the effect of increasing the level of GDP by $5000, since GDP measures the total amount of spending in our economy. This is referred to as the **expenditure multiplier.** The change in spending (ΔAD) is multiplied by an amount $\frac{1}{1 - \text{MPC}}$ in order to determine the final effect on GDP. The formula used above is referred to as *the multiplier formula.*

The multiplier formula can also be used when a decrease in spending or in aggregate demand occurs. The impact of a decrease in consumer spending of $7000 on GDP is shown as follows:

$$\triangle \text{ GDP} = \triangle \text{ AD} \times \frac{1}{1 - \text{MPC}}$$

$$\triangle \text{ GDP} = -\$7000 \times \frac{1}{1 - 0.8}$$

$$\triangle \text{ GDP} = -\$7000 \times \frac{1}{0.2}$$

$$\triangle \text{ GDP} = -\$7000 \times 5$$

$$\triangle \text{ GDP} = -\$35\ 000$$

A cut in consumer spending of $7000 led to a decrease in GDP of $35 000. When consumers reduce their spending, less money circulates in the business sector. Less money is then paid out in wages and salaries, and then a further reduction in spending takes place. Ultimately GDP is reduced by $35 000. This example used a MPC of 0.8. If another MPC were used the reduction in GDP would be different. For example, if the MPC were 0.75, then the reduction in GDP would have been $28 000.

6.9 What would be the impact on GDP if consumer spending increased by $1000 and the MPC was 0.75? What would your answer be if the MPC was 0.50?

6.10 What would be the effect on GDP if the business sector decided to increase its spending by $20 million? Assume an MPC of 0.75.

6.11 The multiplier concept works in reverse as well. A decrease in spending will cause GDP to fall by a multiple amount. Can you explain why?

The Tax Multiplier

The tax multiplier is the amount by which any change in the level of taxation must be multiplied by to determine the resulting impact on GDP.

Government tax changes have a multiple effect on GDP. If government lowers the rate of tax, consumers and businesses have more money to spend; this increased spending has a multiple effect on GDP. The effect resulting from the **tax multiplier** is slightly different from the one shown by the expenditure multiplier. Some of the reduction in taxes will not be spent by households, but will be saved. Therefore, the initial increase in spending resulting from a tax reduction will not be equal to the initial reduction in taxes. Since a reduction in taxes affects savings, tax changes do not have the same impact on GDP as do changes in government or other spending. When taxes are increased, some of the money paid in taxes will come out of savings. For example, what would be the effect of a $20 million tax reduction on the level of GDP? Assume that the MPC is 0.75. If $20 million is returned to the public in the form of tax reductions, $5 million will be saved and $15 million will be spent. The effect of an increase of $15 million in spending on GDP is as follows:

$$\Delta \text{ GDP} = (\text{MPC}) \times \$15$$
$$+ (\text{MPC})(\text{MPC}) \times \$15$$
$$+ (\text{MPC})(\text{MPC})(\text{MPC}) \times \$15$$
$$+ \ldots \ldots \ldots$$

Again, this can be added up by the use of a formula. The formula is:

$$\Delta \text{ GDP} = - \left[\Delta \text{ taxes} \times \frac{\text{MPC}}{1 - \text{MPC}} \right]$$

$$\Delta \text{ GDP} = - \left[-\$20 \times \frac{0.75}{1 - 0.75} \right]$$

$$\Delta \text{ GDP} = - \left[-\$20 \times \frac{0.75}{0.25} \right]$$

$$\Delta \text{ GDP} = -[-\$20 \times 3]$$

$$\Delta \text{ GDP} = -[-\$60 \text{ million}]$$

$$\Delta \text{ GDP} = +\$60 \text{ million}$$

The reduction in tax revenues of $20 million had a positive effect of $60 million on GDP. If government had increased the level of taxes rather than decreased them, GDP would decline. The same formula would be used to determine the impact of a tax increase. The formula used to calculate the effect of a tax change on GNP is called the tax multiplier formula.

6.12 What is the impact on GDP of a $10 million increase in taxes? Assume that the MPC is 0.8.

6.13 Which has more impact on the economy—a $20 million increase in government spending or a $20 million decrease in taxes? Use the expenditure and tax multipliers in your answer.

Balanced-Budget Multiplier

Often government increases in tax revenues are used to finance increases in government spending. Increases in taxes tend to decrease the level of GDP, while government spending tends to increase the level of GDP. In order to determine the combined effect of these measures, assume that the government increased taxes by $10 million and then spent the $10 million on job-creation programs. If the MPC is 0.8, the impact will be as follows:

$$\triangle \text{GDP} = -\left[\triangle \text{ taxes} \times \frac{\text{MPC}}{1 - \text{MPC}}\right]$$

$$\triangle \text{GDP} = -\left[\$10 \times \frac{0.8}{1 - 0.8}\right]$$

$$\triangle \text{GDP} = -\left[\$10 \times \frac{0.8}{0.2}\right]$$

$$\triangle \text{GDP} = -[\$10 \times 4]$$

$$\triangle \text{GDP} = -\ \$40$$

The impact of government spending is then as follows:

$$\triangle \text{GDP} = \triangle \text{ spending} \times \frac{1}{1 - \text{MPC}}$$

$$\triangle \text{GDP} = \$10 \times \frac{1}{1 - 0.8}$$

$$\triangle \text{GDP} = \$10 \times \frac{1}{0.2}$$

$$\triangle \text{GDP} = \$10 \times 5$$

$$\triangle \text{GDP} = \$50$$

The balanced-budget multiplier is the amount by which an equal increase in taxes and in government spending increases GDP.

The increase in taxes had the effect of reducing GDP by $40 million. The subsequent increase in spending had the effect of increasing GDP by $50 million. The net effect on GDP is, therefore, an increase of $10 million. This is referred to as the **balanced-budget multiplier,** since the increase in taxes and the increase in government spending were the same amount. The government has balanced the books and GDP has increased by $10 million. When taxes are paid, some of the money comes from a reduction in savings. The government then spends this money along with the money that households would have spent, yet gave up in taxes. The government is spending your savings. When taxes are reduced, the opposite occurs. Not all of the additional money that households receive from tax deductions will be spent. Some of it will find its way into savings. Therefore, if the government is interested in stimulating the economy, a greater stimulus is provided by government spending rather than by reducing taxes.

Government policy that changes expenditures and taxation in order to influence the level of economic activity in Canada is referred to as *fiscal policy.* At the federal government level, fiscal policy is the responsibility of the Department of Finance.

6.14 What is the net effect on GDP of government increasing taxes and spending by $50 million? Assume that the MPC is 0.5.

Foreign-Trade Multiplier

The *expenditure,* or *spending, multiplier* $\dfrac{1}{1 - MPC}$ is the number that any change in spending is multiplied by in order to determine the ultimate effect on GDP. Our previous discussion of the multiplier omitted the impact of exports and imports on the level of GDP. Canada, however, is a major participant in international trade and so it is necessary to discuss this impact. This discussion will require an adjustment to the expenditure multiplier formula.

In our earlier discussion of the multiplier, we assumed that an individual had only two choices in handling money. It could be spent (consumed) or saved. Any increase in income had to be allocated to these choices. International trade is a third element involved in the allocation of money. Households can spend some of their income on imports. This money acts as a leakage in the circular flow. Money spent on imports is not returned to Canadian businesses and is not paid out in wages, rent, or interest to Canadian households. The spending of money on imports reduces the impact of the spending multiplier on GDP. A numerical example will help in the explanation.

Assume MPC = 0.8,   MPS = 0.2, $\triangle$ AD = $100.

$$\triangle GDP = \triangle AD \times \frac{1}{1 - MPC}$$

$$\triangle GDP = \$100 \times \frac{1}{1 - 0.8}$$

$$\triangle GDP = \$100 \times \frac{1}{0.2}$$

$$\triangle GDP = \$100 \times 5$$

$$\triangle GDP = \$500$$

Without taking into consideration the foreign-trade sector, an increase in spending of $100 leads to a $500 increase in GDP. Now let us introduce international trade into our models. If one's income can now be spent on imports, the concept of *marginal propensity to import* (MPM) has to be introduced.

$$\text{marginal propensity to import (MPM)} = \frac{\triangle \text{ imports}}{\triangle \text{ income}}$$

Previously,
     MPC + MPS = 1

Now,
     MPC + MPS + MPM = 1

The introduction of MPM has reduced the value of MPC since some of the money previously spent on domestic items is now spent on imports. Making changes to our example, assume

MPC = 0.6,   MPS = 0. 2,   and, MPM = 0.2

Now,

$$\triangle GDP = \$100 \times \frac{1}{1 - 0.6}$$

$$\triangle GDP = \$100 \times \frac{1}{0.4}$$

$$\triangle GDP = \$100 \times 2.5$$

$$\triangle GDP = \$250$$

The foreign-trade multiplier is the amount by which a change in aggregate demand is multiplied to determine the change in GDP while taking into account the impact of foreign trade.

When international trade is inserted into the model, the resulting increase in GDP is only $250. Therefore, the multiplier effect on total spending when using the **foreign-trade multiplier** is not as great as it was without taking into consideration international trade.

The multiplier $\dfrac{1}{1 - MPC}$ can be rewritten $\dfrac{1}{MPS + MPM}$

since,

MPC + MPS + MPM = 1.

Questions
1 Why does the introduction of foreign trade to the circular flow cause the value of the multiplier to be reduced?
2 What is the change in GDP that results from an increase in government spending of $2 million? Assume MPC = 0.5, MPS = 0.4, and MPM = 0.1.

Full-Employment GDP

The level of aggregate demand in the economy required to ensure that everyone who wants to work can work is called full-employment GDP.

The amount that aggregate demand must increase in order to bring the equilibrium level of GDP up to a full-employment level is the recessionary gap.

As shown in Figure 6.4, it may be possible for the equilibrium level of GDP (**RGDP$_e$**) to be less than the **full employment level of GDP** (**RGDP$_{fe}$**). If this situation exists, then all the resources available to Canadians are not being fully utilized. Some land and equipment remains idle while some workers remain unemployed. Because full employment is a desirable objective, it is necessary to increase the level of aggregate demand so that equilibrium GDP will occur at a full-employment level. The AD curve must shift to the right in order to intersect the AS curve at **RGDP$_{fe}$**. The amount that aggregate demand has to increase in order to raise equilibrium GDP to a full-employment level is referred to as the **recessionary gap.**

We can use the expenditure multiplier in order to measure the size of the deflationary gap. Assume that the equilibrium level of GDP is $400 billion and that **RGDP$_{fe}$** is $450 billion. In other words, if **RGDP$_e$** were $450 billion, there would be enough spending in the economy to provide everyone with a job. Under these conditions, what increase in aggregate demand is necessary in order to achieve full employment? If it is desirable to increase the level of GDP by $50 billion, the expenditure-multiplier formula can be used in order to determine the necessary increase in aggregate demand.

$$\triangle \text{ GDP } = \triangle \text{ AD } \times \frac{1}{1 - \text{MPC}} \text{ (assume MPC } = 0.75)$$

$$\$50 = \triangle \text{ AD } \times \frac{1}{1 - 0.75}$$

$$\$50 = \triangle \text{ AD } \times \frac{1}{0.25}$$

$$\$50 = \triangle \text{ AD } \times 4$$

$$\$12.5 = \triangle \text{ AD}$$

An increase in aggregate demand of $12.5 billion is sufficient to raise the equilibrium level of GDP from $400 billion to $450 billion. The size of the recessionary gap is therefore $12.5 billion.

What reduction in taxes would accomplish the same thing? Using the tax multiplier formula we can show that a $16.67 billion reduction in taxes will result in an increase in GDP of $50 billion. Remember that a greater reduction in taxes than an increase in spending is necessary to bring about the same increase in GDP. Some of the tax reduction will be saved and thus will not circulate in the economy.

$$\triangle \text{ GDP } = - \left[\triangle \text{ taxes } \times \frac{\text{MPC}}{1 - \text{MPC}} \right]$$

$$\$50 = - \left[\triangle \text{ taxes } \times \frac{0.75}{1 - 0.75} \right]$$

$$\$50 = - \left[\triangle \text{ taxes } \times \frac{0.75}{0.25} \right]$$

$$\$50 = - \ [\triangle \text{ taxes } \times 3]$$

$$\frac{\$50}{3} = - \triangle \text{ taxes}$$

$$- \$16.67 = \triangle \text{ taxes}$$

If it is possible for Canadians not to be spending enough money in order to guarantee full employment, is it possible for them to spend too much? Yes, it is possible. If the limit on aggregate supply has been reached, then any further increases in aggregate demand will not increase the amount of goods and services produced. The increases in aggregate demand at this point will only lead to price increases. Once full employment has been reached, increases in aggregate demand will not cause RGDP to increase but will cause the current dollar value of GDP to go up. In order to reduce these inflationary pressures, it would be necessary for the level of aggregate demand to decrease. The reduction in aggregate demand necessary to reduce the level of aggregate demand and still maintain full employment is referred to as the **inflationary gap.** The inflationary gap could be eliminated through either a reduction in spending or an increase in taxes.

The decrease in the level of aggregate demand required to bring the equilibrium level of GDP down to the full-employment level of GDP is referred to as the inflationary gap.

Say's Law and John Maynard Keynes

Say's law states that the supply of products creates its own demand, since all production creates income for households that can be spent on goods and services.

Prior to the 1930s, economists tended to accept the writings on economics of a French economist, J.B. Say. **Say's law** stated that supply creates its own demand. The process of producing goods and services resulted in incomes being paid out to those who contributed to the product process. Say held that this income would always be sufficient to buy what was produced. The theory relied on the flexibility of wages and prices. That is, if there was an over-supply of products, prices would fall and stimulate the consumption of these products. Say's law also assumed that there were no household savings because households spent, or consumed, all of their income. The consequence of Say's law was that there would be no involuntary unemployment. A person was only out of work if he or she chose to be.

The Great Depression of the 1930s pointed out the weakness of Say's law. Levels of production fell and unemployment rose dramatically. The automatic correction of Say's law did not take place. During the 1930s, the writings of a British economist, John Maynard Keynes, began to receive more acceptance. In fact, his book, *The General Theory of Employment, Interest and Money,* has been referred to as the most influential book of the twentieth century.

Keynesian economic theory proposes that government take an active role in the economy, increasing government spending in order to support the demand for goods and services and, therefore, to preserve employment.

It was Keynes' view that the demand for goods and services had to be maintained in order to keep the economy out of a recession. If households decide to save more money, they will spend less and the overall demand for goods and services will be lower. If this demand is not sufficient to provide everyone with a job, it is the responsibility of the government to provide the necessary spending. *Keynes believed that government should take an active role in economic matters.*

The advent of World War II gave support to Keynes' ideas. The need for massive government spending in the war effort stimulated the economy and reduced the level of unemployment that had prevailed throughout much of the 1930s. After the war, many Western governments assumed the responsibility for overall economic conditions in their countries and adopted many of the teachings of Keynes. The economic theories presented in this chapter are often referred to as **Keynesian economics.**

6.15   Will increases in government spending be sufficient to provide everybody with a job? In your answer consider the types of unemployment discussed in Chapter 5.

The Great Depression

The year 1989 was the 60th anniversary of the Great Depression. The depression years were characterized by declining levels of economic activity, by a high unemployment rate, and by the inability of government to take the proper corrective action.

The Great Depression is said to have started on 29 October 1929, known as "Black Tuesday." On this day, stock prices declined drastically on the New York Stock Exchange. The drop in stock prices did not cause the depression to occur, but presaged the downward trend in economic conditions.

The years leading up to 1929 were good, from an economic point of view. In 1927, real GNP grew by 9.5 percent in Canada, and in 1928, it grew by 9.1 percent. The unemployment rate in those years was estimated to be only two or three percent of the labour force. By 1933, real GNP in Canada had declined by 30 percent. In fact, it was to take ten years before the level of real GNP regained the 1929 level. The unemployment situation was drastic. In 1933, the unemployment rate had increased to an estimated 19 percent of the labour force. This figure is only an estimate and many believe that it is too low.

Initial government attempts to deal with the situation were not successful. The government did not initiate spending increases to make up for the decline in spending on the part of consumers, businesses, and foreigners. One attempt by government to solve the crisis was to increase the tariff (tax) on imported products. If imported products became more expensive, consumers would be forced to buy Canadian products and thus preserve Canadian jobs. This approach had two problems. First, if Canadians did not purchase foreign products, foreigners did not have the money to purchase Canadian products. Second, other countries reacted to high tariffs by increasing their own tariff rates. This tended to reduce international trade and prolong the depression by decreasing the level of spending around the world.

Increases in spending were necessary to lift the Western industrialized countries out of the economic doldrums. These increases were proposed by Keynes. It was his belief that government should initiate these spending increases, even if it meant that government had to go into debt in order to get the money. Keynes' ideas received increased support during World War II, when the spending necessary for the war effort stimulated economic activity and reduced the levels of unemployment.

Has Canada experienced a repeat of the 1930s depression? Canada has not had another depression, but there have been a number of recessions. What is the difference between a recession and a depression? There is no single accepted definition of a recession; however, the term is associated with a period of negative economic growth. That is, if GDP declines in two consecutive quarters, the economy is said to be in a recession. In recent times, Canada experienced recessions in 1981-82 and again beginning in April 1990.

Similarly, there is no technical definition of a depression. Economists describe a depression as a prolonged and severe recession characterized by widespread unemployment, declining prices, a lack of capital investment, and many business failures. Apart from the depression of the 1930s, the only other depression to hit Canada occurred between 1873 and 1879.

Questions

1 In light of your knowledge of GDP and its determinants, what policies would you have introduced in order to solve the economic crisis of the Great Depression?
2 Do you believe that a repetition of the depression conditions is possible in Canada?
3 In what sense is war beneficial to a country's economy?

Summary

When GDP is in equilibrium, the level of business activity is steady and unchanging. Equilibrium occurs when the leakages from the circular flow of money are equal to the additions to the circular flow. When the additions are greater than the leakages, GDP starts to increase. When the leakages exceed the additions, GDP begins to decline.

In order to analyse why the level of business activity fluctuates, it is necessary to study the components of business activity. Consumption is the spending by households on goods and services. Investment is the spending by businesses on capital equipment, and includes residential construction and any change in inventories. Government spending on goods and services is also included in national income accounting. Finally, the foreign-trade aspect of our economy, imports and exports, also influences the level of business activity. Changes in any of these components bring about changes in the level of GDP.

The paradox of thrift points out a possible contradiction of savings. If enough people decided to increase their savings, the level of spending in the economy would fall. With reduced spending, less income is earned and the ability to save declines.

Every time that spending takes place, GDP increases. The total impact of any increase in spending on GDP is determined by use of the multiplier. There is a difference in impact on GDP when comparing expenditure changes and tax changes. The difference results from the influence that tax changes have on savings. Part of any increase in taxes is financed through savings, while part of any tax reduction finds its way into savings.

A stable level of business activity (equilibrium GDP) is not necessarily an ideal situation. In certain instances, the level of total spending in the economy may not be enough to provide everyone with a job. The economy may not be at a full-employment level of GDP. The amount that spending has to increase in order to achieve full employment is known as the deflationary gap. When there is too much spending, prices start to rise. The inflationary gap indicates how much total spending exceeds the amount of spending necessary for full employment.

The discussion of macroeconomics contained in this chapter is known as Keynesian economics. It was Keynes' view that the demand for goods and services had to be maintained in order to keep the economy out of a recession. If the total demand was not sufficient, Keynes believed that government should take an active role in influencing economic conditions.

Questions for Review and Discussion

1 How could consumer expectations about future price levels affect the level of GDP? (Hint: think of the effect on consumption.)
2 The development of new products influences consumer spending. Can you list three new products that have altered consumer spending?
3 What determines the level of savings in Canada each year?
4 What factors cause the equilibrium level of GDP to change?
5 How would you use a combination of government spending and taxation to improve our current economic situation?
6 Is the equilibrium level of GDP necessarily an ideal economic situation?

7 How is it possible for people to dissave?

8 How might you react to an increase of $2000 in your income? What is your marginal propensity to consume (MPC)?

9 Savings can have both negative and positive consequences for the Canadian economy. Discuss the potential consequences associated with an increased desire on the part of Canadians to save.

10 Using the appropriate multiplier formula, determine the impact of the following:

    i an increase in investment spending of $200 million on the level of GDP (MPC = 0.8)

    ii an increase in savings by Canadians of $50 million on GDP (MPC = 0.9)

    iii a decrease in taxes of $3 billion on GDP (MPC = 0.75)

    iv an increase in government spending of $15 million on GDP (MPC = 0.75)

11 What change in taxes is necessary in order to eliminate an inflationary gap of $10 billion (MPC = 0.8)?

12 What increase in government spending is necessary in order to increase the level of GDP by $20 billion (MPC = 0.9)?

13 What is the balanced-budget multiplier? Use a numerical example in your answer (MPC = 0.8).

14 Why must the MPC and the MPS always add to the total of one?

15 In a recession, government should not undertake any unnecessary expenditures. Comment on this statement.

16 In order to assist the Canadian mining industry, the government could change the income-tax rules that mining companies must abide by. Discuss the impact on our economy of a tax change that allows mining companies to depreciate new equipment more rapidly.

17 What is the connection between J.M. Keynes and Say's Law?

18 Does advertising affect the overall level of consumption in Canada or simply influence the consumer's choice? Can you think of an advertisement that has resulted in an increase in your spending?

19 Capital goods such as machinery and equipment wear out. Could the replacement of these goods result in a change in economic conditions? Explain.

20 How do technological advances such as robotics in the automotive industry and laser printers in the publishing industry affect GDP? (Hint: think of their impact on investment.)

Suggested Readings

Berton, Pierre. *The Great Depression 1929-1939.* Toronto: McClelland and Stewart 1990

Canadian Foundation for Economic Education. "Canada in Recession: A Backgrounder and Some Perspectives." *Economic Bulletin,* Issue 4, January 1991

Daly, Donald J. *Managerial Macroeconomics: A Canadian Experience.* Homewood: Irwin 1988

Hall, Robert E., John B. Taylor and Jeremy Rudin. *Macroeconomics: The Canadian Economy.* New York: W.W. Norton 1990

Lipsey, Richard G., Douglas D. Purvis and Peter O. Steiner. *Economics.* Seventh Canadian Edition. New York: Harper Collins Publishers Inc. 1991

Parkin, Michael and Robin Bade. *Economics: Canada and the Global Environment.* Don Mills: Addison-Wesley Publishers Ltd. 1991

Rabbior, Gary. "The 'Macro' Economy: An Introduction to How It Works." Canadian Foundation for Economic Education Insight #2 November 1989

Chapter 7

Money and the Canadian Banking System

Chapter Objectives

After successfully completing this chapter, you will be able to:

- discuss the shortcomings of a barter system
- explain the functions of money
- define the Canadian money supply
- explain the various demands for money
- describe how interest rates are determined
- explain how, and under what conditions, banks can create money
- use the money-supply expansion formula
- outline the responsibilities of the Bank of Canada
- describe the various tools of monetary policy
- explain why the money supply would be increased or decreased
- explain the relationship between the money supply and the interest rate

Key Terms

barter
legal tender
fiat money
liquid assets
crude-quantity theory of money
Fisher equation of exchange
chartered bank
deposit insurance
branch banking

unit banking
trust company
caisse populaire
credit union
treasury bills
bank rate
open-market operations
secondary reserve rate
moral suasion

What Is Money?

The Barter System

Barter is the process by which goods or services are exchanged without the use of money.

The importance of money in our economy can best be explained by imagining an economic system without it. Even if money did not exist, exchanges would still take place between individuals by trade, or **barter.** Barter systems are still in use today; however, there are several problems in using a barter system extensively in our advanced economy.

Exchanges that take place through barter necessitate a coincidence of wants. That is, if you have an item to trade you have to find someone willing to sell the item that you desire. With luck, this person will be willing to accept whatever you have to trade. For example, assume that you need a stereo and all that you have to offer is a bicycle. You need to locate someone who is willing to exchange a stereo for your bicycle. This may not be easy to do. Divisibility is also a problem with barter. It is not possible to divide many items up into smaller units. Someone may only be willing to trade part of a stereo for your bicycle. How will the stereo be divided? Since this is very difficult, it is likely that the exchange will not take place.

A barter system functions more effectively in a less industrialized economy than ours. In an industrialized economy, individuals normally work for someone else and simply add to the company's total production. After a week of inserting windshields on new cars, what does the individual have to trade? He cannot use the windshields for barter. In less industrialized countries, workers are more likely to be self-employed. The fruits of their labours will be some agricultural product or another product that they have made—a vase, a knife, or whatever. They can take these products and exchange them for others. In order for barter to take place in the Canadian economy, individuals must be self-employed or have some item to offer for exchange. *In a modern economy, money serves as a medium of exchange.* Workers are willing to offer their services to an employer in exchange for money. Store owners are willing to accept money for the goods and services that they sell. Individuals are willing to accept money in exchange because they know that others will also accept money.

It is difficult to express values or prices in a barter system. With no common denominator there can be as many prices for one item as there are articles for trade. For example, one sheep may trade for three bushels of wheat, or four chickens, or five bushels of corn, or two goats, or three vases, or whatever else anyone is willing to trade. Also to be considered in setting a price is the quality of merchandise. If one sheep is to be traded for four chickens, how much do the chickens have to weigh? How much does the sheep have to weigh? *In the Canadian economy, money acts as the common denominator or the unit of account.* Prices and values are expressed in terms of the same unit. Regardless of what item is for sale, it will have a money price stated in terms of Canadian dollars.

Our industrialized Canadian economy also involves a substantial amount of borrowing. Consumers and businessmen borrow in order to pay for current expenses. How would loan repayment take place in a barter system? Each time a loan is undertaken, specific instructions would have to be set out as to the type of repayment. For example, if I borrowed two sheep in order to complete a transaction, would I have to pay back two sheep? What about interest payments on the loan? Money facilitates the borrowing process and becomes a standard for deferred payments. In addition to simplifying debt repayment, future payments for such matters as salaries, rental payments, and dividends payable are specified in money.

Finally, how does an individual accumulate wealth without money? Wealth would have to be accumulated in physical items. Storage could be a problem if wealthy items are bulky. It is also important that wealth be kept in the form of a durable commodity. It would be unwise to store wealth in a commodity that was sensitive to temperature, or deteriorated after being kept in storage for a long time. In our economy, money performs the function of being a store of wealth, as well as a medium of exchange, a unit of account, and a standard for deferred payments.

The barter system, however, is not dead. It is used more extensively in less-developed countries than in Canada; however, it is gaining favour in our country, too. In order to avoid paying income and sales taxes, individuals have resorted to barter whenever possible. If individuals simply exchange services, and do not exchange money, no tax need be paid. Finally, in industrialized countries there have been situations in which people have lost faith in the current value of money and have resorted to barter.

The History of Money

Since the barter system has its drawbacks, societies have adopted the use of money. One of the first forms of money was cattle. In fact, the Latin word for money, *pecunia*, is derived from the word *pecus*, meaning herd of cattle or sheep. The English word pecuniary (relating to, or consisting of money) has these Latin origins. Cattle were used as money because they had value. Cows could be used for food and the skins could be used for clothing. Since they had value, people were willing to accept cattle in exchange for a good or a service. Cattle skins themselves were also used as money, as were other types of livestock, especially sheep.

In addition to livestock, grains (especially corn and wheat) have been used as currency. In fact, in some American states, legislation was enacted that made corn **legal tender**, or money. The advantage of grain over livestock was that it was easier to divide into small amounts. In ancient Rome, Greece, and Egypt, human beings

Legal tender is that part of the money supply that is acceptable for purchases and for repayment of debt.

were used as money. Slaves were exchanged, with the stronger ones being of greater value.

One difficulty (apart from the moral issues) in using cattle, sheep, and even human beings as money, is that these are not standard items. Not all humans are the same. Not all cattle are the same. There was a time when it was required that taxes be paid in cattle. Individuals would keep old and undernourished animals available for the tax collector, while keeping the healthy animals for themselves. Additional problems arose in the use of cattle and grain as money. Cattle need constant care and feeding. Grain tends to deteriorate over time and requires extensive storage space.

Various minerals have also been used as money. Many minerals— diamonds, gold, silver, copper—had ornamental value and were often used in jewellery. Since jewellery contained precious minerals, it also circulated as money. Again, as long as something is perceived to have value it can perform the main function of money: it can be used in exchanges. Minerals such as copper, gold, and silver were used to make practical items such as utensils, as well as for monetary purposes. The precious metals themselves also circulated as money; however, there were problems connected with weighing metals to determine exact amounts.

The problem of weighing was partly solved through the introduction of coins. The coins, made out of various metals, were stamped with the weight of the metal in them. This was supposed to eliminate the weighing of the coins. However, since pieces of the coins were often clipped (or trimmed) off, weighing them was still necessary. Clipping coins was done with the objective of acquiring enough metal to make a new coin without significantly diminishing the value of the original coins. Scales and measures were as important to earlier businessmen as a cash register is today. At times, coins were stamped with a replica of the monarch's head in order to give them some official status.

Since anyone could make a coin, there were often thousands of different coins in circulation. Yet it was difficult to determine how much precious metal was present in each coin. With so many coins in circulation, no one was sure about the value of a particular coin that they might be offered in exchange. The coins in use today are referred to as "token money." The metallic value of the coin is less than the face value (the purchasing power) of the coin. Other items that have been used as money throughout history include playing cards, books, tobacco, and beaver skins. Indians in North America used beads, or "wampum."

Paper money came into existence because those who began to accumulate money wanted a safe place to store it. Some types of money, such as gold, were very heavy to carry around. The discovery of a safe place to store money was the beginning of banking.

People obtained a receipt for the money they stored in a vault. When it was necessary to get the money for a transaction, the receipt would be turned in at the vault, or bank. After a while, the receipts began to circulate in the economy just as money would. This was the beginning of paper money. People would accept receipts as money because they believed that the receipts, or paper money, were backed by "real money." They believed that the paper money had value. *Today, people accept paper money as money because they believe it has value.*

Fiat money is the currency issued by a goverenment or a bank that is not matched by holdings of gold or other securities.

Our paper money circulates because of people's faith in it. There is no gold backing up our paper money. The term used to describe our paper currency is **fiat money.** It is money because it has been declared to be money and it is accepted as such.

If a commodity is to circulate as money (as paper currency does), it must have certain characteristics; it must be:

Durable: if money is to change hands often during exchanges, it must be sturdy.

Portable: money has to be carried around in order to make exchanges, so it cannot be too heavy or cumbersome.

Divisible: since not every product has the same price, money must be divisible into smaller amounts.

Recognizable and readily accepted: if it is not accepted by the population, the item will cease to function as money.

Not easily copied: the ease of manufacturing counterfeit money would destroy the value of the commodity as money.

Face value greater than actual value: if the metallic value of a coin is greater than the face value of the coin, it will not circulate as money. For example, pre-1967 Canadian silver dollars do not circulate as money since the value of the silver in the coin exceeds one dollar. The same rule applies to paper currency.

7.1 Why did coins replace other forms of money?

7.2 What is the most important characteristic of anything that continues to circulate as money?

Money: Demand and Supply

Since money is a commodity, there is a market for it. There are individuals who are willing to buy (borrow) money and there are those individuals who are willing to supply (lend) money. These groups represent the demand and supply sides of the money market.

The Demand for Money

Individual demand for money can be divided into the following categories:

Transactions: it is necessary to have money in order to carry on day-to-day business. People need money in order to purchase food, clothing, recreation, and other items. The business sector needs money in order to pay for the services it requires. This need for money is referred to as the *transactions demand.*

There are a number of factors that influence the transactions demand for money. One factor, from an individual point of view, is the size of family to be supported. There is a greater demand for money on the part of individuals who support families than among single persons. The financial needs of a family are clearly greater than those of a person who is responsible solely for himself or herself.

The consumer's decision to pay cash or to buy on credit influences the demand for money. The recent increase in the number of credit cards for gasoline, department stores, and other goods and services has probably reduced the amount of money needed to carry out transactions. Finally, the amount of money held for transaction purposes depends on the *level of income.* The higher the level of individual income, the more money that can be kept on hand for transaction purposes.

Precaution: money is also held by individuals in case of an emergency or in order to meet unexpected situations. For example, a major household repair may require attention immediately. In these situations, money is needed at once. The precautionary demand for money simply represents a desire to be ready for unexpected circumstances.

The amount of money held for precautionary purposes depends on the level of income. As individuals' incomes increase, they have more money to keep on hand for emergencies. Individuals in lower income brackets will probably use most of their income for transactions and have little left over for precautionary purposes.

Speculation: holding money involves a cost. This is the opportunity cost of the interest that is lost by not putting this money into an *interest-earning asset.* For example, if you buy a $1000 Canada Savings Bond, you earn interest on your money. If you keep $1000 in your pocket, you earn nothing. The speculative demand for money depends on the rate of interest. If the interest rate is relatively low, the opportunity cost of holding money is low. If the cost of holding money is low, there is a greater quantity of money demanded. At low interest rates, individuals are also willing to borrow more money. Expectations about the future also influence the speculative demand for money. If there is the expectation that interest rates will increase in the near future, individuals may be unwilling to put their money into an interest-bearing asset at the present time and will instead hold on to their money. At high interest rates, the speculative demand for money is low. Individuals may find it too expensive to hold money in terms of the opportunity costs. They will not be willing to borrow and will want to earn interest on any extra money that they have available. Money will be transferred into interest-earning assets. Therefore, the demand for money is lower at high interest rates.

**Figure 7.1
The demand for
money**

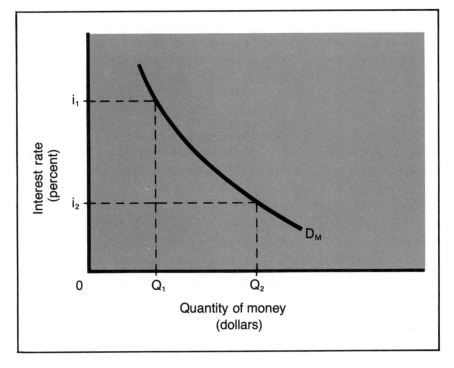

The quantity of money demanded is inversely related to the interest rate.

A liquid asset is one that can be readily converted into money.

The demand for money is referred to as *liquidity preference*. It represents a willingness to make assets liquid. A **liquid asset** is one that can be converted into money quickly, and the most liquid asset is money itself. The liquidity-preference curve is shown in figure 7.1. In the diagram, D_M represents the liquidity preference, or demand-for-money curve. As interest rates (i) fall from i_1 to i_2 the quantity (Q) of money that individuals want to hold increases from Q_1 to Q_2. The interest rates that are measured on the vertical axis of this graph can be considered to be the price of money. If you want to borrow money, the interest rate is the price that you pay. When the interest rate is considered to be the price of money, the D_M curve in figure 7.1 becomes similar to the demand curves introduced in Chapter 2. The lower the interest rate, the greater the quantity of money demanded.

7.3   Why do people hold money instead of some other asset?

7.4   Divide the money that you have available into transactions, precautionary, and speculative amounts.

The Supply of Money

The crude-quantity theory of money is a mathematical identity that states that the price level is directly related to the amount of money in circulation (P =KM).

The supply of money in our economy is an important determinant of economic conditions. It represents the amount of *purchasing power* available. If the supply of money were to increase, then purchases of goods and services would increase as well. The increased spending would mean more jobs and possibly higher prices.

Early economists believed that the relationship between the supply of money and the price level was a direct one. Changes in the money supply would cause changes in the price level. Economists believed that the relationship between money and prices was also constant, and that no other variables affected the price level. The relationship put forth by these economists is known as the **crude-quantity theory of money:**

$$P = KM$$

where P = average level of prices
           M = money supply
           K = a constant value

Assume that the value of the constant, K, is 2.0. If the money supply (M) doubled, then the price level (P) would increase four times. If the money supply tripled, then the price level would increase six times, and so on. The task of the classical economists was to discover the value of the constant, K.

The Fisher equation of exchange states that the money supply multiplied by the velocity of money is equal to the number of transactions that take place in the economy multiplied by the average price level (MV = PT).

This relationship proved to be much too simple, but represented a good starting point for further study. Later a more sophisticated relationship between prices and money was developed. This is referred to as the **Fisher equation of exchange,** named after Irving Fisher, an American economist who developed it. The equation states that

$$MV = PT$$

where M = money supply
           V = average velocity of circulation of money per period of time
           P = average price level
           T = number of market transactions or exchanges per period of time

Two variables, V and T, were added to the earlier theory. The velocity of money (V) can be defined as the average number of times that each unit of the money supply changes hands during a given period. The variable T represents the number of business transactions that take place in a certain period of time. This provides an indication of the level of business activity. The right-hand side of the equation, PT, represents the value of all transactions that took place in the economy. In other words, the right-hand side of the equation is equivalent to GDP. The equation could therefore be rewritten as follows:

MV = GDP

If the money supply (M) increases, then GDP should increase as well.

$$\underset{\uparrow}{\textbf{M}}V = \underset{\uparrow}{\textbf{GDP}}$$

If the velocity of money (V) increases, the level of GDP should also increase.

$$M\underset{\uparrow}{\textbf{V}} = \underset{\uparrow}{\textbf{GDP}}$$

The velocity of money is the key to this equation. Increases in V would cause GDP to increase even if the money supply (M) remained constant. If the velocity of money does not change, then only changes in the money supply will result in changes in GDP.

The significance of the velocity of money will be discussed further in Chapter 8. If the velocity of money can be proved to be stable, then changes in the money supply would be an effective way to control the level of economic activity.

Let us assume that the velocity of money is stable and the money supply doubles in size. According to the Fisher equation of exchange, the level of GDP would also double. This would increase the number of jobs available as well as the price level. If the money supply was to be cut in half, the level of GDP would be halved as well. If the velocity of money does not remain constant, then it will be difficult to determine the impact on GDP of any change in the money supply.

7.5 What changes did Fisher make to the crude-quantity theory of money?
7.6 Why is the velocity of money important?

The Money Market

The demand for and the supply of money make up the money market, shown in figure 7.2. The intersection of the liquidity-preference curve (D_M) with the supply of money (S_M^1) will give an equilibrium price, or interest rate (i_1). The supply-of-money curve in this diagram is shown as a vertical line since the supply of money is constant at any point in time and is not dependent on the interest rate. Any changes in the demand for or the supply of money will cause the rate of interest to change. For example, in the diagram, an increase in the supply of money has lowered the interest rate to i_2.

**Figure 7.2
The money
market**

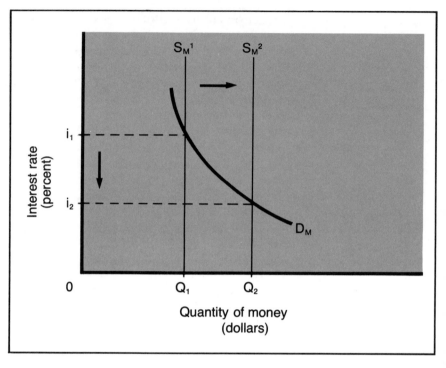

An increase in the supply of money lowers the equilibrium interest rate.

The diagram in figure 7.2 helps explain more fully the impact that changes in the money supply would have on the level of GDP. Any increase in the money supply would result in lower interest rates. Lower rates would encourage more borrowing and less saving on the part of the public. The increase in spending would cause the level of economic activity, GDP, to increase.

$\Delta M \rightarrow \Delta i \rightarrow \Delta spending \rightarrow \Delta GDP$ (where Δ means "change in")

**Definition of
Money in Canada**

The most recognizable form of money in Canada is *paper currency,* which is issued by the Bank of Canada. These paper notes are referred to as legal tender, and must be accepted as a medium of exchange and for the payment of debts. *There is no gold or precious metal behind the issuing of paper money.* As long as Canadians are willing to accept Bank of Canada notes in exchange for goods and services, the notes will continue to circulate as money. This points out one of the major characteristics of any commodity that circulates as money: it must be perceived as having value. If Canadians did not believe these notes had value, they would not accept them.

The federal government in Canada also operates a mint that produces coins. These coins also circulate as money. The value of the metal in the coin is less than its face value, but the coins are still accepted as money. Interestingly, if the face value of the coin was less than the value of its metal content, it is unlikely that the coin would circulate as money. People would tend to hoard the coins and not use them as currency. For example, if the value of the silver contained in a nickel was greater than five cents, people would not spend their nickels. By spending a nickel they would only receive five cents worth of product and would be giving up more than five cents worth of silver. Thomas Gresham formulated a hypothesis to describe this practice of hoarding money that has an actual value greater than the face value. Known as Gresham's Law, it states that bad money forces good money out of circulation.

One final form of money in Canada is *bank deposits,* especially chequing deposits. It is possible to purchase goods and services with a cheque. Therefore, the cheque is a medium of exchange and performs a monetary function. Other bank deposits are not strictly money, but are close to it. For example, you cannot spend money directly from your savings account, yet it is a simple process to withdraw this money and spend it.

The Bank of Canada is concerned with the amount of money in Canada at any given time. In order to determine this amount, a definition of the money supply is necessary. This definition reflects the total purchasing power available in the country at any given time. Included in the Bank of Canada definition are coins and paper currency in circulation, plus chartered bank deposits. Only coins and currency in circulation are counted as money. When coins and currency are put into a bank, they no longer are referred to as money. The deposit that was created becomes part of the money supply.

The inclusion of bank deposits in the money supply creates some problems because not all bank deposits are the same. Some deposits are *demand deposits* in that the depositor can get his or her money back on demand. These deposits have chequing privileges and may pay no interest on the money in the deposit. Savings deposits, on the other hand, usually pay interest. Savings deposits are referred to as *notice deposits,* because the depositor may be required to give notice before withdrawing money. A true savings account does not have chequing privileges. At most banks, a combination of these two accounts is available.

The existence of several types of deposits makes the definition of the money supply complicated. Demand deposits are very close to currency, since cheques can be written against the money in these deposits. Also the money in the deposit can be obtained on demand. Savings accounts are not as close to our definition of money, since they are not readily spendable. Yet these accounts are very liquid and can be converted into money quite readily. In order to accommodate the various types of deposits, the Bank of Canada has developed several definitions of the money supply. These definitions are presented in table 7.1. All of the definitions refer to deposits at chartered banks and not to deposits at any other type of deposit-accepting institution. In this chapter, the money supply definition M1 will be used in all the examples.

Table 7.1 / The Canadian money supply, February 1991

	($ millions)
Currency outside banks	18 863
M1 currency and demand deposits less private-sector float	38 230
M2 M1 plus personal savings deposits and non-personal notice deposits	263 536
M3 M2 plus other non-personal fixed-term deposits plus foreign-currency deposits of residents booked in Canada	315 269
Currency plus total Canadian dollar privately held chartered bank deposits	304 639

Source: *Bank of Canada Review, March 1991* (Ottawa: Bank of Canada, March 1991), p. S70.

7.7   Why are there several definitions of the Canadian money supply?
7.8   Why are bank deposits included in the money supply?

Canadian Chartered Banks

Chartered bank *is the term used to describe a financial institution operating under the authority of Parliament that accepts deposits and lends money to businesses, government, and households.*

By far the largest financial institutions in Canada are the **chartered banks** (see table 7.2). They are referred to as chartered banks since they operate under a charter granted by the Parliament of Canada. The chartered banks are privately-owned companies whose purpose is to make a profit for shareholders. Bank profits are earned by charging a fee for financial services and by charging interest on loans. Banks accept deposits from individuals, businesses, and government, and lend the money to these same groups. The difference between the rate of interest paid to depositors and the rate of interest received on loans represents profits for the bank.

Types of Deposits

Individuals have a number of choices when depositing their money in a bank. These choices consist of the various types of deposits available. The most popular type of deposit is the personal savings deposit (see table 7.3). When an individual puts money into a savings deposit, it is expected that the money will remain in the deposit for a period of time.

Table 7.2 / Total assets of chartered banks and selected deposit-accepting institutions, 1990

Institution	Assets ($ millions)
chartered banks	609 682
trust and mortgage companies (excluding bank mortgage subsidiaries)	135 400
mortgage loan companies associated with banks	126 375
local credit unions and caisses populaires [1989]	67 092

Source: *Bank of Canada Review, March 1991* (Ottawa: Bank of Canada, March 1991), pp. S33-S60.

Table 7.3 / Major assets and liabilities of Canadian chartered banks, January 1991

Assets	($ millions)
Bank of Canada deposits and notes	5 684
treasury bills	20 928
Government of Canada direct and guaranteed bonds	5 843
call and short loans	1 416
loans in Canadian dollars	290 042
Canadian securities	19 180
Canadian dollar deposits with other banks	10 174
customers' liability under acceptances	42 060
all other assets	12 717
Total Canadian dollar assets	408 044
Total foreign-currency assets	196 340
Total assets	604 384

Liabilities	
deposits: personal savings deposits	204 509
non-personal term and notice deposits	67 651
gross demand deposits	21 224
Government of Canada	3 090
advances from Bank of Canada	304
bankers' acceptances	42 060
bank debentures issued and outstanding	4 048
other liabilities	23 801
shareholders' equity	31 890
Total Canadian dollar liabilities	398 577
Total foreign-currency liabilities	205 808
Total liabilities	604 384

Source: *Bank of Canada Review, March 1991* (Ottawa: Bank of Canada, March 1991), pp. S32-S35.

Since the bank will have the use of these funds over time, the depositor is paid interest on the amount of money deposited. The individual has, in fact, lent money to the bank and the rate of interest represents the fee that the bank is paying for the use of that money. In most cases, an individual can withdraw this money at will. Banks may, however, request notice of 30 days before a withdrawal is made, although this is not usually done. Money may also be deposited into a fixed-term deposit (e.g. three months, six months, nine months, one year, or five years). If the individual agrees to leave money in the bank for a specified period of time, a higher rate of interest is usually paid on the deposit.

Money may also be placed into a demand deposit. With such a deposit, the individual can get back his or her money on demand. Usually no interest is paid on demand deposits. The advantage of the deposit is that chequing privileges accompany it. There are no chequing privileges with a true savings account nor with fixed-term deposits. As mentioned, combinations of these types of deposits are also available.

Although chartered banks lend out the money that they receive in the form of deposits, they are not allowed to lend out all the money. According to the Bank Act, chartered banks must keep a reserve representing ten percent of demand deposits. The reserve requirement for most term and notice deposits is three percent. On the first $500 million of term and notice deposits, the legal reserve requirement is two percent. These reserves must be kept in the form of cash or in a deposit at the Bank of Canada. The purpose of the reserve is not only to ensure that the chartered banks have some money to meet the needs of their depositors, but to control the amount of money that banks can lend out. In order to determine whether a chartered bank has sufficient reserves, a *reserve ratio* is calculated monthly from three figures:

a   the dollar value of deposits, computed as the average value out standing on four consecutive Wednesdays ending with the last Wednesday but one in the preceding month;

b   the amount of Bank of Canada notes, computed as the average holdings on four consecutive Wednesdays ending with the last Wednesday but one in the preceding month;

c   the amount of the bank's deposit with the Bank of Canada, computed as the average amount on each legal business day of the current month.

The sum of *b* and *c* has to represent at least two or three percent of *a* in the case of savings deposits and at least ten percent in the case of demand deposits.

The Bank of Canada may also insist on the chartered banks maintaining a secondary reserve. This reserve is kept by the banks in liquid assets, or assets that can readily be converted into cash (e.g. day-to-day loans). The range of the secondary reserve requirement can be anywhere from 0 to 12 percent of deposits. That is, the Bank of Canada at times may not require that the chartered banks keep any secondary reserves. Yet, at other times, it may require the holding of a secondary reserve of anywhere up to 12 percent of total deposits.

Chartered bank reserves as of 6 March 1991 are shown in table 7.4. At this time, the chartered banks were required to keep $5222 million in reserve. These reserves were kept in coins, Bank of Canada notes, and Bank of Canada deposits. The banks were also required to keep secondary reserves, which represented four percent of deposits. A large percentage of secondary reserves is kept in government treasury bills, discussed later in this chapter.

Table 7.4 / Chartered bank reserves 1–6 March 1991

	($ millions)
cash reserves	
required minimum[a]	5 222
actual	
statutory coin and Bank of Canada notes	3 923
Bank of Canada deposits	1 563
excess cash reserves	1 586
other reserves[b]	
treasury bills, excess	13 135

[a]required as a ratio of statutory deposits (%) = 3.81
[b]required secondary reserve ratio of total statutory deposits (%)= 4.00

Source: *Bank of Canada Review, March 1991* (Ottawa: Bank of Canada, March 1991), p. S49.

7.9 Why is there a higher level reserve requirement on demand deposits than on personal savings deposits?

Total Assets of Domestic Banks, Canada, 30 April 1991

Bank	Total assets ($ millions)	Percent
Royal Bank of Canada	131 906.1	21.60
Canadian Imperial Bank of Commerce	119 270.0	19.60
Bank of Montreal	96 762.0	15.90
Bank of Nova Scotia	88 292.0	14.50
Toronto-Dominion Bank	70 199.0	11.50
National Bank	36 357.0	5.90
Laurentian Bank of Canada	6 349.4	1.00
Canadian Western Bank	456.4	0.10
Total domestic banks	549 592.0	90.10
other domestic banks[1]	121.1	0.00
Total foreign banks	60 355.9	9.90
Total all banks	610 069.1	100.00

[1] Reflects the residual balances of Continental Bank of Cda and B.C. Bancorp.

Source:*Detailed Financial Statistics (domestic banks), The Second Quarter ended April 30* (Canadian Bankers' Association, June 1991) p.1.

Foreign Banks Operating in Canada, September 1990

ABN Bank Canada
Amex Bank of Canada
Bank of America Canada
Bank of Boston Canada
Banco Central of Canada
Chemical Bank of Canada
Banca Commerciale Italiana
of Canada
Bank of Credit and Commerce
Canada
Credit Suisse Canada
Daiwa Bank Canada
Deutsche Bank (Canada)
First Interstate Bank of
Canada
Fuji Bank Canada
Hanil Bank Canada
Hongkong Bank of Canada
International Commercial Bank
of Cathay (Canada)
Korea Exchange Bank
of Canada
Mellon Bank Canada
Mitsubishi Bank of Canada
Morgan Bank of Canada
National Bank of Greece
(Canada)
ANZ Bank Canada
Barclays Bank of Canada
BT Bank of Canada
The Chase Manhattan Bank
of Canada
Citibank Canada
Comerica Bank Canada
Credit Lyonnais Canada
Dai-Ichi Kangyo Bank
(Canada)

Dresdner Bank Canada
The First National Bank of
Chicago (Canada)
Bank Hapoalim (Canada)
The Industrial Bank of Japan
(Canada)
Irving Bank Canada
Israel Discount Bank of Canada
Bank Leumi Le-Israel (Canada)
Manufacturers Hanover Bank
of Canada
The Mitsui Taiyo Kobe Bank
(Canada)
Banque Nationale de Paris
(Canada)
Overseas Union Bank of
Singapore (Canada)
Sanwa Bank Canada
Security Pacific Bank Canada
Standard Chartered Bank
of Canada
The Sumitomo Bank of Canada
Swiss Bank Corporation (Canada)
United Overseas Bank (Canada)
NBD Bank, Canada
National Westminster Bank
of Canada
Banca Nazionale del Lavoro
of Canada
Paribas Bank of Canada
Republic National Bank of New
York (Canada)
Société Générale (Canada)
State Bank of India (Canada)
Tokai Bank Canada
The Bank of New York Canada
The Bank of Tokyo Canada

Source: Canadian Bankers' Association.

Can Banks Go Bankrupt?

Canadians have faith in their bank system. Prior to 1985, the last bank collapse in Canada was that of the Home Bank of Canada in1923. Since that time, other banks that were in financial difficulty have merged with a larger bank—preventing any loss of confidence on the part of the Canadian public. But the confidence that Canadians have in their banks was shaken in September 1985, when two banks based in western Canada—the Canadian Commercial Bank and the Northland Bank—were declared no longer to be viable financial institutions. The liquidation of the Canadian Commercial Bank proceeded immediately. The Northland Bank was given time to reorganize or amalgamate with another bank. Eventually the Northland Bank failed as well.

What circumstances would lead to a bank going out of business? In the case of the Canadian Commercial Bank (CCB), it was a combination of factors. The bank conducted most of its business in western Canada and the economy in that part of Canada was having trouble recovering from the recession. Real-estate prices had dropped substantially. In some areas, house prices had dropped by 25 percent or more. People were walking away from houses rather than paying off a mortgage on an inflated house price. Farmers were receiving low prices for their products. The oil and gas industry was still suffering from the federal government's National Energy Program (1980), lower world oil prices, and high interest rates. Many of the loans made by the Canadian Commercial Bank were not being paid back because of the poor economic conditions.

The situation at the CCB was aggravated because of the loans made by a subsidiary bank in California. The Westland Bank had made a large number of loans to oil and gas drilling companies in the southwestern part of the United States. Low oil prices discouraged drilling and made many of these loans non-performing. (A loan is referred to as non-performing when payments are not being made to the bank by the borrower; neither the principal nor interest is being paid.) Non-performing loans had reached 10.2 percent of eligible assets by 31 January 1985 —an unacceptably high level.

Apart from the depressed economy, poor management at the bank was also cited as a reason for its downfall. The CCB had too many loans in the energy and real-estate areas. The bank was also criticized for not making adequate loss provisions on major problem loans. Banks set aside a certain amount of money in order to cover non-performing loans. This money is referred to as a loan-loss provision. A House of Commons committee report accused the bank of questionable accounting practices, inadequate disclosure of its financial position, and poor supervision.

In spite of the difficulties that the CCB was facing, the Bank of Canada continued to lend money to the bank. A total of $1.316 billion was loaned to the Canadian Commercial Bank by the Bank of Canada. The Bank of Canada was repaid as the assets of the bank were liquidated.

Prior to the collapse of the Canadian Commercial Bank, the federal government had tried to save it. In March 1985, the federal government arranged a $255 million bail-out package to prevent the CCB from folding. The federal government, the government of Alberta, and the main Canadian chartered banks contributed this money. The news of the bail-out package, however, had a negative impact on bank confidence. Depositors began to withdraw their money. In order to remain in business, a bank must be able to attract money from depositors.

Why did the federal government want to assist the CCB financially so that it could remain in business? Since the bank is a private company, why not let the shareholders take financial responsibility? The federal government was concerned about a drop in confidence in the Canadian banking system. If the CCB failed, would depositors take their money out of other small banks, most of them located in western Canada, as well? If depositors were not able to get their money back, more bankruptcies could result. Experience has shown that some banks that are in financial trouble can be saved. The Continental Illinois National Bank and Trust Company of Chicago, the eighth largest bank in the United States, survived under even more difficult circumstances. There was also political motivation associated with the decision to assist the Canadian Commercial Bank. The Progressive Conservative government had received strong support from western Canada in the 1984 federal election. Western Canada had desperately wanted to establish a banking industry in order to escape the domination of the eastern financial institutions. The federal government was compelled to help out.

The financial problems at the CCB caused further trouble for the Northland Bank. This bank also had an alarming percentage of bad loans. When word got out that the Northland was in trouble, depositors began removing their money. The Bank of Canada advanced $510 million to the Northland Bank in order to keep it afloat, but the federal government would not arrange any further bail-out packages for the bank. Since no other bank wanted to take over the Northland, it also collapsed.

Questions

1   The CCB was Canada's tenth largest chartered bank. The Northland was the eleventh largest. Together their assets represented one percent of bank assets in Canada. Why were these banks, based in western Canada, more likely to fail than the larger banks?

2   Depositors at banks are insured up to $60 000 by the Canada Deposit Insurance Corporation. The federal government introduced legislation to compensate depositors for uninsured deposits. Why would the federal government do this?

3   The Canadian Commercial Bank offered slightly higher interest rates on deposits than did other banks. As a result, it continued to

attract some depositors in spite of its financial trouble. How much risk should depositors have to take when putting their money into a bank?

4 Would the collapse of these two banks affect other small Canadian banks?

Deposit Insurance

Deposit insurance is insurance on the deposit liabilities of chartered banks and other financial institutions.

If chartered banks can lend out 98 percent of all of the money deposited in savings deposits, will there be any money in the bank when you want to withdraw your money? In most cases the answer is yes. The legal reserve requirement normally provides the bank with more money than the bank needs in order to carry out its daily business. As some people are withdrawing their money, others are depositing money; therefore, the banks do not have to keep a high percentage of deposits at the bank. The banking system in Canada is based on the trust that individuals have in being able to get their money back at any time. If everyone showed up at the bank at the same time to get their money, there would be insufficient funds to pay off all the depositors.

In order to provide some protection for depositors, the Canada Deposit Insurance Corporation (CDIC) was established in 1967 by an Act of Parliament. The purpose of the corporation is to provide **deposit insurance** for depositors in the case of the insolvency of a bank or other financial institution. The CDIC accepts memberships from banks, trust companies, and mortgage loan companies. Only the deposits with member institutions are insured.

It is not necessary for a depositor to apply for deposit insurance. The depositor is covered automatically if his or her money is deposited in a member institution. The maximum amount of insurance is $60 000 for each person, regardless of the number of deposit accounts that each individual has. The $60 000 amount applies to the combined total of principal and interest. That is, if a $60 000 deposit earned $3000 in interest by the time the institution became insolvent, the depositor would only receive $60 000 from the CDIC.

Deposit insurance covers demand deposits, savings and chequing accounts, guaranteed investment certificates and term deposits that are redeemable within five years after the date of deposit. There are a number of deposits that are not covered, including pooled funds, mortgage and real-estate investments, foreign-currency deposits, and stocks and bonds. Money in registered retirement savings plans (RRSPs) is covered separately. These plans have insurance coverage up to $60 000 if the money is deposited in an account eligible for insurance, such as a personal savings account. RRSPs based on stocks, bonds, and mortgages are not covered under the insurance plan. If a depositor has $60 000 in a RRSP and another $60 000 in a savings account, both amounts are covered.

The Bank Act

The Bank Act is federal government legislation that regulates the banking industry in Canada. The act describes the procedure that banks must follow in order to become incorporated. The act also outlines some of the arrangements that must exist between the bank's shareholders, directors, and management. It determines the services that banks may provide to the public and sets controls on the banks, such as the legal reserve requirement. Under the 1967 Bank Act, chartered banks were required to keep reserves equal to four percent of their Canadian dollar term-and-notice deposits and 12 percent of their Canadian dollar demand deposits.

The Bank Act in Canada has an interesting feature. Every ten years the act has to be reviewed and enacted again. This provides an opportunity for officials to review Canada's financial system in light of possible changes in economic conditions. The changes to the 1967 Bank Act were not made until November 1980. At that time, the Banks and Banking Law Revisions Act was passed. This new legislation introduced some changes into Canada's banking industry.

The main thrust of the new legislation was to increase the competition among Canadian banks. One such change is the acceptance of subsidiaries of foreign banks locating in Canada. In previous banking legislation, even foreign ownership of Canadian banks was restricted. A single non-resident could own no more than ten percent of the bank's outstanding voting shares. Prior to 1980 some foreign banks were established in Canada, but only on a limited basis. The local offices of foreign banks made business loans but were not allowed to accept deposits. With the new legislation, foreign banks are now allowed to conduct business in a manner similar to Canadian banks.

Although foreign-controlled banks will be allowed to operate in Canada, they will still be subject to certain restrictions. Foreign bank subsidiaries must get a licence from the minister of finance before they can begin operating. This licence comes up for renewal once a year for the first five years and every three years thereafter. Foreign-owned banks are also restricted in terms of the assets and the number of branches that they may have. For example, no foreign bank will be allowed to open more than one branch without the consent of the minister of finance. Some of the concessions to foreign-banking interests were made in the new legislation because of the Canadian banking industry's involvement in foreign countries. As of January 1981, Canadian chartered banks maintained over 290 branches and 38 percent of their total assets in foreign countries. The provision of Canadian banking services abroad is an important Canadian export and so concessions had to be made to foreign banks operating in Canada.

There has also been a change in the cash-reserve requirement for chartered banks. The legal reserve dropped from 12 percent to ten percent on demand deposits. The reserve ratio for most Canadian term-and-notice deposits dropped from four percent to three percent. For a bank's first $500 million of term-and-notice deposits, the reserve requirement decreased from four percent to two percent.

Changes to the Bank Act were introduced in Parliament in December 1990 as part of the government's financial reform package. The proposals would allow banks, trust companies, insurance companies, and brokerage firms to protect their core business while allowing some cross-over into each other's areas of business. The proposed amendments to the Bank Act would insist on disclosure of service charges and would prohibit banks from direct selling of insurance through branches. Banks would be allowed to own trust and insurance companies. Reserve requirements for banks are also being phased out over a two-year period. As this book goes to press, these changes have not been enacted into law.

Questions

1 Would domestically owned chartered banks be anxious to see the introduction of foreign-owned banks into Canada? Why or why not?
2 Would the Canadian consumer be anxious to see the introduction of foreign-owned banks into Canada?
3 What effect do you think a reduction in the reserve requirement will have i) on bank profits; ii) on the Canadian economy; and, iii) on the ability of the depositor to remove his or her money from the bank?

Canada versus the United States: Banking

Branch banking is a system of banking in which a commercial bank is permitted to operate branches of the main bank.

Unit banking is the system in which commercial banks are either not permitted to operate branches or to operate only a limited number.

The system of banking in Canada is referred to as **branch banking.** There are eight domestic chartered banks operating in Canada. The changes to the Bank Act 1980 permitted foreign banks to operate in Canada. Foreign banks are not, however, allowed to establish the extensive system of branches that Canadian-owned banks have. In the United States, there is a **unit-banking system.** In that country, there are no banks with offices all across the country. Some banks are regulated by federal law and others are regulated by state law. Some states allow branches; others do not. Where branches are allowed, they are usually within a restricted area. For example, in some states, a bank may not have a branch further away than 25 miles from the head office. In comparison to Canada's small number of chartered banks, there are in excess of 13 000 commercial banks in the United States.

There are a number of advantages to each system. A bank that has a number of branches spread over a wide area is likely to be more stable than a bank with only one office, because it will have more diversified assets and liabilities. Funds can be transferred between branches to accounts where they are needed the most. If each bank branch is independent, it is likely that the majority of its loans are in one area or are concentrated in certain industries. This can be more risky from the point of view of bank stability.

Branch banks may be better able to respond to the loan demands of large borrowers due to the ease of transferring assets from other branches. A large bank may be able to open a branch in a location that would not be feasible for a one-office bank.

The main advantage of a unit-banking system is that it protects against the centralization of financial power. In Canada, the head offices of chartered banks are located mainly in Toronto and Montreal. If the United States had adopted a branch-banking policy, the head offices of the major banks would probably be located in the eastern cities of New York, Boston, and Philadelphia. As it is now, major banking centres are spread all across the United States. A further argument for unit banking is that each bank has a big stake in its community and will thus be better able to respond to local needs.

Deposit-Accepting Institutions

Although they are the largest financial intermediaries in terms of total assets, chartered banks are not the only deposit-accepting institutions in Canada. Other institutions have been set up for specific purposes. These include trust companies, mortgage loan companies, caisses populaires and credit unions, and government savings institutions.

Trust Companies

A trust company is a financial institution that acts as a trustee for property interests and conducts other confidential business.

Trust companies were established to act as trustees for property interests and to conduct other confidential business. The most important sources of funds for trust companies are estates, trusts, and agency accounts. Estates are usually established under wills and are administered for a fee according to the instructions contained in the will. *Trust funds* are assets for which the trust company assumes a responsibility during the lifetime of the beneficiary. The most important category of trusts is *pension funds*. Also, *agency funds* are administered by trust companies under the orders of clients. The trust company acts as an agent for the client in the area of investments. Trust companies obtain other funds from the public in the form of deposit accounts and investment certificates, and by the sale of share capital. Term deposits and guaranteed investment certificates comprise the bulk of trust company liabilities. Demand and savings deposits are also available. The amount of a company's deposits and certificates is limited to 20 times its shareholders' equity. Trust companies are required to maintain reserves in cash, in deposits with other institutions (e.g. chartered banks), and in short-term government securities equal to 20 percent of their deposits and borrowed funds coming due in less than 100 days. The main assets of trust companies are *mortgage loans*. They also invest in government securities.

Caisses Populaires and Credit Unions

A caisse populaire is a financial institution that is usually organized on the basis of Roman Catholic parish boundaries, and that receives funds by selling shares and accepting deposits from members.

Similarly, a credit union sells shares and accepts members' deposits. These institutions are oriented toward consumer lending.

Caisses populaires and **credit unions** were established in order to enable groups of individuals to combine their savings, and thus to provide loans to members at relatively low interest rates. They receive their funds by selling shares and accepting deposits from members. Credit-union shares are similar to non-chequing savings deposits in a bank. Their deposits are similar to a bank's current account. The shares in a caisse populaire resemble term deposits at trust companies. Their deposits are similar to chequing savings deposits at chartered banks. Caisses populaires were founded in 1900 in Quebec. They are organized on a territorial basis, usually consisting of parish boundaries of the Roman Catholic church. Caisses populaires stress the advantages of thrift. Credit unions, on the other hand, stress the availability of credit, and are oriented toward consumer lending. Credit unions are often established along occupational or industrial lines.

The difference in orientation between these institutions is also reflected in a difference in their assets. Caisses populaires have a larger percentage of *residential mortgages* than do credit unions. They are also larger purchasers of bonds issued by municipalities and school boards. Credit unions have a greater percentage of their assets in *consumer loans*. They also have a higher loan-to-deposit ratio than do caisses populaires. In some provinces credit unions have initiated the use of a debit card. Through a debit card, money is withdrawn from the card-holder's account when a purchase is made.

Other Institutions

The major sources of funds for *mortgage loan companies* are term deposits and debentures. Debentures are usually one to five years in length. Most of the assets of mortgage loan companies are in residential mortgages. There is a close association between trust companies and mortgage loan companies, with one being the other's parent or subsidiary.

Alberta treasury branches were started in 1938 in order to provide financial services to communities that were too small to warrant a chartered-bank branch. The treasury branches are still primarily located in rural Alberta. These institutions accept demand, term, and savings deposits and issue guaranteed investment certificates. Any profit earned by the treasury branches is split with the government of Alberta.

In Ontario, the government established a deposit-accepting institution in 1921. *Ontario savings banks* offer only a combination savings/chequing account to customers. This account pays interest at 0.5 percent higher than chartered banks pay on their premium savings accounts. The savings banks were originally established to provide low-cost loans to farmers and small business, but now only lend money to the Ontario government. Any profits made by the savings banks are turned over to the Ontario government.

7.10 What are the major differences between chartered banks and other deposit-accepting institutions?

The Creation of Money

Since chartered bank deposits are considered to be money, it is actually possible for the chartered banking system to create money. *The banking system can create deposits through loans—-and thus create money.* This process works in the following manner. Assume that you deposit $1000 in a demand deposit at a chartered bank. The chartered bank is required to keep ten percent of the deposit, or $100, as a reserve against the deposit. Assuming that there are no secondary reserve requirements, the bank can lend out $900. When the $900 is taken out of the bank in the form of a loan, money has been created. The person who took out the loan can spend the $900, and you can spend the $1000 that you have in your deposit. Therefore, money has been created.

The changes that these transactions would have on bank A's balance sheet are as follows:

Chartered bank A

Assets	Liabilities
Reserves + $1000	Demand deposits + $1000

After keeping $100 back for required reserves, the bank has $900 worth of excess reserves. If the $900 were loaned out, the balance sheet would read as follows:

Chartered bank A

Assets	Liabilities
Reserves + $100	Demand deposits + $1000
Loans + $900	

It is likely that the $900 loan will be spent. Once this is done, it may find its way back into a chartered bank. Assume that the

$900 goes towards the purchase of a new chesterfield. The furniture store owner would deposit the $900 in chartered bank B. The bank would be required to keep the legal reserve (ten percent) and would be in a position to lend out any excess reserves.

The changes to bank B's balance sheet are as follows:

Chartered bank B

Assets	Liabilities
Reserves + $900	Demand deposits + $900

Chartered bank B

Assets	Liabilities
Reserves + $90	Demand deposits + $900
Loans + $810	

If bank B lends out the $810 in excess reserves, more money has been created. This process of deposits and loans continues until there are no excess reserves to be loaned out. The amount of money created as a result of your initial deposit of $1000 is as follows:

$900 (first loan)
+ $810 (second loan)
+ $729 (third loan)
+ $. . . (subsequent loans)

If this process were to continue uninterrupted, the amount of money created from the $1000 deposit would be $9000. A short formula allows for the calculation of the change in the money supply.

$$\Delta M = \frac{\text{excess reserves}}{\text{reserve ratio}}$$

where ΔM represents the change in the money supply

The change in the money supply from our example can be written as follows:

$$\Delta M = \frac{\$900}{0.10} \text{ (reserve ratio for demand deposits)}$$
$$\Delta M = \$9000$$

The money supply would increase by $9000 if all the money taken out in loans were put back in demand deposits. If some of the money were deposited into savings deposits, then the reserve requirement on the deposit would change. Since the reserve requirement is only two percent on savings deposits, more money could be loaned out. If more money were loaned out, then more money would be created. If your $1000 was initially deposited in a savings account, the potential increase in the money supply would be:

$$\Delta M = \frac{\$980}{0.02} \text{ (reserve ratio for savings deposits)}$$

$$\Delta M = \$49\ 000$$

Several assumptions have to be made when using this formula. The first assumption is that all loans will eventually be redeposited in savings accounts. This also assumes that savings deposits are included in the definition of the money supply. In order for the money supply to expand by the maximum amount, other conditions must be present. Banks must be willing to lend out all their excess reserves. If banks decide to hold back more money for reserves than is required, then less money will be created. People also have to be willing to borrow money. It is also assumed that all the money that is loaned out eventually finds its way back into a chartered bank. If some of the loan money moves in hand-to-hand circulation and is not redeposited in a bank, less new money will be created. Further, if chartered banks are required to keep any secondary reserves, then even less money will be created.

The example of money creation refers to chartered banks only. There is a difference between the money-creating power of the chartered banks and that of other financial institutions. First, the official Bank of Canada definition of the money supply includes only chartered bank deposits. Second, the majority of deposits in Canada are with chartered banks. There is a greater likelihood that money will be redeposited into a chartered bank than into another deposit-accepting institution. The money-creating potential of other institutions is further restricted by some legal controls on their ability to make loans.

7.11   Assume that $500 is put into a demand deposit. What is the potential effect on the money supply? What conditions are necessary for the money supply to expand by this amount?

7.12   If chartered banks decide to keep excess reserves, the potential of the banking system in creating money is reduced. Are banks likely to keep many excess reserves? Why or why not?

The Bank of Canada

The amount of money in circulation influences the levels of unemployment, inflation, and economic growth. In Canada the banking system has the ability to expand the money supply. This gives the banking system the ability to influence economic conditions. Are there any controls over the ability of Canadian chartered banks to create money? The answer to this question is yes. The control of the Canadian money supply rests with an independent institution, the Bank of Canada. The Bank of Canada is not a chartered bank but a central bank. Its responsibilities are outlined in the preamble to the Bank of Canada Act.

> ... it is desirable to establish a central bank in Canada to regulate credit and currency in the best interests of the economic life of the nation, to control and protect the external value of the nation-al monetary unit and to mitigate by its influence fluctuations in the general level of production, trade, prices and employment, so far as may be possible within the scope of monetary action, and generally to promote the economic and financial welfare of the Dominion ...

The primary responsibility of the Bank of Canada is to regulate the money supply in order to promote the economic and financial welfare of the country. We discussed earlier in the chapter how changes in the money supply can influence economic conditions. The crude-quantity theory of money pointed to a direct relationship between the money supply and prices. The Fisher equation of exchange showed the relationship between the money supply and the level of GDP. It is the Bank's responsibility to control the growth of the money supply in order to influence unemployment and inflation.

The Bank of Canada is an independent institution and is not under the direct authority of the federal government. The independence of the Bank, however, can cause some difficulties. It is possible that policies followed by the Bank may conflict with those followed by the federal government. For example, if the federal government was to see unemployment as the most serious problem facing Canadians, it would undertake steps to increase the level of spending in the economy. These steps may include an increase in government spending and possibly a tax cut. If the Bank of Canada saw inflation as a more serious problem, it would take steps to reduce the money supply and would try to reduce spending. It has been agreed that where policies differ, the federal government has the responsibility of directing the Bank toward policies it would like to see carried out. The Bank of Canada is, therefore, an independent institution making its own economic policy, unless the federal government disagrees with its decision!

The relationship between the Bank of Canada and the government is a close one. The Bank holds some of the government's bank deposits. Federal government deposits in the Bank of Canada amounted to $11 million in 1990 (table 7.5). The Bank provides the federal government with economic advice and lends it money on occasion. The Bank of Canada acts as an agent for the federal government and manages the government's borrowing requirements. It sells government bonds to the public. As part of its role in handling government bond issues, the Bank conducts the weekly auction of treasury bills (see below).

The Bank also serves as a banker's bank, in that it holds deposits for chartered banks. Part of the legal reserves that chartered banks must have are kept in the form of deposits at the Bank of Canada. The Bank has more than $1.4 billion in chartered bank deposits (table 7.5) and can also make loans or advances to the chartered banks. The Bank is referred to as a lender of last resort. The interest rate that the Bank of Canada charges is referred to as the *bank rate*. The bank rate is determined by adding 0.25 percent to the average yield on treasury bills determined each Thursday. Chartered banks do not borrow a significant amount of money from the Bank of Canada; however, the bank rate serves as an indicator of what is going to happen to interest rates. As shown in table 7.3, chartered banks had advances from the Bank of Canada of $304 million in January 1991.

Table 7.5 / Bank of Canada, assets and liabilities, end of 1990

Assets	($ millions)
Government of Canada direct and guaranteed securities	19 998
advances to members of Canadian Payments Association	471
foreign-currency deposits	368
other investments	3 864
accrued interest on investments	392
all other assets	182
Total assets	25 275

Liabilities	($ millions)
notes in circulation	22 970
Canadian dollar deposits	
Government of Canada	11
chartered banks	1 458
other members of the Canadian Payments Association	134
foreign central banks and other institutions	294
other	112
foreign-currency liabilities	210
Bank of Canada cheques outstanding	48
all other liabilities	38
Total liabilities	25 275

Source: *Bank of Canada Review, March 1991* (Ottawa: Bank of Canada, March 1991), pp. S24-S25.

The Bank is also part of the Canadian Payments Association. In 1980, this association was created in order to establish and operate *a national clearings and settlement system* for cheques and other payments orders. Any financial institution that offers accounts on which a customer can write cheques payable to someone else is eligible for membership in the Canadian Payments Association. What is a clearings and settlements system? When someone at a financial institution cashes a cheque that was drawn on an account at another institution, an exchange of funds must take place between the institutions. The drawer's account must be debited and the institution where the cheque was cashed must be reimbursed. The physical exchange of paper items and magnetic tapes between different institutions, and the accounting and balancing involved, make up the clearings and settlements system. Millions of such transactions occur each day.

What role does the Bank of Canada play? Most members of the Canadian Payments Association have settlement accounts and lines of credit at the Bank of Canada. The Bank effects the final settlement of accounts between institutions each day by crediting and debiting member accounts accordingly.

One final responsibility of the Bank of Canada deserves mention: the bank is responsible for the external value of the Canadian dollar. That is, it is responsible for the value of the Canadian dollar in terms of the currencies of other countries. A further discussion of the Bank of Canada's role in influencing the foreign-exchange value of the Canadian dollar is contained in Chapter 9.

Treasury Bills

Treasury bills are short-term government bonds that are sold by auction each Thursday.

Treasury bills are short-term promissory notes issued by the Government of Canada. The 91-day (three-month) bill is the most common; a 182-day (six-month) bill is also issued. The bills are auctioned on a weekly basis and are sold on a discount basis. That is, the government offers to pay the face value of the treasury bill at maturity. Bills come in varied denominations: $1000, $5000, $25 000, $100 000, and $1 000 000. No interest is paid, but the return for the investor is the difference between the purchase price and the face value. For example, it may be possible to purchase a $100 000 treasury bill for $96 000. On the maturity date, the holder of the treasury bill receives $100 000.

The Bank of Canada acts as the federal government's agent in issuing these bills. It conducts a weekly auction of treasury bills on Thursdays. The size of the weekly issue varies and depends on the financial needs of the government and the state of the market. Each week the Bank sends out a notice of the amount of maturities of the current week's auction. Chartered banks and investment dealers are referred to as primary distributors and are asked to submit bids on their own behalf and on behalf of their clients.

The Bank receives the bids in the form of sealed tenders. At 12 noon on Thursday, the sealed tenders are opened. The tenders are arranged in descending order. They are first offered to the highest bidder, and then to the next highest, and so on, until the entire weekly issue has been allocated. The tenders give the price per $100 to three decimal places. For example, a bid of $98.426 on a $100 000 treasury bill means that the bidder would pay $98 426 and receive $100 000 at maturity. Primary distributors may submit multiple bids and there is clearly no advantage to being the highest bidder since everyone receives the face value at maturity.

The Bank of Canada also bids on treasury bills. First, it submits a competitive bid similar to other primary distributors. It then submits a reserve bid, which is usually not successful. The reserve bid is to ensure that the government receives its money if the bids are not enough to buy up the entire issue. The reserve bid also ensures that the government borrows the money at a reasonable cost. If the reserve bid was not there, it would be possible for all the primary distributors to submit very low bids.

The Bank of Canada calculates the average price and the average rate of return and usually makes the information available at about 2 p.m. on the day of the auction. Information on the highest and lowest bids is also made available.

Questions

1   What would be the reason to bid on a treasury bill?
2   Could a treasury bill be considered a liquid asset?
3   Could the Bank of Canada influence the average yield on treasury bills?
4   What factors could influence the bids that are submitted at the weekly auction of treasury bills?

Monetary Policy

Changes in the rate of growth of Canada's money supply influence economic conditions. The Bank of Canada monitors changes in the money supply on a regular basis and takes steps to alter the growth in the money supply when necessary. The action taken by the Bank of Canada to alter the money supply, and ultimately economic conditions, is referred to as monetary policy.

Which definition of the money supply should the Bank of Canada concentrate on? As shown in table 7.6, Canada's money supply has been growing at a variety of rates depending on which definition of money is chosen. For example, in 1990, M1 decreased by 1.9 percent, while M2 increased by 10.6 percent. For the previous year, 1989, M1 increased by only 4.6 percent whereas M2 increased by 13.1 percent.

The selection of a money-supply definition to act as the focus of the Bank of Canada's actions is a difficult decision. Traditionally, changes in M1 have been the focus of the Bank's activities. However, depositors may transfer money out of demand deposits into other deposits that pay interest and also have chequing privileges. By paying attention to M1 only, the Bank may underestimate the purchasing power in the economy. Regardless of the money-supply definition chosen, how does the Bank of Canada influence the rate of growth of the money supply?

Table 7.6 / Rates of change (percentage) in Canada's money supply, 1974-90

Year	M1	M2	M3
1974	9.3	20.5	26.1
1975	13.9	15.2	15.3
1976	8.0	13.0	18.8
1977	8.6	14.3	16.5
1978	10.1	11.1	14.3
1979	6.9	15.8	19.8
1980	6.2	18.7	16.3
1981	3.3	15.1	13.2
1982	-0.1	9.4	4.3
1983	10.1	5.8	0.7
1984	3.4	4.4	2.1
1985	4.3	9.5	5.8
1986	5.0	8.7	6.5
1987	12.9	10.1	8.7
1988	6.1	7.6	7.9
1989	4.6	13.1	11.2
1990	-1.9	10.6	9.8

Source: *Bank of Canada Review, July 1986* (Ottawa: Bank of Canada, August 1986), p. S20; ibid., February 1987, p. S20; ibid., May 1990, p. S20; ibid., March 1991, p. S20

The Bank Rate

The bank rate is the rate of interest paid by chartered banks on money borrowed from the Bank of Canada.

The **bank rate** is the rate of interest that the Bank of Canada charges the chartered banks when they borrow from it. The bank rate is used as a signal for the direction that interest rates are taking. When it increases, other interest rates follow. Chartered banks usually increase their prime lending rate. The prime lending rate is the rate that a bank charges its most credit-worthy customer on loans. When the interest rates go up, people are less likely to borrow money. They are also more likely to want to save money, since the return for savings is greater. Increases in the interest rate are likely to decrease the amount of spending, and can be used to fight demand-pull inflation. Conversely, decreases in the bank rate would lead to lower interest rates. The overall spending in the economy would likely increase, which would decrease the level of demand-deficient unemployment.

How can the Bank of Canada influence the bank rate if the rate is set weekly at the treasury bill auction? The Bank of Canada submits competitive and reserve bids at the weekly auction of treasury bills. The bids of the Bank of Canada influence the average yield on the bills and, since the bank rate is determined by adding 0.25 percent to the average yield, the Bank of Canada does have an influence on the bank rate.

Open-Market Operations

Open-market operations refer to the buying and selling of government bonds by the Bank of Canada in order to influence the money supply.

Open-market operations are the buying and selling of government bonds on the money market by the Bank of Canada. If the Bank wants to reduce the size of the money supply, it will sell government bonds on the open market. The open market simply means that selling is not restricted to certain groups. By selling bonds, spendable money is removed from circulation. Individuals or institutions who purchase government bonds from the Bank of Canada give up money in return for a non-spendable asset (the bond). If the Bank wants to increase the amount of money in circulation, it will buy bonds back from the public, giving individuals and institutions money in return for bonds. This will increase both the money supply and the purchasing power in the economy.

**Figure 7.3
The impact of the Bank of Canada selling a bond to a life insurance company**

Bank of Canada		Chartered Bank	
Assets	Liabilities	Assets	Liabilities
Bonds −$100 000	Chartered bank Deposit −$100 000	Deposit at Bank of Canada −$100 000	Deposits −$100 000

Whitby Life Insurance Company	
Assets	Liabilities
Bonds +$100 000 Deposit at chartered bank −$100 000	

Suppose that the bank sells a $100 000 government bond to the Whitby Life Insurance Company. The balance sheet transactions of the life insurance company, the chartered bank where the life insurance company has its deposit, and the Bank of Canada are presented in figure 7.3. The assets of the insurance company will be transferred from a bank deposit to a $100 000 government bond. In order to pay for the bond, the company had to reduce the amount of money in its bank deposit. The reduction in chartered bank deposits by $100 000 means that the money supply has decreased by this amount.

What does the Bank of Canada do with the cheque from the life insurance company? Since the cheque was written against an account with a chartered bank, the Bank of Canada will present the cheque to the chartered bank for payment. The chartered bank has a deposit at the Bank of Canada and, therefore, this deposit will be reduced by the amount of the cheque. In figure 7.3, the assets of the chartered bank have been reduced by $100 000 (the reduction in its deposit at the Bank of Canada). The liabilities of the Bank of Canada have also been reduced by $100 000 with the reduction in the chartered bank deposit.

What is the effect on the money supply if the $100 000 bond is sold to a chartered bank? The bank would purchase the bond by taking the money out of its deposit at the Bank of Canada (see figure 7.4). The bank exchanges one asset for another. There is actually no change in the money supply since deposits in chartered banks have not changed. Although the money supply has not been directly affected, the ability of the chartered bank to lend money has been reduced because the reserves (deposits at the Bank of Canada) of the chartered bank have been reduced. If the Bank of Canada wanted to expand the money supply, it would buy government bonds in the open market. This would provide the chartered banks with more reserves to be

**Figure 7.4
The impact of
the Bank of
Canada selling a
bond to a
chartered bank**

Bank of Canada		Chartered Bank	
Assets	Liabilities	Assets	Liabilities
Bonds −$100 000	Chartered bank deposit −$100 000	Deposit at Bank of Canada −$100 000 bonds +$100 000	

loaned out. The expansion of the money supply would lead to increased spending and increased gross domestic product.

Secondary Reserve Rates

The secondary reserve rate is the amount of secondary reserves (liquid assets held by chartered banks as a reserve against deposits) required by the Bank of Canada.

The Bank of Canada may require that chartered banks maintain a reserve of liquid assets in addition to the required legal reserves. This **secondary reserve rate** may range from 0 percent to 12 percent of total deposits. If the Bank of Canada wants to take steps to reduce, or slow, the growth of the money supply, it will increase the secondary reserve requirement. If chartered banks are required to keep more money in liquid assets, then they cannot lend out as much money in the form of consumer and business loans. If loans are reduced, then the money supply will not expand as quickly. Conversely, if the Bank of Canada wants the money supply to expand more rapidly, it will lower the secondary reserve requirement.

Transferring Federal Government Deposits

The Bank of Canada acts as a banker for the federal government, which maintains bank deposits in both chartered banks and the Bank of Canada. By transferring federal government deposits between itself and the chartered banks, the Bank of Canada could change the money supply. How could a transfer of federal government deposits affect the money supply? *If the Bank of Canada wanted to increase the money supply, it would transfer federal government deposits to the chartered banks.* This would give the chartered banks more reserves and more money to lend out. The process of lending money begins the multiple expansion of the money supply. If the Bank of Canada transferred $100 000 out of a federal government deposit to a similar deposit at the chartered banks, the chartered bank reserves would increase by $100 000. After keeping the required legal reserves, the banks would be able to lend out the rest. If the Bank of Canada wanted to reduce the expansion of the money supply, it would transfer federal government deposits from the chartered banks back to itself. This would reduce the reserves of chartered banks and give them less money to lend out.

Moral Suasion

Moral suasion describes an informal approach to monetary policy whereby the governor of the Bank of Canada expresses his views on policy to the presidents of the chartered banks with the goal of influencing their decisions on behalf of the country.

It has been suggested that the relatively small number of chartered banks in Canada enables the Bank of Canada to conduct a more informal monetary policy. The governor of the Bank of Canada should be able to call the presidents of the chartered banks in for a meeting to discuss his views about monetary policy. The governor may want certain types of loans increased while others are reduced. This informal discussion approach is referred to as **moral suasion,** and may be used to affect certain industries or regions in Canada. For example, certain chartered banks may be asked to make more loan money available to farmers or small businessmen. Banks may also be encouraged to grant more loans in less-developed regions of the country.

Moral suasion is more likely to be an instrument of monetary policy in Canada than in the United States. The large number of commercial banks in the United States makes an informal policy an impossibility. Although more likely to be used in Canada, moral suasion is rarely used as it is an inefficient way to achieve monetary objectives. The influx of foreign banks into Canada as a result of Bank Act changes will make moral suasion even less effective.

7.13 Work through the balance-sheet approach for a situation in which the Bank of Canada buys a government bond back from the public. What will be the effect on the money supply?

7.14 List three things that the Bank of Canada could do in order to reduce the money supply in Canada. Would this action be undertaken to counteract inflation or unemployment? Explain.

Summary

The existence of money removes our reliance on a barter system. The main function of money is to facilitate transactions between individuals. Apart from acting as a medium of exchange, money also performs other functions. Money serves as a common denominator for prices, which are expressed in terms of a country's currency. Money is also a means whereby individuals can store their wealth.

Throughout history, many commodities have served as money. Regardless of what item is used as money, it must possess certain characteristics. It must be divisible into smaller amounts, easily recognizable, durable, easy to carry, and not easily copied. However, above all else, if an item is to circulate as money, it must be seen as having value.

There is a market for money similar to the market for other products. Individuals demand money primarily for carrying out day-to-day business transactions. Money is also demanded for speculative and precautionary reasons. The supply of money in Canada is composed of coins, Bank of Canada notes, and deposits at chartered banks. The interaction of the demand for and the supply of money determines the interest rate, which in turn influences economic conditions. When the level of business and consumer spending responds to changes in the interest rate, the level of GDP is altered.

Since chartered bank deposits are considered to be money, it is possible for the chartered banking system to create money. When banks lend out their excess reserves, money is created. When loans are redeposited into other banks, it is possible for more money to be created. The banks create money in the sense that they can create deposits.

The Bank of Canada is responsible for the regulation of the money supply in Canada. When the Bank of Canada regulates the money supply in order to influence economic conditions, this is referred to as monetary policy. The tools of monetary policy include bank-rate changes, open-market operations, changes in the secondary reserve requirement, and the transferring of government deposits.

Questions for Review and Discussion

1 What effect do credit cards have on the demand for money? Will credit cards ever replace money?
2 What are some liquid assets with which you are familiar? What type of assets cannot be classified as liquid?
3 Why aren't 1967 Canadian silver dollars circulating in our economy as money?
4 In a newspaper advertisement in February 1979, Dr. Franz Pick stated that the United States would issue a new currency as early as 1980. As yet, a new currency has not been issued. Why would Dr. Pick believe that a new currency was necessary?
5 Why would chartered banks pay a higher rate of interest on specified term deposits than on personal savings deposits?
6 In one sense, the legal reserve rates on demand and savings represent a penalty for the chartered bank. Why is the secondary reserve requirement considered to be less of a penalty?
7 Apart from making exchanges easier, what other uses does money have?
8 If the velocity of money remains constant, does it make the Bank of Canada's task of regulating the economy easier? Explain.
9 What limits the Canadian banking system's ability to expand the money supply?
10 Examine the following balance sheet for bank A:

Assets		Liabilities
Reserves	$25 000	Demand deposits $50 000
Loans	$25 000	

   i What level of excess reserves does bank A have?
   ii If this bank were to lend out its excess reserves, what effect would this have on the money supply?
   iii If a depositor withdrew $10 000 from a demand deposit, how would this affect the assets or liabilities of bank A?
11 Show the impact on a bank's assets and liabilities of the bank purchasing a $20 000 government bond from the Bank of Canada.
12 Are travellers' cheques considered to be money? Are credit cards money?

13 Would you expect the rate of interest paid on a one-year term deposit to be greater than the rate of interest paid on a three-month term deposit? Why or why not?

14 Since 1980 a large number of foreign banks have been operating in Canada. Does this make directing monetary policy by moral suasion a more difficult alternative? Explain.

15 What makes money a valuable commodity?

16 What impact will an increase in the money supply have on
   i   interest rates
   ii   business investment
   iii aggregate demand
   iv   employment in Canada
   v   prices?

17 The chartered banks in Canada are perfectly safe places in which to put your money. Discuss this statement.

18 Some analysts have suggested that deposit insurance be scrapped. Would the elimination of deposit insurance change the lending practices of chartered banks? How would it change the decisions of depositors with regard to where they choose to put their money?

Suggested Readings

Boreham, Gordon F., Eli Shapiro, Ezra Solomon, and William White. *Money and Banking: Analysis and Policy in a Canadian Context*. 2nd ed. New York: Holt, Rinehart and Winston 1979.

Galbraith, John Kenneth. *Money: Whence It Came, Where It Went*. New York: Bantam Books 1976.

McCullough, A.B. "Funny Money." *Horizon Canada* 4, no. 43 (December 1985). Quebec: Centre for the Study of Teaching Canada Inc.

Stewart, Walter. *Towers of Gold, Feet of Clay*. Toronto: Totem 1982.

Stabilization Policy

Chapter Objectives

After completing this chapter, you should be able to:

- explain the unemployment/inflation trade-off
- describe the shortcomings of both monetary and fiscal policies in regulating the economy
- explain the supply-side approach to economic stabilization
- understand the possible problems of large amounts of government borrowing
- relate the shortcomings of long-term wage and price control policies
- explain how manpower policies can be used as economic stabilization policies

Key Terms

Phillips curve
stagflation
fiscal policy
automatic stabilizer
discretionary fiscal policy
public debt

monetary policy
supply-side economics
Laffer curve
wage and price controls
manpower policies

Approaches to Stabilization Policy

The constant flow of injections and leakages associated with the circular flow of money (see Chapter 6) results in changes in the level of gross domestic product (GDP). Changes in GDP have an influence on the levels of inflation and unemployment in Canada. When the level of GDP is increasing, the demand for goods and services is increasing as well. Employers need workers, and as more jobs are created, unemployment is reduced. The reduction in unemployment caused by increased spending will, however, lead to higher prices. On the other hand, when the level of GDP is falling, the opposite results occur. The decreases in spending cause unemployment to rise and inflation to be reduced. A comparison of rates of inflation and unemployment from 1966 to 1989 are presented in figure 8.1.

The federal and provincial governments are concerned about high levels of unemployment and inflation. Both levels of government continually introduce programs aimed at influencing GDP in order to ensure that jobs are being created, and that prices do not rise too rapidly. Programs that are introduced to regulate unemployment and inflation are referred to as *economic stabilization* programs. We have already seen economic stabilization policies at work earlier in the text: in Chapter 6, the effects of government spending and taxation (fiscal policy) on GDP were analysed. At the federal government level, **fiscal policy** is the responsibility of the Department of Finance. Similar departments responsible for fiscal policy exist within each provincial government.

Fiscal policies employ changes to the level of government spending and taxation with the goal of influencing economic conditions.

How does fiscal policy act as economic stabilization policy? If unemployment were seen as the major economic problem in Canada, governments would endeavour to increase their spending and/or reduce the level of taxation. The subsequent increase in spending by government or by households would create new jobs. One example of increased spending would be an initiative by the government to modernize or expand an existing airport. The money spent on design and construction would have a multiplier effect on the economy. An example of an initiative by government in the area of taxation would be the lowering of personal income tax rates. As shown in Chapter 6, both increased spending and lower taxes lead to increases in GDP.

If inflation were the country's main economic concern, the opposite steps would be undertaken. Government spending would be reduced and/or the level of taxation increased. Government spending could be reduced in a number of ways. For example, purchases of office supplies could be cut back, new construction programs on government buildings could be eliminated, the travel expenses of civil servants could be limited, and so on. These steps, along with taxation increases, would reduce the overall amount of spending in the economy. This would put less demand pressure on prices and

International Economics

Chapter Objectives

After successfully completing this chapter, you will be able to:

- appreciate Canada's major trading partners and trading commodities
- explain the law of comparative advantage and use it in a numerical example
- describe the impact of international trade on resource and product prices and on resource allocation
- relate the arguments for and against tariff protection
- relate the protective conditions of the Canada-United States Automobile Agreement
- discuss the advantages and disadvantages of Canada entering into a free-trade agreement with the United States
- relate the objectives of GATT
- differentiate between the capital and current accounts in the balance of payments
- relate deficits and surpluses in the balance of payments to changes in the foreign-exchange value of the Canadian dollar
- describe how foreign-exchange rates are fixed

Key Terms

law of comparative advantage
tariff
countervailing duties
non-tariff barriers
infant industry
dumping
mercantilism
GATT
European Economic Community
Canada-United States
  Automobile Agreement
free trade

international balance
  of payments
current account
capital account
foreign-exchange rate
arbitrage
depreciation/appreciation
devalued/revalued
International Monetary Fund
cabotage
adjustable-peg system
stabilization fund

Canada's Trade Abroad

Canadians carry on business not only with other Canadians, but also with residents of other countries. We buy foreign products such as oranges, cameras, automobiles, clothing, cheese, and wine; we travel in foreign countries, buy foreign bonds and deposit money in foreign banks, hire foreign engineers, and transport products on foreign ships. Residents of other countries purchase Canadian products such as wheat, automobiles, minerals, and lumber, travel in Canada, and carry on a wide variety of business transactions with Canadians.

Market transactions with foreign countries have some unique characteristics, which is why we study them separately from other transactions. First, each country has its own currency. In order for an exchange to take place, an acceptable medium of exchange, or currency, must be found. Individuals and companies who are selling products in international markets prefer to be paid in their own currency in order to pay taxes, rent, the wages of their employees, and the other costs of being in business. If, for example, Canadians are buying products from Great Britain, it will be necessary for Canadians to obtain British pounds in order to pay for the products. British pounds are purchased in the foreign-exchange market (discussed later in this chapter).

Second, international trade brings different languages and customs together. Canadians who hope to conduct business with residents of other countries must attempt to understand different and unfamiliar behaviour patterns. For example, the treatment of time varies around the globe. North Americans tend to react quickly to business requests, whereas Latin Americans are more casual about time and are in less of a hurry. In some African countries, the amount of time required to make a decision is directly proportional to the importance of the decision. If Canadians try to speed up the process, Africans may see it as an attempt to downgrade their work.

Third, political considerations are extremely important in international dealings. In Canada, there are very few barriers to trading across provincial boundaries. A business person in Quebec City may telephone another business person in Winnipeg to order some equipment. Most products can be shipped across provincial boundaries easily. However, this is not the case with international boundaries. *National governments may choose to restrict certain products from entering or leaving their country.* Canada also has some restrictions about what can be allowed into or out of the country. For example, we have had a quota on the amount of shoes and clothes that can be brought into Canada each year. The Canadian government has also restricted the amount of foreign investment into Canada on an annual basis. In addition, Canada has restricted the amount of a product that can leave the country. In recent years, the export of natural gas, for example, has been regulated by the government.

Political differences can also severely restrict or stop trade in certain areas. When the USSR invaded Afghanistan in 1979, several nations including Canada stopped grain shipments to the Soviet Union. The racial policies of South Africa have led to certain restrictions on trade with that nation. When Argentina invaded the Falkland Islands in 1982, the European Economic Community (EEC) imposed restrictions on imports into Europe from Argentina. When Iraq took over Kuwait in 1990, the United Nations imposed sanctions on trade with Iraq.

The movement of workers from job to job in Canada is basically not restricted by provincial borders. If a worker in Regina, Saskatchewan, sees a good job possibility in Victoria, British Columbia, that person is free to apply for the job, and if successful, to relocate. Workers are not, however, free to move across international borders. Canadians cannot work in other countries without receiving work permits. These permits, issued by the foreign country, may not be easy to obtain—just as work permits for non-Canadians may not be easy to obtain.

For these reasons, international trade must be treated as a separate topic. In Chapter 6, international trade was first introduced during the discussion of the circular flow of income. Exports were regarded as an addition to the circular flow, while imports were seen as a leakage. The importance of these items to the Canadian economy can be seen by pointing out that Canada produces about one-quarter of its GDP for export. Therefore, any fluctuations in the amount we sell to foreigners will have a definite impact on our economy.

What products do Canadians sell abroad? A list of exports for 1990 is presented in table 9.1. Our biggest export in terms of dollars is passenger automobiles. Most of our motor vehicles are destined for the United States and fall under the Canada-United States Automobile Agreement. Automotive exports, including cars, trucks, car parts, and engines, account for almost one-fifth of the dollar value of our exports. The forest industry is also a major part of the export scene with three products—newsprint, wood pulp, and lumber—composing almost 12 percent of export sales. Canada also is known for its production of wheat, and wheat sales comprise 2.3 percent of our export dollars. Apart from automotive products, Canada's major exports are derived from the resource industries.

Table 9.1 / Major merchandise exports and imports by commodity, Canada, 1990

Commodity	Exports $ (millions)	Percent
passenger automobiles and chassis	16 162	10.9
trucks, truck tractors, and chassis	7 513	5.0
motor vehicle parts, except engines	7 363	5.0
newsprint paper	6 460	4.3
wood pulp and similar pulp	6 115	4.1
crude petroleum	5 529	3.8
lumber, softwood	5 250	3.5
telecommunications and related equipment	4 505	3.0
aircraft, engines, parts	4 062	2.7
wheat	3 358	2.3
aluminum, including alloys	3 040	2.0
office machines and equipment	2 751	1.9
precious metals, including alloys	2 387	1.6
Total exports	148 664	

Commodity	Imports $ (millions)	Percent
motor vehicle parts, except engines	12 764	9.4
passenger automobiles and chassis	10 714	7.9
electronic computers	5 958	4.4
telecommunications and related equipment	5 631	4.1
crude petroleum	5 405	4.0
electronic tubes and semi-conductors	2 727	2.0
motor vehicle engines	2 676	2.0
aircraft and parts	2 259	1.7
organic chemicals	2 078	1.5
outerwear, except knitted	1 522	1.1
plastics materials, not shaped	1 517	1.1
inorganic chemicals	1 308	1.0
paper and paperboard	1 281	0.9
Total imports	136 224	

Source: *Exports: Merchandise Trade 1990*, publication no. 65-202 annual, (Ottawa: Statistics Canada, May 1991), pp. 32-215. *Imports: Merchandise Trade 1990*, publication no. 65-203 annual, (Ottawa: Statistics Canada, May 1991), pp. 34-182.

Imports into Canada are also listed in table 9.1. Our biggest import item is motor vehicles and parts, again due to the Automobile Agreement, which allows for specialization of production in each country and duty-free access of automobiles and new parts into each country. Automotive imports accounted for almost 20 percent of all imports in 1990. Canada's other major imports are basically manufactured products. In fact, Canada is regarded as an exporter of primary or unfinished products and an importer of finished or manufactured products.

What countries does Canada trade with? Canadians trade with countries all over the globe, but some countries are more important *trading partners* than others. As shown in tables 9.2 and 9.3, our biggest customer is the United States, which imports approximately 75 percent of all our exports. We, in turn, receive more than 64 percent of our imports from that country. As a result, economic conditions in the United States will have a significant impact on Canada's economy. If total spending drops in the United States, spending on Canadian products will also drop. Since the United States is our biggest customer, our exports would be severely affected. Inflation in the United States is also of concern to Canada. If prices in the U.S. are rising, the prices of imported products into Canada will also rise. This could result in a higher inflation rate for Canada.

Table 9.2 / Canada's total exports by destination, 1990

Country	Total exports $ (millions)	Percent
United States	111 380	74.9
Japan	8 230	5.5
United Kingdom	3 536	2.4
Germany	2 322	1.6
China	1 655	1.1
Netherlands	1 641	1.1
South Korea	1 554	1.0
France	1 304	0.9
Belgium	1 249	0.8
Italy	1 188	0.8
U.S.S.R.	1 125	0.8
Australia	902	0.6
Total exports	148 664	

Source: *Exports: Merchandise Trade 1990,* publication no.65-202, annual, (Ottawa: Statistics Canada, May 1991), pp. 2-4.

Table 9.3 / Canada's imports by country of origin, 1990

Country	Total imports $ (millions)	Percent
United States	87 894	64.5
Japan	9 523	7.0
United Kingdom	4 841	3.6
Germany	3 837	2.8
France	2 448	1.8
South Korea	2 254	1.7
Taiwan	2 109	1.5
Italy	1 954	1.4
Mexico	1 748	1.3
Norway	1 683	1.2
China	1 393	1.0
Hong Kong	1 058	0.8
Total imports	136 224	

Source: *Imports: Merchandise Trade 1990,* publication no. 65-203, annual, (Ottawa: Statistics Canada, May 1991), pp. 2-4.

Canada's second-largest trading partner is Japan. In 1990, our exports to Japan represented 5.5 percent of total exports, while imports from Japan were 7.0 percent of total imports. In Canada's very early years, its major trading partner was the United Kingdom. But as early as the 1880s, the United States replaced the United Kingdom as the major source of our imports. We imported mainly manufactured products and the United States was a cheaper source of these products. Still, the United Kingdom remained the main destination of our exports until World War II. It was an importer of the primary products in which Canada specialized, whereas the United States was more self-sufficient in these products.

9.1 In what ways are business transactions with foreign nations different from business transactions within Canada?

9.2 Can you explain why motor vehicles are our major export item, as well as our major import item?

9.3 Is Japan a bigger trading partner for Canada than France? Why?

9.4 What is significant about the fact that we export raw materials and import finished goods?

International Trade Theory

Why is it necessary for Canadians to trade with foreign countries? The main reason is that Canadians want goods that are not available in this country. If Canadians want orange juice for breakfast, it must be brought in from outside Canada. If we want to drink tea or coffee, again, these must be imported. Different countries have different climates and different geographical make-ups; some are good for growing certain products, but not others.

Even though we may be able to buy a certain product in Canada, some Canadians may prefer the uniqueness of a foreign item. For example, wines from different countries have different characteristics and tastes. French and German wines are popular in Canada, but so are wines from Italy, Spain, Portugal, Australia, and so on. In Canada we produce automobiles, yet some Canadians prefer imports. Certain luxury automobiles, such as those built by Rolls Royce and Mercedes Benz, must be imported. The uniqueness of certain products means we must import Cuban cigars, Swiss watches, Scotch whisky, English china, and other special products.

A second major reason for buying a foreign product is that the import may be cheaper or of better quality. The resources available to a certain country may make it efficient at certain types of production. Canada is very abundant in farmland and, therefore, we can specialize in certain agricultural products, such as wheat. We are also surrounded by water and have a fishing industry that exports around the world. Some countries, for example, Japan, are not blessed with a large land mass but have a skilled labour force and a great deal of technological innovation taking place. This makes certain products cheaper to produce in such a country than in Canada. Buyers look for the best bargain for their money, whether they buy a domestic product or a foreign one.

Canadians will buy imported products when they are cheaper than Canadian products and of comparable quality. Foreigners will buy Canadian products when they are cheaper than those produced elsewhere. Under this market situation, Canadians would profit by specializing in developing products that they do best, and by having foreigners do likewise. Through trade, each country could receive products at the lowest possible price.

It makes economic sense to specialize in the development and creation of products that you do best. What if a country cannot produce anything more efficiently than another country? Will such a country be able to trade? The answer would appear to be no, yet a theory addressing this question was developed in 1817 by David Ricardo, an English economist and stockbroker. He suggested that even though one country may not be efficient at producing anything, it can still participate in trade. Countries that are more efficient at

The law of comparative advantage is a theory of international trade that states that a country should specialize in and trade those items that it can produce relatively more efficiently than other countries.

producing everything can still benefit from trading with others. This theory is referred to as the **law of comparative advantage.**

An example may best explain this law. Assume that we are considering two countries: Canada and Mexico. Assume further that we are only talking about two products: wheat and radios. In order to show that trade in these two products can benefit both Canada and Mexico, let us assume that Canada produces both of these products more efficiently than Mexico. In order to *compare efficiencies,* the production of one worker in one week will be used. One worker in Canada can produce either six bushels of wheat or ten radios in one week. In Mexico, one worker can produce either two bushels of wheat or six radios in a week. It is necessary to assume that all workers are equal within each country in terms of what can be produced. Also, these production levels have to remain the same regardless of how much is produced.

Table 9.4 / Production of one worker in one week

Product	Canada	Mexico
wheat	6 bushels	2 bushels
radios	10	6

As shown in table 9.4, Canada is more efficient at producing both wheat and radios than Mexico (three times more efficient at producing wheat and 1.67 times more efficient at producing radios). Would it pay Canada to trade with Mexico in these two products? If a Canadian were to work in the fields growing wheat, he or she could produce six bushels a week. In order to do this, the Canadian worker gives up the opportunity of producing ten radios. The opportunity cost of six bushels of wheat is, therefore, ten radios. The opportunity cost of one bushel of wheat is therefore 1.67 radios.

In Mexico, if a worker produces wheat, he or she must sacrifice radios as well. In order to produce two bushels of wheat, six radios must be sacrificed. The opportunity cost of one bushel of wheat is three radios. Consequently, in Mexico, one bushel of wheat is more costly than in Canada since more radios have to be sacrificed. If wheat is cheaper in Canada, why not try to exchange Mexican-made radios for Canadian wheat? If Canada were to send one bushel of wheat to Mexico, how many radios would they want in return? In Canada, if one worker produces one bushel of wheat, 1.67 radios must be given up. If we can get more than 1.67 radios by sending a bushel of wheat to Mexico, it would be a good deal. In order to produce a bushel of wheat, Mexico has to sacrifice three radios. If Mexico can get a bushel of wheat from Canada for less than three radios, it would be better off.

According to these figures, both countries can benefit from trade. The terms of trade are difficult to predict with any accuracy; however, it is likely that Canada will send one bushel of wheat to Mexico for more than 1.67 radios, but less than three radios.

This example does not take into consideration transportation costs or the value of each country's currency. Yet it shows that even when one country, Canada, is more efficient at producing both products, it can still benefit from trade with a less-efficient country. Both countries get more wheat and radios than they would have without trade. Both countries will benefit from trade as long as a comparative advantage exists.

9.5 Do Canadians only trade with foreigners because of our comparative advantage?

9.6 What does opportunity cost have to do with comparative advantage?

Effects of International Trade

What are the effects of international trade on Canada and Mexico? The potential effects of trade involve three important factors.

Resource Allocation

The advent of international trade and specialization may result in changes in the way that resources such as land and labour are used in any country. Resources will move out of industries in which the country has a *comparative disadvantage,* and into industries where the country has a *comparative advantage.* In Mexico, workers will move from wheat production to the radio factories. Land will no longer be used for wheat, but may be taken over by a radio factory. In Canada, the results would be opposite. Workers would leave the radio factories in order to work in the wheat fields. More land would be turned over to wheat production.

The shift that takes place in resource allocation due to *specialization* will have an additional effect. The total output of wheat and radios produced in the two countries will increase. With specialization, more output is achieved from the same amount of resources. It follows from our example that if all countries in the world engaged in foreign trade and specialized more in production, then the total output of goods and services would increase.

The impact of international trade on a country's production-possibilities curve is shown in figure 9.1. The curves for Canada and Mexico show the possible production of one worker in one week for each country. Assuming that the terms of trade are one bushel of wheat for two radios, the production-possibilities curves for both countries have shifted to the right after trade. One worker

**Figure 9.1
International trade
and the production
-possibilities curve**

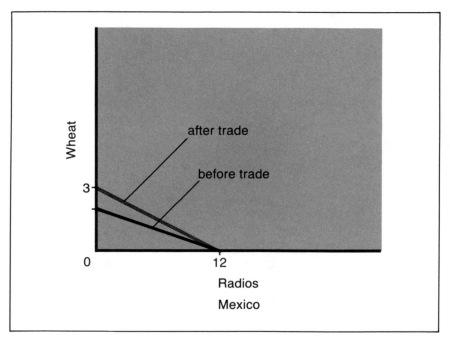

The impact of international trade on the production-possibilities
curves for Canada and Mexico. The production-possibilities curves
have shifted to the right.

in Canada could produce either six bushels of wheat or ten radios in one week before trade. If the Canadian worker produced only wheat, the possibility exists of trading six bushels of wheat to Mexico for twelve radios. For Mexico, the option is three bushels of wheat or six radios after trade. The production and consumption possibilities for both countries have been enhanced by trade.

Product Prices

The prices of wheat and radios will also be affected by international trade. The demand for wheat produced in Canada will go up. The demand for wheat produced in Mexico will decrease. This will cause the price of Canadian wheat to increase as a result of increased demand, and the price of wheat in Mexico to decrease because of an increased supply from Canada. International trade will bring the prices for wheat in the two countries closer together. This example assumes that transportation costs are zero. In reality transportation costs are not zero and will have some impact on the price. The relative prices will also be affected by the exchange values of the Mexican peso and the Canadian dollar.

The *relative price* of radios in Canada and Mexico will also change. The demand for Canadian-made radios will decrease and the demand for Mexican-made radios will increase. The price of radios in Canada will decrease because of increased supply and the price of radios in Mexico will increase because of increased demand. Again, international trade will bring the relative price of radios in Canada and Mexico closer together. If this analysis is extended around the globe, we can assume that international trade will bring prices for all products in different countries closer together.

Resource Prices

Foreign trade will also affect the prices that suppliers have to pay for workers, land, etc. In Canada the demand for land will increase since wheat is a *land-intensive product*. The demand for land in Mexico will decrease. This will result in higher prices for land in Canada and lower prices for land in Mexico. Radios, in contrast, are a *labour-intensive product*. The demand for workers will be reduced in Canada and will increase in Mexico. Some Canadian workers displaced from the radio factories will find work in the wheat fields. Since wheat-growing relies more heavily on land than on workers, not all workers will be re-employed producing wheat. The unemployment among Canadian radio workers will tend to lower the wage rate among radio workers as supply exceeds demand. In Mexico, workers who leave the wheat fields should find new employment in the radio factories because the total demand for workers has increased, and thus would increase the *wage rate* in Mexico.

Assume that workers were allowed to move freely across international borders. What difference would this make? Prior to international trading, wages for radio workers would be higher in

Canada than in Mexico. This circumstance would encourage Mexican radio workers to move to Canada. There would now be a greater supply of radio workers in Canada, resulting in lower wages for radio workers in Canada. In Mexico, the reduced supply of radio workers would force up wage rates. The results are similar to those achieved through trading. Wages in Canada are lowered and wages in Mexico are increased. *International trade is a substitute for the movement of resources.*

9.7 Why does international trade result in a more efficient allocation of the world's resources?

9.8 Why does international trade result in changes in the price of Canadian resources?

Barriers to International Trade

In spite of the advantages of international trade, all countries have erected some barriers to trade. These barriers are aimed at restricting the amount of foreign products that can be imported. Barriers come in one of two forms. **Tariffs** are the most common trade restriction and represent a tax on the imported product. This tax may be imposed as a source of revenue for the government, but more than likely it is for the protection of domestic suppliers. If the tax raises the price of the import, the domestic supplier will be more competitive.

Countervailing duties are a type of tariff. If the product being imported into Canada has received government financial assistance in the exporting country, it may be subject to a countervailing duty. Canada may argue that the imported product has an unfair advantage in the competition with Canadian-made products. The countervailing duty may be applied in order to allow Canadian products to compete in price. In 1986, Canada and the United States exchanged countervailing duties. The United States imposed a duty on imports of Canadian lumber and Canada imposed a duty on the importation of American corn. In 1989, the United States imposed a countervailing duty on steel rails exported to the U.S. by Sydney Steel Corporation of Nova Scotia. This duty was imposed as a result of the subsidies that the company had been receiving from both the federal and provincial governments.

The impact of a tariff on hockey sticks is shown in figure 9.2. The supply curve S_d represents the domestic supply of hockey sticks. The supply curve S_{d+f} represents the total supply, domestic and foreign, of hockey sticks on the market. The addition of foreign suppliers drops the price from P_d to P_{d+f}. The share of the market held by domestic suppliers also drops from Q_d to Q_1. If a tariff is imposed on imported hockey sticks, the new supply curve is S_t. The new price is P_t and the new quantity is Q_t. As a result of the tariff,

**Figure 9.2
The impact of a
tariff on hockey-
stick sales**

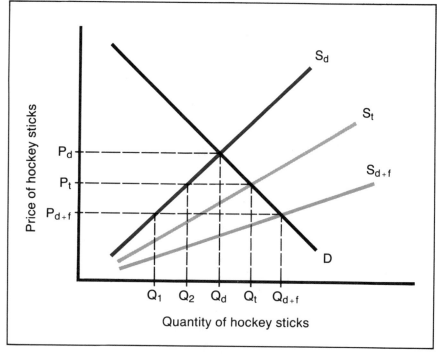

As a result of the tariff, the price has increased and the quantity of
hockey sticks exhanged in the market has decreased.

the price has increased and the quantity of hockey sticks exchanged
in the market has decreased ($Q_{d+f} - Q_t$). Consumers get fewer hockey
sticks. The amount of the market supplied by domestic firms has increased from Q_1 to Q_2. The increase in market share awarded to domestic suppliers is referred to as the protection effect of the tariff.

*Non-tariff barriers
impede the flow of
international trade
through the use of
quotas, restrictive rules
and regulations.*

Non-tariff barriers (NTBs) also impose restrictions on international trade. The most common form of NTB is the quantitative import
restriction, or quota, which places a limit on the value or quantity of
an import. Voluntary export restraints are agreements between importing and exporting countries on the maximum value or number of
items to be exported during a set period. This type of NTB became
better known as a result of the restrictions on Japanese car sales to the
United States in the 1980s. Various rules and regulations in the importing country can also restrict trade. For example, the importing country
may ban a certain type of food additive. Any imports containing the
additive will not be allowed to enter the country. Non-tariff barriers
have expanded as nations agree to reduce tariffs. In a sense they
have replaced tariffs as a form of protectionism.

Some interesting examples of non-tariff barriers come from
Europe. France has held up British meat imports in order to test for
synthetic hormones, even though such hormones are banned in

Britain. Italy prohibits the importation of apple vinegar because of an Italian law that states that vinegar can only be made from wine. In Belgium, margarine can only be sold in square cups even though it is sold in cups of other shapes elsewhere in Europe. Germany requires that all wool be sold in 40-gram packets. Other European nations use 50-gram packets.

Why are countries motivated to construct trade barriers? The reasons for this protection are numerous and are listed below.

Unequal Benefits from Trade

Although there are overall benefits from international trade between two countries, certain groups within one country may be hurt by trade. In our example, Canada would have found it advantageous to import radios from Mexico. This would result in the unemployment of radio workers in Canada. Although some of the workers may go to work in the wheat fields, not all will be able or willing to do so. The owners of Canadian radio companies will not be happy about the situation either. The owners and workers may, therefore, approach the federal government and ask for some protection against the importation of Mexican radios. The federal government may respond by erecting a barrier to trade, such as a quota on the import of Mexican radios. This would reduce the competition for Canadian radios. Both owners and workers would benefit. Many industries in Canada have formed national associations representing their manufacturers. These associations have their offices in Ottawa so that they can lobby the federal government for assistance to their industry; the erection of trade barriers is one such type of assistance.

It should be pointed out that the erection of trade barriers is not without costs. These costs are primarily borne by the consumer who will pay a higher price and receive less of the product after the barrier is in place. Tariffs add a cost to the product that will show up in higher prices. Quotas and other non-tariff barriers reduce the supply of the product and thus increase the price. Also, in our example, Mexico may retaliate by limiting the importation of Canadian wheat. This would hurt Canadian farmland owners and farm workers who would have sold the wheat to Mexico. Trade barriers, therefore, help some Canadians while hurting others.

Protection of Domestic Living Standards

For numerous reasons, workers around the world do not receive the same wage or salary. These *wage differences* between countries may prompt governments to adjust to the differences through trade barriers. For example, if the average wage in Hong Kong was 50 cents per hour and the average wage in Canada was $7 per hour, products leaving Hong Kong for Canada would be much cheaper due to the difference in wages, and would therefore have a definite labour-cost advantage. In order to protect the high wages and living standards in Canada, and to allow Canadian companies to compete for the consumer's dollar, the federal government may place a tariff on all products imported from Hong Kong. The argument for the tariff would be that if Canadian companies had to compete directly with cheaper products from Hong Kong, Canadian wages would have to be lowered and our standard of living would fall.

This argument overlooks the fact that the wages paid to workers are not the only cost of production and also that wages are tied to *worker productivity*. In industries where workers are paid more, the costs of production may not be any higher than in comparable industries where they are paid less. If the more highly-paid workers produce more than the workers receiving a lower wage, the high-paying company could have even lower per-unit costs. Workers in Canada may be paid more and may be able to produce more because they are more skilled or because they have more sophisticated machinery and equipment to work with. Higher wages do not necessarily produce a higher price for an item, nor do they necessarily reflect a competitive disadvantage.

Trade barriers increase the price of the product to the consumer. It is hard to imagine how higher prices can improve domestic living standards.

Infant Industry

When a company is starting out in an industry, it faces tough competition from existing companies in the industry. The existing firms will already have a clientele established and will be producing on a large enough scale in order to have lower per-unit costs. In many cases the new company will not survive unless it receives some type of *government assistance.*

At times, government may be anxious to see a new domestic company or a new industry develop. New companies and indus-tries create jobs and increase gross domestic product. It may be difficult for this new industry to get started if it has to compete with those companies that are already established around the world. The newcomer is referred to as an **infant industry**. In order to help the infant industry get on its feet, governments may impose a tariff or quota on the foreign competition. It is argued that as soon as the industry is large enough and competitive in the world markets, the trade barrier will be dropped.

A newly established industry is referred to as an infant industry.

Suppose that some Canadians wanted to cultivate a banana industry in Canada. They may approach the government for assist-ance. One of the steps taken to promote this industry would be the imposition of a high tariff on all imported bananas. It would be hoped that the Canadian banana industry, producing costly bananas at first, would grow, achieving *economies of scale*. This would make the industry internationally competitive within a number of years. At that time, it might be expected that the tariff on imported bananas could be removed.

There are several difficulties with the argument for imposing a trade barrier in this situation. First, how do we know if the industry will ever become internationally competitive? In the case of bananas, it is highly unlikely. Consumers would continue to pay higher prices for bananas than they would if there were no tariff on imported bananas. Second, if an industry grows up under the protection of a tariff, it may not be forced to develop its efficiency. If it remains inefficient, the tariff is not likely to be removed. Finally, if this industry is eventually going to be successful, why would private individuals not invest in it? Individuals are continually taking risks by putting their money into business ventures with an uncertain future. What rationale is there to treat the infant industry differently from other industries?

Another reason for promoting infant industry is that the economies of some countries are very specialized, relying basically on one product. Fluctuating international markets affect the incomes that these countries receive. In order to add some stability to their economy, these nations would like to develop other industries. To develop these industries, protection must be provided in the form of tariffs and quotas. The argument is that the result—a more diversified economy—would provide economic stability for the country over the long run and that this would override the high costs of the trade barriers.

Military Self-Sufficiency

Trade barriers may be imposed for *strategic reasons*. Some industries may be important for military purposes and, as a result, should not be subject to import competition. The automobile industry would be an example. If military conflict broke out, the automobile industry would be required for vehicle production. The textile industry would be required for uniform production, and so on. The difficulty with this argument is that in times of military conflict, all industries are likely to be important. Special trade barriers cannot be set up for all of them.

Reaction to Dumping and Foreign Assistance

Dumping is the practice of selling a product in a foreign market at a lower price than is charged in the domestic market.

Charging different prices in different markets is referred to in international trade as **dumping**. It refers to a situation in which a product sells for a lower price in the foreign market than it does in the domestic market. For example, it is argued that the Russian-built automobile, the Lada, is being dumped into Canada. The argument is that the Lada sells for more money in the USSR than it does in Canada.

Importing countries are concerned about dumping since the products dumped are often in competition with domestically produced products. There is a fear that once an import becomes established and has possibly driven some domestic producers out of business, the prices will be increased. When it can be shown that dumping exists, the importing countries usually respond with special tariffs in order to raise the price and protect domestic manufacturers.

Trade barriers in the form of tariffs are also imposed when it is discovered that an imported product was produced with the aid of government assistance in the exporting country. If this assistance leads to lower prices and unfair competition, then the importing country may impose a countervailing duty or tariff on the import. An example in which a countervailing duty was applied was in Michelin's decision to export tires to the United States. The Canadian government had given the Michelin Tire Company financial assistance to locate in Nova Scotia. The Americans argued that giving financial assistance to Michelin gave that company an unfair advantage in the American automobile tire market, and they imposed an additional tariff on Michelin tires.

Diffusion of Technology

In order to be competitive in international markets, companies are forced to spend significant amounts of money on *research and development*. Government assistance is often available to companies that are improving their technology. Once the technology is developed, however, there is no guarantee that it will always benefit the country that helped to finance it. Many companies are multi-national in nature and can transfer their technology across international boundaries. It is not possible for countries to duplicate another country's climate or natural resources, yet it is possible to duplicate technology.

Assume that Canada were to give some financial assistance to a multi-national company in Canada in order to help the company develop a new computer diskette. Once the diskette is developed, the company may decide not to have the diskette produced in Canada but in another country. The diskette would then be imported into Canada from abroad. Such a situation would not be beneficial to Canada. The federal or provincial government in this case helped finance the technological advance, yet Canadians would not have received any of the benefits. In this case a heavy tariff could be placed on the importation of this diskette in order to encourage the company to produce it in Canada.

Increase in Domestic Employment

As discussed in earlier chapters, economic conditions are continually fluctuating. At times, the economy may be in a recession with high levels of unemployment. A possible cure for unemployment may be to raise trade barriers on imports and force Canadians to buy domestically-made products. This argument appears to make sense, since if money is spent on Canadian-made products, the money stays in Canada and creates employment here. One problem that may arise with this approach, however, is that Canadian exports may be affected.

If foreign countries cannot sell their products in Canada, they will not have money to spend on Canadian products. If our exports decline, then jobs may be lost. *The trade barrier may protect some jobs, while sacrificing others.* In our earlier Canada-Mexico example, any attempt to protect Canadian radio manufacturers would hurt Canadian wheat producers. What would happen if all countries imposed trade barriers simultaneously in order to increase domestic employment? World trade would be drastically reduced and all the benefits from trade would be lost. Further, it is unlikely that the overall level of employment would increase.

Trade barriers may be imposed for any of the above reasons. In each instance, the level of international trade is reduced. When trade is reduced, the total output of goods and services that could be achieved is not reached. Prices also remain higher than need be for certain products. Therefore, any decision to erect a trade barrier should take into consideration all of the positive and negative aspects of such a move.

9.9 Explain some of the problems with the infant-industry argument to trade restrictions.

9.10 What do we mean when we say that the benefits from international trade are not spread equally throughout the population?

9.11 Why may higher tariffs not help a country out of a recession?

Mercantilism

From the sixteenth to the eighteenth centuries, a school of thought called mercantilism held the view that if a nation promoted exports and limited imports, an inflow of gold and silver would result.

Nations were not always aware of the advantages of free trade. During the years 1500-1750, countries established many barriers to international trade in an attempt to gain economic superiority. This economic philosophy was known as **mercantilism.** The objective behind international trade was to have exports greater than imports. This favourable balance of trade would cause gold and silver bullion to flow into the exporting country. The inflow of gold and silver would stimulate domestic employment and provide money for the production of military equipment.

The countries that were influenced by mercantilist thought were England, France, Holland, Portugal, and Spain. Each was experiencing the same type of economic changes. Industries were starting to develop and people were moving from the farms to the towns. Manufacturers and merchants were becoming prominent members of the community. These nations were also involved in exploring the New World and establishing colonies. Again, the inflow of gold and silver from trade was necessary to expand the navy in order to protect colonial interests.

The mercantilists proposed several measures to ensure that exports exceeded imports. They urged government to establish quotas and tariffs and to prohibit the importation of certain products. They proposed that government provide subsidies to domestic producers so that they could better compete with foreign goods. In some countries it became illegal to export certain products. In Spain, the punishment for sending gold and silver out of the country was death. In England, it was illegal to export woollen goods. Again, severe punishment was handed out for infractions.

Eventually the mercantilist doctrine began to lose favour with business people who were interested in acquiring wealth. The business community believed that more freedom in international dealings would help them achieve their goal of getting rich. A move began toward less government regulation of trade. In 1776, Adam Smith's writings told of the advantages of free trade, and the mercantilist philosophy began to decline.

Early Canada was affected by the mercantilist philosophy. France saw its colony of New France only as a source of raw materials. One task performed by Samuel de Champlain was to report on the resources available in the New World. His list included fish, fur, timber, flax, and hemp. New France was a source of raw materials but was prevented from establishing industries that would compete with those in France.

Questions

1 Why were the five countries mentioned above interested in protecting their colonies?
2 Did Canada have a role to play in the inevitable conflicts between these nations?
3 Would it be possible for all countries to have more exports than imports?
4 If the amount of money circulating in a country was based on the amount of gold and silver in that country, what impact would the mercantilist philosophy have on the money supply? What impact would it have on prices ?(See Chapter 7.)

General Agreement on Tariffs and Trade

An international agreement called the General Agreement on Tariffs and Trade (GATT) is aimed at reducing the barriers to international trade.

In order to profit from the advantages of international trade, 23 countries signed the **General Agreement on Tariffs and Trade (GATT)** in 1947. The agreement was aimed at removing the barriers to international trade. *If international trade flourished, specialization would result in improved standards of living.* GATT became effective in January 1948. Since that time, membership has increased from the original 23 to the present 100 members. GATT was based on a few fundamental principles:

Non-discrimination: the contracting parties agreed that trade between nations should be conducted on a non-discriminating basis. Each nation was to apply any tariffs or trade policy equally to all countries. There were exceptions to this rule only in unusual circumstances. Existing preferential trading arrangements such as the British Commonwealth preferences were allowed to continue. That is, products entering Britain from Commonwealth countries were subject to lower tariff rates than products from other nations.

Multilateral negotiations: GATT provided a mechanism for the discussion of trade problems and for the reduction of trade barriers. Reductions in tariffs were to be undertaken by multilateral negotiations. These are negotiations in which all GATT signatories take part. GATT also established a review panel to examine trade disputes.

Quantitative restrictions: GATT hoped to have countries use only tariffs as a barrier to trade. Quantitative restrictions, such as quotas, were to be prohibited. Although quantitative restrictions have not been eliminated, the use of quotas has been reduced. GATT did provide for the use of quantitative restrictions in situations in which the country was having persistent balance of payments problems.

GATT has assisted in reducing the level of tariffs between trading nations. Tariffs are reduced through multilateral negotiations. The Kennedy Round of negotiations (1964-67) was named after U.S. President John F. Kennedy. The tariff reductions negotiated at this time were phased in from 1967 to 1972. The Tokyo Round, (1973-79), focussed a great deal of attention on non-tariff barriers. The tariff reductions negotiated during the Kennedy Round had forced countries to look for other types of protection. Non-tariff barriers in the form of rules and regulations began to spring up.

In many ways, non-tariff barriers are more effective than tariffs. Whereas tariffs simply increase the price of the imported article, non-tariff barriers can effectively prevent the article from being imported. Many non-tariff barriers are hard to identify. Some are imposed by government and others by corporations. Non-tariff barriers that were a major concern of the Tokyo Round negotiations can be classified into three types:

Technical barriers to trade: certain technical specifications may be attached to imported products that make it difficult for them to be imported. For example, a West German regulation calls for five-ply, three-eighths-inch-ply plywood. This effectively eliminates Canadian exports of plywood to West Germany.

Government procurement practices: some governments may insist that government purchases be made from domestically-produced products. Since government spending is a major component of total spending in countries, imports are eliminated from competing in this area.

Customs valuation: different countries have different procedures for valuing imports for tariff purposes. Most trading countries use the Brussels system, which accepts the value of the product as listed on the invoice. Canada, the United States, New Zealand, and South Africa use their own valuation systems. If the tariff is represented as a percentage of the price, then the amount of the tariff depends on what price is established for tariff purposes. If a higher price were selected for tariff purposes, then the tariff would be higher and a stronger barrier to trade.

The GATT agreement that came out of the Tokyo Round was signed in 1979. The tariff reductions commenced on 1 January 1980 and were to be phased in over a seven-year period. In terms of non-tariff barriers, Canada adhered to the international agreement on customs valuation. Canada received permission to wait for four years before introducing the new system. The Canadian government was also required to change some regulations and administrative procedures as a result of international agreement. The United States agreed to prove injury to domestic firms before applying countervailing duties. This change benefitted Canada in particular.

Canada benefitted from the reductions in tariffs negotiated during the Tokyo Round. Canada also had to reduce tariffs. The average rate of Canadian industrial tariffs was reduced by between nine and ten percent. No reductions were made, however, in the level of Canadian tariffs on such items as textiles, clothing, footwear, and ships.

The eighth round of GATT negotiations got underway in Uruguay in September 1986. Non-tariff barriers were still a concern for countries associated with GATT; however, the emphasis in the new round of talks shifted to subsidies and market-sharing agreements. Food-exporting counties were upset over the subsidies given to farmers in the European Economic Community (EEC) and the United States. Market-sharing agreements, such as voluntary export-restraint agreements, are at odds with GATT's principle on non-discriminatory behaviour. That is, if action is taken against one country, it should be taken against them all. Many developing countries wanted the topics of increased trade in financial information and investment services discussed at these talks. The Uruguay Round of trade talks was also concerned about intellectual property rights and performance requirements set on foreign investment.

The meetings in Uruguay developed guidelines for that round of GATT negotiations. New commodities were covered in the talks, including food and services. Agreements were made allowing GATT to become more of a watchdog over domestic trade policies. This means that it will have the power to monitor and regulate revisions to domestic microeconomic policies. In December 1990, the GATT discussions broke down over the question of agricultural subsidies.

A study released by the Economic Council of Canada in 1989 suggests that Canada would have faced less upheaval than other industrial nations if the Uruguay Round of talks had been successful in lowering barriers to trade. The study estimated that if all developed countries eliminated trade barriers, just over 0.5 percent of Canada's workforce would need to change jobs. The relative impact in Europe would be twice as great and in Japan eight times as great. In addition to facing less dislocation as a result of trade liberalization, Canada would gain access to markets that are disproportionately larger than those gained by the United States and Europe.

In the past, nations have complained that Canada is not living up to the principles of the GATT. The European Economic Community has complained that provincial liquor boards use discriminatory pricing practices when marking up European liquor. The GATT ruling went against the provincial pricing practice. The United States has argued that Canadian pricing practices discriminate against imported beer. A 1988 GATT panel found that Canadian beer practices violate international trade obligations. The United States also complained about a Canadian requirement that west coast fishermen sell their salmon and herring to Canadian processors only. United States processing firms wanted to be able to bid for this fish as well since Canadian processors can bid for U.S. salmon and herring. The GATT ruled that Canadian restrictions violated international trade law. The GATT also ruled against Canada in a complaint from the United States about Canadian import quotas on ice cream and yogurt. Canada has the right under the GATT to control imports of milk and other raw foods where production is controlled by a marketing board; however, ice cream and yogurt are classified as processed foods.

Not all GATT rulings have gone against Canada. The GATT ruled that the United States was in violation of international trade law by allowing U.S. producers to block the importation of goods that they viewed as an infringement of intellectual property. Canada is anxious that the United States bring this legislation into line with the GATT. Canada and several other nations also appealed to the GATT over a U.S. tax that imposed a higher levy on petroleum imports than on domestic production. A GATT panel backed Canada's complaint.

9.12   What were the original objectives of GATT?

9.13   Describe the non-tariff barriers that were a concern during the Tokyo Round negotiations.

9.14   What were the main issues of the Uruguay Round of negotiations?

European Economic Community

The European Economic Community (EEC) consists of a group of European nations that have eliminated barriers to trade among themselves, and have established common external tariffs on products from non-member countries.

After World War II, countries in Europe started discussing the possibility of an economic union. First, Belgium, Luxembourg, and the Netherlands signed an agreement that eliminated internal tariffs between them and set up a common external tariff on goods entering any of these three countries from elsewhere. In 1951, these countries, along with France, West Germany, and Italy, signed a treaty in Paris that created the European Coal and Steel Community. This treaty established a common market in coal and steel. The success of this treaty led these countries to further discussions on economic co-operation. In 1957 in Rome, Italy, two treaties were signed. The first treaty established the European Atomic Energy community, which encouraged the co-operative development of nuclear energy for peaceful purposes. The second established the **European Economic Community (EEC).**

The EEC's objective is to develop the economies of countries in the community and improve their standards of living. The belief was that these objectives could best be achieved through the elimination of tariffs and non-tariff barriers. This would allow for the free movement of products between countries. The EEC also established a common external tariff that would apply to imports from non-member countries. In addition to goods, the plan was that people and money would also be allowed to move freely among member nations, although initially this was not the case.

The community has expanded since 1957. In 1973, the United Kingdom, the Republic of Ireland, and Denmark joined the EEC. Greece became the tenth member in 1981, and in 1986, Portugal and Spain joined the EEC. The population of the EEC member countries is approximately 320 million.

The EEC countries are taking advantage of the benefits of international trade. Countries are specializing in the production of certain products in order to maximize total output. This also means lower prices for consumers. The decision on which country should specialize in which product is not an easy one. Even though the formation of an economic union provides overall benefits for member countries, disadvantages exist because certain groups are hurt by the specialization process. In each country there are producers of dairy products. What determines which country specializes in dairy production? Several EEC countries are wine producers. Who should specialize in wine? French grape farmers, for example, have resisted the importation of Italian wine into France. French farmers have also blocked and hijacked imports of British lamb into France. Germany has banned the importation of Italian beer, and Italy has impounded some German imports. Nevertheless, the EEC has made overall improvements in the movement of goods among member countries.

As of December 31, 1992, the EEC will take another step

toward a single trading market. Barriers will be removed to allow people, goods, services and capital to move freely between member nations. Certain non-tariff barriers currently in place will be removed and companies will be able to sell their products anywhere in the European Community without trade barriers. The European Community is to develop 279 directives by the 1992 deadline. Once the directives have been passed, member countries must change their national laws to conform. These directives include agreements on a common electrical current, common tomato-grading standards, a standard rule on lawnmower noise, and many others.

How will companies adapt to the new Europe after 1992? Instead of producing for the domestic market only, companies will find it necessary to compete on the European market. Those companies currently being sheltered from competition by trade barriers will be hurt by the new rules unless their efficiency is improved. Other companies will enjoy the new freedom associated with a broader market. Some analysts predict that the potential gains of the new single trading market are great because there is so much inefficiency at present in the various markets.

Where does the Europe of 1992 leave those European nations that are not part of the EEC? Some nations still may apply for membership in the EEC. Any democratic European country with a market economy can apply. Austria has already applied for membership, however, a decision on its application will likely wait until after 1992. Even though they may not apply for membership, other European countries such as Sweden and Norway would like some input into EEC decision-shaping if not into decision-making. To date, no official arrangements have been made concerning the relationship between the EEC and other European countries.

There is also talk of economic and monetary union (EMU) in the EEC. The plan is to have a single European currency with an independent "Eurofed" (central bank) setting Europe's interest rates. The objective of monetary policy would be price stability. Banking supervision would be left to the national authorities. There is still discussion on the exact nature of the EMU. Not all member nations see the same role for a European central bank.

Questions

1 Why would a country such as Austria want to be part of the European Economic Community?
2 Does the EEC have anything to do with the law of comparative advantage?
3 Would former communist countries like Poland and Hungary be able to apply for membership in the EEC?
4 What difficulties can you foresee in having twelve nations agree on a single currency and a single European central bank?

Canada-United States Automobile Agreement

During the 1920s, Canada was the world's second largest manufacturer of automobiles. Production of automobiles declined during the 1930s, but picked up during World War II. After the war, it became more difficult for North American automobile manufacturers to export their cars. Other industrialized countries were anxious to rebuild their economies and introduced discriminatory treatment against our auto exports. The Canadian industry began to decline.

The Canadian government was anxious to develop the domestic automobile industry. There was concern that the population of Canada was not large enough to support the large-scale manufacture of cars. Therefore, in order for the industry to grow, it was necessary to increase the export market.

The Canada-United States Automobile Agreement allows for the duty-free movement of most vehicles and parts between the two countries.

In 1965, Canada and the United States signed an agreement regarding automobile production and trade. The **Canada-United States Automobile Agreement** allowed for the duty-free movement of most vehicles and parts between the two countries. Canada had several objectives in signing the agreement. It wanted to increase automobile production in Canada. It also wanted to increase the productivity of the Canadian automobile worker. This strategy would lead to lower prices for cars and higher wages for workers.

American automobile manufacturers also benefitted from the agreement. They did not have to pay the tariff on exports to Canada. They could organize their production in order to make the most efficient use of their factories in both Canada and the United States. Canadian subsidiaries of American companies began to specialize in certain lines of cars, rather than to produce a wide range of cars for the entire market.

Canada and the United States both had certain conditions that they wanted included in the agreement. The main condition imposed by the United States was that automobiles and parts that were destined for the U.S. be composed of at least 50 percent Canadian content. This was to protect against European manufacturers setting up a small assembly plant in Canada in order to gain duty-free access to the American market. By setting up a small plant in Canada, the foreign company could send cars to the United States free of the U.S. tariff instead of exporting them directly to the United States and paying the tariff.

Canada limited the duty-free access of automobiles into Canada to authorized manufacturers. Authorized manufacturers were those who maintained at least 0.75 production-to-sales ratio for each class of vehicle in Canada. This condition was to ensure that some automobile production was undertaken in Canada and that American companies did not return all of their automobile production to the United States. It also kept out imports from other countries that may have entered the United States before coming to

Canada. If automobile companies did not make cars in Canada as well as elsewhere, they could not export them free of tariff to Canada.

In certain respects, the automobile agreement has been a success. Employment and output in the industry have increased since the agreement was signed. Much of this increase would likely have occurred anyway because of a larger and wealthier population. Price differentials that existed between cars sold in Canada and those sold in the United States have been reduced. Longer production runs in the Canadian industry since 1965 have increased efficiency. However, since population increases would have brought about more automobile production in spite of the agreement, it is difficult to attribute all increases in efficiency to the agreement alone.

There are some negative aspects of the agreement, however. Canada has continually had a *deficit* in the trade of automobile parts. That is, we have imported more automobiles and parts from the United States than we have exported to that country. Under the agreement, replacement parts were not permitted duty-free access to either country. Canadian parts manufacturers must face tariffs when trying to sell in the United States. This has led to an overall deficit in automobile trade for Canada, and in recent years, the deficit has been getting larger.

Employment has grown in the Canadian arena of the North American car industry. There is some concern, however, that the percentage of jobs located in Canada is less than the percentage of auto sales in Canada. The type of jobs created in Canada may also be considered a negative aspect of the agreement. In the United States, approximately eight percent of the jobs in this industry are considered to be skilled jobs. In Canada, the corresponding number is two percent. The percentage for semi-skilled jobs is 43 percent in the United States and 23 percent in Canada. This means that Canada has a greater percentage of the unskilled, lower-paying jobs. The lack of research and development undertaken in Canada means that many of the more highly-skilled jobs are not required.

The agreement states that either country can cancel the agreement on one year's notice. It is doubtful that the Canadian government would want to cancel the agreement, even though Canada is not satisfied with all aspects of it. In recent years, the United States has shown more interest in a renegotiated agreement.

The future of the Canada-United States Automobile Agreement is uncertain. The North American automobile industry is not as insulated from competition as it was in 1965. Automobiles from offshore producers have captured a significant portion of the market. In addition, foreign producers have established assembly plants in both Canada and the United States. By 1990, Japanese and Korean assembly operations had been established in Canada. What impact these foreign operations will have on the Canadian automobile industry, especially on the parts manufacturers, is uncertain.

The Canada-United States Automobile Agreement was altered slightly with the signing of the Free Trade Agreement (FTA) between Canada and the United States. The FTA recognized the automobile agreement and incorporated it into the free trade agreement.

9.15   Explain why both countries would benefit from signing the automobile agreement.

9.16   Would Japanese cars assembled in Canada be exported to the United States duty-free?

Freer Trade Between Canada and the United States

Free trade is trade between countries that is unrestricted by tariffs or non-tariff barriers.

International trade benefits those nations that participate. The success of GATT has permitted more than 100 countries to benefit from specialization and the concept of comparative advantage. Even if a country is relatively more efficient at producing all products than other countries, it may still benefit from trade. The benefits from international trade have prompted several people at times to propose the idea of completely **free trade** between Canada and the United States. That is, trade would take place across the border free of tariffs and quotas.

As early as 1857 a free-trade area existed that encompassed Upper and Lower Canada, New Brunswick, Prince Edward Island, Newfoundland, Nova Scotia, and the United States. Not long after, however, John A. Macdonald's National Policy of 1879 established a series of tariffs on imports in order to encourage Canadian manufacturing. In 1911, the federal election was fought over the idea of free trade with the United States. Robert Borden's Conservative Party, which campaigned on an anti-free-trade platform, defeated Wilfrid Laurier's policy of reciprocity. After World War II, Canadians sought freer trade through GATT. In recent years, interest in free trade has come from the American side of the border as well. What are the advantages and disadvantages of freer trade with the United States from Canada's point of view?

Advantages

The advantages of freer trade are many. The removal of barriers to the United States market provides Canadian producers with duty-free access to more than 250 million people. This change allows Canadian companies to become more efficient by producing on a larger scale. Greater efficiency could lead to lower prices and higher wages for Canadian workers. Duty-free access to a larger market should also increase employment in Canada. The removal of tariffs protecting Canadian manufacturers will also have an impact. Canadian companies will be forced to become more efficient if they wanted to compete. This circumstance should also lead to lower prices.

The direction of trade will probably change with freer trade. There will also be certain *cost savings*. Some Canadian cities are in close proximity to major U.S. markets. Atlantic Canada and Quebec are very close to the heavily-populated northeastern portion of the United States. British Columbia is closer to west-coast markets than many American cities. Under these circumstances, Canadian manufacturers have a cost advantage in terms of transportation costs.

If freer trade makes Canada economically stronger, it is likely to make Canada politically stronger as well, by strengthening Canadian unity. Provinces will be anxious to remain part of the free-trade area and would also be interested in remaining part of a united Canada. If a province were to separate from Canada, it would face tariff barriers from both Canada and the United States.

Freer trade can also bring other advantages to Canada. First, it may stimulate *research and development activity*. This type of activity is essential if Canada is to remain competitive in world markets. It will also help to increase employment. Second, some economists argue that more processing of our raw materials will be done in Canada if access to foreign markets were made easier. This would also create more jobs. Third, others believe that our manufacturers would be in a better position to handle non-tariff barriers that are springing up in many countries and that can be more detrimental to trade than tariffs.

Freer trade between the two countries will not necessarily mean similar economic policies. Canada will maintain an independent fiscal and monetary policy, though it will not be able to ignore U.S. policy. Workers will not be free to move between countries, as each country has its own immigration laws. If Canadian wage rates could remain below those in the United States, Canada will have a competitive advantage. Finally, there would undoubtedly remain an exchange-rate differential between the two currencies. At the present time, the Canadian dollar is equivalent to approximately $0.86 of an American dollar. This fact gives Canadian products a slight cost advantage.

The signing of a bilateral trade agreement between Canada and the United States should protect Canadian industry from sudden protectionist forces arising in the United States. In 1986, the United States imposed countervailing duties on cedar shakes and shingles and on softwood lumber imports into the United States from Canada. These duties substantially reduced export sales to the United States, and reduced employment in these industries in Canada.

If access to the U.S. market were secure, business will be more willing to invest in Canada. It would be willing to undertake the long-term investment in plants, technology, and human resources that is required in order to successfully compete in a larger market. Firms are unlikely to make major investment commitments in an uncertain trading environment.

Disadvantages   Certain disadvantages for Canada may accompany freer trade. Some economists believe that Canadian markets would be swamped with lower-priced American products. If Canadian companies are not able to compete, they may be forced out of business. Unemployment will increase. In order to reduce the negative impact of freer trade, it will be phased in over a number of years.

If the major markets are south of the border, Canadian companies may locate close to their markets. American companies might close down their Canadian subsidiaries and locate closer to these major markets. Free trade has been present in agricultural products since 1944, and some Canadian companies, such as Varity Corporation, have moved their head offices to the United States.

Some economists argue that tariffs are no longer the major impediment to trade. The main barriers to trade are *non-tariff barriers* such as the "buy American" laws that have been passed in a number of U.S. states. The removal of tariffs will not tackle the problem of non-tariff barriers. Even when Canadian companies are efficient, they may be prohibited from competing.

Canada is very much a *branch-plant economy,* as many of our companies are simply subsidiaries of American companies. Under a free-trade arrangement, will the branch plants compete with the parent company for business? Why would the American parent company continue the operation of the Canadian plant? The only reason for the Canadian subsidiary to remain in operation would be if it specialized in the production of a certain item or product line that is not produced in the United States. Otherwise many Canadian branch plants may shut down.

Finally, freer trade may alter the lines of communication in Canada. Communication in North America will be strengthened in a north/south rather than an east/west direction. Central Canada may find more in common with the central United States than with other parts of Canada. British Columbia may have more in common with the states of Washington, Oregon, and California. The Atlantic provinces will be oriented to the east coast of the United States. Some argue that this situation will lead to the destruction of Canada. Why would Canadians find it necessary to communicate with Canadians in other parts of the country?

In 1986, Canada and the United States began negotiations on a bilateral free-trade agreement. A Canada-U.S. trade agreement was signed on January 2, 1988 and the agreement came into effect on January 1, 1989. The objectives of the agreement are as follows:

a) to eliminate barriers to trade in goods and services between the territories of the Parties;
b) to facilitate conditions of fair competition within the free-trade area;
c) to liberalize significantly conditions for investment within this free-trade area;
d) to establish effective procedures for the join administration of this Agreement and the resolution of disputes; and
e) to lay the foundation for further bilateral and multilateral co-operation to expand and enhance the benefits of the Agreement.

The reduction of tariffs between Canada and the United States is a major part of the agreement. Tariff cuts began on January 1, 1989; after that date, no existing tariff could be increased unless specifically provided for in the agreement. Tariffs are to be eliminated by January 1, 1998 on the basis of three formulas:

a) Tariffs were eliminated January 1, 1989 on goods that were deemed ready to compete on an international basis. Some of these goods include:

computers and equipment	some pork
some unprocessed fish	fur and fur garments
leather	whiskey
yeast	animal feed
unwrought aluminum	ferro alloys
vending machines and parts	needles
airbrakes for railroad cars	ski
skates	motorcycles

b) Tariffs for other goods are being eliminated in five equal steps that began on January 1, 1989. Some of these goods include:

subway cars	furniture
printed matter	hardwood plywood
explosives	aftermarket auto parts
paper and paper products	

c) All other tariffs are being eliminated in ten steps, with most reductions having begun on January 1, 1989. Some of these goods include:

railcars	steel
softwood plywood	appliances
textiles and apparel	tires
most agricultural products	pleasure craft

There are several conditions attached to the reduction of these tariffs. Reference should be made to the agreement itself, which can be obtained from the Department of External Affairs.

The impact of the Free Trade Agreement is difficult to determine. Other factors, such as tax changes, interest rates, exchange rates, and political stability, can influence the Canadian economy. Also, the cuts in tariffs are to be phased in over a ten-year period. Some early indications are that Canada is benefitting from the FTA. A study by the Royal Bank of Canada found that more jobs were created than lost during the first year of the agreement. The bank concluded that free trade had spurred investment, both foreign and domestic, in Canada. Prices of products which were among the first to receive tariff cuts have declined. The bank also found that most of the early effects from the deal were felt in the Windsor to Quebec City corridor. Both the United States and Canada have received petitions from companies asking that the tariff cuts be implemented more quickly. Another study, this one by the accounting firm KPMG Peat Marwick Thorne, indicates that Canadian firms are investing more in Canada now than before the agreement was signed.

Not all observers are happy with the FTA. The Canadian Labour Congress blamed the FTA for dozens of plant closings and thousands of layoffs. The Ontario Centre for International Business argued that the dispute settlement mechanism is not designed to take consumer interests into account. Some companies have stated that the regulations, including documentation and research, have reduced some of the intended benefits of the FTA.

9.17 Discuss the potential advantages to Canada that may result from the FTA.

9.18 The branch plants of many American-controlled companies are located in Canada. How would this influence the consequences for Canada of the Free Trade Agreement?

Cabotage

Cabotage rights would allow airlines to pick up and deliver passengers between any two points in North America.

Canada and the United States began negotiating a new bilateral aviation agreement in April 1991. It is possible that the treaty will permit almost unlimited access for carriers to operate in both countries. The treaty could negotiate **cabotage** rights, which would allow U.S. carriers to pick up and deliver passengers between Canadian cities, and Canadian carriers to pick up and deliver passengers between U.S. cities. This practice is currently not permitted. Also to be renegotiated are treaties involving charter flights, air-cargo services, security, customs, and immigration.

Why is there interest in deregulating airline traffic between the two countries? One objective is to provide quicker access to U.S. cities for Canadians. Passengers from Canada would be less likely to change planes when travelling to U.S. destinations. Interest in deregulation also came from smaller municipal airports such as Kelowna and Hamilton. These airports would like access to flights to and from U.S. cities. Canada's major carriers are also interested in a new treaty. Air Canada argues that U.S. airlines have access to a larger share of the Canadian market than Canadians have of the U.S. market. Air Canada wants cabotage rights between U.S. cities. Canadian Airlines wants more trans-border routes.

Although both airlines see some advantages to cabotage, they are concerned about the potential consequences for their companies. The pilots' association is against cabotage. Operators of small airlines fear that an "open skies" treaty would make it impossible to compete with U.S. carriers that have lower operating costs. Some analysts argue that safeguards should be negotiated to protect Canadian carriers. The first advantage that U.S. carriers have is size. The seventh-largest carrier in the United States is bigger than Air Canada and Canadian Airlines combined. U.S. carriers also have cost advantages because of lower fuel costs, more liberal tax laws for leasing aircraft, and lower marketing costs. The cost advantage has been estimated to be approximately 25 percent on long hauls and over 10 percent on shorter flights. U.S. carriers have a marketing advantage through their access to major connecting points in the United States such as Boston and Chicago. U.S. carriers also have a marketing edge through their ability to "pre-clear" passengers through U.S. customs in Canada. This pre-clearance allows passengers to go directly to connecting flights when they arrive in the United States. Passengers flying with Canadian airlines currently must clear customs before going to connecting flights.

Questions

1   What is meant by the term "cabotage"? Why would Air Canada be interested in exercising cabotage rights in the United States?
2   Why is it important that Canadian carriers have access to connecting hubs such as Chicago?
3   Will the consumer benefit from an open skies treaty? Explain.

International Balance of Payments

In order to assist with economic planning, the federal government records Canadian foreign trade. Statistics Canada maintains a record of all economic transactions between residents of Canada and the residents of foreign countries. This is referred to as the **international balance of payments.** Essentially, the balance of payments is a record of the amount of money entering Canada and the amount of money leaving Canada. Money enters Canada for a variety of reasons. Some foreigners want to buy our products such as newsprint and wheat. Others want to travel in Canada or invest in Canadian companies.

The international balance of payments documents all financial transactions between residents of one country and residents of the rest of the world.

The current account is the section of the international balance of payments that records the inflows and outflows of money for merchandise and service items.

The section that records the inflow and outflow of investment dollars is the capital account.

Some foreigners purchase bonds that are issued by our various levels of government. Money leaves the country for many of the same reasons. Canadians buy foreign products and travel in foreign countries. Others send money to relatives elsewhere. All of these transactions, and more, make up the balance of payments.

Statistics Canada divides the balance of payments into two sections: the **current account** and the **capital account.** The current account records trade in goods and services. Purchases of merchandise as well as payment for services are included in this account. The merchandise part of the account includes those items that are commonly referred to as exports and imports. These are visible or physical items. The service part includes payment for such services as travel, the use of borrowed money, and freight and shipping.

A breakdown of Canada's current account for 1990 appears in table 9.5, which shows that Canada had a negative balance, or *deficit*, in the current account for that year. More money left the country (payments) than entered the country (receipts) for the items in the current account. This deficit amounted to $15 989 million. Further investigation of the table reveals some of the reasons for the deficit. The merchandise section of the current account actually showed a positive balance, or *surplus*, in 1990. Exports exceeded imports by $10 798 million.

Table 9.5 / Current account, Canadian balance of international payments, 1990

Item	In $ (millions)		
	Receipts	Payments	Balance
merchandise trade	146 057	135 259	10 798
non-merchandise trade			
services	22 378	30 205	-7 827
travel	7 437	11 961	-4 524
freight and shipping	5 332	5 370	-38
other	9 609	12 874	-3 265
investment income	8 701	32 923	-24 222
interest	5 617	26 554	-20 937
dividends	3 085	6 370	-3 285
transfers	10 613	5 350	5 262
inheritances and immigrants' funds	8 114	1 423	6 691
personal and institutional remittances	907	1 015	-108
Canadian withholding tax	1 592	1 592	
foreign withholding tax		248	- 248
official contributions		2 665	-2 665
balance on non-merchandise trade			-26 787
balance on current account			-15 989

Source: *Bank of Canada Review,* March 1991 (Ottawa: Bank of Canada, March 1991), pp. S120 -S121.

However, that surplus was countered by a large deficit in the service sector. In 1990, Canadians paid out $24 222 million more in interest payments and dividends than they received from foreigners. Canadians and Canadian governments have borrowed money in foreign countries. The interest payments on these loans are recorded in the service sector of the current account. Foreigners also invest in Canada by purchasing shares in Canadian corporations. When these corporations make a profit, they distribute part of those profits to shareholders in other countries in the form of dividends. Canadians also have a significant deficit in travel. In 1989, Canadians spent $4 524 million more on foreign travel than foreigners spent travelling in Canada. The role that the foreign-exchange value of the Canadian dollar plays in the determination of these figures is discussed later in this chapter.

A historical perspective of Canada's current-account balance is presented in table 9.6. As shown in the table, Canada has had a deficit in the current account for most years from 1970 to 1990.

Table 9.6 / Current account balance and net capital movements, Canada, 1970 – 1990

| Year | In $ (millions) | |
	Current account balance	Net capital movements
1970	1 033	-717
1971	370	919
1972	- 283	1 847
1973	312	538
1974	-1 299	2 331
1975	-4 631	5 957
1976	-4 096	7 876
1977	-4 322	6 546
1978	-4 903	8 049
1979	-4 864	7 372
1980	-1 130	2 306
1981	-6 131	14 587
1982	2 824	- 713
1983	3 066	2 626
1984	2 695	3 742
1985	-1 991	8 209
1986	-10 155	12 729
1987	-9 168	12 254
1988	-10 162	14 200
1989	-16 688	22 070
1990	-15 989	20 959

Sources: *Bank of Canada Review,* March 1991 (Ottawa: Bank of Canada, March 1991) pp. S121-123

As the name implies, the long-term capital account records money flows of a long-term nature. For example, if a foreign company that operates a factory in Canada puts money into the expansion of that factory, the money is included in the long-term capital account and represents a flow of money into Canada. In contrast, if a resident of Canada buys shares in an American company, the purchase represents an outflow of money and is also recorded in the long-term section. International purchases of long-term bonds are also recorded here. In 1990, Canada had a net capital inflow of $20 959 million.

Table 9.6 also presents a historical perspective of Canada's capital account. Net capital movements is the sum of the long-term and the short-term capital accounts for each year. As shown in the table, Canada has had a net inflow of capital for most years from 1970 to 1990. Only in 1970 and 1982 did Canada experience a net outflow of capital.

9.19 What is the difference between the current and capital accounts in the balance of payments?

Foreign-Exchange Rates

In order for an economic transaction to take place, a *medium of exchange* is necessary. In Canada, this medium of exchange is the Canadian dollar. Our currency is used to buy food, travel, household articles, and other goods and services. What currency, or medium of exchange, is used if Canadians wish to purchase an article outside of Canada? Since the Canadian dollar is not considered legal tender outside Canada, a new medium of exchange must be found.

The foreign-exchange rate is the value of a nation's currency in terms of another nation's currency.

Assume that a Canadian company wants to import cheese from a company in France. Since Canadian dollars are not legal tender in France, the French company will want payment for the cheese in French francs. In order to complete the transaction, the Canadian company must acquire French francs. It does this by going to a market where French francs are sold. This is called the foreign-exchange market. The Canadian company offers to trade Canadian dollars for French francs. Before the exchange in this market can take place, a price or **foreign-exchange rate** has to be established. How is this exchange rate determined?

When Canadians want to purchase French francs, they increase the demand for francs on the foreign-exchange market. This increase in demand tends to put upward pressure on the price of French francs. Canadian dollars are offered in exchange for the francs. As a result, the supply of Canadian dollars on foreign-exchange markets is increased. When the supply of Canadian dollars increases, there is a tendency for the price to fall. If nothing else changes, this foreign-exchange transaction would increase the price, or *value,* of the French franc and lower the value of the Canadian dollar. If a French company were buying Canadian steel, the opposite would occur. The demand for Canadian dollars would increase and so would the foreign-exchange value of the Canadian dollar. The supply of French francs on the market would increase and the price of francs would tend to fall.

Each day thousands of purchases of foreign currencies take place and, therefore, the values of these currencies are constantly changing. Each day the Canadian dollar is exchanged for a new price on foreign-exchange markets. These fluctuations in price are a result of constantly changing demand and supply conditions. Still, regardless of what happens to the value of the Canadian dollar on world money markets, it maintains its value within Canada. A dollar is still a dollar, and the only factor that influences the value of the Canadian dollar domestically is the rate of price increases. When prices increase in Canada, the dollar purchases fewer goods and services than before.

Where is the foreign-exchange market located? There is not just one foreign-exchange market, there are many. Any place in which foreign currencies are exchanged can be classified as a foreign-exchange market. In Canada, chartered banks and foreign-exchange dealers are the major participants in this market. If there are many markets, then there can be many prices. The Canadian dollar may trade for a different price in London, England, than in New York. Nevertheless, prices for the Canadian dollar and other currencies are not likely to vary much from market to market. They are kept close

Arbitrage, a system based on international communications, keeps the foreign-exchange value of a currency approximately equal in all markets.

together through a system called **arbitrage.** This system, based on good international communications, works in the following manner. Assume that the Canadian dollar was trading at a higher price in London than in New York. Individuals could buy Canadian dollars in New York and sell them in London at a higher price. If many people did this, the demand for Canadian dollars would increase in New York and so would the price. The supply of Canadian dollars would increase in London and the price there would come down. Since these transactions can be made by telephone, they can be made quickly—as soon as any major price differences appear in the two markets. This system of arbitrage, in which currencies are bought "low" in one market and sold "high" in another, tends to keep the value of the Canadian dollar the same in all markets around the world.

Since the Canadian dollar's foreign-exchange value is determined in the marketplace, it is possible to analyse changes in the value of the dollar through demand and supply curves. These curves are presented in figures 9.3a and 9.3b. The price of the Canadian dollar is presented on the vertical axis in terms of U.S.

dollars. The price of the Canadian dollar has to be presented in terms of another currency, and the U.S. dollar is commonly used for this purpose. The quantity of Canadian dollars is presented on the horizontal axis. The demand and supply curves take on their traditional shapes. The demand curve slopes down to the right. As the price of the Canadian dollar falls, a greater quantity of Canadian dollars will be demanded. A cheaper Canadian dollar makes Canadian products and services less expensive for foreigners. The supply curve slopes up to the right. As the value of the Canadian dollar rises, more dollars will be offered to the foreign-exchange market. Canadians can now buy more foreign products with the same amount of our currency. As the value of the Canadian dollar increases, Canadians are more likely to travel outside Canada, buy imported wine, hire foreign architects, etc.

**Figure 9.3a
The foreign-
exchange market**

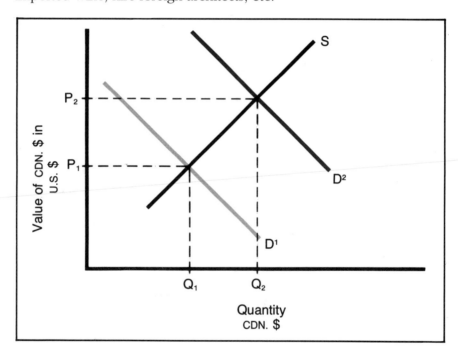

An increase in the demand for the Canadian dollar increases its value.

Any economic transaction that causes money to enter Canada will cause the demand for Canadian dollars to increase. This is represented in figure 9.3a. If Canada exports more natural gas, the demand for Canadian dollars increases because foreigners need Canadian currency to buy the Canadian natural gas they want. This is shown by a shift in the demand curve from **D^1** to **D^2** in figure 9.3a. The price of the Canadian dollar would increase from **P$_1$** to **P$_2$**. The same result would be achieved if foreigners decided to purchase Canadian government bonds or to travel more in Canada. Any transaction that increases the demand for Canadian dollars on foreign-exchange markets will also increase the price, or value, of the Canadian dollar.

The results of more Canadians travelling abroad are shown in figure 9.3b. In order to travel outside Canada, Canadian dollars must be exchanged for other currencies. This exchange increases the supply of Canadian dollars on foreign-exchange markets. The foreign-exchange value of the Canadian dollar will fall from P_1 to P_2 as the supply curve shifts from S^1 to S^2. The same result would occur if Canadians purchased more foreign products or sent money to relatives in other countries. Any transaction that increases the supply of Canadian dollars on foreign-exchange markets decreases the value of the Canadian dollar.

**Figure 9.3b
The foreign-
exchange market**

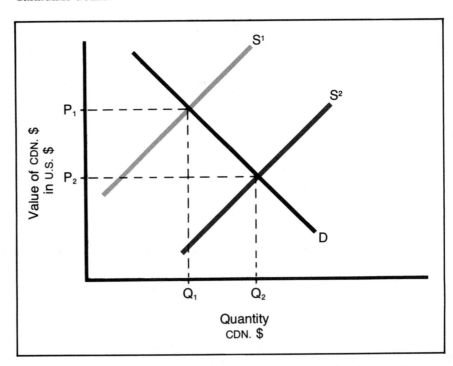

An increase in the supply of the Canadian dollar on foreign-exchange markets decreases its value.

The foreign-exchange value of the Canadian dollar is directly related to the balance of payments. If Canada has a surplus in the balance of payments, then more money is coming into Canada than is going out. The demand for Canadian dollars on foreign exchange markets is greater than the supply. This increases the *exchange rate* of the dollar. If Canada is incurring a balance of payments deficit, more money is leaving the country than is coming in. The supply of Canadian dollars on foreign-exchange markets is greater than the demand. Thus, the value of the dollar falls.

Any activity or government policy that affects Canada's balance of payments will affect the foreign-exchange rate of the dollar. Canadian trade policies, in the form of tariffs, quotas, and non-tariff barriers directly influence the flow of money out of and into Canada. Canada's participation in GATT and the Canada-United States Automobile Agreement are also important. In addition to these international policies, domestic policies and activities can influence the dollar's foreign-exchange value. For example, if the federal government decides to stimulate economic activity through increased spending, one of the consequences may be inflation. If the prices of Canadian products begin to rise, foreigners may stop buying them in favour of competing products. If our exports go down, less money comes into Canada and the foreign-exchange value of the dollar drops. Canadian government policy on gasoline prices will also affect the dollar. The decision by the federal government in the 1970s to keep Canadian gasoline prices below world levels attracted tourists from south of the border. Higher gasoline prices in recent years have discouraged tourists from vacationing in Canada.

Private-sector activity may also influence the dollar. A new discovery of oil reserves in Canada's north may cause investment money to flow into the country. The development of a new tourist attraction in Canada will attract more visitors to our country and increase the value of the dollar, as well as increasing GDP. A Canadian architect, musician, engineer, or other professional who attracts international attention could also bring money into the country. *Again, any transaction that has an influence on the balance of payments has an influence on the foreign-exchange value of the dollar.*

A history of Canadian dollar exchange rates from 1973 to 1990 is presented in table 9.7. The Canadian dollar value is given by referring to the amount of Canadian dollars required to purchase a U.S. dollar, a British pound, a French franc, a German mark, a Swiss franc, and a Japanese yen. In 1973, the Canadian dollar was virtually at par with the U.S. dollar. In 1974 and 1976, it was worth more than a U.S. dollar, but it has steadily declined in value since then. In comparison to the British pound and the French franc, the Canadian dollar has appreciated in value since 1973. However, in comparison with the German mark, the Swiss franc, and the Japanese yen, the Canadian dollar has depreciated since 1973. In other words, it required more Canadian dollars to purchase these currencies in 1990 than it did in 1973.

Table 9.7 / Canadian dollars required to purchase foreign currencies, 1973-90

Year	U.S. dollar	British pound	French franc	German mark	Swiss franc	Japanese yen
			Canadian dollars per unit			
1973	1.00	2.45	0.23	0.38	0.32	0.0037
1974	0.98	2.29	0.20	0.38	0.33	0.0034
1975	1.02	2.26	0.24	0.41	0.39	0.0034
1976	0.99	1.78	0.21	0.39	0.39	0.0033
1977	1.06	1.86	0.22	0.46	0.44	0.0040
1978	1.14	2.19	0.25	0.57	0.64	0.0055
1979	1.17	2.49	0.28	0.64	0.70	0.0054
1980	1.17	2.72	0.28	0.64	0.70	0.0052
1981	1.20	2.43	0.23	0.53	0.61	0.0055
1982	1.23	2.16	0.19	0.51	0.61	0.0050
1983	1.23	1.86	0.16	0.48	0.59	0.0052
1984	1.29	1.73	0.15	0.46	0.55	0.0055
1985	1.37	1.77	0.15	0.47	0.56	0.0058
1986	1.39	2.04	0.20	0.64	0.78	0.0083
1987	1.33	2.17	0.22	0.74	0.89	0.0092
1988	1.23	2.19	0.21	0.70	0.84	0.0096
1989	1.18	1.94	0.19	0.63	0.72	0.0086
1990	1.17	2.08	0.21	0.72	0.84	0.0081

Source: *Bank of Canada Review,* August 1986 (Ottawa: Bank of Canada, September 1986), p. S129; ibid., March 1991, p. S116.

9.20 Using graphs in your answer, show the impact of the following transactions on the foreign-exchange value of the Canadian dollar:

   i Japanese tourists visit British Columbia

   ii a Canadian company hires an American architect to design their new office building

   iii a Canadian citizen buys a U.S. government bond

   iv a rich uncle in Europe sends money to relatives living in Canada.

Flexible versus Fixed Exchange Rates

Appreciation describes an increase in the value of the currency in relation to another currency under the conditions of a flexible exchange rate system.

The foreign-exchange value of the Canadian dollar fluctuates on a daily basis depending on the demand and supply conditions in the market. The exchange rate is said to be *flexible* or *floating.* When the value of the Canadian dollar increases, the increase is called an **appreciation.** When it falls, the decrease is a **depreciation.**

Depreciation *is the term used to describe a reduction in the value of the currency in relation to another currency.*

At one time, the Canadian dollar was fixed in value in relation to other currencies. Regardless of the changes in demand and supply that took place in international foreign-exchange markets, the Canadian dollar kept the same exchange rate. How was this possible, since changes in demand and supply would cause the value of the dollar to change? Under a fixed exchange-rate system, it is necessary for the Bank of Canada to influence market conditions in order to keep the value of the dollar at its fixed rate.

In 1962, the Canadian government set the value of the Canadian dollar at $0.925 U.S. dollars. How did the Bank of Canada ensure that the rate remained at this level? If market forces were acting to raise or lower the value of the dollar, it would be necessary for the Bank of Canada to influence the market in such a way that the value of the dollar returned to $0.925 U.S. First, the Bank could purchase or sell Canadian dollars on foreign-exchange markets. If the Bank were to buy Canadian dollars in the foreign-exchange market, the demand for Canadian dollars would increase. This would cause the exchange rate of the Canadian dollar to rise. How would the Bank buy Canadian dollars? It would purchase Canadian dollars with foreign currencies that it has at its disposal. For example, the Bank could offer to sell Japanese yen or British pounds for Canadian dollars. What happens if the Bank does not have any foreign currencies available? If this happens, then it will be necessary for the Bank to borrow foreign currencies from other countries.

If the foreign-exchange value of the Canadian dollar rose above $0.925 U.S. as a result of market forces, then it would be necessary for the Bank of Canada to sell Canadian dollars on the foreign-exchange market. This action would lower the exchange value of the dollar, by increasing the supply of Canadian dollars on the market.

A second method of influencing the foreign-exchange value of the dollar would be to change the level of *interest rates* in Canada. If the value of the Canadian dollar was lower than the desired value, an increase in Canadian interest rates would increase the demand for Canadian dollars. People with money to lend would want to lend it in Canada in order to get a high return. The inflow of money into Canada would increase the demand for Canadian dollars. This would, in turn, increase the value of the dollar. If the value of the Canadian dollar was too high, interest rates would be reduced. Lower interest rates in Canada than in other countries would result in money leaving Canada for a better return elsewhere. With money leaving Canada, the supply of Canadian dollars on foreign-exchange markets would increase and the value of the dollar would fall.

A third option for influencing the value of the dollar would be *foreign-exchange controls*. The Canadian government could regulate the amount of money that Canadians would be able to take outside the country. If there is a limit on the amount of dollars that Canadians can supply to foreign-exchange markets, the value of the dollar will remain at a higher level. In past years, Great Britain and Jamaica have had foreign-exchange controls.

What is the ideal value for the dollar? This is a very difficult question to answer. If the dollar is increasing in value, foreign products and foreign vacations are cheaper for Canadians. Our products become more expensive to residents of other countries. With a Canadian dollar decreasing in value, the reverse is true. The ideal value of the Canadian dollar depends on the elasticity of demand for Canadian and foreign products. If we continue to purchase foreign products regardless of the price (inelastic demand), a cheap dollar means that our import costs will increase. Such an increase will cause prices to be higher for products that we use. If foreigners also have an inelastic demand for our products, then we receive less total revenue for our products when the dollar is low. The ideal exchange rate depends on how Canadians and others react to changes in the exchange rate.

Is it better to have a fixed or a flexible exchange-rate system? There is still considerable debate on this point. The primary advantage of the flexible exchange-rate system is that it is automatic. It operates according to demand and supply forces. The Bank of Canada need not interfere with a flexible exchange-rate system. However, the disadvantage of this system is that it creates uncertainty. The exchange rate changes on a daily basis and businesses are less certain about what the costs of foreign purchases will be. This uncertainty may interfere with trade.

Having a fixed exchange rate solves the problem of uncertainty. Fixed rates, however, create other problems. How do you decide what the exchange rate should be? How do you adjust the rate when it needs to be changed? A fixed exchange-rate system requires that the Bank of Canada play an active role in determining the value of the dollar on a daily basis.

We use a combination of the two systems. The rate fluctuates daily, yet these fluctuations are influenced by the Bank of Canada. The Bank uses interest rates and Canadian dollar purchases to influence the value of the dollar. If the value of the Canadian dollar is falling too quickly on foreign-exchange markets, the Bank will increase interest rates and increase its purchases of the dollar in order to boost its value. If the value of the Canadian dollar is increasing too rapidly, the Bank will lower interest rates and sell Canadian dollars. *Our present foreign-exchange system is flexible, yet the fluctuations are managed by the Bank of Canada.*

9.21 Explain how the Bank of Canada could participate in maintaining a fixed value for the Canadian dollar in foreign-exchange markets.

The International Monetary Fund

A devalued currency is one that has decreased in value in relation to another currency under the conditions of a fixed exchange rate system.

During the depression years of the 1930s, many countries **devalued** their currency in order to stimulate exports. A cheaper currency was aimed at making domestic products less expensive to foreigners, and imports more expensive. If exports increased and imports were reduced, then domestic employment would increase as well. With many countries devaluing their currency, international trade became a confusing business. The uncertainty about exchange rates reduced, rather than stimulated, foreign trade.

The International Monetary Fund (IMF) is an international agency established in 1944 with the objective of stabilizing foreign-exchange rates.

In 1944, an international conference was held in Bretton Woods, New Hampshire, in order to find a solution to trade problems. The conference proposed a system of fixed exchange rates aimed at providing stability in the international scene. The **International Monetary Fund (IMF)** was created to oversee the new exchange rate system and to ensure that the system worked. The purposes of the IMF, as set out in article 1 of the Articles of Agreement are as follows:

i   to promote international monetary co-operation through a permanent institution which provides the machinery for consultation and collaboration on international monetary problems;

ii to facilitate the expansion and balanced growth of international trade, and to contribute thereby to the promotion and maintenance of high levels of employment and real income and to the development of the productive resources of all members as primary objectives of economic policy;

iii to promote exchange stability, to maintain orderly exchange arrangements among members, and to avoid competitive exchange depreciation;

iv to assist in the establishment of a multilateral system of payments in respect of current transactions between members and in the elimination of foreign exchange restrictions which hamper the growth of world trade;

v   to give confidence to members by making the general resources of the Fund temporarily available to them under adequate safe guards, thus providing them with the opportunity to correct maladjustments in their balance of payments without resorting to measures destructive of national or international prosperity;

vi in accordance with the above, to shorten the duration and lessen the degree of disequilibrium in the international balances of payments of members.

An adjustable-peg system is a system of fixed foreign-exchange rates that can be adjusted if necessary.

The exchange-rate system was called an **adjustable-peg system.** Exchange rates were pegged at a certain par value, but could be adjusted when conditions warranted a change. Nations agreed to maintain a certain par value for their currency in terms of gold or U.S. dollars. The Canadian dollar was set at par with the U.S. dollar. The value of a country's foreign-exchange rate was only allowed to vary by one percent above or below the par value. If a country was experiencing persistent balance of payments problems, it could adjust its par value by ten percent without approval from the IMF. Any larger adjustments required IMF approval. In 1949, Canada dropped its exchange rate to $.909 U.S.

Stabilization funds were established in support of the adjustable-peg system. Each country maintained a fund of domestic and foreign currencies and gold that allowed the country to purchase its currency on world markets to keep the exchange rate at the par value.

In order for the adjustable-peg system to work, it was necessary for each country to maintain a **stabilization fund.** This fund, affiliated with the nation's central bank, was comprised of domestic and foreign currencies and gold. The currencies in the fund were to be used to buy that nation's currency on world markets in order to keep the exchange rate at the par value. For example, if the value of the Canadian dollar fell below the par value, it would be necessary for the Bank of Canada to use some of the currencies in the stabilization fund to buy Canadian dollars in the foreign-exchange market. This action would raise the value of the dollar to its par value. In case a country's stabilization fund became too small, the IMF was empowered to make loans to countries with short-term balance of payments problems.

The need to maintain adequate reserves was a serious problem for the adjustable-peg system. If a country was experiencing a continuous balance of payments deficit, it would not have sufficient reserves with which to buy back its currency. It could borrow money from the IMF, but if the balance of payments deficit continued, it would soon run out of reserves again. It would be necessary to borrow more reserves from the IMF. Borrowing could not continue indefinitely, and eventually the country's currency would have to be devalued in order to correct the deficit.

The second problem with the adjustable-peg system was that an adequate scheme for adjusting exchange rates was not set up. A country's international balance of payments is constantly changing. Since the exchange rate of its currency is closely tied to the balance of payments, the exchange rate should also change. In actual fact, the exchange rate was rarely adjusted and the rates remained fixed. When the rates did change, they were usually adjusted by a very large amount.

The problems of the IMF and the system of adjustable pegs reached a climax in the early 1970s. Many countries began to put their currencies on a flexible exchange system. The final straw that broke the adjustable-peg system came when the United States decided to float its dollar. From the beginning of the IMF, the U.S. dollar had been pegged to gold: it took $35 U.S. to buy an ounce of gold. Today the flexible exchange-rate system is predominant. However, foreign-exchange rates are not totally free to move according to the forces of demand and supply, as the central banks of most countries are taking steps to manage or influence the foreign-exchange value of their currency.

In recent years the focus of the IMF has changed. It is now a vital lending institution for debtor countries. Since the resources of the IMF are limited, the Fund may not actually lend money to countries in need of assistance but may help them gain access to other sources of finance. A precondition of receiving aid from the IMF is usually an agreement permitting the IMF to play a major role in the development of the country's monetary and fiscal policies. Whereas in the 1970s, few conditions were attached to IMF financial assistance, the situation has reversed in the 1990s. The Fund now takes an active role in the economic management of many of its developing-country members.

9.22 What is a stabilization fund? Why is it necessary to the system of adjustable-pegged rates established by the IMF?

Gold

As mentioned in Chapter 7, one of the earliest forms of money was gold bullion and gold coins. It was possible for gold to serve as a medium of exchange, since many people regarded gold as valuable. People were willing to accept gold as payment for goods and services because they believed that others would also accept gold.

What characteristics of gold made it attractive? Gold is a very durable metal. In comparison with other metals, gold is relatively lightweight and therefore easy to carry. It is expensive to mine gold and, as a result, the supply of gold on the market does not increase drastically. This keeps the value of the metal high.

These attributes of gold have given it importance on an international scale, as well as domestically. Individuals in other countries were willing to accept gold as payment for goods and services. Gold became the main international currency. Central banks stored gold, believing that someday they would be able to sell gold to the monetary authorities in other countries. Storing gold was seen as a safer means of storing wealth than keeping national currencies such as the American dollar and the British pound. The values of these currencies were likely to fluctuate more than the value of gold.

When the International Monetary Fund was established, and a system of adjustable exchange rates set up, gold and the U.S. dollar were seen as the primary international reserves. The price of gold was set at $35 (U.S.) per ounce and remained at that price until 1971.

Gold has since declined in importance as an international currency and a medium of exchange. Most currencies are on a floating exchange-rate system and their values are stated in terms of other currencies and not in terms of gold. Central banks only infrequently use gold for international payments. Those who hold gold today do so as a way of keeping wealth or as an investment. The price of gold has varied since 1971; in January 1980 it rose to over $800 (U.S.) per ounce. The price has since dropped, and at time of publication is approximately $365 (U.S.) per ounce.

Questions

1 Why would gold serve as an international currency? What else could serve as an international currency? Why?
2 Those who hold gold today do so as a store of wealth or as an investment. Why would buying gold be seen as an investment?
3 Apart from the uses mentioned in question 2, what other uses does gold have?

Summary

Canadians not only trade with each other but with residents of other countries as well. For several reasons, international trade is treated as a separate topic in the study of economics. International trade involves currencies, languages, and customs that are different from our own, and trade is also heavily influenced by political considerations. Because workers are not free to cross national borders in the same way that they cross provincial borders in Canada, international economics has a different context from domestic economics.

Canada's major trading partner is the United States. Approximately 75 percent of our exports are sent to the United States, while about 65 percent of our imports are from that country. Our major export item is road motor vehicles and parts. Apart from these manufactured items, most of Canada's export items are primary products requiring very little processing in Canada. Our major import also is road motor vehicles, engines, and parts.

It is beneficial for all countries to participate in international trade. The law of comparative advantage proves that even in a situation where a country is efficient at producing all items, it can still benefit from trade. In spite of the benefits from trade, countries still erect barriers to imports. These barriers are in the form of tariffs or non-tariff barriers.

Recognition of the value of freer international trade led to the development of the European Economic Community, GATT, the Canada-United States Automobile Agreement and the FTA.

A record of all financial transactions between residents of Canada and residents of other countries is called the balance of payments. Canada's deficit and surplus in international trade transactions are recorded in the balance of payments. Whether a deficit or surplus exists determines the change in the value of the Canadian dollar. If the balance of payments is in a deficit position, the exchange value of the Canadian dollar is falling. If a surplus exists, the value of the dollar is rising.

Questions for Review and Discussion

1 Many Canadian companies are subsidiaries of foreign companies. What impact do you believe this situation has on Canada's imports? Exports?

2 Identify comparative advantage and the terms of trade in the following example. The numbers represent the production of one worker in one week.

Product	Norway	Sweden
skis	20 pairs	10 pairs
snow tires	16 tires	4 tires

3 What effect would international trade have on a country's production-possibilities curve?

4 The Canada-United States Automobile Agreement provides for free trade in automobiles between the two countries. Would you like to see a similar agreement extended to other products? Explain.

5 Why would a country like Norway not want to join the European Economic Community?

6 Replacement parts were not included in the automobile agree-ment. Why might Canadian parts manufacturers be more concerned about this than American parts manufacturers?

7 What impact does a decline in the foreign-exchange value of the Canadian dollar have on Canada's exports? On imports?

8 In past years, Canada has asked the Japanese to put voluntary quotas on the shipment of automobiles to Canada. Who benefits from these quotas? Who loses due to the imposition quotas?

9 In 1986 the United States placed countervailing duties on a number of Canadian lumber products. Why would American consumers want to pay more for Canadian lumber?

10 If Canada were divided into four regions—West, Ontario, Quebec, and East—with no free trade between the regions, what would happen to the standard of living of Canadians? Explain.

11 In 1986, in response to a U.S. countervailing duty on Canadian softwood lumber, the Canadian government imposed a 15-percent export tax on this product. The United States agreed to drop the countervailing duty. What are the advantages for Canada of an export tax? What are the disadvantages? What would have happened to the price of softwood lumber in the United States? In Canada?

12 Using a graph in your answer, show the impact of the Canadian government imposing a $1 per bottle tariff on imported wine.

13 Explain the impact that higher interest rates in Canada may have on the foreign-exchange value of the Canadian dollar.

14 What are the advantages of flexible as opposed to fixed foreign-exchange rates?

15 The Toronto Blue Jays and Montreal Expos pay their players' salaries in U.S. dollars. In order to protect their payroll costs from fluctuations in the foreign-exchange value of the Canadian dollar, the teams buy futures contracts in U.S. dollars. From the information provided on futures contracts in Chapter 2, explain how buying futures contracts in foreign currencies works.

16 Canada has been participating in discussions with the United States and Mexico about the possibility of including all three countries in a free-trade area. What implications would free trade with Mexico have for Canada?

Suggested Readings

Canadian Foundation for Economic Education. *The Canada-U.S. Free Trade Agreement: Background, Overview and Perspectives.* Economic Bulletin 2, May 1988

Curtis, Christopher. "The Free-Trade Free-for-all" *Horizon Canada* 7, no. 83 (1986): 1969-77.

Jackson, John H. *Restructuring the GATT System.* New York: Council on Foreign Relations Press, 1990.

Kenen, Peter B. *Managing Exchange Rates.* New York: Council on Foreign Relations Press 1988.

Lipsey, Richard G., and Murray G. Smith. *Taking the Initiative:Canada's Trade Options in a Turbulent World.* Toronto: C.D. Howe Institute 1985.

Mathieu, Jacques. "Industry in New France." *Horizon Canada 1*, no. 12 (1985): 278-83.

Morici, Peter, ed. *Making Free Trade Work: The Canada-U.S. Agreement.* New York: Council on Foreign Relations Press 1990.

Ontario Federation of Labour. *It's Not Free: The Consequences of Free Trade with the U.S.* Don Mills: OFL 1986.

Rabbior, Gary. *The Canadian Economy: Adjusting to Global Change.* Toronto: Canadian Foundation for Economic Education 1990.

Royal Commission on the Economic Union and Development Prospects for Canada. Volume One, pp. 229-385. Ottawa: Minister of Supply and Services 1985.

Taylor, Joan Kennedy, ed. *Free Trade: The Necessary Foundation for World Peace.* Irvington-on-Hudson, NY: Foundation for Economic Education 1986.

Chapter 10

Industrial Organization in Canada

Chapter Objectives

After successfully completing this chapter, you will be able to:

- differentiate between the types of business ownership
- discuss the advantages and disadvantages of small business and of franchising
- describe the characteristics of the competitive groupings
- describe the role of entrepreneurs in the Canadian economy
- define concentration ratios
- discuss the impact of foreign investment on the Canadian economy

Key Terms

microeconomics
sole proprietorship
partnership
corporations
small business
entrepreneur
franchising

perfect competition
monopoly
oligopoly
many differentiated sellers
concentration
foreign ownership

Introduction to Microeconomics

Microeconomics is the area of economics that emphasizes smaller decision-making units, such as business firms, consumers, and workers.

The first part of this textbook introduced the idea of economic decision-making. It concentrated on the decisions that must be made by Canadians regarding the use of their resources. The issues discussed earlier were those affecting the entire country: unemployment, inflation, economic growth, money and banking, and international trade. That area of economics is called macroeconomics, which is derived from the Greek word "macro," meaning large. In this part of the book, we switch to economic decision-making on a smaller scale. We will discuss the area of **microeconomics,** which emphasizes smaller decision-making units, such as business firms and individual consumers and workers. The term microeconomics is derived from the Greek word "micro," meaning small.

Types of Business Enterprises

Discussions in the text thus far have made reference to business without defining what we mean by the term. In the Canadian economy, types of businesses vary, ranging from a corner convenience store to a telephone company, from a farmer to an automobile manufacturer, from a self-employed barber to a mining company.

Sole proprietorship is the simplest form of business organization with one owner, usually a small business.

Sole proprietorship: **sole proprietorships** are the simplest form of business enterprise and are well suited to the small business. Examples of proprietorships are businesses run by doctors, dentists, store owners, farmers, insurance agents, restaurateurs, painters, garage operators, and other self-employed people. Apart from its simplicity, the sole proprietorship has several other advantages. This type of business has no separate existence in legal terms, and all the income earned by the business goes to the single owner. The management of the business is flexible, since the owner need not consult with anyone else on business decisions.

Proprietorships have certain disadvantages as well. First, the owner is liable for the business, and personal assets may have to be used to meet business obligations. Second, the amount of money available to the business is limited to what the owner can provide or borrow. Finally, the owner does not necessarily have the expertise to solve all the problems that may arise in the course of trying to operate a business. If the owner is not skilled in various aspects of business, such as accounting, finance, or marketing, and cannot employ extra people who are skilled to assist in these matters, the business may well fail.

Partnerships: **partnerships** are similar to proprietorships except that there is more than one owner. Professionals such as accountants

A partnership is a form of business enterprise in which two or more persons own and operate the business firm and are liable for its debts.

and lawyers often use partnerships as a form of business enterprise. The Income Tax Act does not recognize the existence of partnerships and each partner is taxed individually on the basis of his or her income.

With a partnership, the skills of a number of people are brought into the business. The partnership will also be able to attract more financial resources than a sole proprietorship. It may be easier for a partnership to get a loan from the bank. Liability under a partnership must be determined by the partners involved. It may be that one partner is liable for something that another partner did. Partnerships cannot sue or be sued, so any legal action will have to be undertaken in the name of (or against) one of the partners. Decision-making may take longer in a partnership than in a sole proprietorship, since all partners will want to have their say.

A corporation is a business organization created by law that is owned by its shareholders.

Corporations: **corporations** are created in Canada only by permission of the government. Both federal and provincial governments have the legal authority to grant charters to corporations. If the business is to be conducted solely within one province, a provincial charter will suffice. If the corporation is formed under a federal charter, it can do business in any part of the country.

The owners of the corporation are referred to as the *shareholders.* They are entitled to attend corporation meetings and share in corporation profits by receiving dividends.

There are several advantages to the corporate form of business enterprise. For one thing, it is easier to acquire large amounts of money than in other forms of business. It addition, lawsuits can be undertaken in the corporation's name, which means that individual shareholders are not responsible for corporation liabilities. Finally, the death of one of the shareholders does not end the corporation.

The main disadvantage of the corporation lies in the rules and regulations that have to be followed. This makes it a more expensive form of business enterprise. Another disadvantage is that, depending on earnings, the level of taxation on corporation income may be quite high.

Crown corporation: A Crown corporation is defined as a corporation that is directly owned by a government, either federal or provincial. There are in excess of 300 Crown corporations in Canada at the federal government level alone. These corporations are divided into three main categories based on their administration and their method of financing.

Departmental corporations are similar to government departments and perform a variety of administrative, regulatory, and supervisory functions. Most of the employees of these Crown corporations are civil servants; each corporation reports annually to

Twenty Top Industrial Companies in Canada According to Revenue, 1990

Rank by revenue	Company	Revenue ($ thousands)
1	General Motors of Canada Ltd.	18 458 171
2	BCE Inc.	18 373 000
3	Ford Motor Company of Canada	13 706 200
4	George Weston Ltd.	10 856 000
5	Canadian Pacific Ltd.	10 499 700
6	Imperial Oil Ltd.	10 223 000
7	Alcan Aluminium Ltd.	10 217 000
8	Noranda Inc.	9 565 000
9	Brascan Ltd	7 163 000
10	Chrysler Canada Ltd.	7 067 000
11	Provigo Inc.	6 525 700
12	Ontario Hydro	6 484 000
13	Thomson Corp.	6 259 000
14	Seagram Company Ltd.	5 865 000
15	Hydro-Quebec	5 822 988
16	Shell Canada Ltd.	5 508 000
17	Petro-Canada	5 317 000
18	Hudson's Bay Co.	5 041 733
19	Nova Corp.of Alberta	4 736 000
20	John Labatt Ltd.	4 681 000

Source: *The Financial Post 500,* Summer 1991 (Toronto: The Financial Post Company 1990), p. 94.

a Cabinet minister who is directly responsible to Parliament. Examples of departmental corporations are the Economic Council of Canada, the National Research Council, the Atomic Energy Control Board, and the National Gallery of Canada.

Agency corporations perform a variety of commercial and management functions for the government. They hire their own employees, as a private corporation would. Agency corporations have more financial and administrative independence from government than do departmental corporations. Although their budgets are separate from general department budgets, they must be approved by the appropriate Cabinet minister, the president of the Treasury Board, and Parliament. They get money from parliamentary appropriation, statutory grants, and operational income. Examples of agency corporations are the Canadian Mint, the Canadian Film Development Corporation, and the National Capital Commission.

Corporations in the final category, *proprietary corporations,* are not associated with any government department. Many of these corporations are in direct competition with privately-owned companies, and they are expected to finance themselves from their operating revenue. Unlike private companies, however, any deficits that these corporations may have will likely be covered by the taxpayer. Examples are the Canadian Broadcasting Corporation, Canada Post, Air Canada, Petro-Canada, and Canadian National.

Several other Crown corporations have been established by special legislation and do not fall into one of the above categories. These corporations perform certain functions that require independence from government control and include the Bank of Canada, the Canadian Wheat Board, and the Canada Council.

There are large differences in the structure of these types of businesses, but for our purposes the structure of the individual business is not as important as the *market power* that it possesses. Market power is represented by the ability of the business to control the price of the product.

10.1 What are the advantages of a partnership in comparison to a sole proprietorship? What are some disadvantages?

10.2 Which type of Crown corporation is most similar to a privately-owned corporation. Why?

Ten Largest Federal Crown Corporations Ranked by Revenue, 1989	Rank	Company and year end	Revenue ($ thousands)
	1	Petro-Canada (De 90)	5 873 000
	2	Canadian National Railway (De 90)	4 023 016
	3	Canada Post (Mr 90)	3 756 093
	4	Via Rail Canada (De 89)	1 013 368
	5	Canada Mortgage and Housing (De 90)	818 230
	6	Export Development Corp. (De 90)	642 323
	7	Royal Canadian Mint (De 90)	606 162
	8	Farm Credit Corp. (Mr 90)	428 186
	9	Federal Business Devel. Bank (Mr 90)	402 136
	10	Canadian Broadcasting Corp. (Mr 90)	352 973

Source: "The Top 1000 Companies." *The Globe and Mail Report on Business Magazine.* July 1991 p.115

Small Business in Canada

Much of the discussion about the nature of business in Canada centres on the large firm. Yet the small business sector is an essential part of our economy. In Canada, there are more than 700 000 small businesses and an additional 500 000 unincorporated self-employed individuals. The federal government estimates that 97 percent of all businesses in Canada are small.

There are numerous definitions of what constitutes a small business. It is generally accepted that a **small business** is independently owned and operated. However, there is wide variation in terms of the maximum number of employees in a small business and in its maximum annual revenue. The Commercial Clearing House in its *Small Business Guide* defines a small business as any business entity that is managed by the owner, or owners, with fewer than 100 employees and less than $20 million in annual sales. Each government has its own definition of small business when assessing a firm's eligibility for provincial assistance. The Federal Business Development Bank refers to firms with 75 employees or fewer as small, whereas the Ministry of State for Small Business uses the criterion of a 100-employee maximum. In the Atlantic provinces, Quebec, and Manitoba, the maximum number of employees is 50. In Ontario and Alberta, the maximum number is 100. Saskatchewan and British Columbia do not specify a maximum number of employees in their definitions of a small business.

A small business is a firm that is independently owned and operated and that is not dominant in its field of endeavour, usually employing fewer than 100 persons and having annual sales of $20 million or less.

Small businesses are also categorized by annual sales. The Department of Finance sets the cut-off for designation as a small business at a maximum annual revenue of 1.5 million dollars. The federal Small Business Loans Act defines a small business as a company that has gross annual revenue of $2 million or less. The federal Income Tax Act permits a small-business deduction only on the first $200 000 of earned income. Again, provincial definitions differ. In Quebec, firms with annual sales of up to $10 million are considered to be small. Other criteria are also used provincially in order to determine size. In Saskatchewan, a company that requires less than $5 million in capital is termed small. In Alberta, less than $5 million in assets allows a firm to qualify. In Ontario and British Columbia, the management style of the business is also used as a criterion. For some programs in these provinces, the owner must operate the business personally—and not have hired a manager —in order to qualify for provincial assistance.

Small businesses are part of many industries. Possibly the most well-known area of small business is *retailing*. Typical small businesses are drug stores, clothing stores, book stores, and grocery and confectionery stores. Along with retailing, the service sector is also a home for small businesses. Restaurants, dry cleaners, service stations, barbershops, and motels are examples of this type of establishment. Small businesses are also found in agriculture (farms) and in professional areas (lawyers, doctors). Wherever there are few barriers to the entry of new firms, small businesses predominate.

Small businesses have some advantages over their larger competitors. Smaller companies are usually located close to their customers. In an age when energy costs are significant, smaller companies have fewer transportation costs. Smaller companies may also provide an outlet for new entrepreneurs and may motivate people who often feel stifled in a larger organization. The enthusiasm of many small-business owners provides for more competition in the marketplace. Finally, small businesses are often an essential part of many communities and serve community needs.

Despite these advantages, small businesses account for the vast majority of bankruptcies each year in Canada. In 1981, 97 percent of all businesses that went bankrupt had assets of less than $250 000. An earlier study on business failure pointed out that 90 percent of all bankrupt companies had ten or fewer employees. Firms that have been in business less than five years also have a higher failure rate. Why the high failure rate among small businesses? One reason is *undercapitalization*. In other words, more money needs to be put into the operation of the firm. Many small businesses see banks as their only source of funds. Banks may not be willing to lend the firm the necessary amount of money, or, in fact, any money at all. The owner may not be willing to take on a partner or additional shareholders in order to get extra cash. Another reason for the high failure rate of small business is poor management. This may result in poor planning, poor inventory control, and high employee turnover. The owner of the business may be a skilled tradesman or highly qualified in a certain area, yet may not be an efficient manager. A study on business failures by Dun and Bradstreet Limited in 1983 revealed that an overwhelming majority of the failures were due to poor management at some point in the life of the business. Finally, small businesses often require a constant flow of money. They may not be as able, as are larger firms, to cope with fluctuations in their accounts receivable. Larger firms may also be better equipped to withstand an economic downturn. For example, large firms can reduce inventories through price cutting, which hurts the smaller competitors in the industry.

Any successful business, large or small, had to start somewhere. In order to get any business off the ground, an individual or group of individuals must be able to recognize a need that has not yet been met by the marketplace. This person, or group of people, must have initiative, be willing to work hard, and also be willing to take risks. Those who fit into this category are referred to as **entrepreneurs.** Risk-taking is necessary for entrepreneurs as the marketplace does not guarantee success for everyone who wants to go into business. If successful, the entrepreneur will then be able to enjoy the reward that accompanies success. In economics this reward is called profit.

An individual willing to take a risk by introducing a new product or service in the marketplace is an entrepreneur.

Entrepreneurs play a vital role in a market-based economy. They have been compared to the motor that allows the car to move.

Entrepreneurs get the economy in motion. They respond to, or create, consumer demand in a wide variety of areas from computer software to toys and from food to household services. The new products and services introduced into the marketplace by entrepreneurs increase the amount of competition. This activity leads to lower prices and better-quality products.

In order to provide goods and services to the marketplace, resources—land, labour, and capital—must be combined in the production process. This is also the function of the entrepreneur. The ability to combine resources effectively in order to provide goods and services is the mark of an entrepreneur.

Are you a potential entrepreneur? Do you have the personality to succeed at your own business? The importance of entrepreneurship to our economy has led to various studies on the characteristics of successful entrepreneurs. A summary of these characteristics follows:

– they tend to be very self-confident while recognizing that failure is a possibility;
– they like to be in control of the business;
– they realize their personal limitations and rely on experts in areas where they are weak;
– they are willing to make personal sacrifices for long periods of time without becoming discouraged;
– they are attracted to a challenge and are very achievement oriented;
– they have the ability to see relationships among independent events;
– they need to be in good health both physically and mentally; and
– they need to be in the right place at the right time.

The following reading discusses a Canadian entrepreneur, Kaaydah Schatten. After reading about her success, match her apparent traits with those listed above.

10.3   What advantages does a small business have over a large corporation?

Kaaydah Schatten: Entrepreneur

Like many women entrepreneurs, Kaaydah Schatten first ventured into business not to realize a dream but out of necessity. At the age of seven, she started her first business to help support her family, delivering a local farmer's fresh eggs and produce to customers in a nearby town for a fee. She soon learned her first business lesson: that she could increase her profits significantly by buying the produce directly and then re-selling it. On finishing high school, Kaaydah volunteered to help out in the office of a real estate developer, from whom she learned the basics of that industry. When she was involved in a serious automobile accident at seventeen, Kaaydah saw the opportunity represented by the $7000 settlement she received, and purchased her first real estate investment, a four-plex apartment building. She quickly learned the fundamentals of office accounting through a junior administrative job, and though she was offered a promotion, she decided to return to her dream of developing real estate. By 1981, she had 1001 units under construction. Unfortunately, Canada was entering a recession at the time, and when the banks called in several loans, Kaaydah was unable to pay off her debts. She lost everything.

Once again taking advantage of a seemingly disastrous situation, Kaaydah took some time to think about her next direction. She reflected on what she had heard about the difficulties in cleaning ceiling tiles in office buildings, which become soiled by dirt, fungus, and bacteria. The chemical then used to clean the tiles was toxic. It would circulate in the building's air system for days, and would be flushed into the sewer system. This chemical also corroded the "T-bars" that support the ceiling tiles. Kaaydah decided to investigate whether there might be another, safer way to clean these ceilings.

First, she drove from Vancouver to Toronto, home of many head offices. She developed a system of biodegradable cleaning solutions that would do the job without harming the office workers or their environment. Formula in hand, Kaaydah approached potential clients directly–she called them at home. Though they did not understand the benefits of Kaaydah's "green" approach at that time, the company CEOs she contacted were interested in her promise of lower overhead costs.

Though she had contracts, Kaaydah needed capital to finance her new company, The Ceiling Doctor. In order to get this money, she returned to real estate. She purchased a condominium for only $3000 down and sold it immediately for a profit. She also bought condominiums from agents who could not sell them at the high mortgage rates of the time. She then rented out 50 such units and applied the money left over after carrying charges to financing her new firm.

By 1984, The Ceiling Doctor was launched as an international franchise. The company now has franchises located in the U.S., Pacific Rim, and Eastern Europe. In addition to ceilings, The Ceiling Doctor now cleans historic buildings, underground garages, and heavy machinery. Today, more and more clients respect her "green" business practices, and Kaaydah is often invited to share her skills, experiences. and success in business with aboriginal and women's groups.

Questions

1 What general characteristics of an entrepreneur are illustrated by Kaaydah Schatten's career?
2 Can you think of a product or service not currently being provided in the marketplace that may be attractive to consumers?

Franchising

Franchising is a contractual privilege in which the owner of a particular product or service grants to a person or company the right to sell that product within a specified territory.

For those interested in starting a small business, the safest approach may be to purchase a franchise. There are more than 1500 individuals or companies offering franchises in Canada. **Franchising** currently exists in the restaurant, computer, real estate, insurance, home repair, and retail trade industries. In the future, it is expected that franchising will expand into the areas of law, veterinary medicine, dentistry, architecture, and accounting. For these professions, franchising may help reduce start-up costs. Some well-known companies that currently offer franchises are McDonald's, Mister Transmission, Living Lighting, Century 21, Canadian Tire, Color Your World, Ramada Inns, and Stedman's.

Franchising is not an industry or a business. It is a contractual privilege granted by one person or company (the franchisor) to another person or company (the franchisee). The franchisor grants to the franchisee the right to sell, in a specified manner, a particular product or service within a specified territory. The product or service is usually identified by a trade name over which the franchisor has exclusive control.

Franchise arrangements have been subdivided into three broad classes:

a   establishing a selective and limited distribution system for particular products (for example, automobiles, gasoline, tires, appliances, cosmetics) to be distributed under the manufacturer's name and trademark;

b   franchising of an entire retail business operation, including the licence of a trade name, trademark, method and format of doing business (for example, fast-food restaurants, motels, car rentals);

c   trademark and brand-name licensing for processing plants (for example, soft-drink bottlers).

The franchise owner, or *franchisee,* usually pays a licence fee or royalty, or both, for the right to operate a franchise. The franchisee may also be required to pay a regular fee for common advertising. In return, the owner can take advantage of entering into an established business. A noted advantage of franchising is that small businesses operating under a franchise agreement are less likely to go bankrupt in the first five years than are independent businesses. The franchise owner may have access to a common pool of financial and managerial resources, shared advertising, better inventory control, easier debt collection, and central purchasing. In some cases, bank loans may be guaranteed by the franchisor. Banks are more willing to lend money, and at lower interest rates, to franchise purchasers than to independent businesses just starting out.

By entering into an agreement with a reputable franchisor, the franchisee can expect a great deal of help while learning to plan ahead, to control inventory, and to understand the industry. The franchisor is concerned that the owner/operator be successful in order to maintain the reputation of the company. The franchisee remains relatively autonomous but must operate within the franchise guidelines. Strict adherence to the franchisor's operations manual is essential and may be a drawback for independently-minded persons.

What type of people are likely to purchase a franchise? The franchisee must have some entrepreneurial spirit and be willing to promote the business. Purchasers of franchise operations are often people in their early 30s with a marketing background. Women returning to the labour force after raising children are also attracted to franchising. Parents have purchased franchises for their children in order to help them start a business once they graduate from school. Mid-level managers in large corporations, who are frustrated with their position or who have been laid off because of economic conditions, are also potential franchisees.

10.4   What are some advantages to buying a franchise as opposed to starting an independent business?

McDonald's

A success story in the field of franchising is McDonald's restaurants. In 1989 there were more than 600 McDonald's restaurants in Canada with sales in excess of $1.3 billion.[1] McDonald's has approximately one-half of the hamburger business in Canada and approximately one-quarter of the entire fast-food market. Close to 55 percent of McDonald's Canadian restaurants are operated as franchises, with the remainder being either company-owned or operated in conjunction with local business people.

There are no set age or educational requirements in order to be a franchisee, although one must have an entrepreneurial spirit. The potential franchisee must complete a six-month screening and training procedure before being allowed to open a McDonald's restaurant. The cost of obtaining a McDonald's franchise is around $950 000, which includes equipment, seating, and decor. The company requires a debt-to-equity ratio of 1 to 1; in other words, McDonald's will not lend the franchisee more money than the franchisee can provide him- or herself. The cost of obtaining a franchise includes a $22 500 licensee fee and a $15 000 security deposit. Once the restaurant is open for business there are the operating expenses of any licensees. In all cases, McDonald's leases the land and building to the franchisee.

Why would a company like McDonald's franchise its restaurants? McDonald's franchises its restaurants so it can maximize its

[1] The figures used in this section are subject to change.

purchasing power ability, achieve optimum marketing exposure, and influence the financial resources of its franchise holders.

Source: Text prepared by McDonald's Restaurants of Canada Ltd., January 1991.

Questions
1 What possible advantages are there to purchasing a McDonald's franchise?
2 Why might a potential franchise purchaser not be interested in a McDonald's franchise?
3 Why would McDonald's not want all their restaurants to be company owned and operated? In other words, why bother with franchises?

Types of Competition

The type of competition that a firm faces will influence the price that is charged for the product. It will also affect the amount of the product available on the market. Grouping Canadian industries according to four competitive models allows for a clearer discussion on the nature of competition faced by businesses in Canada. These groupings are established for discussion purposes only, and it is not expected that a certain industry will be exactly described by the characteristics of the group with which it is associated. The models are intended as aids in analysing the *price and quantity decisions* of business firms.

The four competitive models are perfect competition, monopoly, oligopoly, and many differentiated sellers. Each model is reviewed under the following headings:

a the number of firms in the industry
b the type of product
c ease of entry into the industry
d the firm's control over price
e the firm's use of non-price competition

Perfect Competition

In industries characterized by **perfect competition,** there are many firms, each one producing only a small percentage of the total output. With a large number of firms, no individual firm has any control over the price of its product and must accept the *market price.* The firm's control over the price of its product is further reduced by the fact that each firm produces an identical product. It is not possible to identify one firm's products from among the

Perfect competition is a competitive situation in which there are many thousands of firms, each selling an identical product.

products of other firms in the industry. This eliminates the need for non-price competition, such as advertising.

An important aspect of perfectly competitive industries is the relative ease with which new firms are able to enter the industry. Entrance into any industry is going to require a certain amount of money; however, in perfect competition, the financial barriers to entry are less restrictive than in other industries. There are virtually no other barriers to entry.

Entry into an industry is considered easy when certain conditions exist. Established firms must have no price advantage or other advantages when purchasing the necessary resources for production. Further, there can be no advantages for established firms resulting from buyer preference for brand-name products. Finally, it is relatively easy to enter an industry when the production-cost advantages that come from mass production are negligible.

Canadian agriculture is an industry closely associated with perfect competition, with many farmers each producing an identical product. That is, you cannot tell one farmer's beans from another farmer's beans. Entry into the agricultural business can be costly for new farmers, the major expense being the price of good farmland. For existing farmers, the ability to enter another line of agriculture is easier than for new farmers to enter the industry. For example, once a farmer owns the land, he or she can switch from one crop to another, depending on market conditions. In some areas of agriculture, marketing boards restrict the entry of new firms; therefore, these products cannot be considered perfectly competitive. A detailed discussion of Canadian agriculture is presented in Chapter 12.

Monopoly

A monopoly occurs when only one seller of a good or service exists in a given industry.

Monopoly is the extreme opposite of perfect competition. In a monopoly industry there is only one firm. Since it is the only company in the industry, it has control over the price of the product. Industries remain in a monopoly position because there are significant barriers to the entry of new firms.

Government is normally involved in monopolies. Government agencies regulate the pricing practices of telephone, natural gas, and cable television companies. Monopolies like public utilities and the post office are operated by the government itself.

Even though there is only one firm in a monopoly, that firm still may have competition. It competes with all other industries for the consumer dollar. The monopoly also faces competition from close substitutes. For example, natural gas companies have been granted monopolies in specific geographic areas. These companies may be the only ones supplying natural gas in the area, but people do not have to heat their homes with natural gas, because other good substitutes are available.

Monopolies do not engage in a great deal of advertising. The advertising done by monopolies is mainly of an informative or public-relations nature. For example, the Bell Telephone System, a monopoly, has advertisements focusing on the quality of telephone service provided to Canadians. One such ad ends with the statement "Bell Canada—one of the best anywhere."

Oligopoly

An oligopoly is a competitive situation characterized by an industry that is comprised of only a few firms.

In an **oligopoly,** there are "a few" firms. Unfortunately, it is difficult to determine the exact number that makes up "a few." The number of firms is small enough that each firm must consider the reaction of the other firms when it changes its price. This is referred to as *mutual interdependence.*

The product in an oligopolistic industry can be identical or differentiated. When products are classified as identical, there are no distinguishing characteristics of each product that would allow the manufacturer of the product to be identified. Steel is an example of an identical product. In contrast, differentiated products are readily identified by manufacturer. Examples of differentiated products in an oligopolistic setting are automobiles, beer, and Canadian chartered banks.

The reason why there are only a few firms in the industry is that barriers limit the entry of new firms. These barriers include such things as brand names and the advantages of large-scale production. Even though barriers exist, they are not as strong as in a monopoly and the entry of new firms is not blocked completely.

Firms in oligopolistic industries use various types of *non-price competition.* These include advertising, sales promotion, product quality, product warranties, and service.

Many Differentiated Sellers

Many differentiated sellers describes a competitive situation with many sellers of a similar, but slightly different, product.

The competitive group called **many differentiated sellers** is similar in some respects to perfect competition. There are a large number of sellers in the same industry and entry into the industry is relatively easy. However, there are significant differences in relation to the model of perfect competition. First, the products are not identical. It is possible to distinguish the products of one seller from another. The differences may be in terms of product quality, brand name, product design, and so on. Second, each firm in the industry has some control over the price of the product. Finally, firms in this competitive structure make extensive use of non-price competition, especially *advertising*. Through advertising, individual firms hope to differentiate their product from that of their competitors. The more their product is different, the more control that the firm has over the price that it charges.

Examples of many differentiated sellers are numerous. They include men's and ladies' clothing, retail stores, restaurants, laundries, barbers and hairdressers, and similar business operations.

10.5 Explain the difference between perfect competition and many differentiated sellers.

10.6 Why would industries characterized by oligopoly and many differentiated sellers use non-price competition like advertising, whereas perfect competitors would not?

10.7 Under what types of competitive structure would you classify the record industry, the furniture industry, and the cable television industry?

Qualifications to Competitive Groupings

The competitive categories that we have defined are meant to serve only as a broad outline. Under certain conditions an industry may be classified as an oligopoly and under other circumstances it may be a monopoly. In many instances, grocery stores are in an oligopolistic situation. In a small town with one grocery store, however, a monopoly situation exists. The competitive nature of an industry may also change over time. For example, at one time there were many more automobile manufacturers than there are today. Let us consider these qualifications further.

Geographic

Depending on geographic boundaries, the competitive grouping of an industry may change. We do not normally consider restaurants and gas stations to be monopolies, yet in a rural area or a small town, a restaurant may well be the only one around. In this situation, the restaurant will behave more like a monopoly than a firm under the conditions of many differentiated sellers. If there are two restaurants, they will act like firms in an oligopolistic setting. Therefore, geographic boundaries have to be taken into consideration when discussing the nature of competition.

International Competition

Imports are an important aspect of many industries. In order to assess the competitive nature of the kinds of industries we've been talking about, foreign companies must be taken into consideration. During the 1960s, the automobile industry was dominated by General Motors, Ford, and Chrysler (Chrysler has since purchased American Motors). New imports have gained a significant share of the North American market. When General Motors is assessing the competition, it has to consider more firms than Ford or Chrysler. It is now possible for consumers to purchase cars made in Japan, Britain, Germany, France, and other countries. This means more competition for all the North American automobile manufacturers.

Inter-industry Competition

All firms, regardless of the kind of industry, are in competition for the consumers' dollar. Not only must they consider other competitors in the same industry, but they have to take into account all other firms vying for consumer attention. There may only be a few companies manufacturing home computers, yet these products have to compete with thousands of other products for sales.

In addition, products in different industries may be substitutes for each other. For example, companies that sell natural gas have a monopoly in a certain region. Yet natural gas is not the only available source of home heat: wood, oil, and electricity are different industries but acceptable substitutes. The post office has a monopoly of postal service in Canada, yet this is not the only form of communication available to the consumer. Airlines must compete with other modes of transportation including trains, buses, and automobiles. There may be only a handful of large grocery store chains, but the consumer does not have to purchase food at one of the chain stores. Food can be purchased at convenience stores, bulk-food stores, farmers' markets, and so on. Restaurants also provide competition for grocery stores. Therefore, the analysis of competition within an industry has to take into consideration the inter-industry competition.

Technological Change

Over time, the competitive nature of an industry is likely to change. Technological advances cause change to take place and can result in brand new industries as well as in changes to existing industries. Pocket and "credit-card" calculators have replaced the larger, less-sophisticated calculating equipment. Foreign expertise in the production of small cars has permitted foreign automobile manufacturers to make great progress in the North American market. Cotton and wool now share a market with a variety of synthetic fibres. Companies are now selling kits with which you can assemble your own computer. Monopolies and oligopolies may not remain that way forever unless the barriers to the entry of new firms are substantial.

10.8   Why may the nature of competition change as a result of techno-logical improvements?

10.9   Why must geography be considered when determining types of competition?

Measures of Concentration

In attempting to categorize industries into one of four competitive types, the measure of competition that we used was the number of firms in the industry. If there was only one firm, the industry was a monopoly. If there were a few firms in the industry, it was an oligopoly, and so on. The number of firms in an industry is not a precise measure of competition. It tells us nothing about either the size of the firms in the industry or the percentage of the industry's business each firm commands. Knowing that there are eight breweries in Canada tells us something about the competition in that industry. Knowing that four of those firms control 99 percent of the business tells us more about the competitive nature of the industry.

The measure of concentration within an industry indicates the degree to which the industry is dominated by a few firms.

Economists have developed measures of concentration in order to determine the *competitive nature* of an industry. **Concentration** refers to the degree to which business activity in an industry is dominated by a few firms. One measure of concentration is the proportion of total *industry sales* or output that can be attributed to the industry's four largest firms. Measures of concentration for Canadian manufacturing industries are given in table 10.1. The number of enterprises, or firms, in each industry is listed along with the value of shipments for the four largest firms. In 1985, the most concentrated industry was tobacco products manufacturing, in which 99.4 percent of industry shipments were concentrated in only four firms. Although this is the highest-concentration industry, there were only ten firms in the industry. By contrast, there were 51 firms in the aluminium rolling, casting, and extruding industry. In this industry, the top four firms had 88.8 percent of the market.

The concentration ratios shown in table 10.1 improve our knowledge of the competitive conditions in certain industries. Yet these ratios do have their shortcomings. The ratios published by Statistics Canada do not contain information on foreign suppliers who compete in the Canadian market. As pointed out in Chapter 9, imports are an important part of certain industries. When imports are not included in concentration ratios, industries will appear to be more concentrated than they actually are.

In addition, concentration figures refer to national markets only, counting the number of firms on a Canada-wide basis. For some industries, it may be more appropriate to calculate regional or local concentration ratios. *Transportation costs* may make it impractical for firms in one part of Canada to compete with firms thousands of miles away. Transportation costs in many industries are significant. In the cement industry, for example, it has been estimated that transportation costs account for more than 34 percent of every dollar of sales. Other industries in which transportation costs are significant are glass bottles, beer, petroleum products, and steel. If transportation costs restrict competition, then concentration measures on a regional or local basis will be higher than on a national basis. Unfortunately, concentration measures on a regional basis are not readily available.

A further criticism of the concentration ratios refers to the method by which the data were collected. The data on value of shipments are gathered at the individual plant or factory level and all output at the plant is allocated to one industry. If 80 percent of the output at a

Table 10.1 / Concentration ratios for the first four firms (CR4) by enterprises for twenty selected industries, Canada, 1985

Industry	No. of enterprises	CR4
tobacco products	11	99.4
breweries	11	97.7
silver-lead-zinc mines	9	95.8
motor vehicles	15	95.1
gypsum products	14	90.6
rubber hose and belting	13	89.2
paper consumer products	14	89.1
aluminium rolling, casting, and extruding industry	51	88.8
asphalt roofing	11	86.1
major appliances	22	85.0
copper rolling, casting, and extruding industries	34	82.4
potash mines	8	81.9
cement	9	81.7
communications and energy wiring cable	29	81.0
man-made fibre and filament yarn	25	79.4
domestic clay products	26	78.9
railroad rolling-stock industry	22	78.8
biscuits	21	78.8
leather tanneries	32	77.4
metal closures and containers	73	76.4

Source: *Industrial Organization and Concentration in the Manufacturing, Mining, and Logging Industries*, catalogue 31-402, biennial (Ottawa: Statistics Canada, 1989), pp. 2-32.

certain factory was for industry A and the remaining 20 percent of the plant's output was for industry B, the total output of the plant would be listed under industry A. This overstates the value of shipments for industry A and understates the value of shipments for industry B.

If we are to interpret correctly the competitive nature of an industry, we must know whether the industry is expanding or contracting. If the industry is expanding, then it is likely to become more competitive in the future, and increased competition will cause the measure of concentration to decrease. If the industry is contracting, it will become less competitive and concentration measures will increase. Whether or not an industry becomes more competitive depends on the *barriers to entry* for new firms. If major barriers are present, the industry is not likely to become more competitive in the future. Barriers can take several forms. Established firms may be able to take advantage of large-scale production and produce at a lower cost. They may also be able to get a discount if materials are purchased in large quantities. Existing companies may also have an advantage in terms of buyer preference (people prefer to buy a product with which they are familiar).

Another view of industry concentration can be seen by examining the market shares for selected industries as presented in table 10.2.

Royal Commission on Corporate Concentration

In 1975, the federal government appointed a royal commission to investigate the degree of concentration in Canadian industry. The terms of reference were to inquire into, report upon, and make recommendations concerning:

a   the nature and role of major concentrations of corporate power in Canada;
b   the economic and social implications for the public interest of such concentrations; and
c   whether safeguards exist or may be required to protect the public interest in the presence of such concentrations.

The event leading to the creation of this commission was the bid for control of Argus Corporation Limited by Power Corporation Limited. The federal government was uncertain about the impact of such a merger and wanted to ensure that existing legislation would protect the public interest.

Why was the government concerned about possible increasing industrial concentration? There is a concern that large corporations would have extensive control over price and the quantity of products available on the market. There also is concern that large corporations may be able to influence government policy. Finally, some argue that large corporations can shape the tastes and attitudes of consumers through the mass media.

The commission's basic conclusion was that industry is more concentrated in Canada than in other countries. Two types of concentration were studied. *Aggregate concentration* refers to the proportion of overall economic activity in Canada accounted for by the largest firms in the nation. *Industrial concentration* refers to the proportion of business activity in a particular industry dominated by the largest firms. Canadian concentration ratios were high according to both measures.

The commission found that corporations that we believe to be large in Canada are small by international standards. Large firms do

Table 10.2 / Market shares for selected industries, Canada, 1989

Industry	Percentage share	Industry	Percentage share
Cars (by manufacturer)		Hotels, cont.	
General Motors	34.3	Ramada	4.6
Ford	20.1	other	27.8
Chrysler	14.2		
Honda	8.5	Cellular Phones (subscribers)	
Toyota	7.8	Cantel	51.2
Nissan	3.2	Cellnet	48.8
Volkswagen	2.9		
other	8.9	Laser Printers	
		Hewlett-Packard	68.0
		Apple	16.0
		other	16.0
Fast-food Chains (sales)			
McDonald's	28.7	Diapers (sales) (1988)	
Kentucky Fried Chicken	11.3	Pampers	34.0
Harvey's	5.8	Huggies	31.0
Burger King	4.7	Luvs	15.0
A&W	4.2	other	20.0
Dairy Queen	3.6		
Wendy's	2.9	Athletic Footwear (pairs) (1988)	
Pizza Pizza	2.4	Reebok	15.4
Mr.Submarine	2.1	Nike	6.8
mmmuffins	1.7	Sonic	4.7
other	32.6	Adidas	4.1
		Bullit	3.9
Hotels (lodging sales)		Brooks	3.1
Four Seasons	18.1	Wildcat	3.0
Canadian Pacific	12.1	Converse	2.5
Commonwealth	7.5	Trax	2.2
ITT Sheraton	7.1	North Star	1.8
Westin	6.5	Cougar	1.7
Best Western	6.1	Sparx	1.6
Delta	5.2	Kangaroo	0.9
Journey's End	4.8		

have certain competitive advantages, and size may be related to efficiency. Smaller firms may have certain disadvantages in the areas of finance, marketing, and management. It is also more difficult for small companies to undertake the industrial research and product development that is essential in order to remain competitive. As well, larger firms may have a greater ability to take risks in new areas. Since Canadian companies must compete with foreign companies, the commission concluded that the federal government should not be overly concerned about the size of Canadian companies.

Large companies are not always more beneficial for Canadians. In the banking industry in particular, the commission concluded that size has not contributed to efficiency. In fact, the oligopolistic nature of the banking industry has perhaps led to more branches than necessary and a consequent lack of efficiency.

The commission concluded that the trend was toward lower overall concentration in Canadian non-financial corporations. This conclusion was treated with some skepticism by some researchers. They recognized that the commission did not have adequate data with which to work, and basing its conclusion on only the 100 leading companies. Also the commission did not use corporate enterprise data in the analysis of concentration.

After the commission had completed its work, Statistics Canada began to link corporate financial data with ownership information. Statistics Canada introduced the enterprise as the unit of observation. An enterprise is defined as a group of corporations under common control. Using this concept, all corporations controlled by one family would be aggregated and treated as one unit. This change in the data collection by Statistics Canada made it easier to look at the impact of inter-industry merger, vertical integration, and growth in conglomerates on industrial concentration. A clearer picture of concentration in Canada has emerged. From 1975 to 1986, the sales, assets, and profits of Canada's largest 25 enterprises grew significantly faster than those of all other enterprises. This resulted in an increase in the shares of sales, assets, and profits held by the leading enterprises. In recent years, there has been a slight decline in the concentration of sales, assets, and profits.

10.10   What do we mean by industry concentration?

10.11   Why is the number of firms in an industry not a sufficient measure of the competition that exists in an industry?

10.12   Did the Royal Commission on Corporate Concentration believe that Canadians benefit from large-sized companies?

Foreign Ownership of Canadian Industry

Foreign ownership occurs when foreign residents invest in Canadian assets and financial securities.

A unique aspect of Canadian industry is the large degree of **foreign ownership.** The largest company in Canada, General Motors, is completely owned by the parent company in the United States. Of the 50 largest industrial companies in Canada, 25 have some degree of foreign ownership. Canadian dependence on foreign capital is not a recent occurrence, as Canada has traditionally relied on foreigners for much of its investment. The British initially supplied most of the foreign investment. In 1900, approximately 85 percent of foreign investment in Canada came from the United Kingdom. The situation has now changed; the major source of foreign investment in Canada is now the United States, which accounts for approximately 70 percent of the direct foreign investment in this country.

Foreign investment in Canada is divided into two categories. *Foreign direct investment* implies managerial control of a business by persons in a foreign country. Under this type of investment, residents abroad will own the factory or other assets established in Canada. *Foreign portfolio investment* refers to the ownership of debt instruments, such as loans and debentures. It may also apply to minority holdings of shares in Canadian companies. Portfolio investment is not accompanied by any managerial control.

This section discusses the benefits and costs of foreign investment in Canada. Reference will be to direct investment where control over business assets in Canada is exercised by persons in another country.

What are the benefits of foreign investment to Canada? If a foreign company is setting up in Canada, it will bring business experience, new products, and technical know-how. New investment increases Canada's GDP and provides more jobs. Foreign competition also makes the Canadian market more competitive. Canadian firms are forced to adopt the latest technological and management techniques in order to compete. The resulting lower prices and improved quality benefit the consumer. The presence of foreign companies in Canada seems to improve our level of productivity. A strong, direct relationship exists between foreign ownership and productivity. The benefits from higher productivity going to Canadian workers have a positive effect on the Canadian economy.

The benefits of foreign investment, however, are accompanied by certain costs. Those who argue against foreign ownership claim that it results in lower productivity for Canadian workers. They argue that branch plants are not usually large enough to achieve the cost advantages associated with mass production. With the increased competition, Canadian companies also remain small and unable to achieve production economies. Others argue that foreign investment does not cause GDP to increase. If foreign investment is simply a substitute for the Canadian investment that would have taken place, the total level of investment spending, and hence GDP, is not any higher.

Foreign-owned companies may be subjected to some restrictions imposed by their parent country. Some subsidiaries of foreign companies located in Canada are not permitted to export to certain countries. The United States has often forbidden subsidiaries of American companies to sell products to countries it considers to be enemies of the United States. This extraterritoriality of American law was more of a problem in the past than it is now, but problems like these led to the development of the Committee for an Independent Canada in the early 1970s. This non-political committee was interested in restricting the foreign ownership of Canadian industry. Pressure by this committee and others resulted in the formation by the federal government in 1974 of the Foreign Investment Review Agency (FIRA). FIRA had the authority to approve or reject new foreign investment in Canada and foreign purchases of Canadian companies. Foreign investment in Canada had to represent a significant benefit to Canada in order to be approved.

Although foreign investment continued to flow into Canada after FIRA was established, some new investment was discouraged. A survey undertaken in 1983 by the Conference Board of Canada revealed that some foreigners did not invest in Canada because of the added costs, uncertainty, secrecy, and long delays associated with the FIRA process. Other potential investors were unhappy with the political interference in relation to the decision on new investment. They were also worried that in the future more restrictive changes would appear in Canada's legislation regarding foreign ownership and investment. Foreign dissatisfaction with FIRA and an economic recession in Canada led the Progressive Conservative government to scrap FIRA when they came to power in 1984. It was replaced by a new agency, Investment Canada, whose mandate was to attract new investment to Canada.

Foreign subsidiaries are often set up to serve the Canadian market only. The subsidiary is not established for purposes of exporting to other countries. If subsidiaries of foreign firms are not exporting, they will not improve our international balance of payments. Canada is a country that relies on foreign trade, especially exports. Subsidiary companies may only be established in order to perform certain functions. Very little product research and development is done by the subsidiary. This function is usually handled by the parent company. With a limited range of activities performed in Canada, there is only a limited range of jobs available. The more skilled jobs are likely to remain with the parent company. Canada has a good supply of educated and skilled workers and needs more employment opportunities than subsidiary companies are often able to supply.

Foreign ownership of many of our resource industries has created a unique problem. These resources are often exported to the parent country to be used in manufacturing. As a result, Canada has become a major exporter of raw materials but has not developed a strong manufacturing sector geared towards using these resources. The evidence of this was shown in Chapter 9, where Canada's trade statistics were discussed.

Foreign investment in Canada has provided Canadians with a variety of benefits and costs, which vary according to economic conditions. When the economy is good and employment is up, concerns about the ownership of our industry are more abundant. When the level of unemployment is high, and jobs are scarce, there is less concern over who owns the companies that provide employment.

10.13   List some of the benefits and costs of foreign investment in Canada.

Summary

Microeconomics is a section of economics that studies the decision-making process of business firms and individuals. There are various types of business firms operating in Canada. Sole proprietorship is the simplest form of business enterprise and is well-suited to the small firm. Partnerships are similar to sole proprietorships in their appropriateness for small firms. Partnerships differ from sole proprietorships in that they have more than one owner. The corporation is a business firm owned by shareholders. It is suitable for businesses of all sizes, but is especially appropriate for large firms. Canada also has a significant number of Crown corporations. These corporations are divided into three categories, depending on their financial and reporting structure. Proprietary Crown corporations compete directly with corporations in the private sector.

A major segment of the Canadian economy is small business. The definitions of small business vary, but each contains some reference to maximum annual sales and to a maximum number of employees. The advantages of small business include proximity to customers and an outlet for entrepreneurial talent. A market-oriented economy needs entrepreneurs not only to satisfy consumer wants but to create jobs. For those potential entrepreneurs not wishing to start from scratch, the possibility of purchasing a franchise exists.

From an economic point of view, the ownership of the business firm is not as important as the competition that the firm faces. The nature of the competition has a direct impact on the decisions made by the firm. Four competitive models are discussed in this chapter. In perfect competition, there are many sellers, each producing an identical product. Monopolies are characterized by one seller, and oligopolies have a few sellers. In many differentiated sellers, there are many sellers of similar but differentiated products.

Concentration refers to the degree to which business activity in an industry is dominated by a few firms. Concentration measures are described in terms of the percentage of the total business activity in an industry that is undertaken by the four largest firms. Those industries having a high percentage of business activity centred on four firms are described as highly concentrated. For example, in the tobacco-products industry, more than 99 percent of the value of all shipments is concentrated in the four largest firms.

Canadian industry is characterized by a high degree of foreign ownership. Canada has traditionally depended on foreign companies for much of its investment. Foreign ownership of Canadian business has brought with it some costs, as well as benefits, and the desirability of foreign investment in Canada seems to depend on the state of the Canadian economy.

Questions for Review and Discussion

1 Into what competitive grouping would you put the following businesses in your community?

   i a restaurant   iii a dentist

   ii a hotel   iv garbage pick-up services

2 Concentration and competition are the same thing. Discuss the merit of this statement.

3 Would Canadians be as well off if we were without foreign investment in our country?

4 Name five Canadian companies owned by a company in a foreign country. Name the parent company.

5 Is foreign investment more prominent in some provinces of Canada than in others? Discuss.

6 Why does criticism about foreign ownership decline when unemployment is high?

7 It has been suggested that the next industry to offer franchises will be farming. How might franchising work in an agricultural environment?

Suggested Readings

Barnes, Kenneth, and Everett Banning. *Money Makers! The Secrets of Canada's Most Successful Entrepreneurs*. Toronto: McClelland and Stewart Limited 1985.

Canadian Business. Special 60th Anniversary Issue: Guts. Greed and Glory. September 1988. Toronto: CB Media Ltd. 1988.

Financial Post 500. Summer 1991. Toronto: Maclean Hunter Ltd. 1991.

Jennings, William E. *Entrepreneurship: A Primer for Canadians.* Toronto: Canadian Foundation for Economic Education 1985.

Rabbior, Gary. *Bizball.* Toronto: Canadian Foundation for Economic Education 1986.

Ruggeri, G.C. *The Canadian Economy: Problems and Policies.* 3rd ed. Toronto: Gage 1987.

Chapter 11

Production Costs

Chapter Objectives

After successfully completing this chapter, you will be able to:

- define explicit and implicit costs
- define average and marginal costs
- graph average variable cost, average total cost, and marginal cost
- discuss the impact of the law of diminishing returns on the production function
- distinguish between the short run and the long run
- describe how long-run average costs are derived
- distinguish between economies and diseconomies of scale

Key Terms

explicit costs
implicit costs
economic profit
short run
long run
production function
division of labour
marginal product

productivity
multifactor productivity measures
fixed costs
variable costs
economies of scale
diseconomies of scale
marginal cost
marginal revenue

Elements of Production

In this chapter, we begin to analyse the *supply side* of individual markets. The focus of our attention will be on the costs that are faced by individual business firms. As mentioned in Chapter 2, these costs are major determinants of the quantity and price of a product that any firm puts on the market. A change in production costs results in a change in the supply curve. The concept of the supply curve introduced in Chapter 2 will be expanded.

The business firm was defined in Chapter 10. It is an organization that combines various resources into a final product. It can be a sole proprietorship, a partnership, or a corporation. The objective of the owners of the firm is to earn a profit, which is defined as the difference between the total revenue received by the firm and the total costs incurred.

profit = total revenue − total costs

The concept of total revenue is straightforward. It represents the total amount of money received from sales. In order to calculate total revenue, we multiply the quantity sold times the price.

total revenue (TR) = price (P) x quantity (Q)

Payments for productive resources that the firm does not own and must purchase are called explicit costs.

The concept of production costs is not as straightforward as that of revenue. First of all, it is necessary to differentiate between explicit and implicit costs. **Explicit costs** are those payments for resources that the firm must purchase. These resources include labour, materials, transportation, rent, and energy. Since these resources are not owned by the firm itself, they must be purchased from outside.

Payments for productive resources that the firm already owns are called implicit costs.

Implicit costs, in contrast, are payments to resources that the firm already owns. The firm may own the building from which it operates. It may also own a certain amount of machinery and equipment. It could own some land. The firm may also have some money that it is planning to invest in the business. Finally, the talents and time of the owner(s) can be considered resources that the firm owns. How does the firm pay for something that it already owns?

An opportunity cost is associated with each of these resources. If the firm uses its own building, the opportunity cost is the money that it could have received had it rented the building to someone else. The opportunity cost of any money invested in the firm is the interest lost by not putting this money into an interest-earning asset, such as a savings account. Finally, the opportunity cost of the owner's time is the money that he or she could have earned elsewhere. Implicit costs represent the sum of the opportunity costs of those resources owned by the firm.

Why are implicit costs included as costs? Opportunity costs represent the value of what was given up in order to operate the business. If the firm does not earn enough money to cover these costs, then it would be better off to enter another line of business or to do something else with the resources that it owns. Since it is desirable to cover these opportunity costs, they are included in the firm's total costs.

total costs = explicit costs + implicit costs

Economic profit is the excess of total revenue over total costs.

Since the total costs of a business firm include both explicit and implicit costs, a profit will only be earned when total revenue exceeds these costs. This is referred to as **economic profit;** the amount of money that comes into the firm over and above the amount necessary to pay off all costs. It can also be regarded as an amount of money over and above that necessary to keep the firm in business.

economic profit = total revenue – total costs

11.1 Why is it necessary that the firm consider opportunity costs when determining whether or not an economic profit has been made?

Numerical Calculation of Profit

Accountants and economists may look at profits from different points of view. A numerical example highlights these differences. Mr. Doolittle was employed at Dawson's Garage as a mechanic. Though he enjoyed his job, he always wanted to operate his own automotive repair shop. He believed that by working on his own he could earn more money than he could working for someone else. He also liked the idea of being his own boss. One day Mr. Doolittle saw an opportunity to start his own business, so he left Dawson's Garage.

While employed at Dawson's Garage, he had been earning $40 000 per year. He had managed to accumulate $20 000 in savings, which he needed to launch his business. This money had been deposited in a savings account at a chartered bank and was earning ten percent interest annually.

There were certain costs associated with going into business. Mr. Doolittle had to rent a garage, buy machinery and tools, advertise, and hire other mechanics. At the end of one year in the auto-repair business, Mr. Doolittle's costs were as follows:

rent (garage)	$ 10 000
wages to mechanics	$ 60 000
advertising	$ 2 000
tools	$ 4 000
electricity	$ 2 000
Total costs	$ 78 000

During the first year of operation, Mr. Doolittle's garage brought in $130 000 in sales. Did he earn a profit? The traditional calculation of profit is to subtract total costs from total revenue.

profit = total revenue − total costs
= $130 000 − $78 000
= $52 000

The traditional accounting definition of profit would be that Mr. Doolittle had earned a profit of $52 000 in the first year of operation.

Economists would not agree that Mr. Doolittle's profit was this high. From an economist's point of view, certain costs were not included in the calculation of total costs. These are the implicit costs. Mr. Doolittle gave up a job paying $40 000 per year in order to start his own business. If he did not earn at least $40 000 with his own business, he would be better off working for someone else. Mr. Doolittle also took $20 000 out of his savings account for the new business. At an interest rate of ten percent, he would have earned an additional $2000 if this money had remained in the bank. In fact, Mr. Doolittle sacrificed $42 000 ($40 000 + $2 000) in order to go into business for himself. This amount represents his implicit costs.

In order to calculate profit, the economist believes that explicit and implicit costs should be added together.

explicit costs   = $ 78 000
+ implicit costs   = $ 42 000

= total costs   = $120 000

economic profit = total revenue − total costs
= $130 000 − $120 000
= $10 000

From an economic point of view, Mr.Doolittle earned $10 000 profit in his first year of operation. He earned $10 000 more than necessary to keep him in business.

Questions

1   If Mr.Doolittle's garage earned $110 000 in revenue, what would his accounting profit be? His economic profit?

2   Calculate his economic profit if he had been earning $44 000 a year at Dawson's Garage, and if total revenue brought in by his new business was $130 000 per year.

3   Calculate his economic profit in our original example if the interest rate on his savings account was 15 percent annually.

4   Do you think that Mr.Doolittle would be willing to stay in business for himself even if he was earning less than he did at Dawson's Garage? Why or why not?

5 Do you think that company profits reported in the newspaper are accounting or economic profits? Why?

The Production Function

Time Periods

The short run is a period of time in the production process during which at least one resource cannot be altered.

Production costs tend to change over time. When analysing the cost picture of a firm, it is necessary to distinguish between two different time periods: the short run and the long run. The **short run** is defined as a period of time when at least one resource used in the production process remains unchanged. For example, on a farm the amount of land available is usually fixed. For any business there is a period of time when the ability to produce more is constrained by the size of the factory or store. It is impossible to say whether the short run is one month, three months, one year, or five years. This evaluation depends on the nature of the business and the resources that are used. Because firms are always faced with constraints or resources that cannot be changed immediately, they are always producing in the short run.

The period of time in the production process during which all resources are variable is termed the long run.

The **long run** is a period of time when no resources can be called fixed. It is a period of time long enough for the firm to be able to adjust all of its inputs in the production process. All resources, or inputs, that the firm has access to are variable. The firm can buy more machinery, hire more workers, build a new factory, or buy more land. The long run is seen as a planning period, since it is impossible to actually produce in the long run. Production will always take place in the short run because companies are always faced with certain resource constraints that they cannot change.

Because a firm is always operating in a short-run situation, the production costs of the firm will be analysed in this short-run time frame. The ability of the firm to increase production in the short run will be constrained by the fact that at least one resource, or input, will remain fixed. The example of a furniture factory will help to describe the relationship between production levels and production costs in the short run. Assume that the Pinewood Furniture Company has rented a building for a year. This is a short-run cost because one resource, the building, cannot be changed for at least one year. Assume further that the factory contains all the raw material and machinery necessary to make chairs. The only input to the production process that can be changed is the number of workers. Changing the number of workers in order to change output is referred to as the **production function.** It represents the relationship between changes in inputs, or resources, and changes in output.

The production function refers to the relationship between the amount of resources used and the level of output.

11.2 Why is it not possible for a firm to be actually producing in the long run?

Specialization

As more workers are hired to make chairs, the number of chairs produced will increase. As the labour force is increased, a division of labour will take place. The firm will have workers who specialize in certain aspects of chair-making: some workers will be employed in measuring and cutting; some will specialize in lathe work; others will specialize in chair assembly, and so on. *This specialization of labour should permit greater efficiency and greater production.* If one person, working alone, could produce five chairs in a day, two workers should be able to make more than ten chairs in a day, if the workers specialize in certain tasks. Consequently, the company would be in a situation of doubling its labour resource and more than doubling its output of chairs.

The division of labour refers to the speciali-zation in the perfor-mance of tasks by workers in order to permit greater efficiency and greater production.

Why does a **division of labour** result in greater efficiency and more output? Performing the same task over and over would allow the worker to become more proficient at it. If someone's specialty was making chair legs on a wood lathe, the person would develop a certain skill at this job. By continually performing the same task, the worker is likely to find a better way to do the job. Specialization also saves time as workers do not have to move to different work stations and use different tools.

Specialization, however, is not without its costs. These are re-lated to the worker's feelings. The worker may develop a sense of boredom as the same task is repeated over and over again. An indi-vidual may also lack a sense of fulfilment in that this task is only one of several other tasks. One worker does not make an entire chair in our Pinewood example. Making a complete chair by oneself might be more satisfying.

In terms of production, the benefits of specialization seem to outweigh the costs. Without specialization, more hours in a day would be required to achieve the same output. As we will show later, lack of specialization can lead to higher production costs and lower wages for workers.

Diminishing Returns

Would increases in output through increased specialization continue forever? No, at a certain level of output the advantages of specializa-tion would cease. The ability of the Pinewood Furniture Com-pany to produce chairs is limited by the size of the factory. Beyond some point, if more workers are hired, their contributions to the daily output of chairs would decrease. They would have less and less of the fixed resources to work with. If each additional worker has less of the fixed resources to work with, that worker will contribute less to the total output than the previous worker.

This situation is known as the *law of diminishing returns*. The idea of diminishing returns was first introduced in Chapter 1 in connection with Malthus' theory of population. It applies equally well to the production situation of a firm. The law states that when increasing amounts of a variable resource are added to a fixed amount of another resource, after a certain point the additions to total output will become fewer and fewer. In our example, the variable resource was workers and the fixed resource was the factory. Since the law of diminishing returns involves a fixed resource, the situation only occurs in the short run.

Table 11.1 / Production function for Pinewood Furniture Company

No. of workers	Total no. of chairs produced per day	Marginal product	Average no. of chairs per worker
0	0	-	
1	5	5	5.0
2	13	8	6.5
3	22	9	7.3
4	30	8	7.5
5	37	7	7.4
6	43	6	7.2
7	48	5	6.9
8	52	4	6.5
9	54	2	6.0
10	55	1	5.5
11	55	0	5.0
12	54	-1	4.5

The production function of our company that demonstrates the concept of diminishing returns appears in table 11.1. As the number of workers hired increases, the total number of chairs produced increases. Yet starting with the fourth worker hired, the additions to the total number of chairs produced become fewer and fewer. The third worker added nine chairs to the total output, increasing the output from 13 to 22. The fourth worker added only eight chairs to the total. Each successive worker adds fewer chairs because each successive worker has less space to work in, less material to work with, and so on. The addition to the total output of each extra worker is called the **marginal product** of labour and is shown in the third column of the table. The word "marginal" means extra or additional. Looking at the marginal-product column, we can see that diminishing returns set in with the addition of the fourth worker.

Marginal product (MP) is the addition to total output as a result of adding one more unit of a productive resource.

This information is shown graphically in figure 11.1. The marginal-product curve increases as a result of worker specialization, but starting with the fourth worker, diminishing returns set in and marginal product starts to decline. Is it possible for the marginal product of labour to be zero? Yes; since the size of the factory is

**Figure 11.1
Production
function for the
Pinewood
Furniture
Company**

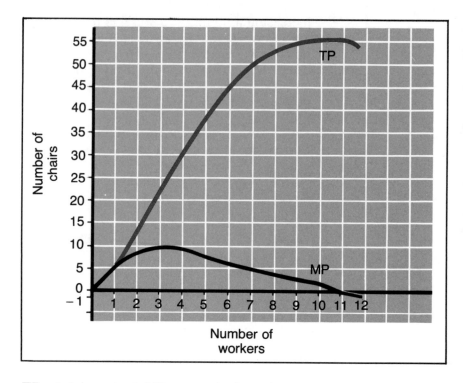

TP = total product, MP = marginal product

fixed, there may be a point at which one more worker does not add anything to the total output of chairs. This is the case with the eleventh worker in table 11.1. It may even be possible to have too many workers and have total output fall. In our example, the marginal product for the twelfth worker is -1. This is shown on the graph by having the marginal-product (**MP**) line fall below the horizontal axis.

In the case of the Pinewood Furniture Company, we theorized that diminishing returns set in after the fourth worker was hired. However, in many production situations, diminishing returns do not occur this soon, and they depend on the size of the firm and the type of operation it is engaged in. A company may have hundreds, or even thousands, of workers before experiencing diminishing returns.

The law of diminishing returns is important in our discussions for two reasons. First, it affects the costs of the firm in the short run. If each successive worker contributes less and less to the daily output of chairs, the cost of making the chairs is going to increase. Second, the contribution of each worker to the total output influences the company's willingness to hire more workers, and the demand for workers strongly affects the wages that workers will earn. Chapter 14 is devoted to a discussion of how wages are determined. The concept of diminishing returns will reappear there.

11.3 In your own words, explain the law of diminishing returns. What conditions must be present for diminishing returns to take effect?

Productivity

Productivity refers to the amount of output produced by a unit of a certain resource during a specified period of time.

The amount of output produced by a unit of a certain input during a specified period of time is referred to as **productivity.** Although productivity can be discussed in terms of any input, or resource, it is most often mentioned in reference to *labour*. It is measured in terms such as output per worker-hour or output per person employed. Other measures of labour productivity are also used, yet none is considered to be the most definitive or accurate.

Why is the concept of productivity important? It is closely related to our standard of living. If productivity is increasing, it means that more goods and services are being provided from the same amount of resources. If productivity is increasing, then production costs can be lower and potential price increases can be held back. This means that increases in labour productivity can be associated with higher incomes for workers without the accompanying increase in prices. Productivity is directly related to one of Canada's economic objectives: a reduced rate of inflation.

Productivity is also an important issue in union/management negotiations. Management is willing to increase wages only if the output per worker increases. In this way production costs will be kept down. Unions try to show how labour productivity has increased in order to justify their demands for higher wages.

What influences labour productivity? Several factors are important. The training, skills, and education of the worker are directly related to the amount produced. Those workers with more experience or greater skills are able to produce more than others. The *quality* of the other resources that labour has to work with is also a significant factor. In many office jobs, a secretary using a word processor is more productive than one using an electronic typewriter. A worker with an automatic sander can finish more wood than one sanding by hand. A homemaker with an automatic washing machine and dryer, a microwave oven, and a dishwasher can accomplish more in less time than a homemaker without these appliances.

The *quantity* of resources that a worker has to work with is also important. A farmer working 200 acres of land can produce more than a farmer working 100 acres of land of comparable quality. The quantity of other resources is related to the law of diminishing returns. In the short run, as production increases, each successive worker has less and less of the fixed resource to work with. As a result, a point is reached beyond which each successive worker produces less than the previous one hired. Due to the law of diminishing returns, labour productivity declines.

The conventional measure of productivity is *labour productivity,* which shows the level of output per employee. This measure ignores any contribution to increased production that results from using more resources along with labour. It is important to consider the contribution of other resources, since using additional resources can also cause labour productivity to increase. In an effort to avoid relying totally on labour productivity figures, economists have been working to develop a measure of total-factor productivity. In June 1990, Statistics Canada released experimental data on new measures of productivity.

Multifactor productivity measures indicate the level of productivity in an industry by taking into consideration all relevant resources, not only labour resources.

The new productivity measures are called **multifactor productivity measures.** The first measure takes into account all changes in factors of production. The second measure includes not only the productivity gains in the industry itself, but also those in the industries supplying it with energy, materials, and services. This latter measure allows for better international comparisons of productivity change, since there are different levels of vertical integration in different countries. For example, does a steel company own the mines that supply it with iron ore, or does the company purchase the iron ore from someone else? Differences in the level of vertical integration can affect productivity calculations. Apart from improving international comparisons, the interindustry productivity measure can identify an industry that is not achieving major productivity gains itself but is using materials from industries in which productivity gains have been significant.

How do the new measures of productivity compare with the former labour productivity measures? In general, the multifactor index of productivity indicates that productivity gains were about half of those calculated for labour productivity for the period 1961-86. The lower figure is likely due to the increase in the capital-labour ratio in Canadian business. Much of the gain for this period can be attributed to the use of more machinery, making workers more productive. According to the new index of productivity, the transportation and communications industries had the highest increase in productivity from 1961-86. The multifactor index showed an increase of 190.1 percent compared to an increase of 242.8 percent for labour productivity alone. Within the manufacturing sector, electrical and electronic products had the highest increase in productivity over this period, followed by chemical products.

There were some interesting contrasts between the labour productivity measure and the new multifactor productivity measure for some industries. Labour productivity measures indicated an increase of 315.4 percent for the plastics industries, while the multifactor index showed a productivity gain of only 132.7 percent. A similar picture is presented for the transportation equipment industry. The labour productivity measure indicated an increase in productivity of 308.9 percent, while the multifactor index shows an increase of only 139.6 percent.

A further discussion of labour productivity and its influence on wage rates appears in Chapter 14.

Short-Run Costs

Fixed costs are production costs that do not vary with the amount produced.

Variable costs are production costs that vary with the amount of output.

The costs faced by a firm can be divided into two groups, based on production levels. **Fixed costs** are costs that remain the same regardless of the level of output. Even if nothing is produced, these costs are present. Examples of fixed costs are rent, real estate taxes, insurance, and interest payments on any loans. **Variable costs,** on the other hand, vary with the level of output. As output increases, more labour, raw materials, and energy are used. If the amount of resources used increases, costs will increase. The total cost faced by the firm in order to produce a given level of output is the sum of the fixed and the variable costs.

total costs (TC) = total fixed cost (TFC) + total variable cost (TVC)

More important than total cost for our purposes will be cost per unit produced. This is called the *average total cost*. In order to calculate average total cost (ATC), the total cost (TC) is divided by the level of output (Q).

$$ATC = \frac{TC}{Q}$$

Remember that TC = TFC + TVC
Therefore,

$$\frac{TC}{Q} = \frac{TFC}{Q} + \frac{TVC}{Q}$$

and,

average total cost (ATC) = average fixed cost (AFC)
+ average variable cost (AVC)

How do the shape of the production function and the law of diminishing returns influence costs? As previously stated, only variable costs will be affected, since fixed costs remain the same regardless of the level of output. As the furniture firm in our example starts to increase the level of chair production by hiring more workers, total costs will increase while average total costs fall. If workers can specialize in certain tasks to increase output, the cost per unit (average total cost) will fall. Look back at the figures in table 11.1. Three workers produced a total of 22 chairs for an average of 7.3 chairs per worker. One worker alone was only able to produce five chairs. Through specialization, the average number of chairs produced per worker increases and the average cost of producing chairs will decrease. After diminishing returns have set in, the average number of chairs produced per worker starts to fall. Diminishing returns set in with the hiring of the fourth worker. The average number of chairs produced per worker falls from a high of 7.5 to 5.5 by the tenth worker. Diminishing returns force the costs associated with producing each chair to rise, assuming that each worker is paid the same wage.

The effects of worker specialization and the law of diminishing returns on a firm's costs are shown in table 11.2. It is assumed that the fixed costs faced by the furniture company are $50. Fixed costs include rent, insurance premiums, and interest payments on loans. Variable costs include labour, raw materials, energy, and transportation. As shown in the table, average variable costs begin to fall until they are affected by diminishing returns. That is, average variable costs decline until a level of output of five units is reached. The extra cost of producing one more unit begins to rise with the fifth unit produced. The addition to the total cost of producing one more unit is known as the **marginal cost,** and is presented in the last column in the table. The impact of diminishing returns is to cause marginal costs to increase. If marginal costs are starting to increase, then average costs will eventually increase as well.

Marginal cost (MC) is the addition to the total cost of producing one more unit of output.

Table 11.2 / Production costs and level of output, Pinewood Furniture Company

Level of output (chairs)	Total fixed costs $	Total variable costs $	Total cost $	Average fixed cost $	Average variable cost $	Average total cost $	Marginal cost $
0	50	0	50	-	0.00	-	
1	50	30	80	50.00	30.00	80.00	30
2	50	54	104	25.00	27.00	52.00	24
3	50	76	126	16.67	25.33	42.00	22
4	50	96	146	12.50	24.00	36.50	20
5	50	122	172	10.00	24.40	34.40	26
6	50	150	200	8.33	25.00	33.33	28
7	50	190	240	7.14	27.14	34.28	40
8	50	240	290	6.25	30.00	36.25	50
9	50	300	350	5.55	33.33	38.89	60
10	50	370	420	5.00	37.00	42.00	70

The data in table 11.2 are plotted in figures 11.2 and 11.3. In figure 11.2, the total cost data are presented. The total-cost (TC) curve is the summation of the total fixed-cost (TFC) curve and the total variable-cost (TVC) curve. In figure 11.3, the average and

**Figure 11.2
Production costs
for Pinewood
Furniture
Company**

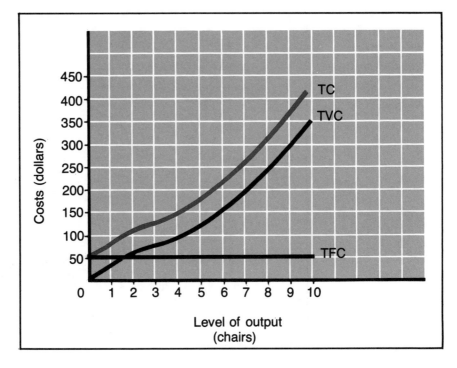

TC = total costs, TVC = total variable costs, TFC = total fixed costs

marginal costs are presented. The average total-cost (ATC) curve is
the sum of the average fixed-cost (AFC) curve and the average variable-cost (AVC) curve. The marginal-cost (MC) curve initially declines because of worker specialization, but eventually begins to rise
when diminishing returns set in. Marginal costs begin to rise with the
fifth unit produced. Eventually the increase in marginal costs begins
to influence average variable costs, which also start to increase.

It should be noted that the marginal-cost curve will always intersect the average variable-cost and average total-cost curves at their
lowest points. As long as the marginal cost of producing one extra
unit of output is less than the average cost, it will bring the average
down. As soon as the marginal cost becomes greater than the average,
it begins to bring the average up. Therefore, the only point where the
two curves can intersect is at the lowest point on the average curve.

In order to better explain the intersection of the curves in the
diagram, an analogy can be made to college test marks. Assume that
on two tests you had an average mark of 70 per cent. If you obtained a mark of 60 on the third test, what would happen to your average? Since 60 is less than 70, your new average would be less than
70. In fact, it would be 66.7 percent. Similarly, when the cost of producing one more unit of output is less than the average cost of the
preceding units, the average cost has to decline. The opposite would

**Figure 11.3
Production costs
for Pinewood
Furniture
Company**

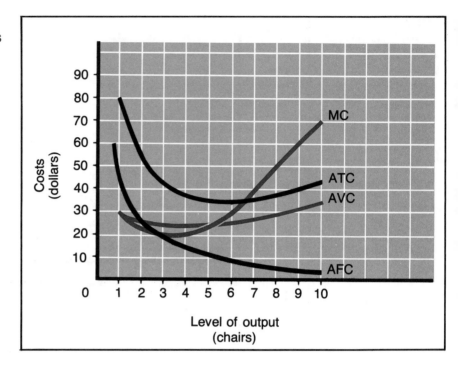

ATC = average total costs, AVC = average variable costs, AFC = average fixed costs, MC = marginal costs

have occurred had you scored 80 on your third test. Your average would then increase to 73.3 percent for the three tests. *Again, if the marginal cost of producing one more unit is greater than the average cost, then the average cost has to increase.* The only possible point where the marginal-cost curve could intersect the average-cost and average variable-cost curves is at their lowest points.

11.4 Explain why diminishing returns would cause marginal costs to increase.
11.5 Why must MC intersect AVC and ATC at the lowest points on the AVC and ATC curves?

**Sunk Costs Are
Irrelevant**

To the economist, one type of cost, called a *sunk cost*, is irrelevant to decision-making, as there are no opportunity costs associated with sunk costs. Further, economists tend to look to the future when confronted with decisions rather than looking back to the past. Still, what are sunk costs? An example is the best way to explain this concept.

Assume that Garson Manufacturing purchased a metal lathe

three years ago for $10 000. At the time of purchase there was an opportunity cost involved in the decision to buy the lathe. What else could the company do with $10 000? Having taken the alternatives into consideration, the company purchased the lathe. There are now newer and more efficient metal lathes on the market. The lathe purchased three years ago needs repairs in order to perform efficiently. Should Garson Manufacturing purchase a new, more efficient lathe, or should the old lathe be repaired? What costs are relevant to the company's decision?

The cost of the new lathe is relevant. What else could be done with the money? The cost of fixing up the old lathe is also relevant. If it is possible to trade in the old lathe or sell it as a second-hand lathe, this, too, is relevant to the decision. If the old lathe could be sold for $4000, there is an opportunity cost to not selling it. What about the original $10 000 spent on the lathe? Where does this cost enter into the decision-making process? The answer is that it does not. The irrelevant factor in this decision-making process is the difference between the original cost of the lathe ($10 000) and the resale value ($4000). This difference ($6000) is called a *sunk cost.* There is no opportunity cost associated with this cost.

Garson Manufacturing may argue that it cannot afford to sell the old machine for less than it paid for it. The company may argue that it cannot afford to take the loss. But the company has already taken the loss on the old lathe. The purchase of the lathe three years ago is in the past and is no longer relevant to today's decision-making. It is a sunk cost. As far as the old lathe is concerned, the only relevant cost is the opportunity cost of the resale.

Was the cost of the old lathe ever relevant? Yes. Before the purchase of the old lathe, the cost was an important factor in making the decision. Once the decision had been made, however, the cost of the lathe was no longer relevant.

Questions

1 Can you reflect on any sunk costs associated with your personal finances?
2 In the 1970s, CN introduced a new train, the *Turbo,* to run between Toronto and Montreal. Were the costs associated with the development of the *Turbo* part of the cost of running it between these two cities? Explain.

Long-Run Costs

In the long run, a firm is not constrained by one factory size. It can expand and build as many factories as necessary. It can hire more workers. It can purchase more equipment. As sales increase, an increase in all resources will be required. In the long run, the law of diminishing returns does not affect costs since no resources that are used in the production process remain fixed. All resources, or inputs, are variable.

The long run can be seen as a planning period. It is composed of a series of short-run situations. It is not possible for the firm to produce in the long run, since the firm will always be constrained by at least one resource that cannot be changed. Therefore we string a series of short-run situations together in order to determine long-run costs. What happens to costs in the long run? As the firm grows in size, its average total costs are likely to fall. Several factors will cause this. First, the firm may take increased advantage of specialization in the use of labour. A larger factory and a larger production run will allow even greater specialization to take place. Second, larger-scale production may permit some cost saving in terms of management. A doubling of the production staff may not require a doubling of managerial staff as well. One supervisor may be able to supervise two, four, six, or even more employees. Third, larger firms may be better able to take advantage of more efficient production equipment. Certain machines may be too impractical and costly for small operations, but may be well-suited to large production runs. Fourth, larger firms may be able to purchase materials in large quantities at a discount. All of these factors tend to reduce average costs. These are referred to as economies of large-scale production, or **economies of scale,** and are more easily attainable in the long run. Economies of scale are present when the firm experiences a more-than-proportionate increase in its output as a result of increasing all its inputs. For example, economies of scale would result if the firm doubled all of its inputs and experienced a more-than-double increase in output. Therefore, in the long run, average costs will decrease as the level of output increases as a result of economies of scale.

Economies of scale are decreases in long-run average costs resulting from the efficiencies of large-scale production.

Economists have determined that economies of scale may be associated with the product, the plant, and the firm. Economies of scale at the product level are associated with the use of more specialized capital equipment. By concentrating on a relatively small number of products, production processes that are well-suited to those products can be set up. While specialized equipment is often expensive, it is usually capable of achieving a greater volume of output for a given level of costs. By focussing on a narrow range of products, the learning, or experience, curve comes into play. As more of a product is produced, costs per unit tend to decline as a result of "learning by doing" on the part of the workers.

Economies of scale at the plant level refer to the effects of a larger plant on per-unit costs of production. The reduction in per-unit costs is associated mainly with the increased specialization of workers and equipment that is a result of larger volumes of output.

Economists have tried to identify minimum efficient scale (MES) plants for various industries. An MES plant has the lowest production costs in an industry. Many Canadian plants are below the MES size. The reasons for smaller plant sizes in Canada are the small size of the domestic market and the large geographic area. High transportation costs encourage companies to build a larger number of small plants, rather than a few large ones.

Firm-level economies of scale occur as a result of a number of factors. These include administrative economies that spread overhead, finance, advertising, and research and development costs over a larger output. Larger firms may be willing to take risks more readily if they are more diversified and can fall back on other products. Such firms may also have dealer networks that provide distribution economies.

Can average costs be expected to keep falling as the company expands? It is unlikely that this will happen. The firm may get so large that certain inefficiencies set in. For example, a large firm may have too many managerial levels between the person who makes a decision and the person who finally puts the decision into operation. Such a situation can result in poorer communication, less efficiency, and higher costs.

The following quote helps to emphasize the communication difficulties in large firms:

> Again, we're faced with an important paradox for management, for the world of big companies is complex. Just how complex is suggested by the fact that as the number of people in a company goes up arithmetically, the number of possible interactions among them goes up geometrically. If our company has ten employees, we can all stay in touch with one another because the number of ways we can interact, say, in one-on-one discussion is forty-five. If our company has 1,000 employees, on the other hand, that same number of possible one-on-one interactions goes up to about 500,000. If there are 10,000 employees then the number rises to 50 million. To cope with the complex communications needs generated by size alone, we require appropriately complex systems, or so it would seem.
> (Peters and Waterman, *In Search of Excellence*, p. 64.)

Mass production facilities do not always guarantee lower costs, as this quote concerning the Ford Motor Company reveals:

> Ten years ago Ford Motor Co. built a plant to produce 500,000 tons of iron engine blocks a year. Erected on the principle that mass production means lower costs, it was four stories high and large enough to enclose 72 football fields. But the plant

designed to produce V-8 engines turned out to be too big and too specialized. When new designs for lighter engines followed the oil crunch, Ford discovered that retooling the huge plant was prohibitively expensive. It shut down the factory, moving operations to a 30-year-old, smaller plant. (*ibid.*, p. 112.)

There is also a high correlation between the size of plants and the degree of labour disputes, labour turnover, and other manifestations of worker dissatisfaction. This correlation is referred to as **diseconomies of scale** and causes average costs to increase. Thus, at a certain level of output, average total costs will begin to rise when diseconomies of scale set in. Just *when* diseconomies of scale will begin to affect costs is difficult to determine. In some firms, diseconomies of scale will take effect at lower levels of output than in other firms. The generalized trends in long-run costs are shown in figure 11.4, which shows the composition of the long-run average cost curve. The long-run cost curve (**LAC**) is derived from a series of short-run cost curves (**SAC₁, SAC₂,** etc.) Each SAC curve relates to a certain factory size. At every possible level of output, there

Diseconomies of scale are increases in long-run average costs resulting from the inefficiencies associated with large-scale operations.

Figure 11.4 Generalized diagram of long-run costs

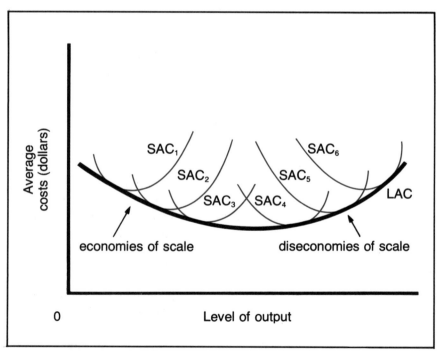

The long-run cost curve (LAC) is derived from a series of short-run cost curves (SAC).

exists a point on a short-run average cost curve (**SAC**) at which this output can be produced. The long-run average cost curve includes those points at which a certain level of output can be produced for the lowest average cost. It should be noted that these points are not necessarily the minimum average cost for each factory size. If a larger factory can achieve lower average costs for a certain level of output, then it makes sense to expand rather than to try to use a smaller factory more efficiently. That is, it is not necessary to include the minimum point of each SAC curve in the LAC curve.

11.6   Do diminishing returns affect costs in the long run? Explain.

11.7   What are diseconomies of scale?

Organization at General Motors

General Motors of Canada was the largest company in Canada in 1986 on the basis of sales. This automobile manufacturer is a wholly-owned subsidiary of General Motors Corporation (U.S.), one of the largest companies in the world. From the beginning, the company was concerned about the cost disadvantages associated with size. The organizational structure developed in the early 1900s was set up in order to counter certain diseconomies of scale.

The organizational plan hoped to preserve the advantages of a decentralized operation, while at the same time maintaining financial control and internal communication. Thus, the company was divided into divisions. Each division was quite autonomous, having responsibility in such areas as product development and promotion, quality control, engineering, and management structure. It was the responsibility of each division to analyse the marketplace and build products for it. It was also intended that there be some interdivision rivalry. In the automobile market, Pontiac, Chevrolet, Oldsmobile, Buick, and Cadillac were to be competitors.

The organization was established so that the head executive of each division would operate within the financial framework and general policy established by the corporation. The organizational plan stressed that certain functions, such as overall planning, had to remain at the head office. The structure has worked quite well, despite a few problems. One problem is that some issues that should be settled at lower levels of the organizational structure find their way to the head office. On the other hand, it is often difficult for head-office personnel to give the chief executive of each division a free hand in running the division.

Even with the decentralization at General Motors, there is still a proliferation of management levels. The following quote from John DeLorean's account of his years at General Motors describes the layers of management:

A plant manager reported to a city manager who reported to a regional manager who reported to a manager of plants who reported to the general manufacturing manager who reported to the works manager who reported to me, the general manager. Consequently, the manager of the Chevrolet Gear and Axle plant on Detroit's near east side who was only a few miles from my office was almost light years away in terms of management reporting channels (Wright, *On a Clear Day You Can See General Motors,* p. 137).

In 1984, General Motors realigned its North American car operations by creating two supergroups: the Buick-Oldsmobile-Cadillac group for more upscale vehicles and the Chevrolet-Pontiac-Canada group for its lower-priced vehicles. In 1985, the company announced a restructuring of the Buick-Oldsmobile-Cadillac group into four separate business units. Each unit is responsible for turning its own profit. This restructuring was designed to allow the company to pinpoint unprofitable operations more easily. In 1989, the company created the Automotive Components Group which centralized the component plants administration.

Questions

1 How would the divisional set-up of General Motors reduce the diseconomies associated with this large corporation?

2 In 1965, Canada and the United States signed an agreement that permitted North American-built cars to cross the border free of tariffs (customs duties). How did this agreement affect General Motors' automobile production in Canada? What impact might this agreement have on Canadian economies and diseconomies of scale?

Making Decisions

Economics is the study of how people go about making decisions regarding the use of scarce resources. In order for a firm to make decisions about the price of its product and the amount produced, it must have a certain objective in mind. Let us assume that all firms attempt to maximize profits as their main objective. They may have other objectives, but it is generally agreed that the assumption of profit maximization is a good predictor of individual firm behaviour. As discussed earlier in this chapter,

economic profit = total revenue − total costs

Marginal revenue (MR) is the addition to total revenue as a result of selling one more unit of output.

In order to maximize profits, the difference between total revenue and total cost has to be maximized. Another way to view this objective is in terms of marginal revenue and marginal cost. **Marginal revenue** is defined as the addition to total revenue resulting from selling one more unit of output. Marginal cost is defined as the total cost of producing one more unit of output. In order to maximize profits, the firm will continue to expand output up to the point at which

marginal revenue = marginal costs

If at a certain level of output marginal revenue exceeded marginal cost, it would pay the firm to expand output. There would be more revenue gained from selling the additional output than there would be costs in producing it. As a result, profits would increase. If the cost of producing more output exceeded the revenue that would be acquired from selling it, then it would not make sense to increase production. In this case, if more units of output were produced, then profits would decrease. Only at the level of output at which marginal revenue is equal to marginal cost will profits be maximized.

It should be noted that when looking at a firm's maximum profit level of output, the cost per unit (average total cost) is not considered. We are not looking for the maximum profit per unit but the maximum profit overall. However, the *average total cost* of output does enter into the firm's decision-making. The average revenue from the sale of the product must equal the average total cost or else the firm will consider closing down. The average total cost is an important statistic, but not in terms of determining the maximum profit level of output.

Do Firms Attempt to Maximize Profits?

In order to study the behaviour of business firms in subsequent chapters, we have assumed that the primary objective of each firm is to maximize profits. We assume that, when a firm is making decisions on price and level of output, the objective of profit maximization is of foremost importance. It should be noted that not all economists agree that firms act in a manner that will maximize profits. Some believe that other objectives are more important. One such objective is to achieve a satisfactory level of profit.

The chief criticism of profit maximization as the sole objective of a business firm is that it is too difficult to achieve. In order to pursue this objective, a firm would have to have perfect knowledge about the demand for its product. This is simply not possible. It is also difficult for this objective to be used in guiding such business decisions as marketing strategy, the direction of future research, and the choice of product line. It is argued that these decisions are too complex and cannot be made by taking into consideration only one objective.

Some economists argue that profit maximization is useful as an objective for the less-complex type of decisions. Shall a certain piece of equipment be purchased? How shall production be scheduled? Other economists believe that the objective holds for analysing the long-run behaviour of a firm but not for the short run. They argue that the goal of profit maximization does not give a prescription for making a decision when the future is unknown. The firm's decision will be based on the assessment of future probabilities. In the long run, profit maximization makes more sense as a goal of business behaviour. In the long run, only certain firms in an industry will remain in business. These firms must have been able to earn sufficient profits in order to continue in business.

If there are so many criticisms of the profit maximization objective, why is it still used? There are two reasons. First, the objective can be readily defined. It is an attempt to maximize the difference between total revenue and total costs. This definition provides economists with a basis for analysing firm behaviour. Second, the objective of profit maximization has proved to be a good predictor of firm behaviour.

Questions
1 Can you identify any other possible objectives of a firm besides profit maximization?
2 Can you define what is meant by satisfactory profits?
3 If firms are trying to maximize profits, why do they donate money to various charities?

Summary

In order to better understand business-firm behaviour, it is essential to know something about production costs and profit. Production costs are divided into two categories: explicit and implicit. Explicit costs are payments for resources that the firm must purchase. Implicit costs are payments to resources that the firm already owns. The total costs of a firm in producing a product are the sum of its explicit and implicit costs.

Profit is defined as the difference between total revenue and total costs. When the total revenue exceeds the sum of explicit and implicit production costs, it is referred to as economic profit.

The production schedule can be divided into short-run and long-run time periods. In the short run, at least one resource remains fixed. This is the reason that the law of diminishing returns begins to influence output and production costs. Since each of the variable resources will have less of the fixed resource to work with as production increases, marginal costs begin to rise.

In the long run, all production resources are variable. Costs are influenced by economies and diseconomies of scale. While economies of large-scale production result in a decrease in average costs, the eventual presence of diseconomies of scale cause long-run average costs to increase.

All business firms are required to make decisions. In order to make decisions, an objective must be present. It is assumed that the objective of all firms is to maximize profits, or the difference between total revenue and total costs. In order to do this, it is necessary for a firm to continue to produce as long as the marginal revenue from increased production exceeds the marginal cost. At the level of production where marginal revenue and marginal costs are equal, profit is maximized.

Questions for Review and Discussion

1 It doesn't matter whether you are an accountant or an economist, profits are profits. Discuss.
2 Is it always true that the more workers you have, the more you produce? Discuss.
3 As soon as diminishing returns set in, average costs will begin to increase. Discuss this statement using the curves in figure 11.3.
4 Fred Quiche had always wanted to get into the restaurant business. He had been working as a restaurant supply salesman and believed that he knew the business well enough to start out on his own. Fred was earning $44 000 per year as a salesman and had accumulated $30 000 in savings. Several years ago Fred had the foresight to purchase a building in the downtown area. He believed that this would make an ideal location for his restaurant. Eventually Fred quit his job and started his own restaurant. He took his savings and purchased the restaurant supplies. At the end of one year in operation his cost structure was as follows:

labour (waitresses)	$40 000
food	$10 000
miscellaneous	$ 2 000
depreciation of building	$ 2 000
hydro	$ 1 500
total cost	$55 500

i Are these costs explicit or implicit costs?
ii Would you include any other costs in calculating Fred Quiche's total costs for the year?
iii How much money would Fred have had to make in sales in order to break even? (If you included any additional costs under (ii), estimate them.)

5 Why might two men be able to dig a hole three times as fast as one man? Why might five men need almost as much time as two men to dig the same hole? Assume that all the men are of equal strength and ability.

6 In what respect does the law of diminishing returns apply to the number of people who can receive swimming lessons at a swimming pool at any one time?

7 Would a firm want to continue producing if variable cost exceeded total revenue? Explain.

8 The accountant at Chipchase Candy Company is trying to determine which costs faced by her firm can be altered and which cannot. From the following list that she has prepared, identify which costs are variable and which costs are fixed.

    i purchase of paper wrappers for candy
    ii wages of night watchman
    iii vehicle maintenance costs
    iv printing of company's annual report
    v purchase of sugar
    vi postage
    vii interest on bank loan

9 In the long run, we need not distinguish between fixed and variable costs. Explain why in the long run all costs are variable.

10 To what economic principle are all the following sayings related?
— Too many cooks spoil the stew
— The straw that breaks the camel's back
— Too much of a good thing
Explain this principle.

11 Much has been written about the differences between Japanese and North American firms. Two of these differences are:
    i   Japanese firms tend to borrow money rather than raise money through issuing shares in the company;
    ii   Japanese employees tend to remain employed by the same firm until retirement rather than be subject to layoffs and recalls, as is the case in many North American industries.

How would these differences influence the shape of the ATC, AFC, and AVC curves for both Japanese and North American firms?

12 If a firm is making no economic profit, will it remain in business? Explain.

13 Do accounting statements for a firm reflect opportunity costs? Explain.

14 Differentiate between diminishing returns and diseconomies of scale. In what respect are they similar? In what respect are they different?

15 Identify the following business costs as either fixed or variable:
    i   salaries   iv   raw materials
    ii   property taxes   v   transportation
    iii fire insurance   vi   energy

16 Copy and complete the following table, then graph the marginal product and average number of bushels of eggplant against labour (days).

Labour (days)	Bushels of Eggplant	Marginal Product	Average number of bushels
0	0		
1	3		
2	8		
3	20		
4	29		
5	36		
6	42		
7	46		
8	48		
9	48		
10	45		

17 Copy and complete the following table, then graph the average costs (fixed, variable, and total) and the marginal cost.

Output	Total fixed cost $	Total variable cost $	Total cost $	Average fixed cost $	Average variable cost $	Average total cost $	Marginal cost $
0	20	0					
1	20	10					
2	20	18					
3	20	24					
4	20	28					
5	20	34					
6	20	42					
7	20	52					
8	20	68					
9	20	88					
10	20	118					

Suggested Readings

Heyne, Paul. *Microeconomics*. Chicago: SRA 1988

Libby, Joyce. *Understanding Productivity*. Toronto: Canadian Foundation for Economic Education 1977.

Mansfield, Edwin. *Microeconomics*. Seventh Edition. New York: W.W. Norton 1991.

Peters, Thomas J., and Robert H. Waterman, Jr. *In Search of Excellence: Lessons from America's Best-Run Companies*. New York: Warner Books 1984.

Wright, J. Patrick. *On a Clear Day You Can See General Motors*. New York: Avon Books 1979.

Chapter 12

Perfect Competition: Theory and Practice

Chapter Objectives

After successfully completing this chapter, you will able to:

- describe how the price is determined for a firm in perfect competition
- graphically show the profit-maximizing point for a perfectly competitive firm
- describe the long-run profit position of a perfectly competitive firm
- relate the trends in Canadian agriculture
- describe the short-run and long-run problems of Canadian agriculture
- describe and graph the cobweb theorem
- describe and graph the attempts at price supports in agriculture
- relate the objectives of marketing boards and the possible methods of achieving these objectives

Key Terms

marginal revenue curve
break-even situation
shut-down point
cobweb theorem

crop restriction
offer-to-purchase
deficiency payment
marketing board

Characteristics of Perfect Competition

Profit Maximization

One of the competitive models introduced in Chapter 10 was perfect competition, which describes a competitive situation in which many sellers each produce an identical product. As a result of this, no individual seller has any control over the price of the product. The price is determined by demand and supply in the marketplace and, consequently, each seller in the industry is faced with deciding how much to produce. This chapter discusses how an individual seller, or firm, goes about making this decision.

The objective of each firm in an industry is to maximize profits. In order to determine how a firm goes about reaching this objective, it is necessary to have some information on the firm's revenue and costs. Since the price of the product is determined in the marketplace, we will begin by reviewing the demand and supply curves for a perfectly competitive industry. These are shown in figure 12.1a. The curves intersect at an equilibrium price of P_1.

Figure 12.1a Industry demand and supply curves

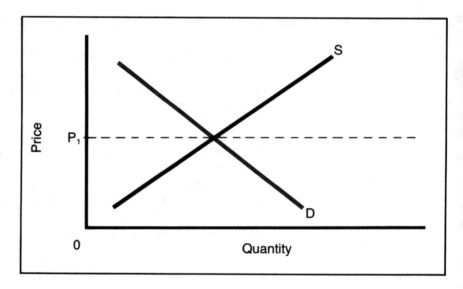

The industry establishes a price P^1 for the product.

The demand curve for each individual firm is shown in figure 12.1b. This demand curve is perfectly elastic, since there is virtually an endless demand for this firm's products at a price P_1. The firm can put as much of this product on the market as it wants without affecting the price. It will not be able to sell this product at a price above P_1, and there is obviously no reason to sell the product at a price below P_1. Because the price is determined in the marketplace, any change

**Figure 12.1b
Firm's demand
curve**

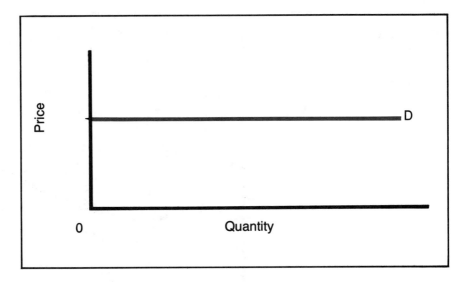

The firm's demand curve is horizontal at price P_1 because the firm
has no control over the price of the product.

in the market price will mean a new demand curve for the firm. The
demand curve represents the revenue side of the profit picture for the firm.

In order to maximize profits, it is necessary to maximize the difference between total revenue and total costs (see Chapter 11). Profits
will continue to increase as long as the extra revenue from increased production exceeds the extra costs. In other words, the
firm will continue to produce as long as marginal revenue exceeds
marginal costs.

The short-run cost side of the picture will be similar to that described in Chapter 11. Over a certain range of output, average costs
will decline because of increased efficiency. Eventually, average costs
will increase as diminishing returns begin to influence the costs. This
situation is shown in figure 12.2. Also included in this figure is the demand curve for the firm.

*A curve relating extra
revenue to the quantity of
output is called a
marginal revenue curve.*

The demand curve in figure 12.2 can be shown to be the
marginal revenue curve for the firm. Since the marginal revenue
refers to the addition of selling one more unit to total revenue, it is
the same as the price of the product. Remember that the price is
determined in the marketplace, and does not change regardless of
how much of its product the firm supplies to the market. With the
price already determined, the firm has only to decide how much to
produce. Profits will be maximized by producing at a level of output where the marginal revenue is equal to the marginal cost (or
where the price is equal to the marginal cost, since price and marginal revenue are identical). The intersection of these two curves in
the diagram occurs at a level of output, **q_1.**

**Figure 12.2
Revenue and
cost curves for a
perfectly
competitive firm**

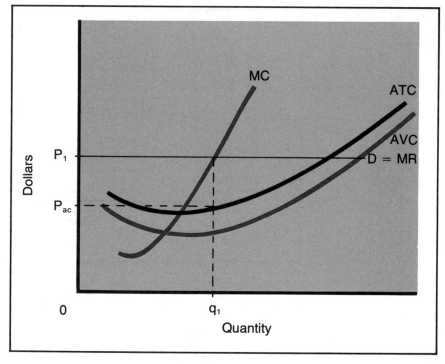

In order to maximize profits, the firm will produce a level of output
(q_1) where marginal cost (MC) is equal to the price (P_1). The firm
in this diagram is making an economic profit since the price (P_1) is
greater than the average cost (P_{ac}) at this level of output.

Is the firm making a profit under the conditions described in figure
12.2? For each unit that the firm produces, it receives a price P_1.
The average cost of producing each of the q_1 units of output is P_{ac},
which is less than P_1. Therefore, the firm is making a profit. This
firm is making an economic profit because economic profit = total
revenue – total costs. The economic profit made on each unit produced is $P_1 – P_{ac}$. The total economic profit as a result of producing
q_1 units is $(P_1 – P_{ac})\, q_1$.

Will this firm continue to make economic profits? The answer
is no. Since it is easy for new firms to get into the industry, the
presence of economic profits will attract new firms. When new
firms enter the industry, the supply of this product on the market
will increase and the price will fall. This situation is shown in figure
12.3a. A shift in the supply curve from S^1 to S^2 has forced a reduction in the price of the product from P_1 to P_2. Our firm now faces a
new demand curve (figure 12.3b), which is perfectly horizontal
at price P_2. It will produce where marginal cost (MC) equals
marginal revenue (MR_2) in order to maximize its profits, yet its
profits have been reduced. Production will fall to a level q_2.

**Figure 12.3 a
Shift in industry
supply curve**

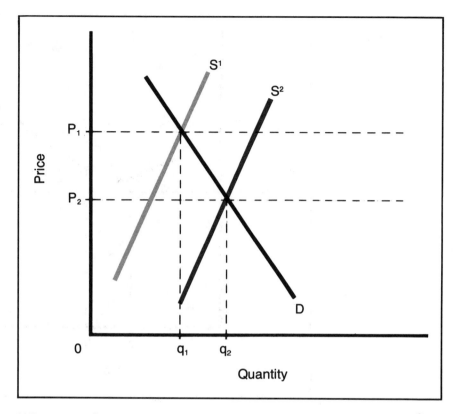

When new firms enter the industry the supply curve shifts to S^2.
This lowers the price of the product to P_2.

*The break-even point is
the level of production for
a firm at which the total
revenue from selling the
product is equal to the
total cost of producing
that quantity of output.*

In fact, new firms may continue to enter this industry until the
price falls so low that all economic profits disappear. This situation is
shown in figure 12.4. If the price had fallen to P_3 the firm would produce a level of output as shown by q_3. At this level of output, P_3 is
just equal to the average costs of production. This is a **break-
even situation,** in which the firm is covering explicit and implicit
costs, but is not earning any economic profits.

break-even point: price = minimum average cost

Will the firm remain in business if the price falls below P_3?
Yes, as long as the price remains above *average variable cost*
(**AVC**). Even at a price between P_3 and P_1, (see figure 12.4), the
firm will continue to produce at a loss because it will cost the firm
more money to shut down. If the firm shuts down, it will have to
pay fixed costs anyway, since fixed costs do not disappear when it
shuts down. Fixed costs remain in the short run even if production
is not taking place.

**Figure 12.3b
New demand
curve**

At the new price P_2, the firm's demand curve becomes D_2. The
level of output that will maximize profits is q_2.

*The shut-down point is
the level of production at
which the average
variable cost of each
unit of output is equal to
the price of the product.*

If the price is greater than the minimum average variable
costs, the firm would be better off to remain in business. It will be
able to cover variable costs and will have some money left over to
put toward fixed costs. If the price falls to minimum AVC, as shown
by **P_4,** the firm may as well shut down, since it is not paying off any
fixed costs anyway. When this happens, the firm is said to have
reached the **shut-down point.**

shut-down point: price = minimum average variable cost

Since a firm in perfect competition that is trying to maximize
profits will always produce where P = MC, the marginal cost curve becomes the supply curve for the firm. In order to determine how much
the firm would produce at any price, simply refer to the MC curve.
Not all of the MC curve, however, would be considered to be the
supply curve. Since the firm will not produce any amount when
the price falls below average variable cost, only the MC above the
AVC curve represents the supply curve for the firm.

**Figure 12.4
Break-even and
shut-down points**

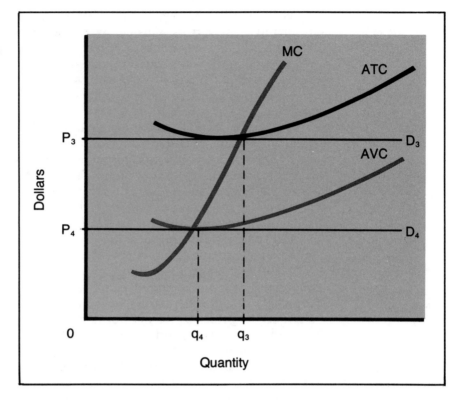

If the price of the product fell to P_3, the new demand curve would
be D_3 and q_3 units of output would be produced. At this level of
output the firm would break even. If the price fell to P_4, an amount
q_4 would be produced. This is known as the shut-down point,
since the price is equal to the average variable cost.

What happens to the profit picture of the firm in the long
run? As noted earlier, if economic profits are being made by firms
in the industry, new firms are likely to enter. With more firms in the
industry, the supply of the product will increase. This will cause the
price of the product to fall. As the price falls, the amount of economic
profits made by firms will begin to decrease, and some firms may
even be operating at a loss. If some firms in the industry continue
to lose money, they will consequently shut down in the long run.
Their exit from the industry will cause the industry supply to decrease
and the price to increase. A higher price will, however, enable
some firms who were losing money to then break even. In fact, in
the long run, there is a tendency for firms in this industry to just
break even. Since there are no barriers to the entry of new firms, existing firms cannot continue to earn economic profits in the long run.

A numerical example may help explain the profit-maximizing

position of a firm in perfect competition. Assume that you own a farm and grow carrots. This year you grew 8000 pounds of carrots that sold for ten cents per pound in the marketplace. The average cost of production for you was eight cents per pound. You made an economic profit of two cents per pound.

You believe that the price of carrots will remain at ten cents per pound next year. Should you increase your carrot production? This decision depends on the marginal cost of producing more carrots. If the marginal cost at your current level of production is eight cents per pound, you should grow more carrots. As long as the price is greater than the extra cost of growing more carrots, you should grow more carrots—and continue to grow them until the marginal cost reaches ten cents per pound. At this level of production, you are maximizing profits. Any increase in production beyond this level would reduce profits because the extra cost of growing more carrots would rise above ten cents—the market price.

What if the price does not remain at ten cents per pound? If economic profits are being made from carrot growing, new suppliers are likely to enter the market. This increase in supply will reduce the market price. If the market price falls below ten cents per pound, your carrot production should still be determined by producing at a level where MC = P. If the price falls to eight cents per pound, you should produce 8000 pounds of carrots. At this level of output, the price is equal to marginal cost and is also equal to your average cost. Here you are just breaking even and earning no economic profit. If the price drops below eight cents per pound, you must decide whether or not to continue growing carrots. Your decision will be based on your average variable costs. If the price is still above AVC, then you may continue in the business for the short run, anyway. If the price drops below your AVC, you would be wiser to stop producing carrots.

12.1 Why does the firm maximize profits by producing a level of output where the price equals the marginal cost?

12.2 Is it possible for a firm in perfect competition to earn economic profits in the long run?

Resource Allocation

Is perfect competition an ideal type of competitive structure for Canadian industry? This is a difficult question to answer. In an industry characterized by a large number of firms, no one firm is likely to be large enough to take advantage of economies of scale, and firms may not be taking advantage of low-cost production techniques. Firms in such an industry are not likely to channel money into product research and development. Also, consumers may not be content with identical, or homogeneous, products and may prefer some variety.

Conversely, there are certain advantages of perfect competition from society's point of view. Perfectly-competitive firms tend to be efficient in their use of Canadian resources and will continue to produce a product until the marginal cost is just equal to the price. The marginal cost represents the value of our resources that are being used up in order to produce the product. It includes the labour, land, and capital, which, if not used to make this product, could be used for making something else. By allocating resources for the manufacture of this product, Canadian society acquires the opportunity cost of not being able to use the resources for other products.

What significance is there in the fact that a perfectly competitive firm keeps expanding output as long as the marginal cost is less than the price? In order to answer this, we have to examine what the price of the product represents. Since the price of a product represents how much people are willing to pay for it, the price represents the *value* that consumers get from the product. It can also be seen as representing the benefit of the product to Canadians. The advantage of perfect competition is that each firm expands output to the point at which the benefit that consumers are getting from the product (P) is just equal to the cost of producing it (MC). The individual firm is not attempting to equalize benefits and costs from society's viewpoint. The firm is interested in maximizing profits in a manner seen as beneficial to society.

Why will the firm not produce beyond the level of output that equates marginal cost and price? Because if it does, it loses profits. Also, if the marginal cost is greater than the price, the cost of making the additional output (MC) is greater than the value of the output (P). This is not an ideal situation for either the firm or for society. As well, if the firm were to restrict output to a level at which the price exceeded the marginal cost, the firm's profits would be less than they could be. The firm benefits by expanding output. Canadians would also want to receive more output of this product because the benefit (P) is greater than the cost of producing it (MC).

A firm in perfect competition allocates resources efficiently by producing a level of output where P = MC. This is exactly the way society would like to see resources used. However, the firm is not producing this level of output in order to please the rest of society but in order to maximize profits. Thus, perfect competition is seen as an ideal way to allocate resources because firms will produce at a level where the benefits from the additional output are equal to the cost of making the product. The P = MC rule does not consider negative third-party effects, however. The costs associated with negative third-party effects are not included in the marginal costs calculated by the firm. Since possible third-party costs are not included, a firm in perfect competition may produce at a higher level of output than is considered socially optimum.

12.3 Why is perfect competition seen as an ideal way to allocate scarce resources? Despite this benefit, why would it not be desirable if all industries were perfectly competitive? (Hint: Think of the characteristics of perfect competition.)

An Example of Perfect Competition: Canadian Agriculture

Trends in Canadian Agriculture

At the turn of the century, the major industry in Canada was farming. In fact, government immigration policy encouraged newcomers to Canada to begin farming the available land, particularly in western Canada. At this time, farms were primarily small, self-sufficient enterprises. Farmers raised a variety of crops and livestock, mainly for their own consumption.

The number of farms in Canada has been steadily decreasing. In 1941, the peak year for farms, there were 733 000 farms in Canada; by 1986 this figure had decreased to 293 089 farms (see table 12.1). The number of Canadians employed in agriculture has also declined. One hundred years ago, 60 percent of all families were farm families, whereas today only three to four percent of all families are farm families. Small, self-sufficient farms are giving way to larger, more specialized, and more capitalized farms. Yet in spite of the reduction in farms and farm workers, agricultural production is increasing. Farm production in 1981 was 175 percent higher than it was in 1941.

Table 12.1 / Total number of farms by province, Canada, 1951, 1971, 1986

Province	Number of farms		
	1951	1971	1986
Newfoundland	3 626	1 042	651
Prince Edward Island	10 137	4 543	2 833
Nova Scotia	23 515	6 008	4 283
New Brunswick	26 431	5 485	3 554
Quebec	134 366	61 257	41 448
Ontario	149 920	94 722	72 713
Manitoba	52 383	34 981	27 336
Saskatchewan	112 018	76 970	63 431
Alberta	84 315	62 702	57 777
British Columbia	26 406	18 400	19 063
Canada	623 087	366 110	293 089

Source: *Farming facts 1986* (Ottawa: Statistics Canada), p.2. Figures for 1951 and 1971 are from the *Census of Agriculture*, Agriculture Census Canada 1986 publication no. 96-102 (Ottawa: Statistics Canada, December 1987) pp. 1-1,1-2.

What has accounted for these trends? Farms have been increasing in size mainly because farming is becoming more mechanized. The introduction of the tractor and other farm machinery has enabled the farmer to handle larger tracts of land. In order to make the new equipment more economical and efficient, larger farms are required. Farms are also becoming more specialized in order to spread the increased costs of farm operation over a larger volume of output.

Along with changes in farm size have come changes in farm incomes. The net income of farm operators has generally been declining as a percentage of the total income earned in Canada each year. Agricultural output has represented a smaller proportion of GDP in recent years. Incomes received by farm operators also fluctuate a great deal from year to year. The following sections in the text analyse the reasons for declining and unstable farm incomes.

Reasons for Low Farm Incomes

Declining farm incomes are a result of the various markets for agricultural products. In these markets, the ability of farmers to supply food has increased faster than increases in the demand for food. Figure 12.5 shows that when the supply increases more than the demand for a product, the price falls. The shift of the supply curve to S^1 and of the demand curve to D^1 has lowered the price of the product to P_1. When the prices of agricultural products decline, farm incomes decline as well. In actual fact, prices of agricultural products have not been declining but have been increasing less rapidly than other prices.

Figure 12.5 Shifts in demand and supply in agriculture

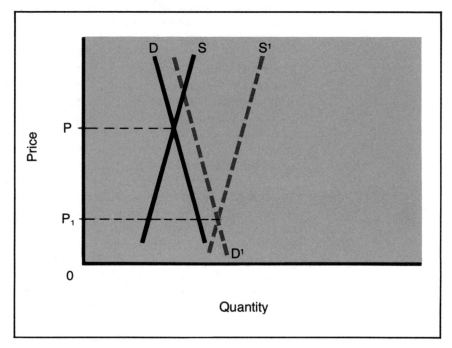

When supply (S^1) increases more than demand (D^1), the price falls.

12.4 What has accounted for the trend toward larger farms?

12.5 Why have farm incomes been declining in relation to non-farm incomes?

Instability of Agricultural Prices

Not only have relative farm prices and incomes been declining, they have also been very unstable. This instability, which can also be traced to market forces, is a result of two factors: 1) the inelastic demand and supply in agricultural markets; and 2) fluctuations in the supply of agricultural commodities.

The inelasticity of the demand and supply for food causes farm prices to be unstable. Since food is a necessity, the demand for farm products is relatively inelastic. Price changes do not drastically influence the quantity of food purchased. On the supply side of the market, the curve is relatively inelastic as well, because once a farmer has planted his crop, there is very little he can do about the volume of output until next year. Also, in farming, fixed costs are a high percentage of total costs. Since a large portion of total costs are composed of fixed costs, farmers would save very little by cutting back on output when prices drop. Therefore, within a short period of time, the supply of agricultural output is inelastic, because it does not respond significantly to price changes.

How does the inelasticity of demand and supply affect prices? Reference to figure 12.6 shows the effect of inelastic demand and supply curves on market prices. In the figure, two demand curves are drawn intersecting the supply curve S^1 at the same point. This provides an equilibrium market price of P. The demand curve D^1 is relatively inelastic, while the demand curve D^2 is relatively elastic. Assume that the supply increases to S^2. Under the conditions of an inelastic demand D^1, the price falls to P_1. Under the conditions of an elastic demand D^2, the price falls to P_2. Given any shift in the supply curve, an inelastic demand will result in a greater change in price than will an elastic demand curve. Since the demand for agricultural products is relatively inelastic, any change in the supply causes food prices to fluctuate greatly. If farm prices fluctuate a great deal, then farm incomes will fluctuate as well.

The curves in figure 12.6 point out another interesting aspect of farm prices. A good crop can depress farm prices and farm incomes, while a poor crop may increase farm income. A large crop will shift the supply curve to the right, causing a drop in price. Under conditions of an inelastic demand, any drop in price results in less total revenue or less money being spent on the product (see Chapter 2). A poor crop will cause the supply curve to shift to the left, causing a higher price. Any increase in price because of a bad crop raises total revenue as well as farm incomes, because of the inelastic nature of the demand curve.

**Figure 12.6
Comparison of
price changes
with elastic and
inelastic demand
curves**

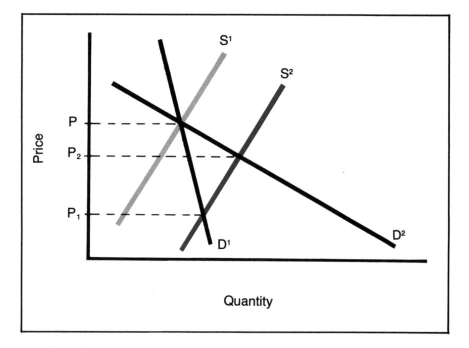

With any shift in the supply curve, the price changes more with an
inelastic demand curve (D^1) than with an elastic demand curve (D^2).

12.6   Does an inelastic demand curve cause farm prices to fluctuate more in
response to supply changes than if the demand was elastic? Explain.

12.7   What would be the effect on farm product prices if one farmer were
to withhold his crop from the market? If all farmers were to withhold
their crops from the market?

The Cobweb Theorem

*The cobweb theorem, an
explanation of price
fluctuations in agri-
culture, assumes that
farmers determine the
size of next year's crop
on the basis of this year's
price.*

In addition to market inelasticities, price fluctuations in agriculture are
due to fluctuations in the supply of agricultural products on the market. Some of these fluctuations are due to changes in weather conditions; however, the main cause of supply variation lies with the
farmers themselves. A possible explanation of farmer reaction to
changing farm prices is provided by the **cobweb theorem.** This
theorem, which has been used to explain changes in hog prices, assumes that farmers determine the size of next year's crop, or number
of livestock, on the basis of this year's price. If prices are high this year,
farmers will plan to increase their output next year. On the other hand,
if prices are low this year, next year's output will be reduced.

An example of the cobweb theorem is presented in figure 12.7. In the diagram, **S** represents the short-run supply curve for the product. The other supply curves **S¹, S², S³,** and **S⁴,** represent the supply curves of the product on the market in years 1, 2, 3, and 4. The amount of crop supplied next year is determined by relating this year's price to the short-run supply curve. When next year's crop is harvested, it becomes the basis for the supply curve for that year. The yearly supply curves determine the price for each year, depending on where they intersect the demand curve. In the diagram, it is assumed that the elasticities of demand (**D**) and supply (**S**) are equal.

Figure 12.7 The cobweb theorem

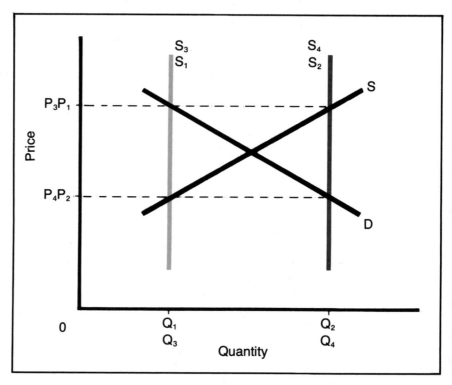

S represents the short-run supply curve for the industry. S¹, S², S³, and S⁴ represent the yearly supply curves. The intersection of the yearly supply curves and the demand curve (D) establishes the price.

Assume that the quantity of this product put on the market in the first year is equal to **Q₁**. With this supply curve (**S¹**), the price of the product in year 1 will be **P₁**. If the price **P₁** prevailed in the market in year 1, then farmers will want to supply **Q₂** to the market in the second year. This result is determined by relating **P₁** to the short-run supply curve. This increase in supply (**S²**) will depress the market price to P_2 in year 2. The lower price in year 2 will convince some farmers to get out of this crop and supply will drop to Q_3 in year 3. This change shifts the supply curve to S^3 and a higher price (P_3). In subsequent years, the trend continues.

The cobweb theorem explains why farm prices fluctuate. It also explains why prices may never reach an equilibrium level. If the demand and supply elasticities for the product are identical, the price will continue to fluctuate around the equilibrium point.

12.8 What is the cobweb theorem trying to explain?

12.9 In order for the cobweb theorem to be an accurate description of agricultural prices, what assumption has to be made?

The Pesticide Dilemma

One of the technological advances that has increased the supply of agricultural products in recent years is the development of pesticides. Of these chemicals, which have the effect of protecting farm crops from insects, the most famous is DDT. Early successes with this chemical pesticide in controlling the spread of diseases (such as malaria) led to more widespread use. Since DDT could increase crop yields, farmers saw it as an unqualified benefit.

In the 1940s, however, some negative aspects of DDT began to emerge. The pesticide was no longer effective against all insects. For example, houseflies began to build up an immunity to DDT. In fact, it is estimated that today more than 400 species of insects and mites are resistant to agricultural pesticides—and the number is growing.

Individuals have become concerned about the effects of DDT on their general environment. Pesticides were responsible for the death of many fish and birds; the chemicals also began concentrating in human fat and mothers' milk. Certain illnesses among farm workers have been linked to extended pesticide exposure. Nineteen studies have found higher rates of blood cancers among farmers; nine have shown increased stomach cancer rates; and six have found a higher incidence of malignant brain tumours.

Agricultural experts are also concerned about the side effects of herbicides. Studies in 1981 and 1983 found that alachlor, a herbicide used on corn and soybean crops, has been linked to cancer. More than one million kilograms of this herbicide were used on Ontario farms alone in 1983. The use of alachlor exposes not only farmers but also consumers to the risk of cancer because alachlor residues are found on food. People living in corn-growing regions face the risk of having their drinking water contaminated with this herbicide. Unfortunately, herbicidal alternatives to alachlor are not themselves entirely free of health risks.

Questions

1 Using demand and supply curves, show the impact on the market for corn as new pesticides are developed. Taking your analysis one step further, discuss the long-run implications of insects becoming more resistant to pesticides.

2 Do consumers benefit from scientific advancement in the area of pesticides and herbicides?

3 How can we, as consumers, be protected from increased levels of pesticides being found in the food that we consume? What about imported foods?

4 What impact would there be on agricultural prices if stricter regulations were imposed on pesticide use?

5 An alternative to the use of chemicals in agriculture is organic farming. What impact might a switch to organic farming methods have on the cost curves of a firm?

Price Supports

From the preceding discussion, it can be determined that the problem of agricultural incomes is twofold: 1) they are generally lower than non-farm incomes; and 2) they fluctuate more than non-farm incomes. In order to overcome these difficulties, a number of government-assisted programs have been introduced.

Crop Restriction

A crop restriction is a government quota designed to reduce the quantity of an agricultural product on the market.

One possible solution to low and fluctuating incomes is to limit the amount of a product that a farmer can produce. This means imposing a quota, or **crop restriction,** on each farmer's output. The effect of this restriction is shown in figure 12.8. As shown in the graph, a shift in the supply curve from S^1 to S^2 raises the price of the product from P_1 to P_2. If the demand for the product is inelastic, then an increase in price will result in an increase in the total revenue that farmers receive.

It should also be noted that any quota system will also prevent wide fluctuations in supply and will limit price-and-income fluctuations as well. A quota system has been introduced in Canada for many agricultural products, including tobacco, milk, and eggs. As a result, consumers are forced to pay a higher price for less output than before the quota was introduced.

Offer-to-Purchase

In the offer-to-purchase program of agricultural price support, the government establishes a price floor and then offers to buy any surplus product not sold in the marketplace.

The **offer-to-purchase** type of program establishes a minimum price for which the product can be sold. The minimum price results in a *surplus,* which government offers to purchase from farmers at the minimum price. In figure 12.9, the minimum price is designated by P_m. At this price, consumers are only willing to purchase Q_d while suppliers are willing to supply Q_s. The surplus (Q_s-Q_d) is

**Figure 12.8
A crop-restriction
program**

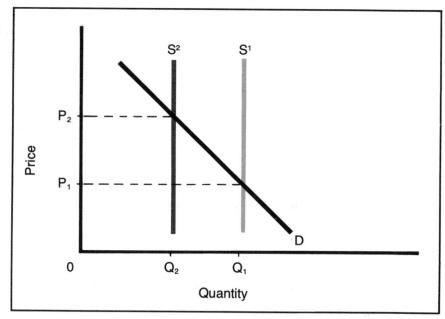

A restriction of the supply from S^1 to S^2 raises the price from P_1 to P_2.

**Figure 12.9
The offer-to-
purchase program**

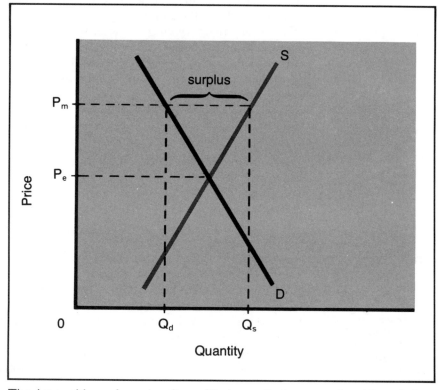

The imposition of a price floor (P_m) results in a surplus (Q_s - Q_d).

purchased by government. The problem then becomes one of disposing of the surplus, or storing it. The size of the surplus will partially depend on the elasticity of demand for the product. The more inelastic the demand, the smaller the surplus. If the demand is inelastic, increases in the price are not going to reduce quantity demanded to a significant degree.

Who pays for the offer-to-purchase price support program? Consumers pay increased prices for farm products compared to the free market price. Taxpayers pay for buying up the surplus and possibly for storing it.

Deficiency Payment

The deficiency-payment system is an agricultural price support program whereby the government pays the farmer the difference between the average market price for a product and the support price.

The deficiency-payment price support system solves the problem of a surplus. Under this system, no minimum price is set. Instead, the government guarantees to pay farmers the difference between the average market price and a specified support price. All farmers receive the same **deficiency payment** per unit regardless of the market price received for their product. This scheme is depicted in figure 12.10. In the graph, P_s is the support price and Q_1 the amount that farmers are willing to produce at this price. However, in order to sell Q_1 on the market, a price of P_m is established. The deficiency payment is then $(P_s - P_m) Q_1$.

Apart from solving the problem of storing and disposing of a surplus, the deficiency-payment price support ensures a lower price for the consumer. One possible disadvantage is that this type of price support could be more expensive than the offer-to-purchase system. If the demand for the product is highly inelastic, it is possible that the cost to government from the deficiency payments program would be higher than under the offer-to-purchase program.

12.10 Why, under an offer-to-purchase system, may quotas on farm production be necessary?

12.11 How does the deficiency-payment scheme differ from the offer-to-purchase scheme?

Marketing Boards

A marketing board is a compulsory marketing organization for primary or processed agricultural products.

Because individual farm operators have no control over agricultural prices, they have been encouraged to co-operate with one another to influence market conditions. Through joint action, farmers have tried to influence the supply of the product on the market, its distribution, the demand for the product, and ultimately its price. One attempt at joint action has been the creation of **marketing boards.**[1] A marketing board is a compulsory marketing organization for primary or processed agricultural products. The compulsory nature

[1] Hiscocks and Bennett, "Marketing Boards and Pricing in Canada," pp. 271-8.

**Figure 12.10
The deficiency-
payment scheme**

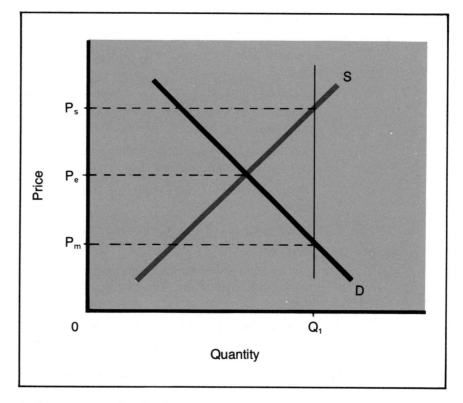

At the support price P_s, farmers decide to produce an amount Q_1.
This brings about a price P_m in the marketplace. Government will pay
to the farmer the difference between P_s and P_m for Q_1 units of output.

of the board means that a specified commodity is subject to the
rules and regulations of the marketing board. The authority that
marketing boards possess over the supply and marketing of a specific agricultural commodity can come from either the federal or the
provincial government.

Marketing boards have been established in Canada since 1929.
At present, there are more than 100 producer-marketing boards in
Canada. The primary purposes of these boards are 1) to maintain or
increase incomes of the producers of a particular product; 2) to stabilize income from the sale of the product; and 3) to standardize the
terms of sale of the product.

Not all marketing boards have exactly the same objectives and
methods of operation. A number of powers and procedures are available to them:

Pooling: all of the proceeds from sales of the product are pooled so
that each producer receives the same average price after adjustments
for such items as grade.

Price setting: a board may have the authority to set wholesale, consumer, or producer prices.

Quotas: marketing and/or producer quotas can be set for each producer.

Licensing: licences may be required of growers, producers, processors, dealers, or any other person involved in any way with the marketing process.

Seizure and disposal: any product marketed contrary to board orders may be seized and disposed of.

Trade regulation: both export and interprovincial trade may be regulated.

Purchase and sell: the product may be purchased by the board and sold through the board.

Market information and development: producers can be supplied with market information, leading to a development of domestic and foreign markets.

Each marketing board operates under a different mandate, with somewhat different goals and methods of operation.

12.12   What are the objectives of marketing boards in Canada?

The Canadian Egg Marketing Agency

The development of provincial marketing boards enabled farm organizations to better control the volume of production. Provincial control over agricultural output, however, is not sufficient control in light of interprovincial trade. As egg producers in each province began to develop control over the supply of eggs, they began to recognize the need for a national egg-marketing plan. The passage of the National Farm Products Marketing Agencies Act in 1971 permitted national marketing agencies in eggs and poultry. The Canadian Egg Marketing Agency (CEMA) became fully operational in June 1973.

Provincial egg-marketing boards divide up their provincial share of the national market by allocating quotas to individual producers. The CEMA determines the market share for each province. Quotas were originally based on the number of eggs but are now based on the number of hens that each producer is allowed to have. With a restriction on hens, but not eggs, there is some incentive for farmers to try and produce more eggs from the same number of hens. The main exemption from the quota system is for small egg-producing operations (defined as having less than 100 to 500 hens, depending on the province). The federal government has also imposed a quota on the importation of eggs and egg products in compliance with the General Agreement on Tariffs and Trade (GATT).

The Canadian Egg Marketing Agency also administers a central-pricing scheme based on the cost of producing eggs. The CEMA's pricing formula is based on a national survey of egg farmers. The survey collects information on the costs involved in producing eggs and determines the weight that each cost factor should have in the pricing formula. The costs taken into consideration are the cost of pullets (laying hens); the cost of feed and the cost to transport it; labour costs; overhead; depreciation; and producer return. On the basis of these production costs, egg prices are established on a monthly basis. Prices are also adjusted to reflect seasonal variation in demand.

The CEMA also tries to find markets for excess table eggs, either in the processing industry or in export markets. The agency stimulates egg consumption through advertising and promotion. It has developed advertising slogans such as "Get Cracking" and "Have Eggs Instead." Finally, the CEMA attempts to improve egg quality and productivity in the egg industry.

Questions

1 Why was it necessary to establish a national egg-marketing agency in addition to provincial egg-marketing boards?
2 Using demand and supply curves in your answer, show the impact of the following:
   i CEMA setting a minimum price for eggs
   ii CEMA imposing a quota on egg production in Canada
   iii the federal government limiting the importation of eggs into Canada.
3 Why would the CEMA find it necessary to advertise in order to increase egg consumption?

A Defence of Supply Management

Canada's system of restricting the output of some agricultural products has received some criticism in recent years as the world discusses freer trade in agriculture. It is argued that this system of supply management restricts competition and increases prices to the consumer. The Consumers' Association of Canada has asked that marketing boards be replaced by a market-driven system that would charge consumers the world price for poultry, eggs, and milk. How do the proponents of supply management defend the restrictions placed on eggs, chicken, milk, and other products?

The defence begins by asserting that supply management sets only the "farmgate" price; the price received by the farmer.

This price is based on a formula which reflects the costs of production. The retail prices are set by the grocery stores. In many cases, there is little competition at the retail level. Prices to the consumer are determined not by supply conditions alone but by the interaction of demand and supply. The quantity of product that is produced is determined not by farmers themselves but by a committee with representatives from processors, consumers, restaurants, and government as well as farmers. The price to the consumer also depends on processing costs. Agricultural representatives have argued that processors should increase their productivity levels and help to keep costs down instead of focussing on supply management as the source of their difficulties. Supply management also results in less price fluctuation in the market.

What would happen to our rural communities without supply management? If supply management keeps Canadian farmers in business, people are kept on the land and rural communities can prosper. Proponents of supply management point to the United States, where large corporations control the production and processing of chicken. They argue that the same scenario will occur in Canada. Without supply management, there is a fear that cheaper foreign products would take over the market. Do Canadians want to depend on foreign sources for food? Supply management prevents the spread of corporate farming, ensures the survival of independent farmers with a committment to the environment, and provides Canadians with healthy food. Even under the supply management system, farmers leave the industry. There is no guarantee that all farmers will be financially well-off within the supply-management system.

If agriculture were to compete on an international basis, foreign exchange rates would play a role in the success of the Canadian industry. Do we want the success of an industry as important as agriculture to be subject to the fluctuations in foreign exchange rates?

Finally, commodity producers under supply management do not receive government stabilization payments as do farmers in other sectors of agriculture.

Questions
1   Do you agree with the arguments put forward by the proponents of supply management? Explain.
2   Why are consumers generally opposed to supply management?

Summary

Perfect competition is a competitive situation in which many firms are producing and selling an identical product. The price of the product is determined by the marketplace; no individual firm has any control over the price. The demand curve for each firm is perfectly horizontal at the market price. Because the price is determined by the market, each firm must decide how much of the product to produce. A firm maximizes profit by producing at a level of output at which the price is equal to the marginal cost.

There is no guarantee that a firm will earn economic profits, or even remain in an industry. If the price of its product falls below the average variable cost, the firm may shut down. If the price is equal to the average total cost, the firm is breaking even. If the price is greater than the average total cost, an economic profit is being made. When economic profits are being made, new firms are attracted into the industry and the market price falls. The decline in price leads to a decline in economic profit. In the long run, firms in perfect competition tend to break even.

The industry most resembling the perfect competition model in Canada is agriculture. Farm prices have been increasing less rapidly than non-farm prices because advances in agricultural technology have allowed the supply of farm products to increase faster than the demand for them. Farm prices also tend to fluctuate a great deal because of the inelastic demand and supply conditions in agricultural markets and of fluctuations in the supply of farm products. In order to assist farmers, governments have introduced a variety of crop restriction, offer-to-purchase, and deficiency-payment programs. Marketing boards have also been established in order to raise and stabilize farm incomes.

Questions for Review and Discussion

1 Do you think that most of the costs facing a farmer are fixed or variable? List various costs of production in agriculture, and state whether they are fixed or variable.

2 Much of the increase in the supply of agricultural products has been attributed to improvements in technology. Does the farmer develop these improvements? Where is most of the research and development related to agriculture undertaken?

3 How can you account for the fact that in Canada the supply of food is increasing faster than the demand, while in many other parts of the world, a shortage of food is the major problem?

4 Should the government undertake programs to encourage people to stay on the farm?

5 Is it fair to offer income and price programs to farmers and not to other business firms?

6   It is likely that price-support programs assist the operators of small farms more than the operators of large farms. Discuss this statement.

7   Using your knowledge of demand and supply curves, discuss the different impacts of the price-support programs considered in this chapter, depending on whether the demand for the product is elastic or inelastic.

8   If the supply of farm products were to decrease, prices would increase. The supply would decrease if a number of farmers decided to leave the industry. Why would some farmers be reluctant to give up farming in spite of low incomes?

9   How would the cobweb theorem apply to livestock? Would prices fluctuate from year to year or could the cycle be extended over a couple of years?

10   Economist: "What crop have you planted this year?"
Farmer: "Barley."
Economist: "Why? Was the price of barley high last year?"
Farmer: "No. The price of corn was low."
Explain this conversation, relying on your knowledge of the cobweb theorem.

11   In this chapter, we described a cobweb-theorem situation in which the elasticities of demand and supply were the same. The theorem also applies to situations in which the elasticities of demand and supply are not the same. Draw cobweb-theorem graphs for the following situations:
  i   the elasticity of demand is greater than the elasticity of supply;
  ii   the elasticity of supply is greater than the elasticity of demand.

12   Why do marketing boards find it necessary to promote the demand for the product as well as to regulate the supply? Use demand and supply curves in your answer.

13   Why do marketing boards require that all producers adhere to the regulations of the board?

14   The presence of economic profits in an industry will attract new suppliers into the industry. With new suppliers entering the market, what will happen to the demand for the resources required to make this product? What might happen to the price of these resources? What might happen to the cost curves in this industry as a result of the expansion of the industry?

15   In professional sports, the fixed cost associated with operating a franchise represents a large percentage of total costs. Does this fact help explain why many sports teams may continue to operate even though they are claiming to lose money?

16   Why is the government more concerned about providing income support for farmers than for other groups, such as service-station owners?

17 It has been stated that Japanese firms have higher fixed costs than North American firms. Does this help explain why Japanese firms may produce large quantities of output? Does it help explain why their prices may be lower than for comparable North American firms?

18 The imposition of quotas in milk farming has had an impact on the cheese industry in Canada. Cheese producers who were unable to acquire sufficient milk have been forced to shut down. Using demand and supply curves, show the impact of milk quotas on the milk and cheese markets.

19 Assume that the federal government gives a 20 cent per kilogram subsidy to Canadian grape growers. Show the impact of this subsidy on the marginal cost, average variable cost, and average total cost curves for an individual grape grower. Would the impact on the curves be different if the subsidy were given in a lump sum as opposed to a per-kilogram subsidy? Explain.

Suggested Readings

Borcherding, Thomas, with Gary W. Dorosh. *The Egg Marketing Board: A Case Study of Monopoly and Its Social Costs.* Vancouver: Fraser Institute 1981.

Bryan, Ingrid A. *Economic Policies in Canada.* 2nd ed. Toronto: Butterworths 1986.

Grubel, Herbert G., and Richard W. Schwindt. *The Real Cost of the B.C. Milk Board: A Case Study in Canadian Agricultural Policy.* Vancouver: Fraser Institute 1977.

Harlow, Arthur A. "The Hog Cycle and the Cobweb Theorem." In D.S. Watson, ed. *Price Theory in Action.* 3rd ed. Boston: Houghton-Mifflin 1973.

Hiscocks, G.A., and T.A. Bennett. "Marketing Boards and Pricing in Canada." In G.C. Ruggeri, *The Canadian Economy: Problems and Policies.* 2nd ed. Toronto: Gage 1981.

Chapter 13

How Imperfect Competition Functions

Chapter Objectives

After successfully completing this chapter, you will be able to:

- describe the barriers to entry into a monopoly
- graph the profit-maximizing point for a monopoly
- differentiate between the socially optimum and fair-return approaches to monopoly regulation
- describe the conditions necessary for price discrimination to exist
- describe how oligopolies come into existence
- graph the kinked demand curve and describe the assumptions behind the curve
- relate illegal activities under the Competition Act
- graph the profit-maximizing position for a firm in many differentiated sellers
- discuss the advantages and disadvantages of advertising on the economy
- describe the long-run position of a firm in many differentiated sellers

Key Terms

natural monopoly
predatory pricing
socially optimum price
fair-return price
price discrimination
horizontal merger
vertical merger

conglomerate merger
kinked demand curve
price leadership
cartel
retail price maintenance
misleading price advertising
Competition Act

What is Imperfect Competition?

The types of competition described by monopoly, oligopoly, and many differentiated sellers are examples of imperfect competition. In contrast to the circumstance of perfect competition, in a situation of imperfect competition, each firm has some control over the price that it charges for its product. This means that in order to sell more, the firm must lower its price. This firm, therefore, deals with a demand curve that is downward sloping to the right. Although each firm has some control over the price, the extent of that control is determined by the exact nature of the competition in that industry.

Characteristics of Monopoly

An industry that is referred to as a monopoly is one in which there is only a single producer of the product. (See Chapter 10.) The product is one for which there are generally no close substitutes. Examples of monopolies are public utilities, daily newspapers, the post office, natural gas, and the telephone service. Although there may not be any close substitutes for the product, monopolies do, in fact, have competition because they must compete for the consumers' dollar along with every other product. In addition, other products may be substituted for the monopoly product in a pinch. For example, there may be only one supplier of telephone service in your area, but you do not have to use the telephone in order to communicate with other people. The post office and courier services provide competition for the telephone company through alternative methods of communication.

Barriers to Entry   The major characteristic of a monopoly from an economist's point of view is that barriers prevent the entry of new firms into the industry. If the monopoly is profitable, new firms would be encouraged to start up. If the industry remains a monopoly, there must be a reason. What are these barriers?

Economies of Scale
In some cases the existing firm that represents the monopoly may be producing on such a large scale that it is realizing economies of scale, and producing with lower average costs. It may not be possible for new firms to enter the industry and to compete on the basis of price. *Economies of scale,* then, become a barrier to the entry of new firms. Where this is the case, the monopoly situation most likely developed over time. As the industry expanded, those firms that began to realize economies of large-scale production drove their competitors out of business. Eventually, only one competitor remained.

An example of this type of monopoly can be found in the newspaper industry. In many cities, there remains only one daily afternoon newspaper. As a newspaper's circulation increases, it starts to achieve economies of scale. The newspaper can then charge a lower price to customers. Also, newspapers whose circulation increases will find it easier to attract advertisers. The newspapers with lower circulation will find it more difficult to compete, and eventually will drop out of the industry.

Advantages to Being Established

In addition to economies of scale, there are certain advantages to being already established in the industry. For example, consumers are familiar with an established company's name and may be reluctant to try a new product. Established companies may find it easier to borrow money, as they are seen to be better risks and may be able to borrow at lower interest rates. The advantages associated with being already established provide another barrier to new firms.

Natural Monopolies

A natural monopoly describes an industry in which it is more efficient to have only one seller of a good or service since average costs decline as output increases.

As we discussed in Chapter 3, in some industries competition may be impractical. It may be more efficient to have only one supplier of a product. With only one supplier, the company will be able to achieve economies of scale and provide the product or service for the lowest possible price. This is known as a **natural monopoly.** Examples of natural monopolies are telephone, natural gas, and public utilities. In the case of natural monopolies, government either regulates or operates the company in the industry. Government ownership or regulation of the industry is the barrier preventing competition.

In Canada, certain companies are granted a monopoly to provide cable television service within a defined geographic area. Competition is not permitted in this market. In the United States cable television companies face competitors in some markets. Technological developments have undermined the label of natural monopoly that has been applied to the cable television industry. These technologies include private cable, wireless cable, direct broadcast satellite, and the use of common carrier lines. In spite of these advances, government regulation maintains a monopoly on the cable television industry in Canada.

Ownership of Raw Materials

In some industries, the company is a monopoly because it owns the raw materials that the industry requires. An example of this is the DeBeers company, which controls the distribution of diamonds worldwide. No one else can compete without owning a diamond mine. In Canada, the International Nickel Company (INCO) has a virtual monopoly in the ownership of that mineral. INCO is the major supplier of nickel in the world. Its position in the industry is maintained because it owns the natural resources that provide its product. In recent years other nations have brought nickel mines into production, threatening INCO's dominance in the industry. Therefore, if certain raw materials necessary to an industry are difficult to acquire or if their supply is scarce, it may be impossible for new firms to enter that industry.

Patents

Patents are another way of maintaining a monopoly. When the inventor of a product takes out a patent, there is a monopoly on the production of that product. This monopoly remains throughout the life of the patent. In Canada, patents last for a period of 17 years (except for some products such as pharmaceuticals).

In some situations it may be possible for potential competitors to circumvent the barrier of a patent. The development of new technology and the creating of new product designs may permit the production of competing products. An example of how a patent may not ensure a monopoly is the case of the ball-point pen. Milton Reynolds took out a patent on the ball-point pen in 1945. He started producing the pens, and sold them for $12.50 each. Reynolds was earning high profits, which attracted competition. The new firms were able to get around the patent and began to compete with Reynolds. Within one year, the price of the pen had been reduced to $2.98. In later years the price of the pen was reduced even further. The competition reduced Reynolds' profits.

This story points out that monopolies will only be able to earn high profits if the barriers to the entry of new firms are invincible. If the barriers can be circumvented, then new firms will compete away much of the economic profit.

Unfair Competition

Large firms may be able to prevent the entry of new firms into the industry through measures that can be considered unfair. For example, a company may purposely reduce the price of its product in order to eliminate the competition. Once the competition has been eliminated, the company is free to increase its prices.

Predatory pricing entails the lowering of prices, usually below the costs of production, in order to eliminate the competition.

This is referred to as **predatory pricing** and, although illegal, is often difficult to prove. For example, it may be difficult to determine whether low prices are aimed at eliminating competition or are a result of lower average costs. If lower prices are a reflection of lower costs, then the charge of unfair competition is not applicable. On the other hand, a monopolist company may argue that low prices are necessary in order to compete effectively.

The *legal barriers* imposed by government are the most formidable of all. If it is illegal to get into the industry, the monopoly situation is ensured. Other barriers may be eliminated over time. For example, product research and development is one way of getting around the barriers that maintain a monopoly. If new products can be developed by others, they may effectively compete with the monopolist.

13.1 Explain how economies of scale provide a barrier to the entry of new firms.

Newspapers: Natural Monopolies?

Natural monopolies occur in situations in which only one firm in an industry is required in order to have low-cost production. That is, economies of scale are achieved by having only one firm in the industry. In this sense, daily newspapers can be considered natural monopolies. As the circulation of the paper increases, the average cost of producing the newspaper falls. The lowest average costs of producing a newspaper can only be achieved if there is only one newspaper. Competition among newspapers reduces the circulation of each newspaper and prevents any one paper from achieving maximum economies of scale.

There has been a trend toward monopolies in the daily afternoon newspaper business. If there are two competing papers, the economics of the newspaper industry tend to eliminate one of the competitors. If one newspaper has a larger and increasing circulation, it will become difficult for the other paper to compete. Also, as circulation increases, advertisers are more willing to buy advertising space, providing an added advantage to the larger company.

The economics of the newspaper industry came to public attention in 1980, when two daily newspapers—the *Ottawa Journal* and the *Winnipeg Tribune*—closed on the same day. A great deal of controversy surrounded these closings. The *Ottawa Journal* was owned by Thomson Newspapers Limited and the *Winnipeg Tribune* was owned by Southam Inc. The remaining newspaper in Ottawa was the *Ottawa Citizen*, a Southam paper. In Winnipeg, a Thomson newspaper, the *Winnipeg Free Press*, remained in business. The closings resulted in newspaper monopolies in each city.

The simultaneous closings led to an investigation by federal government officials under the Combines Investigation Act (now the Competition Act). The investigation centred on two aspects: 1) whether there was a conspiracy to unduly lessen competition, and 2) whether there was a monopoly operating that was detrimental to the public interest. The investigation led to the charge that the two newspaper chains, Thomson and Southam, had conspired to unduly lessen competition and to monopolize the production and sale of major English-language newspapers in four Canadian cities. The activities of the two companies in Montreal and Vancouver were also included in the charges. The companies were acquitted in 1983 of both conspiracy and monopoly charges.

The newspaper industry has also been the subject of a royal

commission (the Kent Commission), which submitted its report in August 1981, with several recommendations. The commission recommended that Canada's newspaper chains should be forced to sell some of their newspaper holdings in order to reduce concentration in the industry. The report was directed primarily at the Thomson and Southam chains. In 1980, Southam had 32.8 percent of the English-language newspaper circulation in Canada. This was an increase of 11.3 percent from 1970. Thomson had 25.9 percent of the circulation, an increase of 15.5 percent from 1970.

In May 1982, the federal government introduced its proposals to the newspaper industry. Although the proposals have not been implemented as legislation, their impact would have been to prevent Canada's two largest newspaper chains from expanding their holdings as long as they each controlled more than 20 percent of the daily newspaper circulation in the country. Smaller chains would have been allowed to expand until they reached a 20 percent share of national circulation. Other proposals were to include:

— the establishment of a Canadian Advisory Council on Newspapers to receive complaints about newspapers;
— non-media companies that wished to acquire newspapers were to demonstrate that they would be managed independently of other company interests;
— the CRTC (Canadian Radio-television and Telecommunications Commission) would prevent newspapers from holding controlling interests in broadcasting outlets in the same area; and
— the federal government would share the cost, with individual newspapers, of establishing new out-of-province or foreign news bureaus.

Questions
1 What are the advantages and disadvantages of having a monopoly in the daily newspaper business in major Canadian cities?
2 Is there any problem in the fact that the ownership of English-language dailies in Canada is highly concentrated in two companies?
3 Thomson claimed that the *Ottawa Journal* was losing money and, as a result, the paper was shut down. Should a paper be allowed to shut down if it means leaving behind a monopoly?

Profit Maximization

If a monopoly is interested in maximizing profits, the company must attempt to produce at a level that equates marginal revenue and marginal costs. We can assume that the cost structure of the company is similar to the one developed in Chapter 11. That is, in the short run, the average costs will initially decline because of specialization, but will later increase as a result of diminishing returns. What does the revenue side of the picture look like for a monopoly?

In order to answer this question, it is necessary to know something about the demand for the product. Since a monopoly is the only seller in an industry, the demand curve for the monopoly's product is the same as the demand curve for the industry. For most products, the demand curve slopes downward to the right and we will assume that it does for the monopoly in our example—the only bakery in a small town. The demand schedule for the bakery's cakes is shown in table 13.1.

Table 13.1 / Demand schedule for cakes per week

Price	Quantity demanded	Total revenue	Marginal revenue
$11	0	$0	
10	1	10	$10
9	2	18	8
8	3	24	6
7	4	28	4
6	5	30	2
5	6	30	0
4	7	28	- 2
3	8	24	- 4

In order to sell more cakes, it is necessary for the bakery to lower the price. Since it is very difficult to sell similar cakes for different prices to different customers, the bakery must lower the price for all customers. Doing so affects the marginal revenue that the bakery receives for selling more cakes. For example, at a price of $10, the bakery would only sell one cake per week. If the price were to be reduced to $9, the bakery could sell two cakes per week, which would increase the bakery's total revenue to $18. The marginal revenue from selling the additional cake is $8. The information in table 13.1 is graphically demonstrated in figure 13.1. The demand curve is plotted from the first two columns in the table, while the marginal revenue curve is plotted from the second and fourth columns. As shown in the diagram, the marginal revenue curve lies below the demand curve.

The table provides some information about the *price elasticity of demand* for cakes. In the price range $6–10, any decrease in the price increases the total revenue received by the bakery. This fact indicates that the demand in this price range is elastic. In the price range $3-4, any reduction in price leads to a decline in total revenue, indicating an inelastic demand. Finally, in the price range $5-6, the drop in price left total revenue unchanged, indicating unitary elastic demand.

It is possible for the marginal revenue to be negative. If the price of cakes was lowered to $4 from $5, there would be a reduction in

**Figure 13.1
Demand (D) and
marginal-revenue
(MR) curves for a
monopoly**

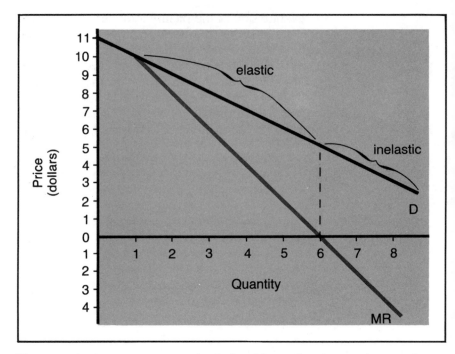

The marginal-revenue curve is derived from the demand curve for a product and refers to the addition to total revenue of selling one more unit of output.

total revenue. If total revenue declines, then marginal revenue must be negative. This occurs in the inelastic portion of the demand curve.

Since the demand curve slopes down to the right, the firm has some control over the price that it charges. In order to determine that price, the revenue and cost situation for this company have to be reviewed together (see figure 13.2).

In order to maximize profits, the firm will produce at a level of output at which marginal revenue and marginal cost are equal (see Chapter 11). For our bakery, this occurs at five cakes. Beyond this point, marginal costs exceed marginal revenue. To produce more than five cakes would be to reduce profits: the extra cost (**MC**) of making more cakes is greater than the extra revenue (**MR**) gained from selling those cakes. If five cakes were produced, the price of the cakes would be $6 each, as indicated by the demand curve.

The monopoly does not charge the highest price possible for its product. The firm is interested in maximizing profits, so it charges a price consistent with that objective. At too high a price no one would purchase the product. Simply because a firm has a monopoly in a certain area does not guarantee that a profit is earned. The product may not be in demand by consumers, or costs of production may be too

**Figure 13.2
Profit-maximizing
position for a
monopoly**

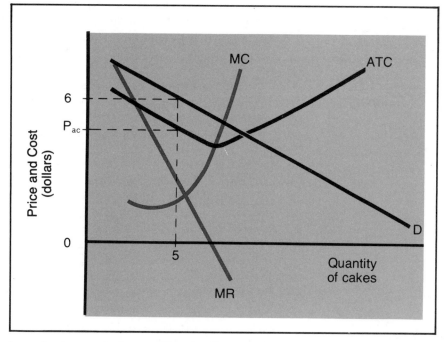

In order to maximize profits, the firm produces a level of output at which marginal cost is equal to marginal revenue. This occurs at five units.

high. In either case, it is quite possible that a loss could occur, and eventually the firm could go out of business unless conditions were to change.

The bakery whose cost and revenue position is shown in figure 13.2 is making an economic profit. The average cost of producing five cakes (P_{ac}) is less than the price (**$6**). Will the bakery continue to earn an economic profit? The ability to earn an economic profit over a long period of time depends on the barriers to entry. If it is relatively easy for new firms to enter the industry, the initial firm's economic profits will be competed away. If the barriers to entry are formidable, then new firms will not enter and economic profits will continue to be earned. In most monopoly situations, the barriers to entry prevent the establishment of new firms and permit economic profits to exist in the long run.

The monopoly does not produce a level of output in the inelastic portion of the demand curve (see figure 13.1). In the elastic portion of the demand curve, any increase in output (and subsequent drop in prices) will lead to increases in total revenue. In the inelastic portion of the demand curve, reductions in price lead to lower total revenue because marginal revenue is negative in this section of the demand curve.

13.2   Why does the demand curve for a monopoly slope down to the right?

13.3   Why could a monopoly continue to earn economic profits in the long run when a firm in perfect competition cannot?

Economic Effects of a Monopoly

When perfect competition was discussed in Chapter 12, we learned that each firm maximizes profits by producing at a level of output at which price equals the marginal cost. *Profit maximization* at this level of output is seen as desirable, since the firm continues to produce more output as long as price exceeds marginal cost. Because the price of the product is representative of its value (or benefit) to society, the firm continues to produce as long as the value (price) exceeds the costs of production (marginal cost). This is an ideal situation from society's point of view, and it is said that perfect competition results in an efficient allocation of resources.

How do monopolies rate according to this criterion? At the level of output at which a monopoly maximizes profit, the price is greater than the marginal cost (see figure 13.2). This circumstance indicates that the value of this product to society is greater than the extra costs of producing more of it. We are willing to pay the price in order to receive more of this product, yet we do not receive any more. If this is so, why does the monopoly not expand production? The answer to this question lies in the monopoly's attempt to maximize profits. If more of the product were produced, it could only be sold by lowering the price, and monopoly profits would drop. The monopoly is withholding some of this product from the market in order to keep up the price and maximize profits.

It can be argued that the actions of a monopoly lead to misallocation of our nation's resources. Consumers are anxious to receive more of this product and want more resources devoted to its production. They are even willing to pay more than the extra cost of producing it. Yet the monopoly withholds some of this product from the market in an attempt to maximize profits. In order to improve the allocation of resources, government often regulates the price that the monopoly can charge. If the government does not like the price that a monopoly charges while trying to maximize profits, then the government must select an appropriate price. Two approaches to monopoly price regulation are discussed below and displayed in figure 13.3.

Socially optimum pricing, an approach to monopoly price regulation, sets the price at a level equal to the marginal cost.

The first approach is called the **socially optimum price.** It is patterned after the results obtained in perfect competition. If government were concerned over the price and the resource allocation effects of monopolies, then it could legislate a price that would be equal to the marginal cost. The monopoly would continue to expand output up to the point at which the benefits from additional output (the price) were just equal to the costs of producing it (the marginal cost). This price would be where the demand curve intersects

**Figure 13.3
Socially optimum
and fair-return
pricing**

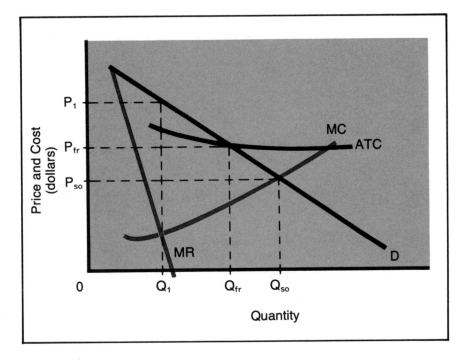

The socially optimum price (P_{so}) occurs where the demand and marginal-cost curves intersect. The fair-return price (P_{fr}) occurs where the demand and average-cost curves intersect.

*The fair-return price,
a price used in the
regulation of a mono-
poly, is equal to the
average cost of
production.*

the marginal-cost curve. This would lower the price to P_{so} and more of the product would be put on the market (Q_{so}). One difficulty with this approach would be the possibility of the monopoly not receiving a high-enough price to cover costs. If the average-cost curve was above the P = MC point, as it is in figure 13.3, the monopoly would operate at a loss. This is not desirable, because the company would go out of business.

The second approach to monopoly price regulation is called **fair-return pricing** and requires that the price be set equal to the average cost. This principle would permit the company to break even. Since implicit costs are included in the average-cost calculation, the firm would be willing to stay in business. Figure 13.3 shows P_{fr} as the point at which the demand curve intersects the average-cost (**AC**) curve. The quantity that would be produced is Q_{fr}.

Fair-return pricing seems to be a more practical approach to monopoly price regulation than socially optimum pricing. A company should be allowed to break even and cover implicit costs as well as explicit costs. The difficulty with this approach lies in determining the exact level of implicit costs. These costs are the sum of the opportunity costs of the resources owned by the firm (see Chapter 11). It may be difficult to determine opportunity costs. If a monopoly invests money in a business, what return on this money should be considered an opportunity cost? For example, if the firm expands its main offices at a cost of $6 million, what is the opportunity cost of this expenditure? Should it be equal to the interest paid on a savings account in a chartered bank? Should it be more because there is more risk attached to investing in your business than in getting a safe return on your money in a bank? Should extra money be made available for product research and development? How should implicit costs be adjusted for inflation? Prior to establishing a fair-return price, these questions must be answered.

Government regulation of a monopoly, although often logical in theory, has some very practical problems, the first of which concerns the estimation of costs and demand for the product. We have mentioned that implicit cost estimates may be hard to determine. Estimates of demand may also be difficult to obtain. A second problem has to do with encouraging efficiency on the part of the company, once regulated. Would the monopoly be interested in lowered costs of production? The answer may be no, if lower costs mean a lower regulated price. In contrast, the company may be willing to accept additional costs as long as these increase the regulated price. Money may be spent on luxuries like new office furniture in order to ensure that costs remain high. This system of price regulation by government may lead to a certain amount of inefficiency. Product quality may also suffer in an attempt by the firm to realize more money. If the firm can charge the same price for a lower quality product, then profits should increase.

The third problem relates to spill-overs, or third-party effects. Additional costs may be present in the case of negative third-party effects. These may inadvertently not be considered in the regulation of the monopoly price. The use of nuclear energy provides a good example. The storage problems and possible nuclear radiation leaks are third-party costs that are difficult to assess. These third-party costs may not be reflected in the product price.

Regardless of whether socially optimum or fair-return pricing is used, the consumer receives more of the product for a lower price than would be the case if the monopoly were not regulated. In figure 13.3, both P_{so} and P_{fr} are below the profit-maximizing price (P_1).

The public tends to have a negative impression of monopolies. It sees the monopoly as a company charging the highest possible price and "ripping off" the consumer. When we compare monopolies to perfect competition, we see that they do lead to a misallocation of resources. Yet this is not the only basis on which to judge a monopoly. Monopolies may have certain advantages compared to other types of competition. They may be large enough to achieve economies of scale and produce at a lower average cost. The consumer may then be able to obtain products at a lower price. A major disadvantage of a perfectly competitive firm is that it may never be large enough to achieve economies of scale. If a firm cannot take advantage of economies of large-scale production, its costs will not be reduced. If costs are not reduced, then prices will not be reduced.

There is a tendency for firms in perfectly competitive industries to break even in the long run. Breaking even leaves no money for modernization and product research and development. The ability of a monopoly to earn economic profits, unless regulated by government, enables the company to undertake product research and development from which the consumer ultimately benefits in the form of new and better products.

Some economists argue that a monopoly will not commit money to product research and development. They believe that there is no incentive to do this, because the firm is already in a monopoly position. Others argue that the monopoly needs to undertake research, to assist in reducing costs and to increase economic profits. However, if it is a government-regulated monopoly, it may be forced to lower prices if costs are reduced, and this may reduce the incentive to be innovative. A monopoly may be interested in developing new products if that will allow the company to maintain its monopoly position. If the company does not develop new products some other company will. Monopolies cannot be expected to last forever.

13.4 Does fair-return pricing allow the monopoly to earn a profit? Discuss.

The Telephone Monopoly

In Canada, telephone companies are granted a monopoly within certain geographic boundaries. Considered to be a natural monopoly, the companies are regulated by the Canadian Radio-television and Telecommunications Commission (CRTC). The largest of these companies is Bell Canada. It has a monopoly over telephone service in Ontario, Quebec, and the eastern Northwest Territories. It owns 98.8 percent of Northern Telephone in northern Ontario, a majority of Telebec in Quebec, the Newfoundland Telephone Company, and Maritime Telegraph and Telephone. The latter owns 41 percent of the Island Telephone Company in Prince Edward Island.

When Bell Canada wants to increase the rates for telephone service, it must apply to the CRTC. The procedure for deciding on appropriate rate increases is not satisfactory to many people. Bell Canada claims that the hearings for rate increases are costly and time-consuming. Consumers argue that they are not adequately represented at the hearings. Consumers also complain that the CRTC does not consider the operations of Bell Canada subsidiaries, the company's construction program, consumer services and practices, and corporate privileges when approving rate increases.

The procedure used by the CRTC in approving rate increases has been to look at Bell's return on capital. When the rate of return falls too low, rate increases are deemed to be appropriate.

Bell Canada has to do a great deal of work in preparing its case for the CRTC. The company has spent millions of dollars in order to present its position. The company argues that its costs of providing telephone service are increasing. These include materials costs, wages, and interest. The company also cites the increase in postage costs associated with sending out phone bills each month. Further cost increases are associated with Bell's program of expanding into non-urban areas with improved service. Bell also points out to the CRTC that its telephone rates are lower than those elsewhere.

Consumer and telephone user groups may also present their positions to the CRTC. These groups are restricted by the expense and time required for the hearings. The major complaints of consumer groups have been about the service in rural areas, the failure of Bell Canada to use the best equipment available, and the failure of the CRTC to take into account the activities of Bell's subsidiaries and the earnings of Bell Canada International, which promotes sales in other countries. Consumer groups argue that the foreign earnings of Bell Canada International should help lower the telephone rates for Canadians.

A challenge to the telephone company monopoly over long-distance calls was made to the CRTC in 1984. CNCP Telecommunications wanted the CRTC to permit them to compete with Bell Canada and British Columbia Telephone Company for long-distance revenues in their territories.

The CNCP proposal would have allowed subscribers in Quebec City, Montreal, Ottawa/Hull, Toronto, Vancouver, and Victoria to obtain long-distance services at least twenty percent cheaper than they were presently paying. CNCP wanted to interconnect with existing Bell Canada and British Columbia Telephone local networks for a monthly fee. The long-distance portion of the call would then be carried on CNCP'S microwave or fibre-optics network.

The decision by the CRTC in August 1985 rejected the CNCP application, stating that it was not in the public interest to accept it. The CRTC was concerned that if competition were permitted in the long-distance market, long-distance rates for the existing firms in the market would come down—but local telephone rates would increase. CNCP offered a payment to the telephone companies in order to reduce the impact on local rates, but the CRTC argued that this payment, if made, would put into question the viability of the CNCP proposal. In addition to rejecting the CNCP application, the CRTC froze long-distance rates for Bell Canada and British Columbia Telephone until it can determine if they are too high.

In May 1990, CNCP (under a new name—Unitel) asked for permission to compete with the six federally regulated telephone companies in British Columbia, Ontario, Quebec, and the Atlantic provinces. Unitel is hoping to phase in its service across Canada over a six year period. The company plans to spend $1.5 billion over five years to expand its national fibre-optic and microwave networks. Unitel expects to pay the local telephone companies for use of their networks. Another application has been submitted to provide long distance service from British Columbia Rail Telecommunications and Lightel Communications of Toronto. At the time of publication, decisions on these applications had not been made.

Will competition be beneficial in the long-distance market? The experience in the United States has shown that long-distance rates will decrease with competition. Canada also needs an efficient telecommunications system in order to be competitive with other nations. Canadian business needs an efficient telephone network, and at present some businesses are re-routeing domestic long-distance calls through the United States. Telemarketing, catalogue shopping, and customer service are all aspects of business in need of an efficient telephone system. If competition is allowed in the long-distance market, it is expected that local rates will increase. Some argue that the increase in local rates will not be excessive and the possibility of an increase in local rates should not deny Canadians the benefits of more competition in long-distance rates. Low-income families and individuals could always be subsidized if affordability is an issue. Cheaper long-distance rates do not only benefit business users. Experience in the United States has shown that as the rates decrease, residential users make more calls outside their area codes. With lower long-distance rates there would be increased communication among Canadians.

The CRTC has rejected competition in the long-distance telephone market for the present and appears to believe that long-distance rates can be reduced through means other than competition.

Questions

1 What factors would you take into consideration in granting Bell Canada a telephone rate increase?
2 Should earnings of Bell Canada subsidiary companies be used to determine appropriate rate increases?
3 If it is expensive for consumers to attend rate-increase hearings, should the CRTC represent the consumers' point of view?
4 Why are telephone companies considered to be natural monopolies?
5 How many technological advances in the communications industry, such as satellites and cellular phones, affect the telephone monopoly?
6 Would lower long-distance telephone rates be an incentive for firms to invest in Canada?

Price Discrimination

Price discrimination is the practice of charging different prices to different consumers for an item produced under similar cost conditions.

The demand curve for a monopoly's product slopes down to the right. This means that if the company wants to sell more of its product, it is necessary for it to lower the price. All consumers benefit from the lower price, even those who were willing to pay a higher price.

Knowing that some buyers would purchase the product at higher prices than others, the monopoly may be tempted to divide up the market and sell to different buyers at different prices, even though the costs of providing the good or the service are the same. This is known as **price discrimination,** and, if successful, will increase monopoly profits. Certain conditions must be present in order for price discrimination to exist.

First, the monopoly must be able to identify separate markets for the product, and they must be kept separate. It must be made impossible for those who purchase the product at the lower price to sell it to those who are willing to pay the higher price. The second condition is that the buyers in each market must have a different reaction to price changes. Those who are able to purchase the product for the lower price will be those with the more elastic demand curve. They may be unwilling to buy the product at the higher price.

Bus tickets provide an example of price discrimination. Local transit companies usually have different prices for adult and student passengers. Students usually pay the lower price, because they are more sensitive to price increases. Different-coloured tickets make it impossible for a student to purchase bus tickets and sell them to an adult. Some companies may even have special rates for senior citizens and children. The different-coloured tickets effectively keep the markets separate. Other examples of price discrimination include theatre tickets, business and residential telephone rates, luncheon specials at restaurants, and excursion air flights.

Professional persons are also in a good position to charge different prices to different customers. Dentists, for example, may charge a lower price for their services to clients who are not in a financial position to pay the regular fees. It is easy to keep the markets separate in this case. Individuals cannot sell their dental work to others. Also, there are different price elasticities of demand for dental services, depending on the patient's income.

Price discrimination also may occur on an international basis. This is referred to as *dumping*. If a Canadian product sells for a lower price in a foreign country than in Canada, we say that it has been dumped abroad. The lower foreign price is usually a result of a more elastic demand for the product in the foreign country. In order to sell the product, its price has to be reduced abroad. Although the foreign country may appear to benefit because it gets the product for a lower price, most countries prohibit the dumping of products on their markets. The prohibition usually comes when the product competes with a domestically produced item. Otherwise, foreign nations would be happy to receive products at the lowest possible price.

13.5 Why are monopolies in a better position to practise price discrimination than firms in other types of competition?.

13.6 Are different ticket prices to a sporting event, e.g. to a hockey game, an example of price discrimination?

Oligopoly

In a competitive situation described as an *oligopoly,* there are only a few firms. When one firm establishes its price, it has to take into consideration the reaction of the other firms. The products in oligopolistic industries can be either homogeneous or differentiated. Examples of homogeneous, or identical, products are steel, sugar, and aluminum. Examples of differentiated products where an oligopoly exists are automobiles and grocery stores. There are two major reasons why there are only a few firms in oligopolistic industries:

Economies of scale: as mentioned in Chapter 11 and earlier in this chapter, economies of scale are cost advantages associated with large-scale production. These cost advantages arise from quantity discounts, increased specialization, and the use of more efficient machinery and equipment. *Technological improvements have been the major factor behind increased economies of scale.* As some firms in an industry expand, they are able to achieve economies of scale and lower-cost production. This gives them an advantage over their rivals. Eventually some rivals drop out of the industry. Not only do economies of scale result in only a few firms being left in the industry, they also prevent new firms from starting up. In order to be able to compete, a new firm would have to start out with large-scale production, which is very difficult for a new company to do. Economies of scale could be considered a barrier to entry into oligopolistic industries, as well as entry into a monopoly industry.

Mergers: a merger can be defined as a circumstance in which one firm acquires another, or in which two or more firms amalgamate in order to make one single firm. The purpose of a merger is usually to increase the share of the market. The newly-combined firm may have more control over setting the price for its product. It may also be able to better achieve economies of scale through quantity purchases of materials and increased specialization.

The combination of two firms engaged in the same activity is called a horizontal merger.

   Mergers may be of different types. A **horizontal merger** is a combination of two firms engaged in the same activity, usually in the same geographic market. For example, two grocery stores that operate in the same city may be merged. A **vertical merger** is one in which firms that engage in different levels of activity are combined. An example of a

The combination of two firms engaged in different levels of the same activity describes a vertical merger.

A conglomerate merger occurs when two firms engaged in different levels of the same activity combine.

vertical merger, or integration, would be an automobile company merging with a tire manufacturer. Tires are one product of the automobile manufacturing process. Finally, a **conglomerate merger** is one in which a firm acquires another firm that is engaged in a different business. For example, a railroad company may purchase a paper mill. Of the three types, horizontal mergers result in fewer firms in an industry and can be a major reason for the existence of oligopolies.

13.7   How do oligopolies come about?

The Beer Oligopoly

Canada's beer industry is clearly an oligopoly. The top two breweries—Molson Companies Ltd. and John Labatt Ltd.—have sales that account for approximately 95 percent of total Canadian beer sales. Imported beer and several smaller Canadian breweries account for the remainder. Why is the Canadian beer industry so concentrated?

A major reason for the high degree of concentration is mergers and acquisitions. Larger companies have acquired smaller breweries, while others have merged to form one company. In Quebec prior to World War I, there were 16 breweries in operation. National Breweries Ltd. of Quebec, over a period of time, consolidated 14 of them into one firm. The large Quebec breweries had fewer brands, higher volume, and better advertising than the smaller Ontario breweries. The Quebec breweries had acquired 12 percent of the Ontario market by 1928.

At this time there were 37 small breweries in Ontario. Most were not operating at capacity. Profits were low and the breweries needed modernization. E.P. Taylor studied the Ontario situation and began a process of mergers and acquisitions using Brading Breweries Ltd. as the starting point. His initial targets were breweries that produced half of the total sales of beer in Ontario. These breweries were Kuntz Brewery in Kitchener, O'Keefe, Canada Bud, Dominion, and Cosgrave's in Toronto, Regal in Hamilton, Carling in London, Taylor & Bate in St. Catharines, British American in Windsor, Kakabeka Falls in Fort Frances, and the Sudbury Brewery in Sudbury. Taylor also wanted to acquire and close breweries that accounted for about 20 percent of Ontario beer sales: Budweiser, Copland, City Club, Heather, Reinhardt, Rock Springs, Grant's, Cronmiller and White, Bixel, Perth, Walkerville, Riverside, Hofer, Tecumseh, Formosa Spring, Gold Belt, Port Arthur, Soo Falls, Lake-of-the-Woods, Fort Frances, and Welland. In 1937 the name of the brewery that amalgamated the smaller firms was Canadian Breweries Ltd. (later Carling O'Keefe Ltd., and now a part of Molson's Breweries).[1]

The industry remains an oligopoly because of the barriers to the entry of new firms. These barriers are in the form of provincial warehousing regulations and advertising costs. In many provinces, a

[1] Rohmer, *E. P. Taylor*, pp. 50-76

beer company must have a brewery in the province before its beer can be sold in the retail outlets. It is difficult for a new company to have a brewery in more than one province.

The advertising expenditures of the three major beer companies also present a barrier to new firms. In 1978 the Henninger brewery opened in Hamilton, Ontario. The company hoped to acquire 3–3.5 percent of the market with an advertising budget equal to eight percent of the industry's advertising budget. Within a year of the opening of the Henninger brewery, the three major companies doubled their advertising budget to $15 million annually. The new brewery found it difficult to compete and ceased its operation. The company claimed that it was also hampered by provincial restrictions on beer advertising.[2]

Questions

1   In what sense would advertising expenditures be a barrier to the entry of new firms?
2   How do provincial warehousing systems represent a barrier to entry?
3   Do you think that beer companies should be allowed to compete on the basis of price?
4   Why might the two major beer companies want some of the smaller Canadian breweries to remain in operation?

Pricing Policies

In an oligopolistic situation each firm must consider the reaction of competitors when setting the price. Although firms may not be certain how their rivals will react, they have to keep possible reactions in mind. For example, if one firm lowers its price and its rivals follow with the price cuts, it is possible that no firm will benefit. Depending on the overall demand for the product, firms may sell approximately the same amount of the product, even after the price cut. In the case of an inelastic demand, price cuts do not lead to large increases in the quantity demanded.

If a firm in an oligopoly does not know how its competitors will respond to changes in its price, then it is impossible to know the shape of the demand curve that it is facing. The firm does not know if its sales will increase as a result of a price reduction, since other firms may lower their prices as well. If the firm raises its price, it is not certain if others will follow. If rivals do not respond with higher prices, then the firm could lose a significant amount of business. If it is, therefore, impossible to describe the demand curve for a firm in an oligopoly, then it is impossible to describe the marginal-revenue curve. If the firm is interested in maximizing profits by equating marginal revenue and marginal costs, the appropriate level of output is more difficult to determine. Observers of oligopolistic industries have noted two

[2] Hunter, "Hard for Small to Survive in Brewing," p. B2.

The kinked demand curve is a demand curve that is composed of two sections—elastic and inelastic—separated by a bend, or kink, and is an attempt to explain price rigidity in oligopolistic industries.

characteristics of prices in these industries. The first is that prices tend to be inflexible, meaning that they do not change very often. Second, when prices do change, all firms tend to change them. A good example of this is the automobile industry. At the same time each year, prices for the new model cars are announced. During the year, if price reductions are required, they appear to happen simultaneously. These characteristics have led to a theory of oligopolistic pricing called the **kinked demand curve** (see figure 13.4), which is an attempt to draw a demand curve for a firm in an oligopolistic setting. The demand curve for an oligopoly appears to be composed of two sections: one elastic and one inelastic. Why does the demand curve in figure 13.4 have a bend, or kink, dividing it into two sections?

**Figure 13.4
The kinked
demand curve**

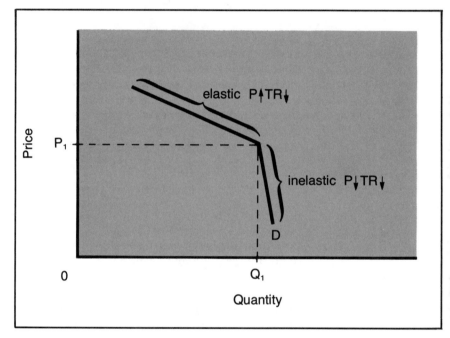

If the firm raises the price above P_1 and other firms in the industry do not, it will lose sales and total revenue will fall. If the firm lowers the price below P_1 and other firms follow, then it may not increase sales substantially and total revenue will decline. Since total revenue declines with either option, the price remains at P_1.

The kinked demand curve represents a situation in which the firm is uncertain about the reaction of its rivals to price changes. If the price is at $\mathbf{P_1}$ the firm may be reluctant to raise the price. If the section of demand curve above $\mathbf{P_1}$ is elastic, any increase in price will result in a drop in total revenue. This will happen if other firms do not follow the price increase. The firm may also be reluctant to lower its prices if it believes that its rivals will not lower their prices. It may perceive the lower portion of the demand curve as being inelastic, and will be unwilling to lower its price if total revenue will fall.

This perception explains why the firm may keep the price at the kink for some time. It does not explain, however, the way in which P_1 was arrived at. The theory of the kinked demand curve also does not explain how the price would change and for these reasons, it is not a totally acceptable theory of oligopoly pricing.

The theory of the kinked demand curve assumes that the firm does not know how rivals will react to price changes. The firm is operating in an atmosphere of uncertainty. In order to eliminate this uncertainty, the firm may try to co-ordinate its pricing policies with its rivals. This activity is referred to as *collusion*. Collusion is easier in an oligopoly than in other types of competition because of the small number of firms. However, its practice is illegal in Canada, and is prohibited under the Competition Act, along with certain other business practices. Even if outright collusion does not take place, oligopolies are often characterized by **price leadership,** which serves to avoid competition. Price leadership is a situation in which one firm raises its price and the other firms in the industry follow with price increases. The price leader may be a dominant firm in the industry. If one firm accounts for a large percentage of industry sales, it may be able to set its price in order to maximize profits. The remaining firms are likely to accept this price for their product. The price leader need not be the largest firm in the industry. It may simply be a firm that has been a good judge of market conditions in the past.

Price leadership occurs in an oligopoly when one firm raises its price and other firms in the industry follow with their own price increases.

The concept of the kinked demand curve also explains why firms in an oligopolistic situation resort to advertising and new-product development in order to compete. If firms are reluctant to change prices, other forms of competition are essential. Through advertising, it is hoped that the upper portion of the demand curve will become more inelastic. When it becomes necessary for prices to rise (under substantial cost increases), the firm would not lose as many sales if advertising is successful in altering the demand curve.

13.8 Why is the price rigid at the kink in figure 13.4?

Cartels

A cartel is a formal arrangement, written or verbal, among producers that regulates the price and total output of a product.

A **cartel** can be described as a formal arrangement, either written or verbal, among producers to regulate the price and total output of a product. Instead of competing, the firms form a monopoly in the sense that they have *sole control* over the market. In Canada, cartels are illegal, yet they have been established for many products on an international scale. These products include oil, bauxite, copper, tin, uranium, coffee, sugar, cocoa, and rubber. Cartels tend to be found in the resource industries or in those that have identical products.

In order to succeed, a cartel must possess certain characteristics. The firms in the cartel must control a major amount of the total output of the product. That is, if strong competition exists from other producers, the cartel is not likely to be successful. The demand for the cartel's product must be growing or at least remain steady. If demand starts to fall, some producers will want to lower prices in order to stimulate sales. It may be difficult to reach agreement on price cuts. Also, close substitutes cannot be readily available; the demand for the product should be inelastic. The final criterion for success is the willingness of individual firms to abide by the decisions of the group. If some firms are unwilling to restrict the amount of the product that they put on the market, or are unwilling to maintain a high price, the agreement will break down.

A look at a real-world cartel points out how difficult it is for a cartel to survive. Possibly the best-known cartel is the Organization of Petroleum Exporting Countries (OPEC). This 13-nation group received international recognition in 1973 as a result of the sharp increases in world oil prices. In fact, oil prices quadrupled in 1973-74 in the wake of a Middle East war. Oil prices increased drastically again later in the decade and prices tripled between the years 1978 and 1980. The OPEC cartel was given much of the credit for these price increases. Beginning in 1981, however, oil prices started to fall.

Was OPEC a successful cartel during these years? There is no doubt that the OPEC nations controlled the majority of the world's oil supplies. It is estimated that they had 80 percent of the non-communist-world's oil reserves. In order to push up prices, the OPEC nations need only reduce their oil production. Yet during the 1970s these countries did not impose production quotas on each other. Many OPEC nations actually increased oil production in response to the higher oil prices. It was only when prices started falling in 1981 that OPEC tried to get its members to agree on production quotas. Agreement on production quotas among members of a cartel is not easily obtained and such was the case with OPEC. Some nations, like Saudi Arabia, have vast oil reserves and want to take a long-term view of oil prices. Others, like Algeria, have small reserves of oil and are more interested in the short-term price for this resource. By the end of 1991, the OPEC nations had not yet reached agreement on permanent production quotas; in fact, the Gulf War and other regional conflicts have made this even less likely.

If high prices were not achieved by reductions in supply, they must have been achieved by increases in demand. During the 1970s the demand for oil was steadily increasing. Also during this decade, many governments were printing money and rapidly expanding the money supply. This led to inflation in certain countries and to increases in the price of oil. When the brakes were put on the expansion of the money supply, and the rate of inflation was reduced, oil prices began to fall. A recession in the Western world in the early 1980s also led to a reduction in the demand for energy. Consumers had also reacted to high energy prices by buying more fuel-efficient cars and living in more fuel-efficient homes.

A cartel will only remain successful if there are no substitutes for its product. The oil price increases during the 1970s were possible because there were few substitutes for oil. By the 1980s, other non-OPEC nations had increased their exploration for sources of oil. Canada, along with the United States, Britain, and Norway, became increasingly self-sufficient in oil. Progress was also being made in the development of other sources of energy, such as solar and nuclear. The future success of OPEC as a cartel will depend on how it deals with the falling demand for oil and with the lower prices of the 1990s.

The Uranium Cartel

Although cartels are illegal in Canada, the federal government did participate in an international uranium cartel in response to a United States ban on imported uranium. The U.S. action had resulted in a drop in uranium prices. The Canadian government then agreed to participation in the cartel in order to protect the Canadian uranium centres of Elliot Lake, Ontario, and Uranium City, Saskatchewan.

The cartel was formed in 1972 at a meeting in Paris. It set pricing schedules, pricing rules, terms and conditions for bids, markets, quotas, and penalties for infraction of rules. Canada participated along with France, South Africa, Australia, and Britain. The federal government passed an order-in-council requiring that Canadian uranium producers follow certain pricing rules and quotas if they wanted to obtain export permits from the Atomic Energy Control Board.

The cartel was successful in raising uranium prices. A pound of uranium cost approximately six dollars in 1971 and over forty dollars in 1975. The cartel did not necessarily have entirely positive effects for Canada. Consumers in Canada were forced to pay the higher world prices as well. This situation affected such companies as Ontario Hydro, the country's largest buyer of uranium. If Ontario Hydro had to pay higher prices, so did electricity users.

The fact that Canadians had to pay higher prices for uranium led to charges in 1981 against six Canadian uranium companies under the Combines Investigation Act (now the Competition Act). The companies—Denison Mines, Gulf Minerals Canada Limited, Rio Algom Limited, Uranez Canada Limited, Eldorado Nuclear Limited, and Uranium Canada Limited—were charged with unduly lessening competition in the purchase, sale, and supply in Canada of uranium, uranium oxide, and other uranium products. The companies argued that they had received federal government assurances that the cartel was legal.

In December 1983 the Supreme Court of Canada decided that the two Crown corporations—Eldorado Nuclear Limited and Uranium

Canada Limited—could not be prosecuted for price-fixing charges. Shortly after this decision, the federal government announced that the charges against the four private companies were to be dropped. The inequity of charging private companies and not charging public companies may have led to the charges being dropped. The charges may have also been dismissed because of lack of evidence that the companies had fixed prices in Canada.

Questions

1   What characteristics of uranium would make it suitable for a cartel arrangement?
2   Why would a United States ban on imported uranium lead to a drop in uranium prices?

Competition Act

Since 1889, Canada has passed legislation aimed at protecting the consumer from unfair business practices. The early legislation was primarily *anti-monopoly* legislation. It was not only directed at single-firm monopolies, but also at those monopolies that result when companies get together to set prices and divide the market.

In 1910, the Combines Investigation Act was passed by the federal government. The act was passed in order to prohibit practices that would unduly restrict competition, including combinations aimed at fixing prices, misleading advertising, and price discrimination.

A major difficulty of the legislation was the interpretation given to the word "unduly." How much did competition have to be reduced in order for it to be unduly lessened? Changing economic conditions may bring about changes in the interpretation of the word, which has been defined as "improperly, excessively, and inordinately." It has also been defined as detrimental to the public interest. *Basically, it is illegal for companies to restrict competition to the point at which these companies can pursue their activities as if they did not have any competition.*

Several amendments have been made to the 1910 legislation—changes directed at preserving competition in Canadian industry. The legislation in its present form prohibits the following business practices:

Amendments to the Early Legislation

Mergers and monopolies: a merger is defined in the act as the acquisition or control over the business of a competitor whereby competition is likely to be lessened to the detriment of the public interest. A monopoly is defined as a situation in which one or more persons control the business that they are engaged in and are likely to operate it to the detriment of the public interest.

Mergers are prohibited where it can be shown that competition is unduly lessened. One such merger to attract public attention was the acquisition of Simpsons department stores by the Hudson's Bay Company. The Thomson newspaper chain then purchased a controlling interest in the Hudson's Bay Company. Neither merger was charged under the act and, in fact, very few mergers have ever been charged under its provisions. The merger of Molson and Carling breweries in 1989 was allowed to proceed as was the sale of Wardair to PWA Corporation in the same year. The merger of Imperial Oil and Texaco was allowed to proceed only after the Competition Tribunal ordered Imperial to divest itself of 600 gas stations, a Nova Scotia oil refinery, and other facilities. In 1991, a proposed merger of the flour and flour-related businesses of Canada Packers Inc. and John Labatt Ltd. was denied by the Bureau of Competition Policy. The bureau refused to approve the merger on the grounds that competition would be excessively reduced in Montreal and in the West.

Monopolies that come into being through legal means are not prohibited. For example, government-owned and regulated monopolies are not illegal. Also monopolies created because of patent legislation are acceptable. The monopoly itself is not illegal, but the abuse of monopoly power is illegal. In 1990, a Competition Tribunal ruled that NutraSweet had effectively maintained monopoly powers over the aspartame market at the expense of potential competitors. Under the tribunal's order, NutraSweet can no longer sign contracts that make it the exclusive aspartame supplier to domestic companies.

Agreements that would restrict competition: agreements between companies that would restrict the entry of new firms, fix prices, or limit the production and distribution of goods and services are prohibited. Generally, anyone who restrains or limits trade is guilty of an offence. The act applies to transporting, producing, manufacturing, supplying, storing, or dealing in any product.

Examples of conspiracies to fix prices are numerous. In 1989, five companies admitted to adopting a policy whereby exhibitors at consumer motorcycle shows would display only manufacturers' suggested prices. Any exhibitor who violated the agreement would be expelled and not permitted to take part in future shows.

The most publicized case of price fixing in recent years was the accusation that Canadian oil companies had overcharged consumers by $12 billion from 1958 to 1973. The charge against the oil companies was that they agreed to fix prices. Criminal charges under the Combines Investigation Act were not laid. Instead an inquiry was held by the Restrictive Trade Practices Commission, which is a quasi-judicial body not bound by the same rules of evidence as a court.

In June 1986, the commission, after five years of inquiry, rejected the accusation that major oil companies had overcharged consumers. The commission did express concerns, however, over certain practices and trends in the industry. It objected to the development of "rack pricing," a policy whereby wholesalers stick to publicly-posted prices for all customers. Since possible discounts would not be allowed on published prices, competition might be adversely affected.

The largest fine ever imposed under the conspiracy provision of the act was $700 000 and was levied in February 1985 against three Canadian advertising companies. The companies conspired to lessen competition in the outdoor billboard market by establishing exclusive territories and effectively dividing up the market. Each company agreed not to own or operate poster panels in the others' "allocated" geographic territory. In addition, each agreed to prevent any other poster-panel owner from owning or operating in the allocated territory.

Not all agreements between companies are illegal. Companies can agree to exchange statistics and credit information, define trade terms and product standards, and co-operate in research and development.

Retail price maintenance: it is illegal for a manufacturer to set the retail price at which the product must be sold. Manufacturers may be interested in maintaining a certain image of their product and may resent price lowering by retailers. In the past, some manufacturers have refused to sell to retailers who lowered the price below the suggested retail price. This practice is also prohibited by the act: companies cannot discriminate against retailers who use the product as a "loss-leader."

Retail price mainten-ance, whereby a manufacturer insists that a product be sold at a specified price, contravenes the Competition Act.

The largest fine ever imposed for **retail price maintenance** was $150 000. The guilty party was Levi-Strauss of Canada. The company took advantage of world denim shortages between 1972 and 1975 to select the retailers that it sold to. These were retailers who sold the company's jeans at prices that the company had set. In 1986, another jeans manufacturer, Blue Bell Canada Inc., was fined $40 000 for putting pressure on retailers to increase the retail price of the company's Calvin Klein jeans. In 1989, Chrysler Canada Ltd. was ordered to recommence supplying automobile parts to a Montreal trading house. The trading house exported parts to Europe, South America, and the Middle East, and Chrysler wanted the operation to expand. When the trading house did not expand, Chrysler refused to supply it with parts. Prosecutions under this section of the act are numerous.

Misleading price advertising, an illegal activity, occurs when the prices actually charged are higher than those advertised.

Misleading price advertising: the act prohibits misleading the public by charging prices higher than advertised prices, a practice called **misleading price advertising.** Some supermarkets have been prosecuted under this section of the act. The lower advertised prices attract consumers to the store. Some items may have the low advertised prices, but others may not. The largest fine imposed for misleading price advertising was $28 000 against a supermarket chain.

Price discrimination: it is illegal to discriminate between buyers who are buying similar quantities and qualities of a product. It is legal to give quantity discounts on bulk purchases, and price reductions for special events such as clearance sales are also acceptable.

Predatory price cutting: predatory pricing is defined as selling a product at a lower price in a certain area in order to eliminate or substantially reduce the competition. After the competition has been reduced, the general practice would be to increase prices. It is often difficult to determine whether prices have been lowered in order to eliminate competition or simply to compete.

Hoffman-La Roche Ltd., a major manufacturer of pharmaceutical drugs, was convicted of predatory pricing in 1980. The company manufactures two tranquilizers, Valium and Librium. It was convicted of selling Valium at unreasonably low prices. The court decision also charged that the practice of discounting and giveaways was in violation of the act. In fact, the company gave away 82 million pills worth $2.6 million in a 12-month period. Hospitals and governments received drugs at prices substantially below cost.

Recent Changes in Competition Law

As economic conditions change, the objectives of legislation designed to ensure competition may change as well. In 1977, several amendments to the Combines Investigation Act came into effect. The act was extended to cover business practices in the service sector of our economy. This sector was exempt from coverage under the previous legislation. Other changes prohibited pyramid selling, bait and switch selling, misleading advertising, and the repricing of goods in stock.

Further changes were deemed necessary in order to ensure that legislation guaranteed competition in our economy. The Combines Investigation Act was enacted under the criminal-code powers of the federal government, making the burden of proof on the part of the government more difficult. The government is required to prove beyond any reasonable doubt that companies colluded in order to fix prices or divide up the market. The government must also prove that the actions of companies unduly lessened competition. These changes make convictions more difficult to achieve. If the legislation were to be placed under civil law instead of criminal law, it would be more effective in preserving competition in the marketplace.

To be effective, competition law should cover areas not currently covered. One area is agriculture. Marketing boards have the legal authority to fix prices, set quotas, and basically to divide up the market. These practices are illegal in all segments of our economy and many economists argue that they should be illegal in agriculture as well. Trade unions and professional organizations are also exempt from competition law. In some instances these groups have been able to restrict entry into their occupation with the effect of keeping the price for their services high. Often these groups argue that restrictions on entry into their area are necessary for public safety and protection. Further discussion of the effects of unions on labour markets is contained in Chapter 14. Crown corporations also need to be covered in the legislation because many of these corporations compete with private corporations in the marketplace.

The Competition Act is federal government legislation prohibiting business practices that unduly restrict competition.

Changes to Canada's competition law were passed in June 1986. The new act is known as the **Competition Act.** The purpose of the Act is to maintain and encourage competition in Canada in order to:

— promote the efficiency and adaptability of the Canadian economy;
— expand opportunities for Canadian participation in world markets while at the same time recognizing the role of foreign competition in Canada;
— ensure that small and medium-sized enterprises have an equitable opportunity to participate in the Canadian economy; and
— provide consumers with competitive prices and product choices.

The major changes from the previous legislation are in the area of mergers and acquisitions. Companies are now required to notify the government before large mergers and acquisitions take place. The new law also gives the competition regulatory authorities a say in bank mergers in addition to the role of the minister of finance in this area. Under the old legislation, mergers were illegal if they were proven to be detrimental to the public interest. Under the new legislation, mergers are illegal if they have substantially lessened competition. The interpretation of the word "substantial" will be very important in these situations. It is not certain if the regulatory authorities will review and consider the competition that continues to exist after the merger in determining whether or not the merger was illegal.

Two other significant changes were introduced under the Competition Act. The old criminal-law standard was replaced with a new civil-law review. A competition tribunal is to be established to replace the courts in the adjudication process. This should speed up the decision-making process. In 1990, the constitutionality of the Competition Act was challenged. A Federal Court of Appeal stripped the tribunal of the power to enforce its own orders. A Quebec Superior Court justice ruled the tribunal unconstitutional because its members do not meet the test of impartiality demanded of judges. In April 1991, the Nova Scotia Court of Appeal reversed a lower court decision and found the Competition Act to be constitutional. Ultimately, the debate over the constitutionality of this act will be decided by the Supreme Court of Canada.

Many Differentiated Sellers

In this type of competitive situation, there is a relatively large number of sellers. As with an oligopolistic structure, the exact number of sellers is difficult to determine. The large number of firms makes it difficult for any collusion to take place on prices. In fact, it can be assumed that the firms in the industry make price and output decisions without regard to the reactions of other firms. Entry into the industry is relatively easy, as is evidenced by the large number of firms. Industries characterized by many differentiated sellers have low concentration ratios.

Each seller offers a similar, yet not identical, product. The products may be differentiated in any number of ways. The differences may be real or simply imagined on the part of the consumer. For example, a consumer may believe one shirt to be of better quality than another, even though their construction is identical. These imagined differences are often created in the mind of the consumer by such things as brand names, trade marks, and advertising.

For other products a real difference may be present: the workmanship, design, materials, and quality of the products could differ. The location of a store or outlet may be another difference. This could be the only advantage that many firms have over other firms. Another difference in products could be the availability of credit. If one store permits payments over time, it may have an advantage over one insisting on cash.

What is the significance of the fact that product differentiation exists? It means that firms have some control over the price of their product. In perfect competition, because of identical products, each firm is forced to accept the market price. In an atmosphere of many differentiated sellers, *product distinction allows for price variation:* in fact, the more that a firm is able to distinguish its products from its competitors, the more control it will have over price.

The second feature of a differentiated market is that there is room for non-price competition. Firms may offer better service or product warranties, or they may get involved in advertising their product.

As with other types of competition, firms in industries characterized by many differentiated sellers will try to maximize profits. This will require that they produce a level of output where marginal cost (MC) is equal to marginal revenue (MR).

We can assume that the short-run cost structure of the firm is similar to other firms. What does the revenue side look like? The demand curve for a firm under these competitive conditions is very elastic. The more substitutes for the product, the more elastic the curve is likely to be. The profit-maximizing position of the firm is shown in figure 13.5.

The diagram is similar to that of a monopoly. The basic difference is the shape of the demand and marginal revenue curves.

Figure 13.5
Profit maximization
for a firm in many
differentiated
sellers

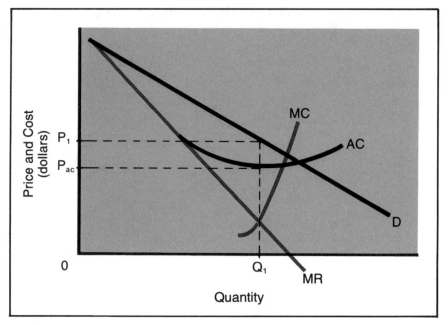

In order to maximize profits, the firm produces a quantity of output (Q_1) where marginal revenue (MR) and marginal cost (MC) are equal. The profit-maximizing price is P_1. In the diagram above, economic profits are being made, since the price (P_1) is greater than the average cost of production (P_{ac}).

The curve is more elastic than that of a monopoly. By equating **MC** and **MR,** the firm will maximize profits. This will occur at a price of **P_1** and a level of output of **Q_1.** In our diagram the firm is making an economic profit since **P_1** is greater than the average cost of production (**P_{ac}**). If economic profits are being earned in the industry, new firms are likely to enter. In this competitive society, there are relatively few barriers to the entry of new firms. As new firms enter, the demand curve for existing firms shifts to the left. The curve also becomes a little more elastic because there are now more competitors and more substitutes for the product. The shift to the left in the demand curve reduces the economic profits to the firm. In fact, as long as economic profits are being made, new firms will enter. The tendency in this industry is for firms to break even in the long run.

　　Even though there is a tendency to break even, some firms may continue to make economic profits, if they can sufficiently differentiate their product from that of their competitors. This differentiation can result from better quality, better styling, or simply better location. It may be hard to compete away the profits earned as a result of superior location.

13.9 Would you expect the demand curve for a firm in this type of competition to be elastic or inelastic? Why?

Non-Price Competition

In order to further differentiate its products from those of its competitors, a firm is likely to resort to various types of non-price competition. Improvements in product quality and design may be undertaken in order to improve the firm's position in the market. Some changes in the product may be simply in packaging. The main type of non-price competition is *advertising*. In addition to providing information, advertising may try to persuade the consumer to buy the product. From an economic point of view, is advertising beneficial to society?

Advantages

The primary advantage of advertising is that it provides *information* to the consumer. As indicated in Chapter 3, better information allows the market system to function more effectively. Advertising can inform a consumer about the ingredients in a product, its safety features, and other favourable attributes. Since fuel efficiency is more important to consumers than it used to be, automobile manufacturers have included kilometres per litre in their product promotion.

Advertising also helps in supporting our communications industry. It pays for television and radio programs as well as for a major part of our newspapers and magazines. In the case of the latter two products, the consumer does pay for part of the product. However, this amount is less than it would be in the absence of advertising.

Some argue that advertising may lead to lower-priced products. If advertising can convince consumers to spend money, the firm may be able to increase production. If economies of scale can be achieved, then lower costs will result and possibly lower prices. If advertising can keep up the level of consumer spending, then employment in the community will be at a higher level. If people are buying products, then workers are needed to produce the products. If foreign firms advertise, then domestic firms will also have to advertise in order to maintain sales. It can also be argued that jobs are created in the advertising business.

Finally, it can be argued that advertising leads to better quality products. In order to have successful advertising, it is necessary that the firm have something to advertise. The demands of advertising could stimulate product research and development.

Arguments against Advertising

The main argument against advertising is that it increases the cost of making and selling a product. This raises the price to the consumer. In spite of the claims that advertising informs the consumer, much advertising is solely aimed at persuading, not informing. Beer advertising provides a good example. Very little information is provided about the product. The ads simply show people having a good time and suggest that the consumer associate good times with the product.

Advertising support for the communications industry may not be a definite advantage. It may lead to some bias in reporting. If one company spends a great deal of advertising money at a radio station, the station may not report any negative stories about that company. It can be argued that advertising diverts resources away from more productive uses. Advertising expenditures do not result in the production of any goods or services, only the promotion of them. Advertising may lead to social costs, such as visual pollution in the form of billboards and neon lights.

Will advertising get the country out of a high unemployment situation by encouraging spending? Advertising tends to be *pro-cyclical* and not *counter-cyclical*. This means that companies traditionally increase their advertising spending in times of high economic activity and cut their spending in poor times. If advertising spending is lower in times of recession, then how can it stimulate employment?

Privately produced goods, such as television and automobiles, are advertised, whereas public goods such as hospitals and roads are not. Does the variation in the use of advertising distort people's ideas about the relative value of these products? Should government advertise these services and solicit funds?

Advertising may, under certain circumstances, be considered a barrier to entry into a market and thus help to reduce competition (see section on the beer oligopoly). If large companies in the industry have large advertising budgets, they may make it difficult for new firms to capture a sizable portion of the market.

13.10   From your point of view, what is the most important advantage of advertising? The major disadvantage?

Professional Advertising

At the present time, medical doctors in Canada are prohibited from advertising such items as their hours of work, whether they participate in medicare, or whether they make house calls. One of the advantages of advertising is that consumers are provided with information. This prohibition of medical advertising denies the consumer access to information. It also reduces competition in this business.

Doctors can list their specialty (ophthalmology, obstetrics, etc.) in the telephone book. This kind of listing does not provide the consumer with enough information to help in selecting a physician. For example, does the doctor believe in preventive medicine? Does the doctor have experience in sports injuries? Recent immigrants may be interested in whether the doctor speaks a foreign language. None of this information is readily available.

Traditionally the medical profession has refused to allow advertising because it is not considered professional. There is a belief that through advertising, doctors would be promoting themselves rather than the service that they provide. By promoting their own virtues, there may be the suggestion that other practitioners are not qualified.

If some doctors were to advertise, others might have to follow suit in order to compete. As a result of incurring increased expenses, doctors might demand higher fees or might reduce the quality of their service. Others argue that if professionals like doctors were allowed to advertise, a spirit of competition would replace that of co-operation in the profession. Intellectual discussions and exchanges of information would be reduced. The profession, as well as the consumers, would suffer.

Despite the negative attitude toward advertising in the medical profession, the consumer may reap some benefits from advertising by physicians. If consumers are aware of the special expertise of individual physicians, they can make a better-informed choice about medical care.

Questions

1 In your opinion should physicians be allowed to advertise? Explain.
2 If physicians were allowed to advertise, what type of advertisements would they use? What media would they use?
3 Would the availability of advertising allow "quacks" to set up practice? Would it permit good doctors more public exposure?

The Function of Profits

The discussion of *pricing behaviour* in this chapter sheds some light on the function of profits in our economy. Profits represent the excess of a firm's revenue over its costs. In one sense, profits are a return to the firm for the effort put forth in producing and selling a product or service. In the case of a sole proprietorship, any economic profit goes to the individual owner. In the case of a limited company, the shareholders are the recipients of profits. It is not necessarily true, however, that the shareholders receive all of the economic profit that a firm earns. Corporate income taxes, both federal and provincial, are based on profit. Much of the remaining profit after taxes is used for business investment. In order to remain competitive, it is necessary for businesses to purchase improved machinery and facilities. The existence of economic profit allows a firm to undertake the research and development of new products.

From an economist's point of view, profits are more than simply a return to the owners of the business. *Profits serve as a signal in the determination of what goods and services Canadians should produce.* If firms in an industry are earning an economic profit, the industry is likely to attract new competitors. The entrance of new firms will reduce the economic profit of existing firms. The existence of an economic profit in an industry indicates that consumers are interested in purchasing this product or service. If new firms enter the industry and survive, it will be because consumers continue to want this product. If firms in an industry are not earning an economic profit, new firms are not attracted to the industry. Also, existing firms will drop out of the industry. The supply of this product on the market will decrease.

Can profits be too high or too low? If the industry is competitive and new firms are free to enter, then it cannot be said that profits are too high or too low. If they are too high, new firms will enter the industry. If profits are not high, then new firms will not be anxious to enter the industry. The existence of profits provides a signal that consumers value this product and want more of it to be produced.

If there are significant barriers to the entry of new firms, then economic profits will not be competed away. For example, one firm may have taken out a patent on a new product. While the patent is in effect, it is illegal for others to produce the product.

In a case like this, the firm with the patent may continue to earn economic profits over a long period of time. If this firm is earning economic profits, there will be an incentive for others to develop products of their own. The consumer will benefit from improved products and more choice in the marketplace. The toughest barriers to break down in entering an industry are imposed by government. In industries, some firms have continued to earn economic profits as a result of government barriers that reduce competition.

13.11   What role do profits play in our economy?

Summary

Imperfect competition refers to a competitive situation in which each firm has some control over the price of the product that it produces. The demand curve for each firm in the circumstances of imperfect competition is downward sloping to the right. In order to sell more output, the firm has to lower the price to all buyers.

An industry in which there is only one seller is referred to as a monopoly. The barriers to entering the monopoly industry are substantial enough to prevent the entry of new firms. These barriers include government legislation, patents, economies of scale, and ownership of raw materials. The presence of barriers to entry ensures that a monopoly that is earning economic profits will continue to do so.

In order to maximize profits, the monopoly produces a level of output at which marginal revenue is equal to marginal cost. At this level of output, the monopoly is producing less than the socially desirable amount. In order to improve the allocation of resources, government often steps in to regulate the price that the monopoly can charge. This can be done through socially optimum pricing or fair-return pricing. Whichever method is selected, the consumer receives more of the product for a lower price.

In an oligopoly, there are a few sellers of an identical or a differentiated product. The presence of only a few sellers in these industries attests to the fact that there are also strong barriers to entry, as is the case with monopoly. Each firm in an oligopolistic setting has to be concerned about the possible reaction of its competitors to any change in its price. The inability to predict the reaction of competitors means that the construction of a demand curve for an oligopolistic firm is very difficult. One attempt to construct a demand curve is demonstrated by the kinked demand curve. This curve is composed of an elastic portion and an inelastic portion, separated by a kink. The curve is drawn under the assumption that other firms do not follow a price increase but do follow a price decrease.

In order to reduce the level of uncertainty in their industry, firms in an oligopoly may collude on prices and output. Any agreement aimed at fixing prices is illegal in Canada under the Competition Act. Other illegal activities under this act include retail price maintenance, misleading advertising, price discrimination, predatory price cutting, and mergers that would unduly lessen competition.

In the many differentiated sellers situation, there is a relatively large number of sellers. Each firm offers a similar yet differentiated product. Since entry into the industry is relatively easy, new firms will start up whenever economic profits are present. The entry of new firms reduces the economic profit of existing firms and in the long run, firms tend to break even.

Advertising is used as a means of competition in situations of oligopoly and of many differentiated sellers. From an economic point of view, there are several disadvantages to advertising. The main advantage is that it provides information and promotes the more efficient functioning of markets. The main disadvantage is that it leads to higher product costs.

Questions for Review and Discussion

1 Explain why different prices for the same meal at lunch-time and at dinner-time is an example of price discrimination. Does this situation meet the conditions necessary for price discrimination?

2 The CRTC grants cable television companies a monopoly in a specific geographic area. How much profit should cable television firms be allowed to make?

3 The major difference between many differentiated sellers and perfect competition is that in the former type of competition, the products are differentiated. Are differentiated products a benefit to society?

4 Would you want hospitals to advertise? Why or why not?

5 Why might it be tempting for firms in an oligopolistic setting to collude on prices?

6 Explain how the easy entry into an industry of many differentiated sellers affects the elasticity of the demand curve that each firm has to deal with.

7 Pharmaceutical manufacturers want the term of a patent on new drugs extended so that the inventor and developer of a new drug will have the exclusive rights to manufacture and sell that drug for a longer period of time. If the term of the patent is extended, what impact may there be on the price of new drugs? Will there be more incentive for pharmaceutical companies to develop new drugs? Explain.

8 Firms in an oligopolistic situation have advertising expenditure as a larger percentage of their products' selling price than do firms in other types of competition. Explain why this is so.

9 The primary difference between perfect competition and many differentiated sellers is the product differentiation that exists in the latter. What implications does this have (i) for the firm's ability to set the price of the product, and (ii) for the firm's need to use non-price competition?

10 During the 1970s, oil prices increased substantially. Much of the credit for these increases was attributed to OPEC, the oil cartel. What conditions must be present in order for a cartel to be successful? Why did oil prices start to fall in the early 1980s? Relate your answer to the success of OPEC as a cartel.

11 The kinked demand curve is an attempt to explain the demand curve for a firm in an oligopolistic situation. Explain the assumptions behind the curve. What are some of the drawbacks in using this curve to explain oligopolistic behaviour?

12 Is it possible for a monopoly to lose money? If so, use a graph to describe this situation.

13 What do we mean by saying that advertising expenditures are pro-cyclical rather than counter-cyclical?

14 Does the kinked demand curve help explain why price wars occur in oligopolies?

15 Restrictions on advertising are being lifted for veterinarians. What form of advertising are veterinary clinics likely to use? Will this lead to increased competition among clinics?

16 During the recession year of 1990, Canadian hotels offered lower room rates to attract customers. One hotel executive was quoted as saying that his hotel chain did not want any rooms to remain empty. In light of your knowledge of costs and pricing, what is the lowest rate that a hotel could offer a customer?

17 In response to lower maple syrup prices, Quebec producers have discussed a supply management system for maple syrup. Would Quebec maple-syrup producers be successful in establishing a cartel? Discuss.

18 The New Democratic Party of Ontario has stated its intention to introduce government-owned car insurance in the province. The objective is to lower car-insurance premiums and to ensure access to fair settlement of claims. At present, there are 80 companies selling car insurance in Ontario. Is it possible for these companies to form a cartel in order to increase car-insurance premiums? Discuss.

Suggested Readings

Armstrong, Donald. *Competition Versus Monopoly: Combines Policy in Perspective.* Vancouver: Fraser Institute 1982.

Consumer and Corporate Affairs Canada. Annual Reports of the Director of Investigation and Research, Competition Act.

Enrico, Roger and Jesse Kornbluth. *The Other Guy Blinked: How Pepsi Won the Cola Wars.* New York: Bantam Books 1986.

Green, Christopher. *Canadian Industrial Organization and Policy.* Second Edition. Toronto: McGraw-Hill Ryerson 1985.

Hunter, Nicholas. "Hard for small to survive in brewing." *The Globe and Mail,* 31 May 1982.

Moskowitz, Milton; Michael Katz; and Robert Levering (eds.). *Everybody's Business: An Almanac.* New York: Harper and Row 1980.

Oliver, Thomas. *The Real Coke, The Real Story.* New York: Penguin Books 1986.

Rohmer, Richard. *E. P. Taylor: The Biography of Edward Plunket Taylor.* Toronto: McClelland and Stewart 1978.

Chapter 14

The Pricing of Resources

Chapter Objectives

After successfully completing this chapter, you will be able to:

- graph and describe both the value-of-marginal-product curve and the marginal-revenue-product curve
- discuss the factors that will cause the demand curve for labour to shift
- discuss the determinants of the elasticity of demand for labour
- describe graphically how wages are determined
- describe union attempts to increase wages
- discuss the various barriers to labour-market mobility
- define equalizing differences

Key Terms

derived demand
value of marginal product
marginal-revenue product
marginal-resource cost
featherbedding
craft unions
industrial unions
collective bargaining

certification
bargaining unit
arbitration
equalizing differences
economic rent
transfer earnings
present value

Analysing Resource Markets

In Chapter 5, we introduced the concept of the circular flow of income (figure 5.1). The upper loop of the diagram illustrated the product markets. In these markets, households exchange money for a variety of goods and services. Households represent the demand side of the market and businesses represent the supply side. The lower loop of the diagram showed the resource markets. In these markets, businesses purchase the resources necessary for manufacturing a product or supplying a service. In the lower loop of the circular flow, households represent the supply side of the market and businesses represent the demand side. Up to this point in the text, our focus has been on the product markets. In this chapter, we will analyse the *resource markets*.

Resources: Demand and Supply

In our analysis of resource markets, we should first review the demand side of these markets. Since the easiest resource to relate to is labour, let us initially focus our discussion on the demand for labour. However, the theory developed in this section also applies to the markets for the other resources—land and capital.

The Demand for Labour

Derived demand is the demand for a resource based on the demand for the good or service that the resource helps to produce.

The primary feature of the demand for any resource is that it is **derived demand,** that is, the demand for the resource depends on the demand for the final product that the resource is used to produce. For example, the demand for automobile workers depends on the demand for cars. The demand for construction workers depends on the demand for new buildings. The demand for other resources such as uranium, nickel, zinc, and fertile land depends on the demand for the final products that these resources are used to produce.

The demand for each resource also depends on the *productivity* of that resource. The term "productivity" was introduced in Chapter 11. It refers to the amount of the final product that the resource can produce. Productivity depends on a number of factors. In the case of labour, it depends on education and training, management techniques, and the quality of other resources with which labour works. In the short run, labour productivity also depends on the law of diminishing returns. As more and more workers are hired in the short run, each successive worker has less and less capital to work with. Thus, the productivity of each additional worker is less than the productivity of the preceding worker.

The relationship between a firm's production function and the law of diminishing returns was first introduced in Chapter 11. Table 11.1 related the number of workers to the number of chairs that could be produced in a day. The productivity of labour is shown in the table: the productivity of each worker is represented by the *marginal product* of labour. After a certain point, the addition to total output (the marginal product) brought on by hiring one more worker becomes less and less. This is because each additional worker has less and less of the fixed resources to work with.

The value of marginal product is an increase in total revenue resulting from employing one more unit of a productive resource in a perfectly competitive industry.

Since each successive worker starts to contribute less than the previous worker to the total output, each successive worker brings in less value to the company. In fact, if we know the price that chairs will sell for, we can calculate the value of the additional output that each worker contributes to the firm. Assume that each chair sells for $20. The value that each worker adds to the firm is referred to as the **value of marginal product** and can be determined by multiplying $20 times the marginal product associated with that worker.

value of marginal product (VMP) = price x marginal product

Using the data presented in table 11.2, we can calculate the value of the marginal product for each worker. This information is presented in table 14.1, and plotted in figure 14.1.

Table 14.1 / Value of marginal product, Pinewood Furniture Company

No. of workers	Total no. of chairs produced per day	Marginal product	Value of marginal product ($20 x marginal product)
0	0		
1	5	5	$100
2	13	8	$160
3	22	9	$180
4	30	8	$160
5	37	7	$140
6	43	6	$120
7	48	5	$100
8	52	4	$80
9	54	2	$40
10	55	1	$20
11	55	0	$0
12	54	-1	$-20

The value-of-marginal-product (**VMP**) curve represents the demand curve for labour in a situation in which the price of the chairs does not change as more chairs are sold. In other words, in the situation of perfect competition, the VMP curve is the demand curve for workers. Why is it the demand curve?

**Figure 14.1
The value-of-
marginal product
curve**

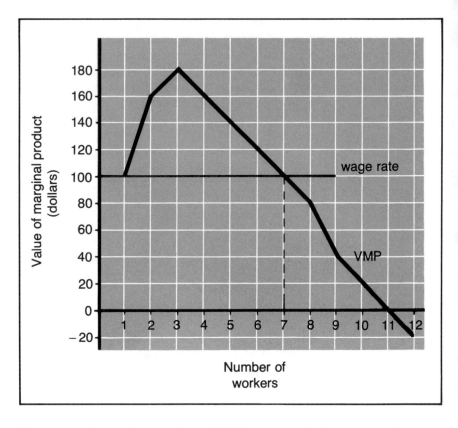

The value of marginal product (**VMP**) represents the demand curve for a certain type of worker. The number of workers hired depends on the intersection of the wage rate and the VMP curve.

A demand curve indicates what quantity of a certain product will be demanded at all possible prices. Assume that the price of labour, or the wage rate, is $100 per day. How many workers would the firm be willing to hire at this wage rate? The answer is seven. The firm would not hire the eighth worker since that worker contributes only $80 worth of output, while being paid $100. As long as the value of the marginal product exceeds the wage rate, the worker would be hired. If the wage rate were to change, the company would equate the wage rate with the value of the marginal product in determining how many workers should be hired.

For example, if the wage rate were to increase to $140 per day, only five workers would be hired. Because the number of workers hired depends on the VMP, this curve represents the demand curve for this type of worker.

A firm in perfect competition will hire workers to the point at which

wage rate = value of marginal product

This assumes that the wage rate remains the same for each worker regardless of how many workers are hired.

If the firm operates in an imperfectly competitive market, then a change has to be made in the derivation of the demand curve for labour. In an imperfectly competitive market, the demand curve for the product produced by each firm slopes down to the right. In order to increase sales, the firm has to lower the price. The contribution that each worker makes to the firm cannot be determined by multiplying the price by the marginal product, since the price is constantly changing as more of the product is sold. Instead, the marginal product of the worker is multiplied by the marginal revenue received from the sale of the additional output that the worker produces. This is called the **marginal-revenue product (MRP).**

Marginal-revenue product (MRP) is the increase in total revenue as a result of employing one more unit of a productive resource (MP x MR).

marginal-revenue product = marginal revenue x marginal product

The MRP curve represents the demand curve for labour for an imperfectly competitive firm. If an imperfect competitor is interested in maximizing profits, then the firm will hire workers up to the point at which

wage rate = marginal-revenue product

The VMP and MRP curves represent the demand curve for a certain type of worker for a single firm. In order to determine the overall demand curve for this type of labour, it is necessary to add up the demand curves of each individual firm. This is referred to as the *market demand curve.* In most cases, a given firm will have more than one demand curve for labour; there would be a different demand curve for each type of worker hired, because the productivity of different types of workers varies.

14.1 What does the value of the marginal product represent? How do you calculate it?

14.2 Why does the value of the marginal product represent the demand curve for labour for a firm in perfect competition?

Changes in the Demand for Labour

What will cause the demand curve for labour to shift? In Chapter 2, demand curves were drawn assuming that the other factors influencing demand remained unchanged. The same holds true when drawing the demand curve for labour. If these factors change, then the demand for labour will also change. What factors are held constant in drawing the demand curve for labour?

The first factor held constant is the *price* of the product that the worker helps to produce. If the price of the product changes, then the demand for labour will change as well. For example, assume that there was an increase in the demand for solar-heating units for houses. This would increase the price of these units in the market-place. The increased demand and price for solar-heating units would increase the demand for workers needed to manufacture and install these units. The demand for labour is derived directly from the demand for product.

Second, changes in the *productivity* of the worker will cause the demand for these workers to change and the marginal-product curve to shift. Since the demand curve for labour is derived by multiplying the marginal product of the worker by the marginal revenue, any change in the marginal product will cause the demand curve to shift. As workers become more productive, the demand for their services will increase. What would cause the productivity of labour to increase? Changes in productivity were discussed in Chapter 11; they are often associated with the equipment that the worker uses. For example, the introduction of word-processing equipment has made secretaries more productive. Alterations to documents and manuscripts can be made more easily and quickly on a word processor than on a typewriter. Changes in productivity can also come from improvements in the quality of the worker. Additional education and training allow workers to increase their output of goods and services. The more a worker can produce, the more the worker is in demand.

A third factor that could influence the demand for labour is a change in the price of a resource that is used along with labour, or that is a substitute for labour. In many situations, labour and another resource are complementary. For example, jewellery-makers use gold, silver, and precious stones in their craft. If the price of gold or silver increases, it will affect the price of the jewellery. As a result of increases in the price of jewellery, consumers may decide to re-duce the quantity they wish to buy (demand). This decision will have an impact on the demand for jewellery workers, and fewer workers will be needed. A change in the price of a complementary re-source will therefore cause a shift in the demand for labour.

In other situations, resources may be substitutes for each other. The introduction of robots in some manufacturing establishments is an example of machinery being substituted for workers. If the price of machinery is attractive, companies could be encouraged to substi-tute machines for workers. A reduction in the price of a substitute re-source shifts the demand curve for labour to the left. The introduction of new machinery may not always result in a reduced demand for la-bour. The new machinery may help reduce production costs and, therefore, reduce the selling price of the product. If prices are reduced, the quantity demanded of the product will increase, and the demand for workers will increase as well.

14.3 Show the impact on the demand for labour of the following:
  i   a decrease in the demand for cars on the demand for auto-mobile workers
  ii a sharp increase in the price of paint on the demand for painters and decorators
  iii the introduction of do-it-yourself medical diagnostic kits on the demand for doctors

14.4 What causes the productivity of labour to change?

Wage-Rate Determination

In order to determine the equilibrium wage rate for a certain type of worker, it is necessary to put the demand and supply sides of the market together. If the firm can hire as many workers as it needs at a constant wage rate, it will hire workers up to the point where the wage rate equals the value of marginal product (or marginal-revenue product). In this situation, the wage-rate line (see figure 14.1) becomes the labour supply curve for this firm in relation to that particular occupation. The supply curve is perfectly elastic, indicating that at this wage rate ($100 in figure 14.1), the supply of workers to the firm is virtually unlimited. In some cases, the firm may not be able to hire an unlimited number of workers at the same wage rate. In this situation, the supply curve for labour to the firm is upward sloping to the right, as shown in figure 14.2. There is a positive relationship between the wage rate and the quantity of workers supplied.

In order to attract workers, the firm may be forced to increase the wage rate. If it becomes necessary to increase wages in order to attract new workers, existing workers will want to receive the wage increases as well. Thus, the cost to the firm of hiring one more worker may be greater than the wage rate paid to that worker, as the firm will have to compensate existing employees. The extra cost of hiring one more worker is known as the **marginal-resource cost (MRC).**

Marginal-resource cost (MRC) is the addition to total cost as a result of adding one more unit of a productive resource.

An example may help the explanation of this process. Assume that the Direct Current Electric Company employs five electricians at a wage of $15 per hour. The company is interested in hiring an additional electrician, although there are no electricians in the local labour market who are unemployed. In order to attract an employee to the company, it will be necessary to increase the wage rate and hire the electrician away from another firm. Assume that $16 per hour is sufficient to attract a new employee.

What is the cost of hiring this employee? It is $16 per hour plus the money necessary to bring existing employees up to the new rate. Each of the five electricians will receive an additional $1 per hour. This brings the marginal-resource cost of hiring another electrician to $21 per hour. The determination of whether or not to hire this worker depends on the contribution that this worker can make to the firm (the marginal-revenue product). The company will hire the worker as long as the marginal-revenue product exceeds the marginal-resource cost.

A diagram representing the determination of wage rates under these conditions is shown in figure 14.2. If it is necessary to increase wages as more workers are hired, then the marginal-resource cost curve (**MRC**) will be upward sloping to the right. The firm will hire the number of workers represented by the intersection of the **MRP** and **MRC** curves, which is L_1 workers. Once it is determined that L_1 workers are to be hired, the wage rate is set by referring to the supply curve. As shown in figure 14.2, L_1 workers will be willing to work at this job for a wage rate of W_1.

A short numerical example helps to explain the shape of the marginal-resource cost curve. In table 14.2, the supply schedule for a certain type of worker appears in the first two columns. As the wage rate increases, the number of workers supplied to the market increases as well. The total-resource cost column shows the cost to the firm of hiring workers at that wage rate. The marginal-resource cost represents the addition to total-resource cost of hiring one more worker. Notice that the marginal-resource cost is greater than the wage rate in every case.

Table 14.2 / Derivation of the marginal-resource cost curve

Wage rate (dollars per hour)	Number of workers supplied	Total resource cost (dollars)	Marginal resource cost (dollars)
15	5	75	
16	6	96	21
17	7	119	23
18	8	144	25
19	9	171	27
20	10	200	29

14.5 Why is the marginal-resource cost (MRC) of hiring one more worker not always equal to the wage rate paid to that worker?

Equilibrium in the Labour Market

The sum of all the marginal-revenue-product curves for all the firms that require a certain type of labour is known as the market demand curve for that occupation. The interaction of the market demand curve and the market supply curve determines the equilibrium wage rate for the occupation (see figure 14.3). Any factors that result in a

**Figure 14.2
Wage-rate
determination in
the firm**

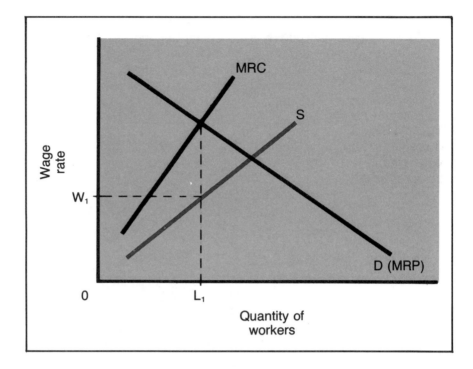

The number of workers hired (L_1) is determined by the intersection of the marginal-resource cost (**MRC**) and the marginal-revenue-product (**MRP**) curves. The wage rate paid to these workers is determined by reference to the supply curve.

shift of the firm's MRP curve will cause the market demand curve for the occupation to shift as well. For example, an increase in the demand for the final product will cause the demand for the labour required to make that product to shift to the right. Any change in worker productivity will also shift the demand curve for labour.

An introduction to the supply of labour appeared in Chapter 5. The Labour Force Survey calculates the *participation rate,* as well as the unemployment rate, on a monthly basis. The participation rate is defined as the percentage of the population who are in the labour force—in other words, the percentage of the population who either have a job or would like to have a job. A detailed discussion of changes in Canada's participation rate appeared in Chapter 5.

In this chapter, we are concerned not about the overall supply of labour, but about the supply of labour to a specific job. The short-run supply of labour identifies the quantity of labour that will be offered to a specific job, depending on the wage rate. In general, the higher the wage rate, the greater the number of people who would be willing to do the job. At very low wage rates, the number of workers willing to do a job is also low. Their time could be better spent working at another job or participating in a leisure activity. As the wage rate increases, the number of workers willing to do the job increases as well. The opportunity cost of not working at this job increases along with the wage rate. The supply curve for workers to most jobs, therefore, is upward sloping to the right (line **S** in figure 14.3).

**Figure 14.3
The equilibrium
wage rate in the
labour market**

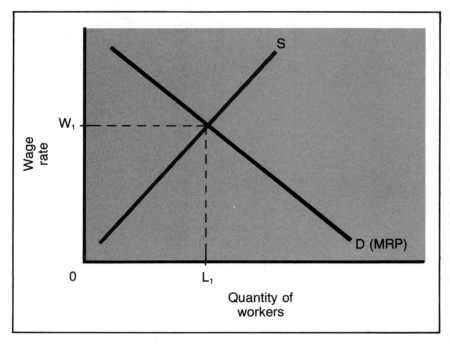

The equilibrium wage rate for a certain type of worker (W_1) is found at the intersection of the demand and supply curves.

Any change in the demand for, or the supply of, labour will result in a new equilibrium wage rate. If the demand for a certain type of labour increases, then the wage rate will increase as well. If the supply of a certain type of labour increases, everything else remaining the same, then the wage rate will fall. It should be remembered that the demand and supply curves in figure 14.3 are *market curves*. That is, they represent the total demand for this type of worker and the total supply of workers available.

**The Elasticity of
Demand for
Labour**

The price elasticity of demand for consumer products, introduced in Chapter 2, is an important concept in the study of markets. The price elasticity of demand indicates exactly how consumers respond to price changes in terms of the quantity that they are willing to buy. The price elasticity of demand for labour is also important in a discussion of resource markets. The more elastic the demand for labour, the more it is likely that employers will respond to changes in wage rates in terms of the number of workers demanded. If the demand for labour is elastic, then a reduction in the wage rate will substantially increase the number of workers demanded. An increase in the wage rate will significantly reduce the number of workers hired. Conversely, if the demand for labour is relatively inelastic, then changes in the wage rate will not affect the quantity of labour demanded to any great extent.

Knowledge of the elasticity of demand for labour is an important aspect in union/management negotiations. If the demand for labour is inelastic, union leaders will be anxious to achieve substantial wage increases for their members. Large wage increases will not greatly reduce the demand for union workers. In contrast, if the demand for labour is elastic, then wage increases may result in reduced employment for union members. The possibility of high unemployment among union members may temper the demand for wage increases. The elasticity of demand for workers clearly influences union demands when bargaining with management.

The government has similar concerns about the elasticity of demand for labour when contemplating minimum-wage increases. Minimum-wage increases will result in a greater decrease in employment if the demand for labour is elastic. That is, the higher the minimum-wage rate, the fewer workers employers will be likely to hire. Increases in the legal minimum wage are meant to be a benefit for workers. Yet if these increases lead to many workers losing their jobs, the increase will have negative rather than beneficial results.

What determines the elasticity of demand for labour? First, it depends on the elasticity of demand for the product that labour produces. *The more elastic the demand for the product, the more elastic the demand for the workers.* If consumers respond to price increases by substantially reducing the quantity of the product demanded, then employers will be forced to reduce their demand for workers when faced with wage increases. For example, the demand for airline tickets is elastic. If the price of airline tickets were to rise, the quantity of tickets demanded would decrease significantly, which would cause a decrease in the number of airline employees required. Since an increase in wages paid to airline employees will lead to an increase in airline ticket prices, the company has to be concerned about the size of the wage increase granted. A sizable wage increase may lead to reduction in staff in order to keep costs, and ultimately prices, down.

Second, elasticity depends on the number of substitutes for labour. If there are few substitutes, the demand is inelastic. If there are several substitutes, the demand tends to be elastic. Where substitutes are available, employers can substitute for workers when faced with wage increases. For example, robots that can paint a car on the production line are now available. If the wages paid to workers on the line increase, it may make more sense economically for the company to use robots instead of workers.

Third, the elasticity of demand for labour depends on the percentage of total costs that labour costs comprise. If labour costs represent only a small portion of total costs, then the demand for labour will be inelastic. Wage increases may not greatly affect the firm's total costs and as a result, wage increases may not affect employment. If labour costs are a large portion of total costs, firms will be forced to respond to wage increases by reducing the number of workers employed. Under these conditions, the demand for labour is elastic. The final condition influencing the elasticity of demand for labour is the shape of the marginal-product curve. This curve shows how fast the productivity of each successive worker declines. If the productivity of each successive worker declines rapidly as new workers are hired, then the demand for labour is likely to be inelastic. If the productivity of each successive worker declines slowly as new employees are hired, the demand for labour is likely to be elastic. In the first case, the marginal-product curve has a steep slope and in the second case, it has a gradual slope.

14.6 Why is some idea of the elasticity of demand for labour important in union/management negotiations?

The Impact of Labour Unions on Wage Rates

One of the main objectives that workers have in joining labour unions is to increase wages. If a union is to be successful at increasing wages, it has the option of trying to increase the demand for its members, or of trying to restrict the supply of workers who can do the job. Let us first analyse the attempts by unions to increase the demand for labour.

Increasing the Demand for Labour

The demand for labour is derived from the demand for the product and the productivity of the worker. If the labour union is to increase the demand for workers, it must increase either of these two factors. Workers do not usually promote the products that they produce. Such promoting is left up to the employer. Yet if unions can increase the demand for the products that they produce, the demand for their services will increase. If the demand for their services increases, the wage rate will increase as well. The International Ladies Garment Workers' Union is one labour organization that has tried to promote the sales of domestically produced women's clothes. This union has advertised on television and has set up booths at shows and exhibitions. The United Automobile Workers has also tried to promote the purchase of domestically produced cars. The union has paid for billboards in some Ontario cities with the slogan "Buy the Cars that Your Neighbours Help to Build."

Featherbedding refers to practices or work rules that may set unreasonable limits on the amount of work employees may perform in a given period of time, or may result in payment for unneeded workers doing jobs that duplicate others' efforts.

There are other ways whereby unions can increase the demand for labour. They can press the federal government to introduce tariffs and quotas on imports. The introduction of these trade barriers should increase the demand for domestically produced goods. Labour unions may also negotiate make-work projects with employers. This procedure, known as **featherbedding,** retains jobs for workers whose jobs have become redundant. Featherbedding, used mainly in the construction and railway industries, maintains the demand for labour, rather than increases it. Still, featherbedding prevents a drop in wages for certain groups of workers.

Labour unions can also take steps to increase the productivity of workers. This effect can be accomplished by providing training and skill development for union members. Encouraging management to introduce better machinery and equipment may also improve productivity. Increases in productivity will lead to increases in the demand for workers.

Influencing the Supply of Labour

A trade union whose members all possess a particular skill is called a craft union.

A trade union that attempts to organize all the workers in a particular industry is called an industrial union.

The ability of a labour union to influence the supply side of the labour market depends on the type of union in question. There are basically two types of unions: craft and industrial. **Craft unions** are made up of workers who have a common skill or craft. Examples of craft unions are the electricians, the plumbers, and the printers. **Industrial unions** organize workers by industry; e.g., automobile, steel, chemical. Members of industrial unions include all workers in the industry, including unskilled, semi-skilled, and skilled workers.

Craft labour unions try to increase the wages paid to their members by reducing the supply of labour. If they can cause the supply curve to shift to the left, the equilibrium wage rate will increase (see figure 14.4). How can unions reduce the supply of labour? This reduction can be accomplished by several means. The unions could press employers to hire only union members. They could insist on long apprenticeships for workers before they are qualified to work at the trade. Craft unions could press government for compulsory retirement programs, for restrictions on hours of work, and for tougher regulations on the immigration of workers.

Industrial unions are not in the same position as craft unions to reduce the supply of labour. They cannot insist on long apprenticeships since many of their members work at unskilled jobs that do not require apprenticeship training. It is also more difficult for industrial unions to restrict membership. In fact, industrial unions are interested in including all the workers in their industry in their membership. Industrial unions must increase wages by ensuring that no members agree to work for less than a certain minimum, or base, wage. In effect, the industrial union tries to establish a wage (price) floor. The setting of a price floor will only work if all members agree and are willing to go out on strike in order to achieve their goal. The difficulty

**Figure 14.4
Restricting the
supply of labour**

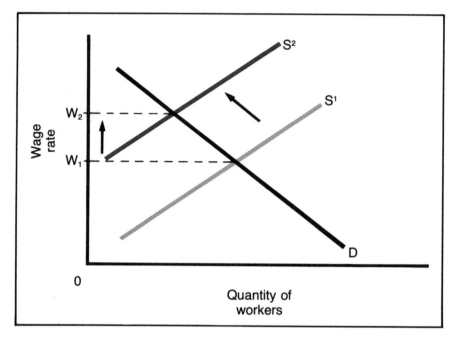

A decrease in the supply of labour from S^1 to S^2 increases the equilibrium wage rate from W_1 to W_2.

**Figure 14.5
Establishing a
minimum rate for
union members**

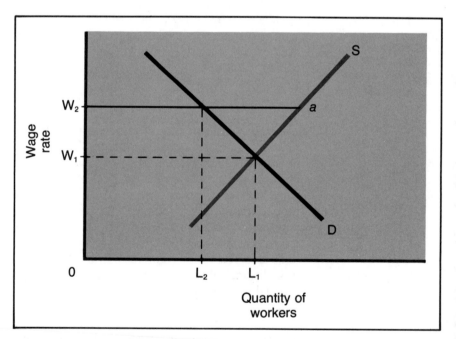

Industrial unions try to set a wage rate (W_2) above the existing equilibrium wage (W_1). This results in a decline in employment from L_1 to L_2.

with price floors is that unemployment results among some members (see Chapter 3). The greater the elasticity of demand for workers, the more likely it is that some workers will lose their jobs as a result of the wage increase.

The impact of an industrial union on wages and employment is shown in figure 14.5. The equilibrium wage rate before the union pushes for a wage increase is W_1. The number of workers hired at this wage is L_1. If the union insists on a minimum-wage rate of W_2, the number of workers hired will fall to L_2. The decline in employment will be greater the more elastic the demand curve. The establishment of a new base rate, W_2, means that a new supply curve for labour is created. The new supply curve is W_2aS, since no one can be employed for a wage below W_2.

14.7 How could trade unions increase the demand for the workers whom they represent?

14.8 How can craft unions restrict the number of members in the union?

Do Unions Raise Wages?

One of the reasons that workers join unions is to increase their hourly wage rate. Through collective action rather than individual action, workers hope to force the employer to pay higher wages. The threat of a strike hangs over the employer's head in the face of union wage demands.

Do unions in fact succeed in raising wages? The answer is not clear. Those who argue that unions do raise wages point to the wage differential that exists between union and non-union workers. Especially in the case of skilled jobs, workers who are union members have a higher hourly wage rate. Those who argue that unions do not raise wages point to the fact that union workers who are highly paid now were highly paid prior to joining the union. They argue that it is not the union but the industry that determines the wage rate. If the industry that employs the workers can afford to pay high wages, then the workers will receive them.

Some situations suggest that union membership is not a guarantee of high wages. In the face of industry problems, workers appear willing to forgo wage and benefit increases. In 1981, 12 unions representing 66 000 Conrail railway workers in the United States agreed to a three-year pay freeze. In the same year, workers at the Firestone Tire Company plant in Memphis agreed to forgo overtime pay on weekends. Employees at a major airline approved a 10 percent cut in wages for one year and a pay freeze for the next year. The United Automobile Workers and the Teamsters have also agreed to major benefit and wage reductions.

More recently, workers at such companies as H.J. Hines, Moore Business Forms, Denison Mines, and Siemens Automotive

Ltd., among others, accepted wage freezes or wage reductions in 1990. These workers were represented by some of the largest and most powerful unions in North America, including the United Steelworkers, the Canadian Autoworkers, and the Food and Commercial Workers unions.

Questions

1 If unions do raise wages, why did the employees of a major airline accept a pay cut?
2 What do you believe is the most important factor in the determination of wage rates?
3 If it was unlikely that a union would improve wage rates in a certain industry, why would workers still want to join a union?
4 What is the association between wage-rate increases or decreases and the elasticity of the demand for labour?

Collective Bargaining in Canada

Collective bargaining involves the negotiating of an employment contract between management and the union representing the employees.

Collective bargaining is the process whereby employees negotiate with an employer as a group, rather than individually, regarding the terms of their employment. Individuals acting alone have very little bargaining power in negotiations with an employer. When employees negotiate with an employer collectively, they are more likely to achieve improvements in working conditions. If a single employee walks away from his or her job because of a dispute over working conditions, the production process is not likely to be adversely affected. If all the employees of a company walk away from their jobs, production will cease.

Governments in Canada have tried to promote the process of collective bargaining between employees and their employers. Legislation requires that an employer negotiate with a certified trade union or group of employees. Legislation also permits compulsory union membership and the compulsory deduction of union dues from the employee's paycheque. Most employees in Canada are covered by provincial legislation in matters pertaining to collective bargaining. Employees in industries such as banking, communications, and transportation are covered by federal government legislation.

Certification

The process by which a labour union acquires the bargaining rights for a group of employees is called certification.

If an employer must negotiate with employees on a collective basis, it first must be determined that the employees want to negotiate their working conditions in this manner. It also has to be determined which employees at the company will be grouped together for bargaining purposes. This process is referred to as **certification.**

Employees who do not presently negotiate with their employer over working conditions, but who wish to do so, must determine if the majority of employees wants to bargain collectively. One procedure to follow is to ask employees to join a labour union. Those employees who want to join the union must sign a membership card and pay a small fee. If enough employees agree to join the union, the union can approach the Labour Relations Board about becoming the certified bargaining agent for the employees of this particular firm.

What number constitutes enough employees? It may be impossible to contact all the employees in the company. It may also be impossible to get all the employees to agree to union membership. In some provinces, when 45 percent of the employees have signed union cards, this percentage is sufficient evidence for holding a representation vote. If as many as 55 percent of the employees have signed union cards, the Labour Relations Board may declare that the union represents the employees and can approach the employer regarding negotiations about working conditions. If a vote is held, the union must get the support of just over 50 percent of the employees in order to represent the **bargaining unit** in negotiations.

A bargaining unit defines those jobs or positions represented in the collective agreement between the employer and the representative of the employees, the union.

What is the bargaining unit? Not all employees of a company are in the union and negotiate collectively with the employer. Persons in supervisory positions such as managers and forepersons are not in the bargaining unit. Security guards are not in the bargaining unit. Other employees such as student workers and part-time workers may be omitted. Office and plant employees are often in separate units and negotiate separately with the employer. Professional engineers often have their own bargaining unit. *The certification process determines which employees are in the bargaining unit.* The determination is made by the Labour Relations Board if the employer and the union cannot agree on the composition of the unit. The representation vote cannot be taken until the bargaining unit is established.

Negotiating a Collective Agreement

Once certified as the bargaining agent for the employees, the union must approach the employer about negotiating a contract of employment conditions. Although the employer must negotiate with the union, the employer does not have to agree to union demands in regard to working conditions. If agreement cannot be reached, a work stoppage may result in order to speed up the process of agreement. A strike occurs when the employees walk off the job in order to put pressure on the employer to accept their demands. A lockout occurs when the employer refuses to allow the employees to enter company premises until an agreement is reached.

The focus of Canada's collective-bargaining legislation has been to prevent work stoppages. In many jurisdictions a third party, brought in to attempt *conciliation,* is made available to assist both parties in achieving an agreement before a work stoppage takes place. The conciliator attempts to persuade both sides to soften their positions before a strike or lockout occurs. It is common for the legislation to insist that the conciliation procedure be exhausted before a work stoppage can occur. The term *mediation* is also used in connection with third-party intervention. Mediation is similar to conciliation.

Arbitration is a procedure whereby an independent third party settles disputes between union and management during the life of a collective agreement.

When the union and employer agree on a set of working conditions, a contract, or collective agreement, is drawn up. Once both sides have signed the agreement, they must adhere to its provisions. There cannot be a strike or a lockout during the term of agreement. Any disputes during the term of the agreement must be settled by **arbitration** if the parties cannot settle the agreement themselves.

Because all firms face different competitive conditions and have varying degrees of control over the price of their products, working conditions for their employees will also vary. Some companies operate in a monopoly situation. Others face tough competition from foreign competitors. The ability of labour unions to improve the working conditions for their members depends on the firm's ability to provide those conditions and still remain competitive.

Contents of Collective Agreements

Working conditions contained in collective agreements cannot conflict with minimum-employment standards contained in legislation. That is, if labour legislation sets a minimum wage of $5 per hour, the collective agreement cannot establish wages at less than $5 per hour. The agreement must also adhere to minimum standards concerning statutory holidays, vacations, hours of work, severance pay, and similar employment standards.

All employer/employee agreements contain three articles. The employer must recognize the union as the bargaining agent for employees in the bargaining unit. The bargaining unit is also defined. There must be no strike or lockout during the life of the agreement. Finally, the company and the union agree to settle any alleged violation of the agreement by arbitration. In the arbitration process, a neutral third party studies the agreement and makes a decision regarding the alleged violation.

Other articles included in collective agreements are:

Wages: this article sets out the rate of pay for each job covered by the agreement.

Hours of work: the standard hours of work, either on a daily or weekly basis, are specified.

Overtime pay provisions: the rate of pay for hours worked in excess of standard hours or for hours worked on a holiday is set out.

Vacations with pay: the amount of vacation with pay to which an employee is entitled is set out. In many agreements, the number of weeks of vacation may increase with the number of years of service.

Seniority: this article establishes the rules by which seniority is recorded. The years of service in the bargaining unit are referred to as an employee's seniority.

Grievance procedure: the procedure for settling alleged violations of the agreement. In most agreements there are several stages set out by which the dispute may be settled before it goes to arbitration.

Union security: this article defines the relationship between the union and the members of the bargaining unit. Under a closed-shop form of union security, the company agrees to hire and employ only members of the union. Under a union shop, all members of the bargaining unit must join the union. A Rand-formula shop requires that all members of the bargaining unit pay union dues whether or not they are union members.

Rights of management: the responsibilities of management are set out in this article. In most agreements, many decisions rest with management except those specifically given up in the agreement.

Glossary of Collective-Bargaining Terms

The following terms are also associated with the practice of collective bargaining in Canada.

accreditation: in the construction industry, employers may join an association in order to negotiate a collective agreement with a trade union. Accreditation of an employers' association as a bargaining agent is similar to certification of a labour union as a bargaining agent.

Canadian Labour Congress (CLC): the largest federation of independent unions in Canada. The CLC has been compared to a "union of unions."

COLA: cost-of-living allowance (or adjustment). An allowance paid, or an adjustment made, to wages set out in the collective agreement in order to compensate for increases in the Consumer Price Index.

contracting out: the practice of having certain stages in the production process or other work functions performed by outside contractors and not by members of the bargaining unit.

decertification: the process of decertification removes the rights of the bargaining agent for members of a bargaining unit from a labour union.

final-offer selection: this is a form of arbitration whereby the arbitrator selects either the company's last offer or the union's last proposal. One proposal only is selected in its entirety. The purpose of such a procedure is to force the parties to submit reasonable proposals.

ratification: the process by which members of the bargaining unit vote on and accept a proposed collective agreement.

unfair labour practices: acts undertaken by the company or the union to thwart the other party's attempt to bargain "in good faith." These include such activities as discriminating against an employee for engaging in union activity and interfering with an employee's right to join a union.

picketing: workers gather outside the plant or office and carry placards announcing that they are on strike.

secondary boycott: the union, during a strike, will try to put pressure on a third party in order to influence the company against which they are striking. The third party may be a supplier or a customer of the company.

Should Civil Servants Be Given the Right to Strike?

Civil servants are employees of the government. In some Canadian jurisdictions, government employees are not permitted to go on strike; in other jurisdictions they have been given the right to strike. Should civil servants be treated in a different manner from other employees in terms of the right to go on strike in order to press for improved working conditions?

There is one major difference between the collective-agreement negotiation process that takes place in the private sector and that which takes place in the public sector involving government employees. The difference concerns the ability of the employer to pay for any improvement in working conditions that the employees receive. In the private sector of our economy, an employer is constrained in presenting an offer to employees on working conditions by the realities of the marketplace. Any improvement in working conditions that increases costs must be translated into higher prices for the product or service. Can the company afford to raise prices? An increase in price may result in a loss of sales to a competitor or in a reduction of the quantity demanded by consumers. The ability of a company to raise the price will depend on the competitive environment that it faces.

In the public sector, ability to pay is not as much of a concern. Taxes can always be increased in order to pay for the improvement in employee working conditions. The federal government could borrow from the Bank of Canada in order to meet an increase in costs. Services provided by government are rarely in competition with similar services in the marketplace. It is less likely that business will be lost to a competitor. The government need not make a profit in order to continue to operate, and will not shut down if it finds itself operating in a deficit position.

Once the government has assumed the responsibility for a service, it also has the responsibility to continue to provide the service. Government services are often in a monopoly position in the marketplace. The consumer has no alternative when these services are interrupted by a strike. In cases such as Canada Post, the government has declared it illegal to establish another post office in Canada. Does the government not have the responsibility to provide this service?

The nature of employment in the public sector is also different from that in the private sector. Employment in the public sector is more stable and not subject to swings in the business cycle. That is, civil servants are not usually subject to the series of layoffs and re-hiring that occur in the private sector.

These distinctions between public- and private-sector employment lend support to the belief that there can be differences in labour legislation affecting the two groups of workers. These differences could extend to denying the right to strike to civil servants.

In contrast, some arguments can be made in favour of giving civil servants the right to strike. Should civil servants not have their employment rights protected in the same manner as other employees? If the right to strike is taken away from civil servants, what bargaining power do they have available in their negotiations with the employer? In the private sector, employees can threaten to go on strike if their demands are not met. What can civil servants do? If government employees are not allowed to strike, government may not be sincere in the negotiation process. The government may not be too anxious to reach a settlement because the employees will continue working even without a contract.

Restrictions have already been placed on civil servants and their right to negotiate. For example, changing some working conditions, such as pension plans, would require changes in legislation to implement and, therefore, cannot be negotiated. Removing the right to strike gives civil servants even less control over their working conditions.

In situations in which government employees are not permitted to strike, disputes over the content of the collective agreement are sent to a third party for a decision. The third party, referred to as an arbitrator, makes a decision that is final and binding on the parties

Figure 14.6
Wage differentials

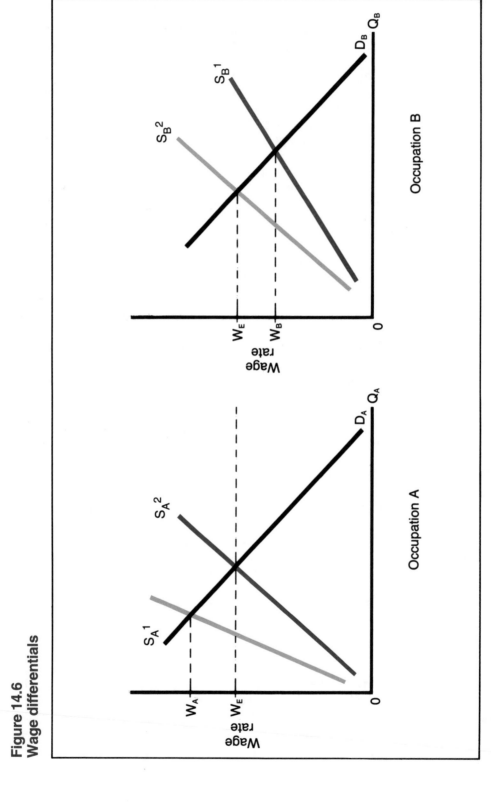

A wage differential between occupations A and B will cause a flow of workers from the lower-wage occupation to the higher-wage occupation. This movement of workers will tend to equalize the wage rates between occupations.

involved. Relegating the decision to an arbitrator is not without its difficulties. Who should be selected as an arbitrator? What criteria should be used in arriving at a decision? Should government be permitted to abdicate its responsibility in this area of government spending?

Questions

1 If strikes are illegal for a certain category of civil servants, what action should government take in the case of an illegal strike? What problems does government face in taking this action?

2 In some cases, civil servants are permitted to go on strike but certain jobs are considered to be essential. Those employees in designated occupations are not permitted to strike. What criteria should determine an essential occupation? Does the classification of essential occupations that are unable to strike reduce the bargaining power of the union?

3 Decisions regarding working conditions for civil servants are often influenced by political considerations. In order to remove politics from the decision-making process, why not hold a referendum of taxpayers on the proposed collective agreement for civil servants? In your answer discuss some of the advantages and disadvantages of such a proposal.

Wage Differentials

Not everyone earns exactly the same hourly wage rate. Why are there wage differences between occupations? Imagine two occupations with market conditions as shown in figure 14.6. The market conditions in occupation A result in a higher wage (W_A) than in the market for occupation B (W_B). If there are no restrictions on workers moving between occupations, then workers in occupation B would move over to the market for occupation A. This would increase the supply of workers in occupation A (S_A^2) and lower the equilibrium wage rate (W_E). The reduced supply of workers in occupation B would cause the equilibrium wage rate to rise to W_E. If workers were free to move between occupations, the equilibrium wage in both markets would eventually be the same.

In real life, there are barriers that prevent the movement of workers from occupation B to occupation A. Wage rates, therefore, are different from occupation to occupation. If the flow of workers from occupation B to occupation A is restricted, the wage will not decline very much in occupation A. In occupation B, the workers who cannot go to occupation A will keep the wage rate for B lower than it would be if workers were mobile. As long as barriers to the mobility of workers exist, occupational wage differentials will remain. What are these barriers?

One barrier is simply *a lack of information*. If workers in occupation B do not know that occupation A exists, or do not know the wages paid in A, then they will not be inclined to move. Labour-market information in the real world is seldom perfect; this is the main reason for establishing Canada Employment Centres and other placement agencies. A second barrier is *skill or education requirements*. Occupation A may require a certain degree of training, which those presently in occupation B do not possess. Not everyone is capable of doing every job. For example, not everyone is qualified to be a dentist. Because there are some restrictions on becoming a dentist, the wages of dentists will remain higher than they would without these restrictions. The limited number of vacancies at schools of dentistry ensures that the market will not be flooded with new dentists. The government also assists in maintaining the wage differential between dentists and other occupations, by not allowing anyone to practise dentistry unless qualified. Any restriction that reduces the supply of labour to an occupation will maintain higher wage rates in that occupation.

A third restriction may be *geographic location*. Occupation A may be located in another part of the country from occupation B. If workers are reluctant to move, then wage differentials will remain. People often do not wish to relocate. They are unwilling to leave family, friends, and familiar surroundings. In fact, worker mobility has declined in recent years. It is possible that government social welfare programs and the unemployment insurance scheme have made relocating to other parts of the country less attractive. If workers are not forced to move due to financial reasons, they may not do so. This applies especially to older workers. If workers do not move to where the higher wages are being paid, wage differentials will continue to exist.

Discrimination may also be a barrier to worker mobility. Employers may refuse to hire workers because of their skin colour, sex, marital status, nationality, or whatever. If discrimination can reduce the supply of workers to an occupation, wage differentials between occupations will be maintained.

Labour unions may also restrict mobility. Some unions have negotiated contracts with employers that state that new employees must be union members before being hired. Since only a certain number of people are union members, this condition restricts the number of people that can do the job. This situation is known as a *closed-shop* arrangement. Labour unions may also encourage government to insist on long apprenticeship periods before a person is qualified to work in a trade. The presence of a long training period may discourage some people from entering that occupation. Unions restrict the mobility of workers into certain occupations in order to maintain wage differentials.

Government has assisted in the maintenance of occupational wage differentials by granting certain professions the statutory power to regulate themselves. That is, certain professional associations can license, control, and govern the members of their profession. The justification for self-regulation is that members of the profession are best suited for setting proper standards of competence. This control gives great powers to the members of such a profession. Licences to practise in the profession may only be given to those who pass the licensing examination. Entrance requirements for schools of training may also be established, as well as restrictions on the number of such schools. The fact that these professions have been given complete monopoly over the practice of the profession means that they are likely to restrict supply in order to keep the wage up. They operate in a fashion similar to monopolies in product markets. Examples of such professions are doctors and lawyers.

If there were no barriers to worker mobility, would all wages be the same? The answer is no. Each occupation has certain characteristics that lend themselves to wage differences. For example, some jobs may involve a certain amount of danger or unsafe conditions. Since not everyone is willing to do this type of work, these jobs are likely to pay higher wage rates than others. Certain occupations may also pay more because they are unhealthy, dirty, involve unusual working hours, have a greater risk of unemployment, and so on. The attractive aspects of some occupations, on the other hand, may result in lower wage rates. These attractive aspects are called **equalizing differences** and include clean and safe conditions, regular hours, job security, and possibly prestige. The idea of equalizing differences is presented in figure 14.7. The heights of the two columns for jobs A and B are equal, indicating that they are equally attractive. Job B is able to pay a lower wage because of the attractive features, or equalizing differences, of the job. Job A is less attractive than job B and must offer a higher wage rate in order to attract workers.

The attractive characteristics of a job, called the equalizing differences, may compensate for lower wages when that job is compared to other jobs.

Figure 14.7 Equalizing differences

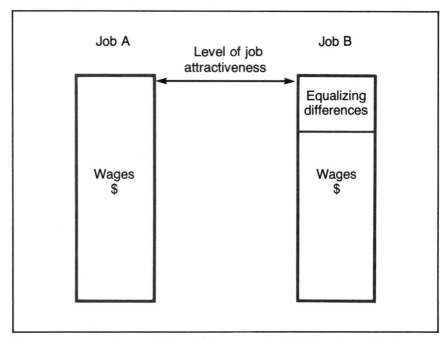

The presence of equalizing differences in Job B makes it just as attractive as Job A even though the wage rate is lower.

Some reasons for wage differentials were introduced by Adam Smith in 1776 in his book *The Wealth of Nations* (p. 100).

The five following are the principal circumstances which, so far as I have been able to observe, make up for a small pecuniary gain in some employments, and counterbalance a great one in others: first, the agreeableness or disagreeableness of the employments themselves; secondly, the easiness and cheapness, or the difficulty and expense of learning them; thirdly, the constancy or inconstancy of employment in them; fourthly, the small or great trust which must be reposed in those who exercise them, and fifthly, the probability or improbability of success in them.

14.9   Identify four barriers to worker mobility between jobs.
14.10 Why would government want to restrict the number of people who could practise a certain trade or profession?

Pay Equity

Research indicates that, on average, women working full-time earn less than men who work full-time. Is this wage differential a result of discrimination against women in the labour market? Is discrimination preventing women from obtaining more highly-paid occupations? The belief that discrimination was present in the labour market led to changes in human rights legislation that were designed to prevent discrimination, and to changes in employment standards legislation that guaranteed equal pay for equal work. According to the equal pay standard, men and women must be paid the same wage if they are performing the same job. Some differences in wages can remain if the wage differential is based on seniority or on the amount of work performed. In spite of these legislative changes, average wages and salaries for women continue to lag behind those of men. Governments across Canada are seeking equality of results and not just equality of opportunity. Equal pay for equal work laws have been criticised as inadequate, since in many cases, men and women do not perform the same job. Thus a series of pay equity laws have been introduced.

Pay equity requires employers to pay men and women the same wage for jobs that are different but are of similar *value.* For example, the secretaries in a company, who are most likely women, may have been earning less than the men working in the warehouse. What are the reasons for the wage differential between secretaries and warehouse employees? Is the secretarial job cleaner, safer, and more pleasant? Is the warehouse job less secure and more subject to lay-offs? Do warehouse jobs require more physical effort?

Whatever the reasons, the market has determined that warehouse employees should be paid more than secretarial workers. The equalizing differences associated with secretarial work must therefore be sufficient to compensate for the lower pay. If the equalizing differences did not exist, secretarial workers would seek warehouse jobs in sufficient numbers to equalize the wage rates. Under pay-equity legislation, secretaries need not apply for warehouse jobs in order to receive higher wages. If a government inspector determines that the secretarial and warehouse jobs are of equal value to the firm, the wages for the two jobs must be equalized. How are different jobs to be evaluated and compared? The market takes all aspects of the job into consideration when determining the wage rate. Government inspectors use the criteria of skill, effort, responsibility, and working conditions for job comparisons and evaluation.

The implementation of pay-equity legislation raises a number of issues for students of economics. What will be the impact of pay equity on employment for women? If employers are required to raise wages to a level greater than the current marginal revenue product, the number of employees will likely be reduced. Unemployment for women would then likely increase. Will employers relocate to jurisdictions that do not have pay-equity legislation, resulting in a loss of jobs for both men and women? Private-sector wages are determined to a great extent by what customers are willing to pay for the product. Will consumers be willing to pay more for the product in order to support the goal of pay equity?

Pay-equity legislation is normally applied to the government sector before being extended to the private sector. Public services provided by government usually have no competition in the marketplace. The increases in costs associated with pay equity can therefore be borne more easily by the public sector.

Will pay equity reduce the incentive to train for higher-paying jobs? If pay equity can improve wages without further education and training on the part of the employee, why go to the trouble of acquiring further skills? Some occupations are more highly-paid because of the relative shortage of workers in those occupations. Canadians should be training for these occupations in order to make the most efficient use of our labour resource.

What about wage differentials between two occupations dominated by men, or between two dominated by women? In some cases, these differences are greater than the differences between typical jobs dominated by either men or women. Can wage differences between two occupations dominated by men be the result of discrimination in the labour market? Should legislation be passed to achieve pay equity between jobs typically held by the same sex?

What causes the differential between average men's and women's salaries to exist? One study determined that most of the salary differential can be explained by the impact of marriage on a woman's career and on her attachment to the workplace. In this study, marital status accounted for all but eight percent of the difference in wages. In fact, in one study, never-married women with university degrees earned 9.8 percent more than comparable men. In another study, these women earned 99.2 percent of what comparable men earned. If a major determinant of wage differentials is a woman's marital status, what role does pay-equity legislation have to play?

Who makes the decision on job comparison? In one U.S. study, similar jobs were ranked according to value by different states. Each state ranked the jobs differently. Which ranking was correct? Clearly the wage rates set by pay equity officers are subjective in nature. Also, should pay-equity officers take such factors as the risk of lay-offs into consideration?

Questions

1 Would employers interested in maximizing profits arbitrarily pay men higher wages than women? Discuss.
2 Should legislation be passed to achieve equity between different occupations that are dominated by men? between those dominated by women?
3 Canadian governments are under spending pressure because of the public debt. In light of the debt, can governments afford to monitor pay equity in the private sector?

The Price of Land

In Chapter 5, rent was included in the calculation of gross domestic product (GDP). *Rent is the income paid to the land resource, and is determined by the interaction of demand and supply in the marketplace.* The demand curve for land for a specific use such as housing is the sum of the marginal revenue product (MRP) curves for the firms that want this resource. As is the case with the labour resource, the demand for land depends on the productivity of the land and the market price for the final product. Although the supply of land in general is fixed, the supply curve for land for a specific purpose slopes upward to the right. For example, when the price of houses increases, the price of land used for housing will also increase. This increase in price results in more land being supplied for housing. Hence, the supply curve for land for this specific purpose has a positive slope. The intersection of the demand and supply curve determines the price of land in the market (see figure 14.8).

Economic rent entails the payment to an economic resource above the amount necessary to attract it to a specified use.

The concept of **economic rent** is also shown in figure 14.8. Rent means something different to an economist than it does to other people, who refer to rent as the price paid for using an apartment, a building, a car, or some other object owned by someone else. To an economist, rent is a payment to the land resource above the minimum amount of money necessary to attract this resource into a specific use. The minimum amount of money required to attract land into a specific use is known as **transfer earnings** (see figure 14.8). The equilibrium price for land in this example is P_1 and all the land receives the same price. Some land would be offered for this use at a lower price than P_1. If that land can attract a price P_1, then it is earning an economic rent.

Transfer earnings are payments to an economic resource just sufficient to attract it to a specific use.

**Figure 14.8
Equilibrium price
of land for
housing**

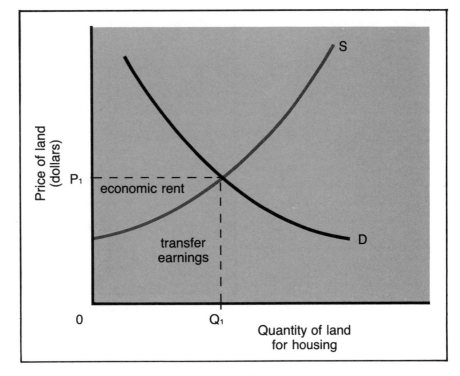

The return to land is divided into transfer earnings and economic rent.

An example may help explain the concept of economic rent. Land located in the heart of a major Canadian city may have more than one use. It may be used for housing, agriculture, commercial or industrial development, or parkland. Some land will be offered for housing even at low prices for the land. Other parcels of land will only be offered for housing if the price of housing land goes up. Once the price of land has been established as P_1 (see figure 14.8), all land used for housing will likely command the same price. The land originally offered for housing at a lower price than P_1 will be earning an economic rent. The economic rent that each parcel of land earns will not be the same.

What happens to economic rent when the supply of land is fixed? When the supply curve for land is perfectly inelastic, the price of land is determined solely by the demand for land (see figure 14.9). In this case, all the income earned by the land is economic rent. Assume that a certain piece of land is only good for growing tobacco and cannot be used for other purposes. The price of this land is determined by the demand for tobacco. If there were no demand for tobacco, this land would have no market price. Therefore any price that this land receives provides the land with economic rent.

Figure 14.9
Equilibrium price
of tobacco land

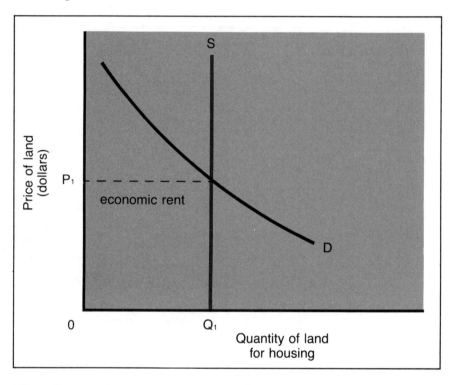

When the supply curve for land is perfectly inelastic, all the income earned from land is economic rent.

The concept of economic rent has been used in connection with other resources as well. In professional sports, for example, many athletes are earning economic rent. Many professional athletes who love their sport would willingly offer their services to an employer for less money than they are currently earning. Many baseball players in the major leagues would be willing to work for less than $200 000 per year even though the vast majority of them earn more than this figure. The income that they earn over and above the amount that they would be willing to work for is called economic rent. For example, if a certain catcher with the Montreal Expos was willing to play baseball for $180 000 per year and the Expos offered him a salary of $380 000 per year, his economic rent would be $200 000. Why do many baseball players and other athletes receive economic rent? The existence of economic rent for athletes is due to the unique ability of the athlete and to the high demand for his or her sport on the part of the viewing public.

14.11 What do we mean by economic rent?

The Market for Capital

Capital goods are man-made resources such as buildings, machinery, and equipment. Since they are durable they can help to produce goods and services for several years after the initial purchase. Eventually capital goods wear out and must be replaced. A demand for new capital is thus created. Technological changes also create a demand for new capital goods by making current machinery and equipment obsolete. For example, rapid changes in computer design and computer software have forced companies to purchase up-to-date equipment if they want to remain efficient and competitive.

    The demand curve for capital goods is influenced by the law of diminishing returns. If both land and labour resources are fixed, then purchases of additional capital goods will eventually contribute less and less to total output. In other words, the marginal productivity of additional capital goods will eventually begin to decline. The firm will only purchase more capital if the price of the capital goes down.

    In making the decision to purchase a capital good, the firm must consider the amount of additional output that can be produced in the future with the aid of this capital good. The dollar value of that future output has to be compared to the present dollar cost of the machinery or equipment. In other words, the money that can be earned in the future from the purchase of a capital good must be discounted to the present. It is necessary to calculate the **present value** of these earnings. The formula for discounting a stream of future earnings follows:

The dollar value today of a future sum of money is called the present value.

$$\text{present value (PV)} = \frac{y^1}{1+i} + \frac{y^2}{(1+i)^2} + \frac{y^3}{(1+i)^3} + \cdots + \frac{y^n}{(1+i)^n}$$

where

  y = earnings obtained from the capital good in a given year
  i = interest rate
  n = year

Assume that a firm is considering the purchase of a new machine at a cost of $3500. In order to determine the feasibility of buying this machine, the firm must determine *the present value of the future earnings* that this machine is likely to bring to the firm. The interest rate is ten percent per annum and the firm estimates that the yearly earnings derived from this machine will be $1000. The machine is expected to last five years. Is this machine a worthwhile purchase? In order to answer this question, the present value of the stream of future earnings must be calculated.

$$PV = \frac{\$1000}{1 + .10} + \frac{\$1000}{(1 + .10)^2} + \frac{\$1000}{(1 + .10)^3} + \frac{\$1000}{(1 + .10)^4} + \frac{\$1000}{(1 + .10)^5}$$
$$PV = \$909.09 + \$826.45 + \$751.31 + \$683.01 + \$620.92$$
$$PV = \$3790.78$$

On the basis of this information, the purchase of the machine makes sense. The present value of the machine is $3790.78 and the purchase price of the machine is $3500, creating a net present value of $290.78. If the purchase price of the machine had been greater than $3790.78, it would not have been a wise decision to buy it.

The decision to purchase the machine is highly dependent on the annual earnings that can be expected from the machine and on the interest rate. In the above example, it was assumed that these annual earnings would be $1000 per year. In reality, this may not be the case. Annual earnings from the machine are likely to decline each year that the machine is in use. The interest rate is also an important factor in this decision. If the interest rate were 14 percent in the above example instead of 10 percent, the present value would be $3433.08. Under these conditions, the firm would not purchase the machine for $3500.

Why is the interest rate so important in making an investment decision? If the firm had to borrow the money in order to purchase this machine, the cost of borrowing would be an important consideration in making the decision. If money could be borrowed at ten percent, then it would be advisable to purchase the machine. However, if money can only be borrowed at 14 percent or more, the present value of this machine is below the purchase price. The machine should not be purchased at this rate of interest. Even if the money does not have to be borrowed in order to make the purchase, the interest rate is significant. The firm must consider the opportunity cost associated with the use of available funds. In our example, if the firm could invest its money in some other manner than by buying the machine, and could get at least 14 percent interest, then it should proceed in that direction. If the firm can only get a return of ten percent on invested funds, then it would be advisable to purchase the machine. *Therefore, the demand for both money and capital goods will be greater at lower interest rates.*

The interest rate also influences the supply of money available to be borrowed. At higher interest rates, more money will be made available. At lower interest rates, less money is made available for borrowing. As discussed in Chapter 7, the intersection of the demand for and the supply of money will determine the equilibrium interest rate.

14.12 Why is the interest rate important in making the decision to purchase capital equipment?

Summary

Labour markets are a good example of how resource markets operate in our economy. Since there are various markets for labour, or workers, the interplay of demand and supply determines wage rates and levels of employment. The demand for labour is referred to as a derived demand, since it is dependent on the demand for the product that labour helps to produce. The demand for labour is also influenced by the productivity of the worker. The greater the productivity, the greater the demand.

Changes in the demand for labour come about as a result of changes in the price of the product that labour helps to produce, and in changes in worker productivity. A change in the price of a substitute for labour would also influence demand. If the price of highly technical equipment falls, employers may be encouraged to substitute that equipment for workers. Finally, any change in the price of a resource that labour works with will affect demand.

The elasticity of demand for labour is an important concept in such areas as union/management bargaining and government wage policy. The greater the elasticity or demand for labour, the more any wage increase will affect employment levels. Elasticity is determined by the following factors: the elasticity of demand for the final product; the percentage of total costs which labour costs comprise; the number of substitutes for labour; and the shape of labour's marginal-product curve.

Wage rates are determined by the interaction of the demand for and the supply of labour. In many instances, the individual firm will have no control over the wage rate paid to certain workers. In other cases, the firm will have an influence on workers' wages, depending on how many are hired. In situations where the firm can influence the wage rate, it has to consider the marginal-resource cost of each worker hired.

Trade unions attempt to increase the wages of their members. They can do this either by increasing the demand for their members or by decreasing the supply of their members able to perform a certain job. Most union activity is directed at the supply side of the labour market. Craft unions try to shift the supply curve to the left, while industrial unions try to reshape the supply curve by imposing a wage (price) floor.

Collective bargaining is the process whereby employees negotiate together with an employer regarding the terms of their employment. In order to ensure that the employer negotiates with employees, a labour union must be certified as the bargaining agent for the employees. The certification procedure establishes that the union has the backing of a majority of employees in the bargaining unit. Once certified, the union approaches the employer to begin the negotiations leading to a collective agreement. If an agreement is reached, the working conditions for the employees are set for the duration of the agreement. If an agreement cannot be reached, a strike or lockout may occur.

Not all occupations pay exactly the same wage. Differences in wage rates are due to two factors: barriers and equalizing differences. Labour-market barriers restrict the flow of workers from one job to another. Equalizing differences are attractive features of certain jobs that make up for lower wage rates.

The income paid to land can be divided into transfer earnings and economic rent. Transfer earnings are the minimum amount of money required to attract land into a specific use. Economic rent is a payment to land above the minimum amount of money necessary to attract this land to a specific use.

The demand for capital is heavily influenced by interest rates. In making a decision to purchase a capital good, the firm must consider the amount of additional output that can be produced in the future with the assistance of this capital good. This future stream of earnings must be discounted to the present, using the interest rate, in order to make the purchase decision.

Questions for Review and Discussion

1. From your knowledge of wage differentials, can you explain the wage differential that exists between wage rates for men and women?
2. What effect would restrictions on immigration have on wage rates?
3. Why are craft unions more interested in reducing the number of workers who can perform a certain job than industrial unions are?
4. Certain negative aspects of a job result in higher wages being paid to people who do these jobs. Discuss these negative aspects.
5. Which of the following activities would result in higher wages for the workers involved?
   i. an increase in the demand for new cars, on autoworkers' wages
   ii. a decrease in the price of Japanese imported cars, on Canadian autoworkers' wages

iii an increase in the number of building permits, on the wages of construction workers

iv an increase in interest rates, on the wages of construction workers

v an increase in the graduates from law school, on the salaries for lawyers.

6 Advances in technology have been cited as the main reason for job losses in some industries. Can you think of a way whereby advances in technology could increase the number of jobs in an industry?

7 Why do companies hire workers? Based on your answer, what is a major determinant of wage rates?

8 Would employers pay all employees the minimum wage if there were no unions? Why or why not?

9 Explain the impact of government imposing a minimum wage on a group of employees in terms of the MRP curve for those workers.

10 Assume that a union organizes apple pickers in Nova Scotia. What impact will this have on

i the wages of apple pickers

ii the employment of apple pickers

iii the price of apples

iv the possible introduction of equipment that can pick apples?

11 A section of land in Northern Ontario can be used only for nickel mining. Using demand and supply, show the impact on the price of land of a decrease in the price of nickel.

12 What effect do future interest rates have on the decision to purchase capital equipment?

13 An article in the Toronto Star in May, 1991 stated that many girls as young as age thirteen decide not to study mathematics and physics. What impact may this decision have on wage differentials for men and women?

14 If there were no barriers to mobility in the labour market, the wages for all occupations would be identical. Evaluate this statement.

15 During World War II, the cost of hiring some employees, for example, domestic servants, increased. Explain why this happened using your knowledge of the labour market.

Suggested Readings

Anderson, John, and Morley Gunderson. *Union-Management Relations in Canada*. Don Mills: Addison-Wesley 1982.

Craig, Alton W.J. *The System of Industrial Relations in Canada*. Scarborough: Prentice-Hall 1983.

Gunderson, Morley and W.Craig Riddell. *Labour Market Economics: Theory, Evidence and Policy in Canada*. Second Edition Toronto: McGraw-Hill Ryerson 1988.

Kehoe, Frank, and Maurice Archer. *Canadian Industrial Relations*. 4th ed. Oakville: Twentieth Century Labour Publications 1985.

King, J.E. *Labour Economics* Second Edition London: Macmillan 1990.

Smith, Adam. *The Wealth of Nations*. New York: Modern Library 1937.

Glossary

Two additional glossaries are presented in this text. A glossary of investment terms appears in Chapter 2 and a glossary of collective-bargaining terms is in Chapter 14.

ability-to-pay: an approach to vertical equity (fairness) in taxation, whereby individuals are taxed on their ability to pay taxes.

adjustable peg system: a system of fixed exchange rates that can be changed to new rates if economic circumstances require it.

aggregate demand: the total demand for goods and services in the economy, including consumption, investment, government spending, and exports.

aggregate supply: the total production of goods and services available in the economy over a certain period of time.

arbitrage: a system based on international communications that keeps the foreign-exchange value of a currency approximately equal in all markets.

arbitration: a procedure whereby an independent third party settles disputes between union and management during the life of a collective agreement.

automatic stabilizers: government programs currently in operation that react automatically to help adjust the level of aggregate demand when economic conditions change.

average fixed costs (AFC): fixed costs divided by the number of units (quantity) produced.

average propensity to consume (APC): the ratio of consumption to gross domestic product.

average propensity to save (APS): the ratio of savings to gross domestic product.

average total cost (ATC): the total cost of producing a certain level of output divided by the number of units (quantity) produced.

average variable costs (AVC): the total variable costs of producing a certain level of output divided by the number of units (quantity) produced.

balanced-budget multiplier: the equivalent increase in government tax revenues and government spending that increases the level of gross domestic product.

Bank of Canada: Canada's central bank, whose primary responsibility is to regulate the money supply in Canada in order to promote the economic and financial welfare of the country.

bank rate: the rate of interest paid by chartered banks on money borrowed from the Bank of Canada.

bargaining unit: the tasks in a company that are covered in the collective agreement between the employer and the representative of the employees, the union.

barriers to entry: obstacles that prevent a new firm from starting operations in a certain industry.

barriers to international trade: obstacles that restrict the amount of foreign products that can be imported into a country. Barriers include tariffs, quotas, and non-tariff barriers like rules and regulations.

barriers to labour mobility: obstacles restricting the movement of workers from one job to another. Barriers include discrimination, government regulations, union restrictions, a lack of information, educational requirements, and geography.

barter: to trade goods and services rather than to purchase them with money.

benefits-received approach: an approach to vertical equity (fairness) in taxation whereby individuals are taxed on the basis of the benefits that they receive from government programs.

bond: a certificate sold by a borrower to a lender of money that promises to pay a certain sum of money, plus interest, at a future date.

bourgeoisie: a group of individuals, according to Karl Marx, who own property, yet do not work.

branch banking: a system of banking in which a commercial bank is permitted to operate branches of the bank.

break-even point: the level of production for a firm at which the total revenue from selling the product is equal to the total cost of producing that quantity of output.

cabotage: rights that would permit air carriers to pick up and deliver passengers between any two points in North America.

caisse populaire: a financial institution usually organized on the basis of parish boundaries of the Roman Catholic church that receives funds by selling shares and accepting deposits from members.

Canada-United States Automobile Agreement: allows for the duty-free movement of most vehicles and parts between the two countries.

Canadian Radio-television and Telecommunications Commission (CRTC): an agency of the federal government responsible for regulating the telephone, television, and radio broadcasting industries.

capital: man-made resources consisting of buildings, tools, and equipment that are used to produce goods and services.

capital account: the section of the international balance of payments that records the inflow and outflow of investment dollars.

capital consumption allowance: a dollar value representing the total amount of machinery and equipment used up in the production process.

capitalism: an economic system in which the free-market principles of private ownership of resources and individual decision-making predominate.

cartel: a formal arrangement, whether written or verbal, among producers to regulate the price and total output of a product.

certification: a process whereby a labour union acquires the bargaining rights for a group of employees.

chartered bank: a financial institution operating under the authority of Parliament that accepts deposits of money and lends money to firms, government, and households.

closed shop: a form of the union security clause whereby all members of the bargaining unit must join the union.

circular flow of money: the directional flow of money in our economy from the business sector to households and back to the business sector.

cobweb theorem: an explanation of price fluctuations in agriculture that assumes that farmers determine the size of next year's crop on the basis of this year's price.

collective agreement: contract signed by the employer and the representative of the employees that sets out working conditions for the employees.

collective bargaining: the negotiating of an employment contract between management and the union representing the employees.

collusion: a secret agreement among business firms to fix prices or share the market.

command approach: the approach to economic decision-making that emphasizes centralized planning and state ownership of resources.

communism: an economic system in which centralized decision-making and state ownership of resources predominate.

Competition Act: federal government legislation that prohibits business practices that unduly restrict competition.

concentration: the degree to which business activity in an industry is dominated by a few firms.

conglomerate merger: a combination of two firms engaged in different levels of the same activity.

Consumer Price Index (CPI): The ratio of prices of consumer products to prices of those products in a base year (1981). The percentage change in this index from year to year is referred to as the rate of inflation.

consumption: household spending on goods and services.

corporation: a business organization created by law that is owned by the shareholders.

cost-push inflation: increases in the general price level that result from firms passing on cost increases to consumers in the form of higher prices.

countervailing duty: an additional tariff placed on an imported item when that item has received government financial assistance during production in the exporting country.

craft union: a trade union whose members all possess a particular skill.

credit union: a financial institution that receives funds by selling shares and accepting deposits from members. These institutions are oriented toward consumer lending.

crop restriction: a government program to reduce the quantity of an agricultural product on the market.

Crown corporation: a corporation directly owned by the government.

crude-quantity theory of money: a mathematical identity stating that the price level is directly related to the amount of money in circulation ($P = KM$).

current account: the section of the international balance of payments that records the inflows and outflows of money for merchandise and service items.

debenture: a certificate of indebtedness issued by a company or a government.

deficiency-payment program: an agricultural price-support program whereby the government pays to the farmer the difference between the average market price for a product and the support price.

delta (Δ): a Greek letter used in mathematics to represent "change in."

demand: the relationship between the amount of a product that consumers are willing to purchase and its price.

demand-deficient unemployment: unemployment that results from a lack of overall spending in the economy.

demand deposit: a deposit at a chartered bank from which the depositor can get his or her money on demand (by writing a cheque).

demand-pull inflation: an increase in the general level of prices that occurs when the aggregate demand for goods and services exceeds the supply.

deposit insurance: insurance on the deposit liabilities of chartered banks and other institutions.

depreciation: describes a reduction in the value of one country's currency in relation to another currency under the conditions of a flexible exchange-rate system. Similarly, *appreciation* describes an increase in the value of the currency in relation to another currency.

depression: a downturn in the level of business activity characterized by large-scale unemployment of resources and declining levels of gross domestic product.

derived demand: the demand for a resource based on the demand for the good or service that the resource helps to produce.

devalued: a devalued currency is one that has decreased in value in relation to another currency under the conditions of a fixed exchange-rate system.

direct tax: a tax imposed on an individual who it is intended should pay the tax.

discounting: the process of calculating the present value from a series of future payments.

discouraged workers: persons interested in employment but not actively seeking a job because they believe that a suitable job is not available.

discretionary fiscal policy: changes in the level of government spending and taxation aimed at altering economic conditions.

diseconomies of scale: increases in the long-run average costs resulting from the inefficiencies associated with large-scale operations.

dissaving: the act of spending more than your income.

dividend: an amount distributed out of a company's profits to its shareholders in proportion to the number of shares that they hold.

division of labour: the specialization in the performance of tasks by workers in order to permit greater efficiency and greater production.

dumping: the practice of selling a product in a foreign market for a lower price than it is sold for in the domestic market.

Dutch auction: an auction at which the price falls rather than increases.

economic profit: the excess of total revenue over total costs.

economic rent: payment to an economic resource above the amount necessary to attract it to a specific use.

economics: the study of how individuals and groups of individuals make decisions regarding the use of scarce resources.

economies of scale: decreases in long-run average costs resulting from the efficiencies of large-scale production.

elastic: a situation in which the quantity demanded (or supplied) of a product responds significantly to changes in the price.

entrepreneur: an individual who is willing to take a risk by introducing a new product or service in the marketplace.

equalization payments: payments made by the federal government to some provinces in recognition of the differing abilities of the provinces to collect taxes.

equalizing differences: attractive characteristics of a job that compensate for lower wages when compared to other jobs.

equilibrium: a situation in which there is no tendency for change to take place.

equilibrium GDP: the level of gross domestic product (GDP) that is stable and occurs when injections from the circular flow are equal to the leakages.

equilibrium price: a price at which the quantity demanded of a product is equal to the quantity supplied.

European Economic Community (EEC): A group of European nations that have eliminated barriers to trade among themselves, and have established common external tariffs to products from non-member countries.

excess reserves: cash reserves held by chartered banks over and above the required amount of reserves.

excise tax: a tax levied on the supplier of a particular product.

expenditure multiplier: the amount by which a change in aggregate demand is multiplied in order to determine the change in GDP.

explicit costs: payments for productive resources that the firm does not own and must purchase.

factors of production: those resources used in the production process.

fair-return price: a price used in the regulation of a monopoly that is equal to the average cost of production.

featherbedding: practices or work rules that set unreasonable limits on the amount of work employees may perform in a given period of time, for example, payment for unneeded workers or jobs duplicating those already done.

federalist system: a system of government in which two levels of government have jurisdiction over each citizen.

fiat money: currency issued by a government or a bank that is not matched by holdings of gold or other securities.

fiscal policy: the use of changes in the level of government spending and taxation to influence economic conditions.

Fisher equation of exchange: a mathematical identity stating that the money supply multiplied by the velocity of money is equal to the number of transactions that take place in the economy multiplied by the average price level ($MV = PT$).

fixed costs: production costs that do not vary with the amount produced.

fixed exchange rate: the foreign-exchange value of a nation's currency set by government to remain constant in terms of another nation's currency.

fixed term deposit: a deposit in a financial institution that remains for a definite period of time, usually at a specified interest rate.

flexible exchange rate: the foreign-exchange value of a nation's currency determined by the interaction of market forces and not set by government.

foreign-exchange rate: the value of a nation's currency in terms of another nation's currency.

foreign ownership: investment by foreign residents in Canadian assets and financial securities.

foreign-trade multiplier: the amount by which a change in aggregate demand is multiplied in order to determine the change in GDP, taking into account the impact of foreign trade.

franchising: a contract granting the right to sell, in a specified manner, a particular product or service.

free market approach: an approach to economic decision-making that stresses private ownership of resources and individual decision-making.

free trade: trade between countries that is unrestricted by tariffs or non-tariff barriers.

frictional unemployment: short-term unemployment characterized by individuals who have voluntarily left one job and are in the process of looking for another.

Friedman, Milton (1912-): a contemporary American economist and author who is regarded as a proponent of the free market approach.

full-employment GDP: the level of aggregate demand in the economy required to ensure that everyone who wants employment has a job.

futures market: a market for commodities in which prices are set in advance of the actual production.

Galbraith, John Kenneth (1908-): a contemporary economist who proposes a significant amount of government intervention in the marketplace.

General Agreement on Tariffs and Trade (GATT): an international agreement aimed at reducing the barriers to international trade.

gross domestic product (GDP): the value of all goods and services produced in a country in a given year.

gross national expenditure (GNE): the sum of all expenditures by households, businesses, government, and foreigners for goods and services.

gross national product (GNP): the value of all goods and services produced by residents of a country in a given year, determined by adding up the value added by firms to each stage of production.

gross public debt: unmatured bonds, treasury bills, and other liabilities of government.

guaranteed investment certificate: a non-transferable deposit receipt issued by a financial situation, usually at a specified rate of interest for a period from one to six years.

hidden unemployed: the number of discouraged workers in the population.

horizontal merger: a combination of two firms engaged in the same activity.

horizontal tax equity: an approach to fairness in taxation stating that taxpayers in similar circumstances should pay the same amount of money in taxes.

hyperinflation: a very rapid increase in the level of prices that leads to a lack of public confidence in money.

implicit costs: payments to productive resources that the firm already owns.

incidence of a tax: the final resting place of a tax. A tax imposed on one party may be partially shifted to another party in the form of higher prices.

indexing: the process of adjusting payments or taxes according to changes in the rate of inflation.

indirect tax: a tax levied against one person in the expectation that it will be paid by another person.

industrial union: a trade union that attempts to organize all workers in a particular industry.

inelastic: a situation in which the quantity demanded (or supplied) does not respond significantly to changes in the price.

infant industry: a newly established industry.

inflation: an increase in the general level of prices.

inflationary gap: a decrease in the level of aggregate demand required to bring the equilibrium level of GDP down to the full-employment level of GDP.

inflationary psychology: an expectation on the part of the public that the current level of price increases will continue into the future.

injections: expenditure in the form of investment, government spending, and exports that is inserted into the circular flow of money.

insurance-induced unemployment: unemployment that is caused by the level of unemployment insurance benefits, making it unattractive to look for work.

interest rate: payment for the use of money on an annual basis, stated in terms of a percentage of the amount borrowed.

international balance of payments: a record of all financial transactions between residents of one country and residents of the rest of the world.

International Monetary Fund (IMF): an international agency established in 1944, whose objective was to stabilize foreign-exchange rates.

inverse relationship: as the value of one variable increases, the value of another variable decreases.

investment: business spending on machines and equipment, new residential construction, and any change in inventories.

invisible hand: a term introduced by Adam Smith to describe the process whereby individual activities in a free market system lead toward a common goal.

Keynes, John Maynard (1883-1946): a British economist whose writings proved that the economy does not always ensure full employment and that government spending may be required to improve economic conditions. These theories form the basis of what is now termed **"Keynesian economics."**

kinked demand curve: a demand curve facing a firm in an oligopolistic industry that is composed of two sections—elastic and inelastic—separated by a bend, or kink, in the curve. The curve is an attempt to explain price rigidity in oligopolistic industries.

labour: the productive services of people. This resource includes the education, skills, and technical training of the population, as well as the size of the population itself.

labour force: those individuals in the population who are either employed or looking for employment.

Labour Force Survey: a monthly measure of the number of unemployed in Canada. This measure provides an indication of the country's economic condition.

Laffer curve: a curve indicating the relationship between the tax rate and the amount of money collected in taxes.

land: a natural resource that includes real estate, minerals, wild animals, vegetation, and water.

law of comparative advantage: a theory of international trade that states that a country should specialize in and trade those items that it can produce relatively more efficiently than other countries.

law of diminishing returns: eventually, when increasing amounts of a variable resource are combined with a fixed amount of another resource, the increases in total output derived from more of the variable resource will become smaller and smaller.

law of downward-sloping demand: states that there is a negative, or inverse relationship, between the price of a good or service and the quantity demanded.

leakages: money taken out of the circular flow of money in the form of savings, taxes, and imports.

liquid assets: an asset that can readily be converted into money.

long run: a period of time in the production process during which all resources are variable.

M1: a definition of the money supply that includes currency outside chartered banks and demand deposits in chartered banks.

macroeconomics: the area of economic analysis concerned with the overall view of the economy, rather than with individual markets.

manpower policy: a stabilization policy aimed at lessening the amount of structural unemployment in the economy.

many differentiated sellers: a competitive situation with many sellers of a similar, but slightly different, product.

marginal cost (MC): the addition to total cost of producing one more unit of output.

marginal product (MP): the addition to total output from adding one more unit of a productive resource.

marginal propensity to consume (MPC): the proportion of any increase in income that is used for consumption.

marginal propensity to save (MPS): the proportion of any increase in income that is used for saving.

marginal-resource cost (MRC): the addition to total cost from adding one more unit of a productive resource.

marginal revenue (MR): the addition to total revenue from selling one more unit of output.

marginal revenue curve: a curve relating extra revenue to the quantity of output.

marginal-revenue product (MRP): the increase in total revenue from employing one more unit of a productive resource (MP x MR).

marginal tax rate: the percentage of any additional income that is paid in taxes.

market: the interaction of buyers and sellers that results in an exchange of a good or a service, and the establishment of a price.

marketing board: a compulsory marketing organization for primary or processed agricultural products.

Marx, Karl (1818-83): a German social philosopher and critic of the free market system, who believed that the conflict between two groups in society—the bourgeoisie and the proletariat—would eventually lead to the destruction of the free market system.

Malthus, Robert Thomas (1766-1834): an English clergyman and economist who argued that the population of the world would increase faster than the ability of the world to produce food.

mercantilism: a school of thought holding the view that a nation should promote exports and limit imports in order to accumulate gold.

merger: the combination of two or more individual firms to make one single firm; one firm acquiring another firm.

microeconomics: the area of economics that emphasizes smaller decision-making units, such as business firms, consumers, and workers.

misleading price advertising: an illegal activity whereby prices charged are higher than advertised prices.

monetary policy: the regulation of the money supply by the Bank of Canada in order to influence economic conditions.

money supply: the amount of purchasing power available in the economy.

monopoly: an industry in which there is only one seller of a good or service.

moral suasion: an informal approach to monetary policy, whereby the governor of the Bank of Canada expresses his views on monetary policy to the presidents of the chartered banks, presumably in the hope of influencing banking decisions for the benefit of the country.

National Accounts: data compiled by Statistics Canada measuring the overall level of business activity in Canada.

natural monopoly: an industry in which it is more efficient to have only one seller of the good or service in the sense that average costs decline steadily as output increases.

net domestic income (NDI): the value of final goods and services produced in a country in a given year, minus an allowance for capital consumption and indirect business taxes.

net public debt: gross public debt after deducting recorded assets.

non-performing loan: a loan is non-performing when payments on the loan are not being made by the borrower.

non-tariff barrier: an impediment to the flow of international trade in the form of quotas and restrictive rules and regulations.

notice deposit: a deposit at a chartered bank for which advance notice may be required before money can be withdrawn.

offer-to-purchase program: an agricultural price-support program, whereby government establishes a price floor and then offers to buy any surplus product not sold in the marketplace.

oligopoly: a competitive situation characterized by only a few firms.

open-market operations: the buying and selling of government bonds by the Bank of Canada in order to influence the money supply.

opportunity cost: the value of the best alternative that is sacrificed when a decision is made to use a resource for a specific purpose.

Organization of Petroleum Exporting Countries (OPEC): an international cartel that controls the production and pricing of oil exports.

patent: a document granting exclusive right to the production, sale, and profit of an invention.

paradox of thrift: an increase in the level of savings in the economy can lead to lower levels of income and ultimately to lower levels of savings.

participation rate: the percentage of the population that is employed or actively seeking employment.

partnership: a form of business enterprise in which two or more persons own and operate the business firm and are liable for its debts.

Peacock-Wiseman hypothesis: a theory of government spending stating that after a military conflict, the level of government spending in the economy remains high because the acceptable level of taxation in the minds of the public has been altered by the military conflict.

per capita GDP: the gross domestic product of a country divided by the population.

perfect competition: a competitive situation in which there are thousands of firms each selling an identical product.

perfectly elastic curve: a demand or supply curve that is perpendicular to the price axis at any quantity.

perfectly inelastic curve: a demand or supply curve that is perpendicular to the quantity axis at a certain quantity.

personal disposable income (PDI): the level of personal income that remains after income taxes have been paid.

personal income (PI): the total of consumption spending and savings in the economy.

Phillips curve: a graphical representation portraying a negative relationship between rates of unemployment and rates of inflation.

positive (or direct) relationship: as the value of one variable increases, the value of another variable increases.

poverty: when an individual or family receives an income less than the minimum necessary to provide a reasonable standard of living.

precautionary demand for money: the desire to hold money for unpredictable expenses.

predatory price cutting: the lowering of prices, usually below the costs of production, in order to eliminate the competition.

present value: the dollar value now of a future sum of money.

price ceiling: a government-legislated maximum price.

price discrimination: the practice of charging different prices to different consumers for an item produced under similar cost conditions.

price elasticity: the responsiveness of the quantity demanded (or supplied) to a change in the price of a product.

price floor: a government-legislated minimum price.

price leadership: a situation in which one firm raises its price and other firms in the industry follow with price increases.

prime lending rate: the rate of interest charged on loans by chartered banks to their most credit-worthy customers.

privatization: the transfer of control of a company from government to private ownership.

production function: the relationship between the amount of resources used and the level of output.

production-possibilities curve: a curve indicating all the possible combinations of two goods that can be produced, using all resources in the most efficient manner.

productivity: the amount of output produced by a unit of a certain resource during a specified period of time.

progressive tax: an approach to taxation in which the percentage of income paid in taxes increases as the level of income increases.

proletariat: a group of individuals, according to Karl Marx, who work, yet do not own property.

proportional tax: an approach to taxation in which the percentage of income paid in taxes remains constant regardless of the level of income.

public debt: the amount of money owed by all levels of government in Canada.

quota: a limit on the amount of a product that can be imported into a country.

Rand-formula shop: a form of the union security clause whereby all members of the bargaining unit pay union dues whether or not they are union members.

real GDP: the level of gross domestic product adjusted for increases in the average price level.

recession: a downturn in the level of economic activity characterized by high rates of unemployment, under-utilized productive capacity, and declining real incomes.

recessionary gap: the amount that aggregate demand has to increase in order to bring the equilibrium level of gross domestic product (GDP) up to a full-employment level of gross domestic product.

regressive tax: an approach to taxation in which the percentage of income paid in taxes decreases as the level of income increases.

rent: income paid to the land resource.

required reserve ratio: the percentage of deposits that chartered banks must keep in cash and deposits at the Bank of Canada.

resource allocation: the use to which a nation's resources are put.

resources: the means available to a country for producing goods and services. Resources are grouped into three categories: labour, land, and capital.

retail price maintenance: an illegal practice, whereby the manufacturer insists that a product be sold at a specified price.

Ricardo, David (1772-1823): an English economist and stock broker, best known for his work on the law of comparative advantage.

savings deposits: an interest-earning notice deposit at a chartered bank.

Say's law: the supply of products creates its own demand, since all production creates income for households that can be spent on goods and services.

scarcity: an insufficient amount or supply. Any item that is available only in a limited supply is considered to be scarce.

seasonal unemployment: unemployment that results from the seasonal nature of some industries, such as agriculture, construction, tourism, and recreation.

secondary reserve rate: liquid assets held by chartered banks as a reserve against deposits, the amount of secondary reserves being set by the Bank of Canada.

short run: a period of time in the production process during which at least one resource cannot be altered.

shut-down point: a level of production where the average variable cost of each unit of output is equal to the price of the product.

small business: a firm that is independently owned and operated and which is not dominant in its field of endeavour, usually employing fewer than 100 persons and having annual sales of $20 million or less.

Smith, Adam (1723-1790): a Scottish philosopher known as the founder of economics.

sole proprietorship: a form of business organization with one owner; well suited to small business.

socialism: an economic system that stresses government ownership of major productive resources and centralized decisions.

socially optimum pricing: an approach to monopoly price regulation by setting the price equal to the marginal cost.

specialization: the division of work into distinct tasks in order to improve worker productivity.

speculative demand for money: a desire to hold money in the expectation that interest rates will increase in the future.

stabilization fund: a fund established in support of the adjustable-peg system. Each country maintains a fund of domestic and foreign currencies and gold that allows the country to purchase its currency on world markets, keeping the exchange rate at the par value.

stabilization payments: payments made by the federal government to the provinces to ensure that provincial taxation revenues do not decline substantially from one year to the next.

stabilization policy: programs introduced by the government to regulate unemployment and inflation.

stagflation: a situation of depressed levels of real output in the economy combined with rising prices.

stock market: a market in which shares, or ownership, in corporations are exchanged.

structural inflation: an increase in the general level of prices due to the fact that some groups in the economy have the ability to raise prices even when aggregate demand is declining.

structural unemployment: unemployment that results from a mismatching of the demand for, and the supply of, workers on an occupational or a geographic basis.

supply: the relationship between the quantity of a product offered for sale and its price.

supply-side economics: an economic stabilization policy that stresses increasing the supply of goods and services in order to reduce the level of prices and to create jobs.

tariff: a tax imposed on imported products.

tax equity: fairness, or justness, in taxation.

tax indexing: adjustments to income tax regulations under a progressive income tax system in order to account for the impact of inflation on incomes.

tax multiplier: the amount by which any change in the level of taxation must be multiplied by in order to determine the impact on GDP.

term deposit: a deposit at a chartered bank for a specified period of time.

third-party effects: the results of a transaction between two parties that have an impact, positive or negative, on a third party.

total costs: the sum of all costs, explicit and implicit, associated with operating a business.

total demand: *see* aggregate demand.

total revenue: the amount of money brought into a firm from the sale of a product; determined by multiplying the price by the quantity sold.

transactions demand for money: a desire to hold money in order to make purchases.

transfer earnings: payment to an economic resource just sufficient to attract it to a specific use.

treasury bills: short-term government bonds sold by auction each Thursday.

trust company: a financial institution that acts as a trustee for property interests and conducts other confidential business.

underemployment: a situation in which individuals are employed but not at a job that fully utilizes their skills.

unemployment rate: the percentage of the labour force that is not employed, but is seeking employment.

union shop: a form of the union security clause whereby all members of the bargaining unit must join the union.

unitary elastic: a situation in which the quantity demanded (or supplied) of a product responds to a price change in exactly the same proportion as the change in price.

unit banking: a system of banking in which commercial banks are either not permitted to operate branches or to operate only a limited number of branches.

unmet public goods: goods and services not provided by the free market system because of the difficulty of charging a fee to the beneficiaries of the good or service.

value of marginal product: the increase in total revenue resulting from employing one more unit of a productive resource in a perfectly competitive industry.

variable costs: production costs that vary with the amount of output.

velocity of money: average number of times that each unit of the money supply changes hands during a given period.

vertical merger: a combination of two firms engaged in different levels of the same activity.

vertical tax equity: an approach to fairness in taxation that states that taxpayers in different circumstances should be treated fairly when paying taxes.

wage and price controls: an anti-inflationary policy, whereby the government puts legal limits on the amount of wage and price increases.

Wagner's law of increasing state activity: a theory stating that government spending can be expected to grow at a faster rate than the total output of goods and services in industrialized economies.

Index

Sources

I am grateful to the following publishers and authors for permission to reprint excerpts from these publications:

Pages 52, 56: Toronto Stock Exchange listings and futures market listings from *The Globe and Mail* and the Toronto Stock Exchange; page 65: from the Candide Model 3.0, Economic Council of Canada, Ottawa, March 1985; pages 76-78: from *An Inquiry into the Nature and Causes of the Wealth of Nations* by Adam Smith, Random House Inc.; page 258: from *The Squeeze* by James Dale Davidson, Summit Books, Simon & Schuster, a Division of Gulf & Western Corporation; pages 328-329: adapted from *Women Like Me,* 8th ed., 1990, published annually by Women Like Me Publications, Toronto; pages 331-332: text prepared by McDonald's Restaurants of Canada Ltd., January 1991; pages 365-366: from *On a Clear Day You Can See General Motors* by J. Patrick Wright, Wright Enterprises, Grosse Pointe, Michigan, 1979; pages 390-392: from "Marketing Boards and Pricing in Canada" by G.A. Hiscocks and T.A. Bennet, in *The Canadian Economy: Problems and Policies,* 2nd ed., edited by G.C. Ruggeri, Gage Publishing Ltd.

Every effort has been made to determine and locate copyright owners. In case of any omissions, the publisher will be pleased to make acknowledgements in future editions.